NEW YORK REVIEW BOOKS
CLASSICS

THE BAD SIDE OF BOOKS

DAVID HERBERT LAWRENCE (1885–1930) was the fourth child born to a coal miner and a sometime teacher in England's rural East Midlands. After a bout of pneumonia when he was sixteen, he began working as a student teacher, then was accepted to Nottingham University to study for a teacher's certificate in 1906; in 1908 he took a teaching job in London. In 1909, with the help of his intimate friend Jessie Chambers, several of his poems and, later, a short story were published in Ford Madox Ford's *The English Review*. Lawrence's first novel, *The White Peacock*, followed in 1911. In 1912, while recovering from another bout of pneumonia, he fell in love with Frieda von Richthofen, the wife of his former professor. The two eloped to Germany, then Italy, where, amid their wandering, he finished *Sons and Lovers* (1913), which was met with enthusiastic reviews and seemed to guarantee some stability. The couple returned to the UK in 1914 to be married. Lawrence's fourth novel, *The Rainbow* (1915), was banned for obscenity upon publication, and he and Frieda spent the war years impoverished, hounded by the British police for their pacifism and perceived German loyalties. In 1919, they embarked on a "savage pilgrimage," traveling first to Italy then sailing east, stopping in Ceylon (now Sri Lanka) and Australia before reaching the United States and settling in Taos, New Mexico, where he completed his *Studies in Classic American Literature* (1923). Lawrence contracted malaria and tuberculosis on a visit to Mexico in 1925; in failing health, he and Frieda returned to Italy, where he finished writing *Lady Chatterley's Lover* (1928). In the late winter of 1930, in Vence,

France, Lawrence died from complications of tuberculosis. In 1935, Frieda had his remains exhumed so that his ashes could be laid to rest in New Mexico.

GEOFF DYER is a fellow of the Royal Society of Literature and a member of the American Academy of Arts and Sciences. He is the author of many books, including *Out of Sheer Rage* (about D. H. Lawrence) and *But Beautiful* (about jazz). His books have won numerous prizes and have been translated into twenty-four languages. He currently lives in Los Angeles where he is a writer in residence at the University of Southern California.

THE BAD SIDE OF BOOKS
Selected Essays

D.H. LAWRENCE

Edited and with an introduction by
GEOFF DYER

NEW YORK REVIEW BOOKS

New York

THIS IS A NEW YORK REVIEW BOOK
PUBLISHED BY THE NEW YORK REVIEW OF BOOKS
435 Hudson Street, New York, NY 10014
www.nyrb.com

Essays copyright © by the Estate of Frieda Lawrence Ravagli and Cambridge
University Press
Introduction, selection, and notes copyright © 2019 by Geoff Dyer
All rights reserved.

This selection first published in the UK by Penguin Books, 2019.
"Elegy" by Rebecca West reprinted by permission of Peters Fraser & Dunlop
(www.petersfraserdunlop.com) on behalf of of the Estate of Rebecca West.

Library of Congress Cataloging-in-Publication Data
Names: Lawrence, D. H. (David Herbert), 1885–1930, author. | Dyer, Geoff,
    editor, writer of introduction.
Title: The bad side of books : selected essays of D.H. Lawrence / edited and with
    an introduction by Geoff Dyer.
Description: New York : New York Review Books, [2019] | Series: New York
    Review Books classics | Includes bibliographical references.
Identifiers: LCCN 2019012598| ISBN 9781681373638 (alk. paper) | ISBN
    9781681373645 (epub)
Subjects: LCSH: English essays—20th century.
Classification: LCC PR6023.A93 A6 2019 | DDC 824/.912—dc23
LC record available at https://lccn.loc.gov/2019012598

ISBN 978-1-68137-363-8
Available as an electronic book; ISBN 978-1-68137-364-5

Printed in the United States of America on acid-free paper.
10 9 8 7 6 5 4 3 2

CONTENTS

INTRODUCTION

I can remember quite clearly how I first encountered D. H. Lawrence as a writer of something other than fiction. We were studying *Hamlet* at school, reading the expected lit-crit by A. C. Bradley, G. Wilson Knight and, more fashionably, Jan Kott (*Shakespeare Our Contemporary*). But my teacher also nudged me towards a strange piece of writing by Lawrence called 'The Theatre', about going to see a production of *Hamlet*, in *Twilight in Italy*. Wanting to reduce the piece to exam-directed utility I didn't know what it was or how it was meant to be read. Obviously it was about *Hamlet* (a 'statement of the most significant philosophic position of the Renaissance') but it was also a kind of story, a re-creation of an actual experience and place.[1] The critical essays I had read up to that point all seemed like more diligent and accomplished examples of what I was reading them for, i.e. homework. There was no suggestion of homework or compulsory diligence about 'The Theatre' and while this had an obvious appeal it also raised doubts as to the legitimacy and value of the piece. On reflection what I missed, I think, was the valorizing dullness that pervaded so much of the criticism that came to define the study of English at university. The gap in enjoyment between the novels or poems and the stuff we were expected to read *about* them was so huge. Until, that is, during the week devoted to Hardy when Lawrence came crashing in again and suddenly there was no gap. One moment he was pointing out, in his rather homely way, that Hardy's characters 'are always going off unexpectedly and doing something that nobody would do' and the next making metaphysical pronouncements about 'the great, tragic power' of Egdon Heath. I read *Study of Thomas Hardy* for the light it shed on Hardy but it was also a revealing expression of who it was by. *Study of Thomas Hardy* was as much mirror as window. Up until then non-fiction existed either as a wholly distinct discipline (history, say) or as a kind of stepladder to help one better get to grips with poetry and novels. These pieces by Lawrence represented the first glimpse of a more labile relationship between criticism and fiction, between the necessary restraints of academic discipline and the vagrant life of the mind. (Lawrence famously went further, rejecting the limiting life of the mind in favour of 'a belief in the blood, the flesh, as being wiser than the intellect'.[2])

The combination of commentary and imaginative writing achieved full expression – or, in Lawrence-ese, was consummated – in *Studies in Classic American Literature* which remains one of the wildest feats of critical mapping ever attempted – not just of the main components of a national canon but the soul of an entire country. Those early pieces on *Hamlet* and Hardy – comparatively early in Lawrence's writing life and very early in my reading of him – were transformative. Forty years later the essays of *Studies in Classic American Literature* remain in constantly surprising proximity to my adult experience. At twenty-five Philip Larkin was too young to know whether his precocious claim that 'no one who has really thrilled to Lawrence can ever give him up'[3] had any validity, but it has proved accurate in my case.

Shortly before writing this introduction I was staying at a

friend's place in Joshua Tree. Late one afternoon we hiked up a nearby hill in the blazing sun to a trailer that had been abandoned by the owner. Inside there were mouse and rat droppings everywhere, on the floor, the bed, all over the kitchen. The scattered remains of what had once been a domesticated life intermingled with the detritus of subsequent drug-use to change the various rooms from a home into 'horrible underground passages of the human soul'. Unchanged in millions of years, the surrounding golden landscape and deep blue sky were tremendous. On a picnic table outside the health-hazard trailer were the brittle pages of a coverless edition of the writings of Edgar Allan Poe. It was impossible to know what 'ghastly story of the human soul in its disruptive throes' had unfolded here but, for me, the mystery itself had been framed by Lawrence's thoughts on Poe. A fortnight earlier, in Colorado, I'd seen the western *Hostiles*, which takes its epigraph from Lawrence's essay on Fenimore Cooper: 'The essential American soul is hard, isolate, stoic, and a killer.'[4] Both experiences were shaped – once deliberately, by filmmaker Scott Cooper, the other randomly – by what Lawrence had written.*

---

* Another example, from literature rather than life, from Europe rather than America, of how Lawrence continues to shape my perceptions: in *T Singer* the Norwegian novelist Dag Solstad writes that the young wife of his eponymous protagonist 'would have liked to see him in bright red trousers'. This seems an obvious allusion to Mellors's claim in *Lady Chatterley's Lover* that men should wear 'close red trousers'. If men wore red trousers, he tells Connie, 'that alone would change them in a month. They'd begin to be men again, to be men!' Singer, for his part, has 'seen men walking around wearing bright red trousers, and that wasn't for him. And honestly, it would have been impossible, it would have been a breach of something deep-seated in him, something he wasn't able to breach.' Is Solstad here using a passage from Lawrence as a way of sending a deliberate message about a failing marriage – or am I using Lawrence to decode what is merely an expression of sartorial

There was a time when this was far from unusual. In 1945 Larkin had gushed to a friend that Lawrence was 'the greatest writer of this century, and in many things the greatest writer of all times'.[5] Born five years after Larkin, the narrator of John Fowles's *The Magus* (1965) raises the bar higher as he leaves school believing Lawrence is 'the greatest human being of the century'.[6] And it wasn't just the guys. Visiting the Lawrence ranch and shrine in Taos in 1939, W. H. Auden noted how 'Cars of women pilgrims go up every day to stand reverently there and wonder what it would have been like to sleep with him.'[7]

The answer, according to Kate Millett in *Sexual Politics* (1970), was probably unpleasant and certainly disappointing. Her devastating and witty analysis laid bare the trowelled-on silli-nesses and 'liturgical pomp' of exactly the thing Lawrence had become famous for, namely his writing about sex.[8] Add in his regrettable – albeit temporary – infatuation with a proto-fascistic cult of 'the leader-cum-follower' and it is easy to see why Lawrence's reputation has been in more or less continuous decline since the 1970s. For a period that has now lasted as long as his short life Lawrence has managed to remain perversely out of step with whatever critical fashions have held sway – though this is not to say that he has been without devotees. Hence the frustrated passion of Tony Hoagland, in his poem 'Lawrence', as he recalls how

> On two occasions in the past twelve months
> I have failed, when someone at a party
> spoke of him with a dismissive scorn,
> to stand up for D. H. Lawrence[9]

---

preference on the part of Singer's wife? (*T Singer* (London: Harvill Secker, 2018), pp. 120–21).

Any attempt at standing up for this 'man who burned like an acetylene torch/from one end to the other of his life' had best begin by conceding not only the poor quality of novels such as *Aaron's Rod* or *The Plumed Serpent* but that some of the canonical works are, in George Orwell's understated words, 'difficult to get through'.[10] As a novelist, it could be argued, Lawrence peaked early, with *Sons and Lovers*. His former friend John Middleton Murry went further, arguing, in a review of *Women in Love,* that Lawrence was one of those novelists who 'appear to have passed their prime long before reaching it'.[11] Thereafter, as Raymond Williams has movingly expressed it, 'What he lost along the way – what I think he knew he had lost and struggled to recover – may in fact be just as important as what he undoubtedly gained.'[12] One way to rebalance the books is to extend the critical catchment area beyond the fictive straits of F. R. Leavis's 'great tradition' to include forms of writings that are considered ancillary or minor. If Lawrence remains a great writer today that is due in no small part because his enduring freshness and force is found in the travel books, in poems that were scarcely even poems, and in the scatter of his essays. For Lawrence the novel, 'the one bright book of life', was the supreme test; that's what he staked his life on. But many of his gifts were best displayed elsewhere. In this regard, in his inability to confine himself to the arena he most valued, he seems a distinctly contemporary writer: Lawrence as loose canon, so to speak.

The present volume aims to bring together the minor works that might be called essays. I put it awkwardly like that because, as an earlier compiler of such a selection, Richard Aldington, concluded, ' "Essays" is a poor word for these brilliantly-varied writings.'[13] Actually, Aldington perhaps understates things for the brilliance and variety often occur *within* a single essay. (Dean Young narrows the focus still further, characterizing Lawrence, in his poem 'Shield of Moon Dust', as someone 'able to write horribly and magnificently/in the same sentence'.[14]) Essays on writers are also essays on places; essays on places are also piece of autobiography and so on. Rebecca West, in the 'Elegy' composed after his death (see p. 472), concluded that Lawrence only ever wrote about the state of his own soul, using as symbol whatever was closest to hand. Persuasive and partly true, West's analysis risks diminishing his uncanny ability to render what Mabel Dodge Sterne called 'the feel and touch and smell of places' – which is why she invited him to New Mexico in 1921.[15] On his circuitous way there from Sicily, in Australia the following May, he seemed immediately to intuit another world, some kind of dream-time: 'a "fourth dimension" and the white people swim like shadows over the surface of it.'[16] While scarcely mentioning politics his 'Letter from Germany' registers something – something 'which has not yet eventuated' – blowing through the trees of the Black Forest in 1924: 'Out of the very air comes a sense of danger, a queer *bristling* feeling of uncanny danger.' Sensations flicker and blaze into ideas that are presented as though they are data from some instrument calibrated to a pitch of receptivity so extreme as to be abnormal or even pathological. The gulf between the ostensible object of enquiry and the direction taken by the investigation is frequently vast, the conclusions routinely drastic. Everything has the potential to become something else. The best parts of 'Art and Morality' are not about art or morality but – via an extraordinary speculative detour into the lives of ancient Egyptians – about how the 'Kodak' habit of photographing oneself all the time has fundamentally changed our sense of ourselves: a prophetic diagnosis of a defining malaise of the iPhone era. In an editorial note to 'Introduction to Pictures' (not to be confused with 'Introduction to These Paintings' included here) the scholar James T. Boulton rightly points out that the essay 'does not once refer to pictures'.[17] This tendency to stray from stated intentions was best expressed by Lawrence himself on 5 September 1914. 'Out of sheer rage I've begun my book about Thomas Hardy. It will be about anything but Thomas Hardy I am afraid – queer stuff – but not bad.'[18]

The *Study of Thomas Hardy* introduces a further editorial complication. Intended as part of a series called 'Writers of the Day', the manuscript which had veered far from any template was not accepted for publication. Lawrence, for his part, wanted to leave the original brief still further behind and began recasting something that had been 'mostly philosophicalish, slightly about Hardy' into a more explicit statement of his '"philosophy" (forgive the word)'.[19] The result, itself much revised, was 'The Crown' but some of the 'sketches' in which *Twilight in Italy* had its origins were also redesigned to bear this heavier philosophical load. Versions of the same concerns crop up in multiple, overlapping forms, some of them unfinished or unpublished. What start out as isolated 'essays' or 'sketches' become the integrated chapters of a book.

My solution to these issues is to have abandoned the subdivisions by ostensible subject favoured by Aldington and Edward D. McDonald (editor of *Phoenix*) in favour of chronological arrangement by date of composition. The gain is twofold: while avoiding the sense that a piece has been miscategorized we are also able to follow the twists and turns of Lawrence's writing and thought over time. Essays that ended up in a book that is currently readily available have been excluded in order to make room for harder-to-find pieces. So while there is nothing from *Studies in Classic American Literature* or *Mornings in Mexico* I have included an early version of what became a section of *Twilight in Italy*. With the exception of the review of Ernest Hemingway's *In Our Time* (the most interesting part of a round-up of American books) I have avoided cutting down longer pieces or chapters from non-fiction books and presenting them as self-contained essays.

Beyond that the present selection comes down to personal

preferences held in check or complemented by the need to be responsibly comprehensive and receptive to the probable needs of students. 'The Crown' is not here because, although Lawrence undoubtedly had a philosophy which he was keen to share with the world (to put it mildly), the effort involved him writing against his strengths. I love the way he took issue with Bertrand Russell for being unable to 'accept in his philosophy the Infinite, the Boundless, the Eternal, as the real starting point', but notwithstanding plans to 'give some lectures on Eternity' Lawrence was always at his best when facing the finite and the particular.[20] However unpalatable they may be to modern readers, his titular 'Reflections' retain their fascination because of the way they are rooted not just in 'the death of a porcupine' but in the agony of the dog with porcupine quills in his nose with which the piece begins. Lawrence was often carried away by stuff about a metaphorical 'river of dissolution' but he noticed, with stunning clarity of vison, all the flora and fauna on the literal riverbank. Baulking instinctively at Joyce's *Ulysses* ('Such effort! Such exertion!') he was often best when most off-the cuff, even if that guaranteed Joyce's reciprocally low opinion: 'That man really writes very badly.'[21] In this respect, although he rewrote his major novels multiple times, the man who scorned Joyce for being 'utterly without spontaneity' is like a proto-Kerouac.[22] He could preach endlessly about man, woman and the need for them to be, as Birkin insists in *Women in Love*, 'like two single equal stars balanced in conjunction', but the best thing he ever wrote about a wife or life-partner occurs as a throwaway line in the poem 'For a Moment' when, sitting and waiting on a hotel terrace, he sees 'the woman who looks for me in the world'.[23] No one has expressed more clearly than that woman, Frieda, what continues to engage readers who have otherwise grown weary of Lawrence's loins of darkness, hard gem-like flames and so forth: 'To me his relationship, his bond with everything in creation was so amazing, no preconceived ideas, just a meeting between him and a creature, a tree, a cloud, anything. I called it love, but it was something else – *Bejahung* in German, "saying yes." '[24]

Yes indeed, there are moments like this in everything he wrote, irrespective of the form, from the description of cypress trees in *Twilight* ('For as we have candles to light the darkness of night, so the cypresses are candles to keep the darkness aflame in the full sunshine') to a kangaroo with her 'drooping Victorian shoulders' in the eponymous poem, to numerous scenes and passages in every one of the novels.[25] You never know, in Lawrence, when or how the next flash of genius will manifest itself. A compulsion to override the usual imperatives of editorial self-restraint is a small price to pay for the unimpeded flow of improvisation we get when he records a Saturday afternoon spent in Malta in the company of Maurice Magnus, as he moves around 'that dreadful island', 'the sun-blazed, sun-dried, disheartening island', 'that bone-dry, hideous island', 'that beastly island'. In passages like this Lawrence's writing floats free from the period of its composition, from the anxiously shared prerogatives of the age, in a way that rarely happens with the modernists who were his contemporaries. The opening of 'Whistling of Birds' reads like a passage from J. A. Baker's *The Peregrine*: 'The frost held for many weeks, until the birds were dying rapidly. Everywhere in the fields and under the hedges lay the ragged remains of lapwings, starlings, thrushes, redwings, innumerable ragged bloody cloaks of birds . . .' Rather than multiply potential comparisons across time like this, one example can be allowed to stand for many. The ink, on the first page of 'Taos', feels as if it has barely had time to dry in the ninety-five years since Lawrence wrote it.

Many of the later essays were written for money when Lawrence lacked the energy and will to concentrate on sustained imaginative work. 'I think perhaps it's a waste to write any more novels,' he wrote to Nancy Pearn at the office of his literary agent Curtis Brown. 'I could probably live by little things. I mean in magazines.' The patient Ms Pearn proved equally adept at finding homes for these pieces and securing invitations to come up with further 'little articles for the newspapers' which he considered '*far* the best way of making money'. [26]

Irrespective of how such things originated, or of Lawrence's motives in undertaking them, the act of writing invariably yields something – and this is the word with which Hoagland concludes his too-late defence – magnificent. Nowhere is this more evident than in the introduction he contributed to Magnus's *Memoirs of the Foreign Legion*. Largely *about* money, it was written to discharge Magnus's debts and recoup money Lawrence had himself lost, but the extended length of the piece effectively wipes out – or writes off – its initiating motive. More generally, when Lawrence was dashing off 'little things' he was in some ways playing to his strengths, unburdening himself, partly in the sense of expressing himself freely but also without the psychic weight of ambition that bears down on *The Rainbow* or *Women in Love*.

In a letter concerning the whereabouts of misplaced manuscripts his friend Dorothy Brett noted astutely that 'When a careless man like Lawrence becomes careful – & has no track of his carelessness – he is apt to fly off the handle.'[27] The carefree attitude he could bring to essay-writing had unexpected advantages. Throughout his career Lawrence threw out bottles containing messages energetically disdaining whatever it was he professed not to care about at any given moment. In one of the last pieces he wrote, an introduction to *The Dragon of the Apocalypse* by Frederick Carter – another example of a piece that outgrew its brief as Lawrence ended up writing his very own *Apocalypse* – he set out some of the reasons why, and the ways in which, we continue to care about him. 'I don't care *what* a man sets out to prove, so long as he will interest me and carry me away. I don't in the least care whether he [Carter] proves his point or not, so long as he has given me a real imaginative experience by the way, and not another set of bloated thought-forms.' He then goes on to anticipate our potential objections: 'What does it matter if it is confused? What does it matter if it repeats itself? What does it matter if in parts it is not very interesting, when in other parts it is intensely so, when it suddenly opens doors and lets out the spirit into a new world, even if it is a very old world!'[28]

Here, on page after page, is Lawrence as a writer of endless renewal: our perpetual contemporary.

1 *Twilight in Italy* (Harmondsworth: Penguin, 1997), p. 144

2 *The Letters of D. H. Lawrence Volume I 1901–13*, edited by James T. Boulton (Cambridge: Cambridge University Press, 1979), p. 503

3 *Selected Letters of Philip Larkin: 1940–85*, edited by Anthony Thwaite, (London: Faber, 1988), p. 154

4 *Studies in Classic American Literature* (Harmondsworth: Penguin, 1971), pp. 88, 71, 68

5 *Selected Letters of Philip Larkin*, p. 101

6 John Fowles, *The Magus* (London: Cape, 1966), p. 1

7 Quoted by Janet Byrne in *A Genius for Living: A Biography of Frieda Lawrence* (London: Bloomsbury, 1995), p. 385

8 Kate Millett, *Sexual Politics* (London: Rupert Hart-Davis, 1971), p. 296

9 Tony Hoagland, *Donkey Gospel* (Minneapolis: Graywolf, 1998), p. 31. (It is interesting to note how Rebecca West was, in part, similarly *provoked* into writing her 'Elegy': 'What I hate is the sniggering about Lawrence and the actual candid joy in his death . . .' *Selected Letters of Rebecca West*, edited by Bonnie Kime Scott (New Haven: Yale University Press, 2000), p. 130)

10 George Orwell, *Collected Essays, Journalism and Letters Volume 4*, edited by Sonia Orwell and Ian Angus (Harmondsworth: Penguin, 1970), p. 52

11 Quoted by Mark Kinkead-Weekes in *D. H. Lawrence: Triumph to Exile* (Cambridge: Cambridge University Press, 1996), p. 684

12 Raymond Williams, *The English Novel from Dickens to Lawrence* (London: Chatto & Windus, 1970), p. 169

13 *Selected Essays*, edited by Richard Aldington (Harmondsworth: Penguin, 1950), p. 8

14 Dean Young, *elegy on toy piano* (Pittsburgh: University of Pittsburgh Press, 2005), p. 61

15 Quoted by Bill Goldstein in *The World Broke in Two* (London: Bloomsbury, 2017), p. 85

16 *The Letters of D. H. Lawrence Volume IV 1921–24*, edited by Warren Roberts, James T. Boulton and Elizabeth Mansfield (Cambridge: Cambridge University Press, 1987), p. 238

17 *Late Essays and Articles*, edited by James T. Boulton (Cambridge: Cambridge University Press, 2004), p. xxvii

18 *The Letters of D. H. Lawrence Volume II 1913–16*, edited by George J. Zytaruk and James T. Boulton (Cambridge: Cambridge University Press, 1981), p. 212

19 *Letters Volume II*, p. 292 and p. 309

20 *Letters Volume II*, p. 363

21 *The Letters of D. H. Lawrence Volume VI 1927–28*, edited by James T. Boulton, Margaret H. Boulton and Gerald M. Lacy (Cambridge: Cambridge University Press, 1991), p. 507; Joyce on Lawrence quoted by Richard Ellmann in *James Joyce* (Oxford: Oxford University Press, 1976), p. 628

22 *Letters Volume VI*, p. 548

23 *The Complete Poems*, edited by Vivian De Sola Pinto and F. Warren Roberts (Harmondsworth: Penguin, 1977), p. 672

24 Quoted by Byrne in *A Genius for Living*, p. 376

25 *Twilight in Italy*, p. 154; *Complete Poems*, p. 393

26 *Letters Volume VI*, p. 29, and *Volume VII*, p. 41

27 Quoted in footnote in *The Letters of D. H. Lawrence Volume VII 1928–30*, edited by Keith Sagar and James T. Boulton (Cambridge: Cambridge University Press, 1993), p. 342

28 *Apocalypse* (London: Penguin 1995), p. 50 and p. 54

THE BAD SIDE OF BOOKS

CHRISTS IN THE TIROL (1912)

The real Tirol does not seem to extend far south of the Brenner, and northward it goes right to the Starnberger See. Even at Sterzing the rather gloomy atmosphere of the Tirolese Alps is being dispersed by the approach of the South. And, strangely enough, the roadside crucifixes become less and less interesting after Sterzing. Walking down from Munich to Italy, I have stood in front of hundreds of *Martertafeln*; and now I miss them; these painted shrines by the Garda See are not the same.

I, who see a tragedy in every cow, began by suffering from the Secession pictures in Munich. All these new paintings seemed so shrill and restless. Those that were meant for joy shrieked and pranced for joy, and sorrow was a sensation to be relished, curiously; as if we were epicures in suffering, keen on a new flavour. I thought with kindliness of England, whose artists so often suck their sadness like a lollipop, mournfully, and comfortably.

Then one must walk, as it seems, for miles and endless miles past crucifixes, avenues of them. At first they were mostly factory made, so that I did not notice them, any more than I noticed the boards with warnings, except just to observe they were there. But coming among the Christs carved in wood by the peasant artists, I began to feel them. Now, it seems to me, they create almost an atmosphere over the northern Tirol, an atmosphere of pain.

I was going along a marshy place at the foot of the mountains, at evening, when the sky was a pale, dead colour and the hills were nearly black. At a meeting of the paths was a crucifix, and between the feet of the Christ a little red patch of dead poppies. So I looked at him. It was an old shrine, and the Christus was nearly like a man. He seemed to me to be real. In front of me hung a Bavarian peasant, a Christus, staring across at the evening and the black hills. He had broad cheek-bones and sturdy limbs, and he hung doggedly on the cross, hating it. He reminded me of a peasant farmer, fighting slowly and meanly, but not giving in. His plain, rudimentary face stared stubbornly at the hills, and his neck was stiffened, as if even yet he were struggling away from the cross he resented. He would not yield to it. I stood in front of him, and realized him. He might have said, 'Yes, here I am, and it's bad enough, and it's suffering, and it doesn't come to an end. *Perhaps* something will happen, will help. If it doesn't, I s'll have to go on with it.' He seemed stubborn and struggling from the root of his soul, his human soul. No Godship had been thrust upon him. He was human clay, a peasant Prometheus-Christ, his poor soul bound in him, blind, but struggling stubbornly against the fact of the nails. And I looked across at the tiny square of orange light, the window of a farmhouse on the marsh. And, thinking of the other little farms, of how the man and his wife and his children worked on till dark, intent and silent, carrying the hay in their arms out of the streaming thunder-rain which soaked them through, I understood how the Christus was made.

And after him, when I saw the Christs posing on the Cross, à la Guido Reni, I recognized them as the mere conventional symbol, meaning no more Christ than St George and the Dragon on a five-shilling-piece means England.

There are so many Christs carved by men who have carved to get at the meaning of their own soul's anguish. Often, I can distinguish one man's work in a district. In the Zemm valley, right in the middle of the Tirol, there are some half-dozen crucifixes by the same worker, who has whittled away in torment to see himself emerge out of the piece of timber, so that he can understand his own suffering, and see it take on itself the distinctness of an eternal thing, so that he can go on further, leaving it. The chief of these crucifixes is a very large one, deep in the Klamm, where it is always gloomy and damp. The river roars below, the rock wall opposite reaches high overhead, pushing back the sky. And by the track where the pack-horses go, in the cold gloom, hangs the large, pale Christ. He has fallen forward, just dead, and the weight of his full-grown, mature body is on the nails of the hands. So he drops, as if his hands would tear away, and he would fall to earth. The face is strangely brutal, and is set with an ache of weariness and pain and bitterness, and his rather ugly, passionate mouth is shut with bitter despair. After all, he had wanted to live and to enjoy his manhood. But fools had ruined his body, and thrown his life away, when he wanted it. No one had helped. His youth and health and vigour, all his life, and himself, were just thrown away as waste. He had died in bitterness. It is sombre and damp, silent save for the roar of water. There hangs the falling body of the man who had died in bitterness of spirit, and the driver of the pack-horses takes off his hat, cringing in his sturdy cheerfulness as he goes beneath.

He is afraid. I think of the carver of the crucifix. He also was more or less afraid. They all, when they carved or erected these crucifixes, had fear at the bottom of their hearts. And so the monuments to physical pain are found everywhere in the mountain gloom. By the same hand that carved the big, pale Christ I found another crucifix, a little one, at the end of a bridge. This Christ had a fair beard instead of a black one, and his body was hanging differently. But there was about him the same bitterness, the

3

same despair, even a touch of cynicism. Evidently the artist could not get beyond the tragedy that tormented him. No wonder the peasants are afraid, as they take off their hats in passing up the valley.

They are afraid of physical pain. It terrifies them. Then they raise, in their startled helplessness of suffering, these Christs, these human attempts at deciphering the riddle of pain. In the same way they paint the humorous little pictures of some calamity – a man drowned in a stream or killed by a falling tree – and nail it up near the scene of the accident. 'Memento mori,' they say everywhere. And so they try to get used to the idea of death and suffering, to rid themselves of some of the fear thereof. And all tragic art is part of the same attempt.

But some of the Christs are quaint. One I know is very elegant, brushed and combed. 'I'm glad I am no lady,' I say to him. For he is a pure lady-killer. But he ignores me utterly, the exquisite. The man who made him must have been dying to become a gentleman.

And a fair number are miserable fellows. They put up their eyebrows plaintively, and pull down the corners of their mouths. Sometimes they gaze heavenwards. They are quite sorry for themselves.

'Never mind,' I say to them. 'It'll be worse yet, before you've done.'

Some of them look pale and done-for. They didn't make much fight; they hadn't much pluck in them. They make me sorry.

'It's a pity you hadn't got a bit more kick in you,' I say to them. And I wonder why in England one sees always this pale, pitiful Christ with no 'go' in him. Is it because our national brutality is so strong and deep that we must create for ourselves an anæmic Christus, for ever on the whine; either that, or one of those strange neutrals with long hair, that are supposed to represent to our children the Jesus of the New Testament.

In a tiny glass case beside the high-road where the Isar is a very small stream, sits another Christ that makes me want to laugh, and makes me want to weep also. His little head rests on his hand, his elbow on his knee, and he meditates, half-wearily. I am strongly reminded of Walther von der Vogelweide and the German medieval spirit. Detached, he sits, and dreams, and broods, in his little golden crown of thorns, and his little cloak of red flannel, that some peasant woman has stitched for him.

'*Couvre-toi de gloire, Tartarin – couvre-toi de flanelle,*' I think to myself.

But he sits, a queer little man, fretted, plunged in anxiety of thought, and yet dreaming rather pleasantly at the same time. I think he is the forefather of the warm-hearted German philosopher and professor.

He is the last of the remarkable Christs of the peasants that I have seen. Beyond the Brenner an element of unreality seems to creep in. The Christs are given great gashes in the breast and knees, and from the brow and breast and hands and knees streams of blood trickle down, so that one sees a weird striped thing in red and white that is not at all a Christus. And the same red that is used for the blood serves also to mark the path, so that one comes to associate the *Martertafeln* and their mess of red stripes with the stones smeared with scarlet paint for guidance. The wayside chapels, going south, become fearfully florid and ornate, though still one finds in them the little wooden limbs, arms and legs and feet, and little wooden cows or horses, hung up by the altar, to signify a cure in these parts. But there is a tendency for the Christs themselves to become either neuter or else sensational. In a chapel near St Jakob, a long way from the railway, sat the most ghastly Christus I can imagine. He is seated, after the crucifixion. His eyes, which are turned slightly to look at you, are bloodshot till they glisten scarlet, and even the iris seems purpled. And the misery, the almost criminal look of hate and misery on the bloody, disfigured face is shocking. I was amazed at the ghastly thing: moreover, it was fairly new.

South of the Brenner again, in the Austrian Tirol, I have not seen anyone salute the Christus: not even the guides. As one goes higher the crucifixes get smaller and smaller. The wind blows the snow under the tiny shed of a tiny Christ: the guides tramp stolidly by, ignoring the holy thing. That surprised me. But perhaps these were particularly unholy men. One does not expect a great deal of an Austrian, except real pleasantness.

So, in Austria, I have seen a fallen Christus. It was on the Jaufen, not very far from Meran. I was looking at all the snow-peaks all around, and hurrying downhill, trying to get out of a piercing wind, when I almost ran into a very old *Martertafel*. The wooden shed was silver-grey with age, and covered on the top with a thicket of lichen, weird, grey-green, sticking up its tufts. But on the rocks at the foot of the cross was the armless Christ, who had tumbled down and lay on his back in a weird attitude. It was one of the old, peasant Christs, carved out of wood, and having the long, wedge-shaped shins and thin legs that are almost characteristic. Considering the great sturdiness of a mountaineer's calves, these thin, flat legs are interesting. The arms of the fallen Christ had broken off at the shoulders, and they hung on their nails, as *ex voto* limbs hang in the shrines. But these arms dangled from their palms, one at each end of the cross, the muscles, carved in wood, looking startling, upside down. And the icy wind blew them backwards and forwards. There, in that bleak place among the stones, they looked horrible. Yet I dared not touch either them or the fallen image. I wish some priest would go along and take the broken thing away.

So many Christs there seem to be: one in rebellion against his cross, to which he was nailed; one bitter with the agony of knowing he must die, his heart-beatings all futile; one who felt sentimental; one who gave in to his misery; one who was a sensationalist; one who dreamed and fretted with thought. Per-haps the peasant carvers of crucifixes are right, and all these were found on the same cross. And perhaps there were others too: one who waited for the end, his soul still with a sense of right and hope; one ashamed to see the crowd make beasts of themselves, ashamed that he should provide for their sport; one who looked at them and thought: 'And I am of you. I might be among you, yelling at myself in that way. But I am not, I am here. And so –'

All those Christs, like a populace, hang in the mountains under their little sheds. And perhaps they are falling, one by one. And I suppose we have carved no Christs, afraid lest they should be too like men, too like ourselves. What we worship must have exotic form.

REVIEW OF *DEATH IN VENICE* BY THOMAS MANN (1913)

Thomas Mann is perhaps the most famous of German novelists now writing. He, and his elder brother, Heinrich Mann, with Jakob Wassermann, are acclaimed the three artists in fiction of present-day Germany.

But Germany is now undergoing that craving for form in fiction, that passionate desire for the mastery of the medium of narrative, that will of the writer to be greater than and undisputed lord over the stuff he writes, which is figured to the world in Gustave Flaubert.

Thomas Mann is over middle age, and has written three or four books: *Buddenbrooks*, a novel of the patrician life of Lübeck; *Tristan*, a collection of six *Novellen*; *Königliche Hoheit*, an unreal Court romance; various stories, and lastly, *Der Tod in Venedig*. The author himself is the son of a Lübeck *Patrizier*.

It is as an artist rather than as a story-teller that Germany worships Thomas Mann. And yet it seems to me, this craving for form is the outcome, not of artistic conscience, but of a certain attitude to life. For form is not a personal thing like style. It is impersonal like logic. And just as the school of Alexander Pope was logical in its expressions, so it seems the school of Flaubert is, as it were, logical in its æsthetic form. 'Nothing outside the definite line of the book,' is a maxim. But can the human mind fix absolutely the definite line of a book, any more than it can fix absolutely any definite line of action for a living being?

Thomas Mann, however, is personal, almost painfully so, in his subject-matter. In 'Tonio Kröger,' the long *Novelle* at the end of the *Tristan* volume, he paints a detailed portrait of himself as a youth and younger man, a careful analysis. And he expresses at some length the misery of being an artist. 'Literature is not a calling, it is a curse.' Then he says to the Russian painter girl: 'There is no artist anywhere but longs again, my love, for the common life.' But any young artist might say that. It is because the stress of life in a young man, but particularly in an artist, is very strong, and has as yet found no outlet, so that it rages inside him in *Sturm und Drang*. But the condition is the same, only more tragic, in the Thomas Mann of fifty-three. He has never found any outlet for himself, save his art. He has never given himself to anything but his art. This is all well and good, if his art absorbs and satisfies him, as it has done some great men, like Corot. But then there are the other artists, the more human, like Shakespeare and Goethe, who must give themselves to life as well as to art. And if these were afraid, or despised life, then with their surplus they would ferment and become rotten. Which is what ails Thomas Mann. He is physically ailing, no doubt. But his complaint is deeper: it is of the soul.

And out of this soul-ailment, this unbelief, he makes his particular art, which he describes, in 'Tonio Kröger,' as '*Wählerisch, erlesen, kostbar, fein, reizbar gegen das Banale, und aufs höchste empfindlich in Fragen des Taktes und Geschmacks.*' He is a disciple, in method, of the Flaubert who wrote: 'I worked sixteen hours yesterday, today the whole day, and have at last finished one page.' In writing of the *Leitmotiv* and its influence, he says: 'Now this method alone is sufficient to explain my slowness. It is the result neither of anxiety nor indigence, but of an overpowering sense of responsibility for the choice of every word, the coining of every phrase . . . a responsibility that longs for perfect freshness, and which, after two hours work, prefers not to undertake an important sentence. For which sentence is important, and which not? Can one know before hand whether a sentence, or part of a sentence may not be called upon to appear again as *Motiv*, peg, symbol, citation or connexion? And a sentence which must be heard twice must be fashioned accordingly. It must – I do not speak of beauty – possess a certain high level, and symbolic suggestion, which will make it worthy to sound again in any epic future. So every point becomes a standing ground, every adjective a decision, and it is clear that such work is not to be produced off-hand.'

This, then, is the method. The man himself was always delicate in constitution. 'The doctors said he was too weak to go to school, and must work at home.' I quote from Aschenbach, in *Der Tod in Venedig*. 'When he fell, at the age of fifty-three, one of his closest observers said of him: "Aschenbach has always lived like this" – and he gripped his fist hard clenched; "never like this" – and he let his open hand lie easily on the arm of the chair.'

He forced himself to write, and kept himself to the work. Speaking of one of his works, he says: 'It was pardonable, yea, it showed plainly the victory of his morality, that the uninitiated reader supposed the book to have come of a solid strength and one long breath; whereas it was the result of small daily efforts and hundreds of single inspirations.'

And he gives the sum of his experience in the belief: '*dass beinahe alles Grosse, was dastehe, als ein Trotzdem dastehe, trotz Kummer und Qual, Armut, Verlassenheit, Körperschwäche, Laster, Leidenschaft und tausend hemmnischen Zustände gekommen sei.*' And then comes the final revelation, difficult to translate. He is speaking of life as it is written into his books:

'For endurance of one's fate, grace in suffering, does not only mean passivity, but is an active work, a positive triumph, and the Sebastian figure is the most beautiful symbol, if not of all art, yet of the art in question. If one looked into this portrayed world and saw the elegant self-control that hides from the eyes of the world to the last moment the inner undermining, the biological decay; saw the yellow ugliness which, sensuously at a disadvantage, could blow its choking heat of desire to a pure flame, and even rise to sovereignty in the kingdom of beauty; saw the pale impotence which draws out of the glowing depths of its intellect sufficient strength to subdue a whole vigorous people, bring them to the foot of the Cross, to the feet of impotence; saw the amiable bearing in the empty and severe service of Form; saw the quickly enervating longing and art of the born swindler: if one saw such a fate as this, and all the rest it implied, then one would be forced to doubt whether there were in reality any other heroism than that of weakness. Which heroism, in any case, is more of our time than this?'

Perhaps it is better to give the story of *Der Tod in Venedig,* from which the above is taken, and to whose hero it applies.

Gustav von Aschenbach, a fine, famous author, over fifty years of age, coming to the end of a long walk one afternoon, sees as he is approaching a burying place, near Munich, a man standing between the chimeric figures of the gateway. This man in the gate of the cemetery is almost the *Motiv* of the story. By him, Aschenbach is infected with a desire to travel. He examines himself minutely, in a way almost painful in its frankness, and one sees the whole soul of this author of fifty-three. And it seems, the artist has absorbed the man, and yet the man is there, like an exhausted organism on which a parasite has fed itself strong. Then begins a kind of Holbein *Totentanz.* The story is quite natural in appearance, and yet there is the gruesome sense of symbolism throughout. The man near the burying ground has suggested travel – but whither? Aschenbach sets off to a watering place on the Austrian coast of the Adriatic, seeking some adventure, some passionate adventure, to which his sick soul and unhealthy body have been kindled. But finding himself on the Adriatic, he knows it is not thither that his desire draws him, and he takes ship for Venice. It is all real, and yet with a curious sinister unreality, like decay, the 'biological decay.' On board there is a man who reminds one of the man in the gateway, though there is no connexion. And then, among a crowd of young Poles who are crossing, is a ghastly fellow, whom Aschenbach sees is an old man dressed up as young, who capers unsuspected among the youths, drinks hilariously with them, and falls hideously drunk at last on the deck, reaching to the author, and slobbering about '*dem allerliebsten, dem schönsten Liebchen.*' Suddenly the upper plate of his false teeth falls on his underlip.

Aschenbach takes a gondola to the Lido, and again the gondolier reminds one of the man in the cemetery gateway. He is, moreover, one who will make no concession, and, in spite of Aschenbach's demand to be taken back to St Mark's, rows him in his black craft to the Lido, talking to himself softly all the while. Then he goes without payment.

The author stays in a fashionable hotel on the Lido. The adventure is coming, there by the pallid sea. As Aschenbach comes down into the hall of the hotel, he sees a beautiful Polish boy of about fourteen, with honey-coloured curls clustering round his pale face, standing with his sisters and their governess.

Aschenbach loves the boy – but almost as a symbol. In him he loves life and youth and beauty, as Hyacinth in the Greek myth. This, I suppose; is blowing the choking heat to pure flame, and raising it to the kingdom of beauty. He follows the boy, watches him all day long on the beach, fascinated by beauty concrete before him. It is still the *Künstler* and his abstraction: but there is also the 'yellow ugliness, sensually at a disadvantage,' of the elderly man below it all. But the picture of the writer watching the folk on the beach gleams and lives with a curious, gold-phosphorescent light, touched with the brightness of Greek myth, and yet a modern seashore with folks on the sands, and a half-threatening, diseased sky.

Aschenbach, watching the boy in the hotel lift, finds him delicate, almost ill, and the thought that he may not live long fills the elderly writer with a sense of peace. It eases him to think the boy should die.

Then the writer suffers from the effect of the *sirocco*, and intends to depart immediately from Venice. But at the station he finds with joy that his luggage has gone wrong, and he goes straight back to the hotel. There, when he sees Tadzin again, he knows why he could not leave Venice.

There is a month of hot weather, when Aschenbach follows Tadzin about, and begins to receive a look, loving, from over the lad's shoulder. It is wonderful, the heat, the unwholesomeness, the passion in Venice. One evening comes a street singer, smelling of carbolic acid, and sings beneath the veranda of the hotel. And this time, in gruesome symbolism, it is the man from the burying ground distinctly.

The rumour is, that the black cholera is in Venice. An atmosphere of secret plague hangs over the city of canals and palaces. Aschenbach verifies the report at the English bureau, but cannot bring himself to go away from Tadzin, nor yet to warn the Polish family. The secretly pest-smitten days go by. Aschenbach follows the boy through the stinking streets of the town and loses him. And on the day of the departure of the Polish family, the famous author dies of the plague.

It is absolutely, almost intentionally, unwholesome. The man is sick, body and soul. He portrays himself as he is, with wonderful skill and art, portrays his sickness. And since any genuine portrait is valuable, this book has its place. It portrays one man, one atmosphere, one sick vision. It claims to do no more. And we have to allow it. But we know it is unwholesome – it does not strike me as being morbid for all that, it is too well done – and we give it its place as such.

Thomas Mann seems to me the last sick sufferer from the complaint of Flaubert. The latter stood away from life as from a leprosy. And Thomas Mann, like Flaubert, feels vaguely that he has in him something finer than ever physical life revealed. Physical life is a disordered corruption, against which he can fight with only one weapon, his fine æsthetic sense, his feeling for beauty, for perfection, for a certain fitness which soothes him, and gives him an inner pleasure, however corrupt the stuff of life may be. There he is, after all these years, full of disgusts and loathing of himself as Flaubert was, and Germany is being voiced, or partly so, by him. And so, with real suicidal intention, like Flaubert's, he sits, a last too-sick disciple, reducing himself grain by grain to the statement of his own disgust, patiently, self-destructively, so that his statement at least may be perfect in a world of corruption. But he is so late.

Already I find Thomas Mann, who, as he says, fights so hard against the banal in his work, somewhat banal. His expression may be very fine. But by now what he expresses is stale. I think we have learned our lesson, to be sufficiently aware of the fulsomeness of life. And even while he has a rhythm in style, yet his work has none of the rhythm of a living thing, the rise of a poppy, then the after uplift of the bud, the shedding of the calyx and the spreading wide of the petals, the falling of the flower and the pride of the seed-head. There is an unexpectedness in this such as does not come from their carefully plotted and arranged developments. Even *Madame Bovary* seems to me dead in respect to the living rhythm of the whole work. While it is there in *Macbeth* like life itself.

But Thomas Mann is old – and we are young. Germany does not feel very young to me.

FROM *STUDY OF THOMAS HARDY* (1914)

CHAPTER 3
Containing Six Novels and the Real Tragedy

This is supposed to be a book about the people in Thomas Hardy's novels. But if one wrote everything they give rise to, it would fill the Judgment Book.

One thing about them is that none of the heroes and heroines care very much for money, or immediate self-preservation, and all of them are struggling hard to come into being. What exactly the struggle into being consists in, is the question. But most obviously, from the Wessex novels, the first and chiefest factor is the struggle into love and the struggle with love: by love, meaning the love of a man for a woman and a woman for a man. The *via media* to being, for man or woman, is love, and love alone. Having achieved and accomplished love, then the man passes into the unknown. He has become himself, his tale is told. Of anything that is complete there is no more tale to tell. The tale is about becoming complete, or about the failure to become complete.

It is urged against Thomas Hardy's characters that they do unreasonable things – quite, quite unreasonable things. They are always going off unexpectedly and doing something that nobody would do. That is quite true, and the charge is amusing.

These people of Wessex are always bursting suddenly out of bud and taking a wild flight into flower, always shooting suddenly out of a tight convention, a tight, hide-bound cabbage state into something quite madly personal. It would be amusing to count the number of special marriage licenses taken out in Hardy's books. Nowhere, except perhaps in Jude, is there the slightest development of personal action in the characters: it is all explosive. Jude, however, does see more or less what he is doing, and acts from choice. He is more consecutive. The rest explode out of the convention. They are people each with a real, vital, potential self, even the apparently wishy-washy heroines of the earlier books, and this self suddenly bursts the shell of manner and convention and commonplace opinion, and acts independently, absurdly, without mental knowledge or acquiescence.

And from such an outburst the tragedy usually develops. For there does exist, after all, the great self-preservation scheme, and in it we must all live. Now to live in it after bursting out of it was the problem these Wessex people found themselves faced with. And they never solved the problem, none of them except the comically, insufficiently treated Ethelberta.

This because they must subscribe to the system in themselves. From the more immediate claims of self-preservation they could free themselves: from money, from ambition for social success. None of the heroes or heroines of Hardy cared much for these things. But there is the greater idea of self-preservation, which is formulated in the State, in the whole modelling of the community. And from this idea, the heroes and heroines of Wessex, like the heroes and heroines of almost anywhere else, could not free themselves. In the long run, the State, the Community, the established form of life remained, remained intact and impregnable, the individual, trying to break forth from it, died of fear, of exhaustion, or of exposure to attacks from all sides, like men who have left the walled city to live outside in the precarious open.

This is the tragedy of Hardy, always the same: the tragedy of those who, more or less pioneers, have died in the wilderness, whither they had escaped for free action, after having left the walled security, and the comparative imprisonment, of the established convention. This is the theme of novel after novel: remain quite within the convention, and you are good, safe, and happy in the long run, though you never have the vivid pang of sympathy on your side: or, on the other hand, be passionate, individual, wilful, you will find the security of the convention a walled prison, you will escape, and you will die, either of your own lack of strength to bear the isolation and the exposure, or by direct revenge from the community, or from both. This is the tragedy, and only this: it is nothing more metaphysical than the division of a man against himself in such a way: first, that he is a member of the community, and must, upon his honour, in no way move to disintegrate the community, either in its moral or its practical form; second, that the convention of the community is a prison to his natural, individual desire, a desire that compels him, whether he feel justified or not, to break the bounds of the community, lands him outside the pale, there to stand alone, and say: 'I was right, my desire was real and inevitable; if I was to be myself I must fulfil it, convention or no convention,' or else, there to stand alone, doubting, and saying: 'Was I right, was I wrong? If I was wrong, oh, let me die!' – in which case he courts death.

The growth and the development of this tragedy, the deeper and deeper realization of this division and this problem, the coming towards some conclusion, is the one theme of the Wessex novels.

And therefore the books must be taken chronologically, to reveal the development and to advance towards the conclusion.

1. *Desperate Remedies.*

Springrove, the dull hero, fast within convention, dare not tell Cytherea that he is already engaged, and thus prepares the complication. Manston, represented as fleshily passionate, breaks the convention and commits murder, which is very extreme, under compulsion of his desire for Cytherea. He is aided by the darkly passionate, lawless Miss Aldclyffe. He and Miss Aldclyffe meet death, and Springrove and Cytherea are united to happiness and success.

2. *Under the Greenwood Tree.*

After a brief excursion from the beaten track in the pursuit of social ambition and satisfaction of the imagination, figured by the Clergyman, Fancy, the little school-mistress, returns to Dick, renounces imagination, and settles down to steady, solid, physically satisfactory married life, and all is as it should be. But Fancy will carry in her heart all her life many unopened buds that will die unflowered; and Dick will probably have a bad time of it.

3. *A Pair of Blue Eyes.*

Elfride breaks down in her attempt to jump the first little hedge of convention, when she comes back after running away with Stephen. She cannot stand even a little alone. Knight, his conventional ideas backed up by selfish instinct, cannot endure Elfride when he thinks she is not virgin, though now she loves him beyond bounds. She submits to him, and owns the conventional idea entirely right, even whilst she is innocent. An aristocrat walks off with her whilst the two men hesitate, and she, poor innocent victim of passion not vital enough to overthrow the most banal conventional ideas, lies in a bright coffin, while the three confirmed lovers mourn, and say how great the tragedy is.

4. *Far from the Madding Crowd.*

The unruly Bathsheba, though almost pledged to Farmer Boldwood, a ravingly passionate, middle-aged bachelor pretendant, who has suddenly started in mad pursuit of some unreal conception of woman, personified in Bathsheba, lightly runs off and marries Sergeant Troy, an illegitimate aristocrat, unscrupulous and yet sensitive in taking his pleasures. She loves Troy, he does not love her. All the time she is loved faithfully and persistently by the good Gabriel, who is like a dog that watches the bone and bides the time. Sergeant Troy treats Bathsheba badly, never loves her, though he is the only man in the book who knows anything about her. Her pride helps her to recover. Troy is killed by Boldwood; exit the unscrupulous, but discriminative, almost cynical young soldier and the mad, middle-aged pursuer of the Fata Morgana; enter the good, steady Gabriel, who marries Bathsheba because he will make her a good husband, and the flower of imaginative first love is dead for her with Troy's scorn of her.

5. *The Hand of Ethelberta.*

Ethelberta, a woman of character and of brilliant parts, sets out in pursuit of social success, finds that Julius, the only man she is inclined to love, is too small for her, hands him over to the good little Picotee, and she herself, sacrificing almost cynically what is called her heart, marries the old scoundrelly Lord Mountclerc, runs him and his estates and governs well, a sound, strong pillar of established society, now she has nipped off the bud of her heart. Moral: it is easier for the butler's daughter to marry a lord than to find a husband with her love, if she be an exceptional woman.

The Hand of Ethelberta is the one almost cynical comedy. It marks the zenith of a certain feeling in the Wessex novels, the zenith of the feeling that the best thing to do is to kick out the craving for 'Love' and substitute commonsense, leaving sentiment to the minor characters.

This novel is a shrug of the shoulders, and a last taunt to hope, it is the end of the happy endings, except where sanity and a little cynicism again appear in *The Trumpet Major*, to bless where they despise. It is the hard, resistant, ironical announcement of personal failure, resistant and half-grinning. It gives way to violent, angry passions and real tragedy, real killing of beloved people, self-killing. Till now, only Elfride among the beloved, has been killed; the good men have always come out on top.

6. *The Return of the Native.*

This is the first tragic and important novel. Eustacia, dark, wild, passionate, quite conscious of her desires and inheriting no tradition which would make her ashamed of them, since she is of a novelistic Italian birth, loves, first, the unstable Wildeve, who does not satisfy her, then casts him aside for the newly returned Clym, whom she marries. What does she want? She does not know, but it is evidently some form of self-realization; she wants to be herself, to attain herself. But she does not know how, by what means, so romantic imagination says, Paris and the *beau monde.* As if that would have stayed her unsatisfaction.

Clym has found out the vanity of Paris and the *beau monde.* What, then, does he want? He does not know; his imagination tells him he wants to serve the moral system of the community, since the material system is despicable. He wants to teach little Egdon boys in school. There is as much vanity in this, easily, as in Eustacia's Paris. For what is the moral system but the ratified from of the material system? What is Clym's altruism but a deep, very subtle cowardice, that makes him shirk his own being whilst apparently acting nobly; which makes him choose to improve mankind rather than to struggle at the quick of himself into being. He is not able to undertake his own soul, so he will take a commission for society to enlighten the souls of others. It is a subtle equivocation. Thus both Eustacia and he sidetrack from themselves, and each leaves the other unconvinced, unsatisfied, unrealized. Eustacia, because she moves outside the convention, must die; Clym, because he identified himself with the community, is transferred from Paris to preaching. He had never become an integral man, because when faced with the demand to produce himself, he remained under cover of the community and excused by his altruism.

His remorse over his mother is adulterated with sentiment; it is exaggerated by the push of tradition behind it. Even in this he does not ring true. He is always according to pattern, producing his feelings more or less on demand, according to the accepted standard. Practically never is he able to act or even feel in his original self; he is always according to the convention. His punishment is his final loss of all his original self: he is left preaching, out of sheer emptiness.

Thomasin and Venn have nothing in them turbulent enough to push them to the bounds of the convention. There is always room for them inside. They are genuine people, and they get the prize within the walls.

Wildeve, shifty and unhappy, attracted always from outside and never driven from within, can neither stand with nor without the established system. He cares nothing for it, because he is unstable, has no positive being. He is an eternal assumption.

The other victim, Clym's mother, is the crashing-down of one of the old, rigid pillars of the system. The pressure on her is too great. She is weakened from the inside also, for her nature is non-conventional; it cannot own the bounds.

So, in this book, all the exceptional people, those with strong feelings and unusual characters, are reduced; only those remain who are steady and genuine, if commonplace. Let a man will for himself, and he is destroyed. He must will according to the established system.

The real sense of tragedy is got from the setting. What is the great, tragic power in the book? It is Egdon Heath. And who are the real spirits of the Heath? First, Eustacia, then Clym's mother, then Wildeve. The natives have little or nothing in common with the place.

What is the real stuff of tragedy in the book? It is the Heath. It is the primitive, primal earth, where the instinctive life heaves up. There, in the deep, rude stirring of the instincts, there was the reality that worked the tragedy. Close to the body of things, there can be heard the stir that makes us and destroys us. The heath heaved with raw instinct. Egdon, whose dark soil was strong and crude and organic as the body of a beast. Out of the body of this crude earth are born Eustacia, Wildeve, Mistress Yeobright, Clym, and all the others. They are one year's accidental crop. What matters if some are drowned or dead, and others preaching or married: what matter, any more than the withering heath, the reddening berries, the seedy furze, and the dead fern of one autumn of Egdon? The Heath persists. Its body is strong and fecund, it will bear many more crops beside this. Here is the sombre, latent power that will go on producing, no matter what happens to the product. Here is the deep, black source from whence all these little contents of lives are drawn. And the contents of the small lives are spilled and wasted. There is savage satisfaction in it: for so much more remains to come, such a black, powerful fecundity is working there that what does it matter?

Three people die and are taken back into the Heath; they mingle their strong earth again with its powerful soil, having been broken off at their stem. It is very good. Not Egdon is futile, sending forth life on the powerful heave of passion. It cannot be futile, for it is eternal. What is futile is the purpose of man.

Man has a purpose which he has divorced from the passionate purpose that issued him out of the earth into being. The Heath threw forth its shaggy heather and furze and fern, clean into being. It threw forth Eustacia and Wildeve and Mistress Yeobright and Clym, but to what purpose? Eustacia thought she wanted the hats and bonnets of Paris. Perhaps she was right.

The heavy, strong soil of Egdon, breeding original native beings, is under Paris as well as under Wessex, and Eustacia sought herself in the gay city. She thought life there, in Paris, would be tropical, and all her energy and passion out of Egdon would there come into handsome flower, And if Paris real had been Paris as she imagined it, no doubt she was right, and her instinct was soundly expressed. But Paris real was not Eustacia's imagined Paris. Where was her imagined Paris, the place where her powerful nature could come to blossom? Beside some strong-passioned, unconfined man, her mate.

Which mate Clym might have been. He was born out of passionate Egdon to live as a passionate being whose strong feelings moved him ever further into being. But quite early his life became narrowed down to a small purpose: he must of necessity go into business, and submit his whole being, body and soul as well as mind, to the business and to the greater system it represented. His feelings, that should have produced the man, were suppressed and contained, he worked according to a system imposed from without. The dark struggle of Egdon, a struggle into being as the furze struggles into flower, went on in him, but could not burst the enclosure of the idea, the system which contained him. Impotent to *be*, he must transform himself, and live in an abstraction, in a generalization, he must identify himself with the system. He must live as Man or Humanity, or as the Community, or as Society, or as Civilization. 'An inner strenuousness was preying on his outer symmetry, and they rated his look as singular . . . His countenance was overlaid with legible meanings. Without being thought-worn, he yet had certain marks derived from a perception of his surroundings, such as are not infrequently found on man at the end of the four or five years of endeavour which follow the close of placid pupilage. He already showed that thought is a disease of the flesh, and indirectly bore evidence that ideal physical beauty is incompatible with emotional development and a full recognition of the coil of things. Mental luminousness must be fed with the oil of life, even if there is already a physical seed for it; and the pitiful sight of two demands on one supply was just showing itself here.'

But did the face of Clym show that thought is a disease of flesh, or merely that in his case a dis-ease, an un-ease, of flesh produced thought? One does not catch thought like a fever: one produces it. If it be in any way a disease of flesh, it is rather the rash that indicates the disease than the disease itself. The 'inner strenuousness' of Clym's nature was not fighting against his physical symmetry, but against the limits imposed on his physical movement. By nature, as a passionate, violent product of Egdon, he should have loved and suffered in flesh and in soul from love, long before this age. He should have lived and moved and had his being, whereas he had only his business, and afterwards his inactivity. His years of pupilage were past, 'he was one of whom something original was expected,' yet he continued in pupilage. For he produced nothing original in being or in act, and certainly no original thought. None of his ideas were original. Even he himself was not original. He was over-taught, had become an echo. His life had been arrested, and his activity turned into repetition. Far from being emotionally developed, he was emotionally undeveloped, almost entirely. Only his mental faculties were developed. And, hid, his emotions were obliged to work according to the label he put upon them: a ready-made label.

Yet he remained for all that an original, the force of life was in him, however much he frustrated and suppressed its natural movement. 'As is usual with bright natures, the deity that lies ignominiously chained within an ephemeral human carcass shone out of him like a ray.' But was the deity chained within his ephemeral human carcass, or within his limited human consciousness? Was it his blood, which rose dark and potent out of

Egdon, which hampered and confined the deity, or was it his mind, that house built of extraneous knowledge and guarded by his will, which formed the prison?

He came back to Egdon – what for? To re-unite himself with the strong, free flow of life that rose out of Egdon as from a source? No – 'to preach to the Egdon eremites that they might rise to a serene comprehensiveness without going through the process of enriching themselves.' As if the Egdon eremites had not already far more serene comprehensiveness than ever he had himself, rooted as they were in the soil of all things, and living from the root! What did it matter how they enriched themselves, so long as they kept this strong, deep root in the primal soil, so long as their instincts moved out to action and to expression? The system was big enough for them, and had no power over their instincts. They should have taught him rather than he them.

And Egdon made him marry Eustacia. Here was action and life, here was a move into being on his part. But as soon as he got her, she became an idea to him, she had to fit in his system of ideas. According to his way of living, he knew her already, she was labelled and classed and fixed down. He had got into this way of living, and he could not get out of it. He had identified himself with the system, and he could not extricate himself. He did not know that Eustacia had her being beyond his. He did not know that she existed untouched by his system and his mind, where no system had sway and where no consciousness had risen to the surface. He did not know that she was Egdon, the powerful, eternal origin seething with production. He thought he knew. Egdon to him was the tract of common land, producing familiar rough herbage, and having some few unenlightened inhabitants. So he skated over heaven and hell, and having made a map of the surface, thought he knew all. But underneath and among his mapped world, the eternal powerful fecundity worked on heedless of him and his arrogance. His preaching, his superficiality made no difference. What did it matter if he had calculated a moral chart from the surface of life? Could that affect life, any more than a chart of the heavens affects the stars, affects the whole stellar universe which exists beyond our knowledge? Could the sound of his words affect the working of the body of Egdon, where in the unfathomable womb was begot and conceived all that would ever come forth? Did not his own heart beat far removed and immune from his thinking and talking? Had he been able to put even his own heart's mysterious resonance upon his map, from which he charted the course of lives in his moral system? And how much more completely, then, had he left out, in utter ignorance, the dark, powerful source whence all things rise into being, whence they will always continue to rise, to struggle forward to further being? A little of the static surface he could see, and map out. Then he thought his map was the thing itself. How blind he was, how utterly blind to the tremendous movement carrying and producing the surface. He did not know that the greater part of every life is underground, like roots in the dark in contact with the beyond. He preached, thinking lives could be moved like hen-houses from here to there. His blindness indeed brought on the calamity. But what matter if Eustacia or Wildeve or Mrs Yeobright died: what matter if he himself became a mere rattle of repetitive words – what did it matter? It was regrettable; no more. Egdon, the primal impulsive body, would go on producing all that was to be produced, eternally, though the will of man should destroy the blossom yet in bud, over and over again. At last he must learn what it is to be at one, in his mind and will, with the primal impulses that rise in him. Till then, let him perish or preach. The great reality on which the little tragedies enact themselves cannot be detracted from. The will and words which militate against it are the only vanity.

This is a constant revelation in Hardy's novels: that there exists a great background, vital and vivid, which matters more than the people who move upon it. Against the background of dark, passionate Egdon, of the leafy, sappy passion and sentiment of the woodlands, of the unfathomed stars, is drawn the lesser scheme of lives: *The Return of the Native*, *The Woodlanders*, or *Two on a Tower*. Upon the vast, incomprehensible pattern of some primal morality greater than ever the human mind can grasp, is drawn the little, pathetic pattern of man's moral life and struggle, pathetic, almost ridiculous. The little fold of law and order, the little walled city within which man has to defend himself from the waste enormity of nature, becomes always too small, and the pioneers venturing out with the code of the walled city upon them, die in the bonds of that code, free and yet unfree, preaching the walled city and looking to the waste.

This is the wonder of Hardy's novels, and gives them their beauty. The vast, unexplored morality of life itself, what we call the immorality of nature, surrounds us in its eternal incomprehensibility, and in its midst goes on the little human morality play, with its queer frame of morality and its mechanized movement; seriously, portentously, till some one of the protagonists chances to look out of the charmed circle, weary of the stage, to look into the wilderness raging round. Then he is lost, his little drama falls to pieces, or becomes mere repetition, but the stupendous theatre outside goes on enacting its own incomprehensible drama, untouched. There is this quality in almost all Hardy's work, and this is the magnificent irony it all contains, the challenge, the contempt. Not the deliberate ironies, little tales of widows or widowers, contain the irony of human life as we live it in our self-aggrandized gravity, but the big novels, *The Return of the Native*, and the others.

And this is the quality Hardy shares with the great writers,

Shakespeare or Sophocles or Tolstoi, this setting behind the small action of his protagonists the terrific action of unfathomed nature; setting a smaller system of morality, the one grasped and formulated by the human consciousness within the vast, uncomprehended and incomprehensible morality of nature or of life itself, surpassing human consciousness. The difference is, that whereas in Shakespeare or Sophocles the greater, uncomprehended morality, or fate, is actively transgressed and gives active punishment, in Hardy and Tolstoi the lesser, human morality, the mechanical system is actively transgressed, and holds, and punishes the protagonist, whilst the greater morality is only passively, negatively transgressed, it is represented merely as being present in background, in scenery, not taking any active part, having no direct connexion with the protagonist. Œdipus, Hamlet, Macbeth set themselves up against, or find themselves set up against, the unfathomed moral forces of nature, and out of this unfathomed force comes their death. Whereas Anna Karenina, Eustacia, Tess, Sue, and Jude find themselves up against the established system of human government and morality, they cannot detach themselves, and are brought down. Their real tragedy is that they are unfaithful to the greater unwritten morality, which would have bidden Anna Karenina be patient and wait until she, by virtue of greater right, could take what she needed from society; would have bidden Vronsky detach himself from the system, become an individual, creating a new colony of morality with Anna; would have bidden Eustacia fight Clym for his own soul, and Tess take and claim her Angel, since she had the greater light; would have bidden Jude and Sue endure for very honour's sake, since one must bide by the best that one has known, and not succumb to the lesser good.

Had Œdipus, Hamlet, Macbeth been weaker, less full of real, potent life, they would have made no tragedy; they would have comprehended and contrived some arrangement of their affairs, sheltering in the human morality from the great stress and attack of the unknown morality. But being, as they are, men to the fullest capacity, when they find themselves, daggers drawn, with the very forces of life itself, they can only fight till they themselves are killed, since the morality of life, the greater morality, is eternally unalterable and invincible. It can be dodged for some time, but not opposed. On the other hand, Anna, Eustacia, Tess or Sue – what was there in their position that was necessarily tragic? Necessarily painful it was, but they were not at war with God, only with Society. Yet they were all cowed by the mere judgment of man upon them, and all the while by their own souls they were right. And the judgment of men killed them, not the judgment of their own souls or the judgment of Eternal God.

Which is the weakness of modern tragedy, where transgression against the social code is made to bring destruction, as though the social code worked our irrevocable fate. Like Clym, the map appears to us more real than the land. Shortsighted almost to blindness, we pore over the chart, map out journeys, and confirm them: and we cannot see life itself giving us the lie the whole time.

CHAPTER 7
Of Being and Not-Being

In life, then, no new thing has ever arisen, or can arise, save out of the impulse of the male upon the female, the female upon the male. The interaction of the male and female spirit begot the wheel, the plough, and the first utterance that was made on the face of the earth.

As in my flower, the pistil, female, is the centre and swivel, the stamens, male, are close-clasping the hub, and the blossom is the great motion outwards into the unknown, so in a man's life, the female is the swivel and centre on which he turns closely, producing his movement. And the female to a man is the obvious form, a woman. And normally, the centre, the turning pivot, of a man's life is his sex-life, the centre and swivel of his being is the sexual act. Upon this turns the whole rest of his life, from this emanates every motion he betrays. And that this should be so, every man makes his effort. The supreme effort each man makes, for himself, is the effort to clasp as a hub the woman who shall be the axle, compelling him to true motion, without aberration. The supreme desire of every man is for mating with a woman, such that the sexual act be the closest, most concentrated motion in his life, closest upon the axle, the prime movement of himself, of which all the rest of his motion is a continuance in the same kind. And the vital desire of every woman is that she shall be clasped as axle to the hub of the man, that his motion shall portray her motionlessness, convey her static being into movement, complete and radiating out into infinity, starting from her stable eternality, and reaching eternity again, after having covered the whole of time.

This is complete movement: man upon woman, woman within man. This is the desire, the achieving of which, frictionless, is impossible, yet for which every man will try, with greater or less intensity, achieving more or less success.

This is the desire of every man, that his movement, the manner of his walk, and the supremest effort of his mind, shall be the pulsation outwards from stimulus received in the sex, in the sexual act, that the woman of his body shall be the begetter of his whole life, that she, in her female spirit, shall beget in him his idea, his motion, himself. When a man shall look at the work of his hands, that has succeeded, and shall know that it was begotten in him by the woman of his body, then he shall know what fundamental happiness is. Just as when a woman shall look at her child, that was begotten in her by the man of her spirit, she shall know what it is to be happy, fundamentally. But when a woman looks at her children that were begotten in her by a strange man, not the man of her spirit, she must know what it is to be happy with anguish, and to love with pain. So with a man who looks at his work which was not begotten in him by the woman of his body. He rejoices, troubles, and suffers an agony like death which contains resurrection.

For while, ideally, the soul of the woman possesses the soul of the man, procreates it and makes it big with new idea, motion, in the sexual act, yet, most commonly, it is not so. Usually, sex is only functional, a matter of relief or sensation, equivalent to eating or drinking or passing of excrement.

Then, if a man must produce work, he must produce it to some other than the woman of his body: as, in the same case, if a woman produce children, it must be to some other than the man of her desire.

In this case, a man must seek elsewhere than in woman for the female to possess his soul, to fertilize him and make him try with increase. And the female exists in much more than his woman. And the finding of it for himself gives a man his vision, his God.

And since no man and no woman can get a perfect mate, nor obtain complete satisfaction at all times, each man according to his need must have a God, an idea, that shall compel him to the movement of his own being. And then, when he lies with his woman, the man may concurrently be with God, and so get increase of his soul. Or he may have communion with his God apart and averse from the woman.

Every man seeks in woman for that which is stable, eternal. And if, under his motion, this break down in her, in the particular woman, so that she be no axle for his hub, but be driven away from herself, then he must seek elsewhere for his stability, for the centre to himself.

Then either he must seek another woman, or he must seek to make conscious his desire to find a symbol, to create and define in his consciousness the object of his desire, so that he may have it at will, for his own complete satisfaction.

In doing this latter, he seeks with his desire the female elsewhere than in the particular woman. Since everything that is, is either male or female or both, whether it be clouds or sunshine or hills or trees or a fallen feather from a bird, therefore in other things and in such things man seeks for his complement. And he must at last always call God the unutterable and the inexpressible, the unknowable, because it is his unrealized complement.

But all gods have some attributes in common. They are the unexpressed Absolute: eternal, infinite, unchanging. Eternal, Infinite, Unchanging: the High God of all Humanity is this.

Yet man, the male, is essentially a thing of movement and time and change. Until he is stirred into thought, he is complete in movement and change. But once he thinks, he must have the Absolute, the Eternal, Infinite, Unchanging.

And Man is stirred into thought by dissatisfaction, or unsatisfaction, as heat is born of friction. Consciousness is the same effort in male and female to obtain perfect frictionless interaction, perfect as Nirvana. It is the reflex both of male and female from defect in their dual motion. Being reflex from the dual motion, consciousness contains the two in one, and is therefore in itself Absolute.

And desire is the admitting of deficiency. And the embodiment of the object of desire reveals the original defect or the defaulture. So that the attributes of God will reveal that which man lacked and yearned for in his living. And these attributes are always, in their essence, Eternality, Infinity, Immutability.

And these are the qualities man feels in woman, as a principle. Let a man walk alone on the face of the earth, and he feels himself like a loose speck blown at random. Let him have a woman to whom he belongs, and he will feel as though he had a wall to back up against; even though the woman be mentally a fool. No man can endure the sense of space, of chaos, on four sides of himself. It drives him mad. He must be able to put his back to the wall. And this wall is his woman.

From her he has a sense of stability. She supplies him with the feeling of Immutability, Permanence, Eternality. He himself is a raging activity, change potent within change. He dare not even conceive of himself, save when he is sure of the woman permanent beneath him, beside him. He dare not leap into the unknown save from the sure stability of the unyielding female. Like a wheel, if he turn without an axle, his motion is wandering neutrality.

So always, the fear of a man is that he shall find no axle for his motion, that no woman can centralize his activity. And always, the fear of a woman is that she can find no hub for her stability, no man to convey into motion her full stability. Either the particular woman breaks down before the stress of the man, becomes erratic herself, no stay, no centre; or else the man is insufficiently active to carry out the static principle of his female, of his woman.

So life consists in the dual form of the Will-to-Motion and the Will-to-Inertia, and everything we see and know and are is the resultant of these two Wills. But the One Will, of which they are dual forms, that is as yet unthinkable.

And according as the Will-to-Motion predominates in race, or the Will-to-Inertia, so must that race's conception of the One Will enlarge the attributes which are lacking or deficient in the race.

Since there is never to be found a perfect balance or accord of the two Wills, but always one triumphs over the other, in life, according to our knowledge, so must the human effort be always to recover balance, to symbolize and so to possess that which is missing. Which is the religious effort of Man.

There seems to be a fundamental, insuperable division,

difference, between man's artistic effort and his religious effort. The two efforts are mixed with each other, as they are revealed, but all the while they remain two, not one, all the while they are separate, single, never compounded.

The religious effort is to conceive, to symbolize that which the human soul, or the soul of the race, lacks, that which it is not, and which it requires, yearns for. It is the portrayal of that complement to the race-life which is known only as a desire: it is the symbolizing of a great desire, the statement of the desire in terms which have no meaning apart from the desire.

Whereas the artistic effort is the effort of utterance, the supreme effort of expressing knowledge, that which has been for once, that which was enacted, where the two wills met and intersected and left their result, complete for the moment. The artistic effort is the portraying of a moment of union between the two wills, according to knowledge. The religious effort is the portrayal or symbolizing of the eternal union of the two wills, according to aspiration. But in this eternal union, the features of one or the other Will are always salient.

The dual Will we call the Will-to-Motion and the Will-to-Inertia. These cause the whole of life, from the ebb and flow of a wave, to the stable equilibrium of the whole universe, from birth and being and knowledge to death and decay and forgetfulness. And the Will-to-Motion we call the male will or spirit, the Will-to-Inertia the female. This will to inertia is not negative, and the other positive. Rather, according to some conception, is Motion negative and Inertia, the static, geometric idea, positive. That is according to the point of view.

According to the race-conception of God, we can see whether in that race the male or the female element triumphs, becomes predominant.

But it must first be seen that the division into male and female is arbitrary, for the purpose of thought. The rapid motion of the rim of a wheel is the same as the perfect rest at the centre of the wheel. How can one divide them? Motion and rest are the same, when seen completely. Motion is only true of things outside oneself. When I am in a moving train, strictly, the land moves under me, I and the train are still. If I were both land and train, if I were large enough, there would be no motion. And if I were very very small, every fibre of the train would be in motion for me, the point of rest would be infinitely reduced.

How can one say, there is motion and rest? If all things move together in one infinite motion, that is rest. Rest and motion are only two degrees of motion, or two degrees of rest. Infinite motion and infinite rest are the same thing. It is obvious. Since, if motion were infinite, there would be no standing-ground from which to regard it as motion. And the same with rest.

It is easier to conceive that there is no such thing as rest. For a thing to us at rest is only a thing travelling at our own rate of motion: from another point of view, it is a thing moving at the lowest rate of motion we can recognize. But this table on which I write, which I call at rest, I know is really in motion.

So there is no such thing as rest. There is only infinite motion. But infinite motion must contain every degree of rest. So that motion and rest are the same thing. Rest is the lowest speed of motion which I recognize under normal conditions.

So how can one speak of a Will-to-Motion or a Will-to-Inertia, when there is no such thing as rest or motion? And yet, starting from any given degree of motion, and travelling forward in ever-increasing degree, one comes to a state of speed which covers the whole of space instantaneously, and is therefore rest, utter rest. And starting from the same speed and reducing the motion infinitely, one reaches the same condition of utter rest. And the direction or method of approach to this infinite rest is different to our conception. And only travelling upon the slower, does the swifter reach the infinite rest of inertia: which is the same as the infinite rest of speed, the two things having united to surpass our comprehension.

So we may speak of Male and Female, of the Will-to-Motion and of the Will-to-Inertia. And so, looking at a race, we can say whether the Will-to-Inertia or the Will-to-Motion has gained the ascendancy, and in which direction this race tends to disappear.

For it is as if life were a double cycle, of men and women, facing opposite ways, travelling opposite ways, revolving upon each other, man reaching forward with outstretched hand, woman reaching forward with outstretched hand, and neither able to move till their hands have grasped each other, when they draw towards each other from opposite directions, draw nearer and nearer, each travelling in his separate cycle, till the two are abreast, and side by side, until even they pass on again, away from each other, travelling their opposite ways to the same infinite goal.

Each travelling to the same goal of infinity, but entering it from the opposite ends of space. And man, remembering what lies behind him, how the hands met and grasped and tore apart, utters his tragic art. Then moreover, facing the other way into the unknown, conscious of the tug of the goal at his heart, he hails the woman coming from the place whither he is travelling, searches in her for signs, and makes his God from the suggestion he receives, as she advances.

Then she draws near, and he is full of delight. She is so close, that they touch, and then there is a joyful utterance of religious art. They are torn apart, and he gives the cry of tragedy, and goes on remembering, till the dance slows down and breaks, and there is only a crowd.

It is as if this cycle dance where the female makes the chain with the male becomes ever wider, ever more extended, and the further they get from the source, from the infinity, the more distinct and individual do the dancers become. At first they are only figures. In the Jewish cycle, David, with his hand stretched forth, cannot recognize the woman, the female. He can only recognize some likeness of himself. For both he and she have not danced very far from the source and origin where they were both one. Though she is in the gross utterly other than he, yet she is not very distinct from him. And he hails her Father, Almighty, God, Beloved, Strength, hails her in his own image. And with hand outstretched, fearful and passionate, he reaches to her. But it is Solomon who touches her hand, with rapture and joy, and cries out his gladness in the Song of Songs. Who is the Shulamite but God come close, for a moment, into physical contact? The Song may be a drama: it is still religious art. It is the development of the Psalms. It is utterly different from the Book of Job, which is remembrance.

Always the threefold utterance: the declaring of the God seen approaching, the rapture of contact, the anguished joy of remembrance, when the meeting has passed into separation. Such is religion, religious art, and tragic art.

But the chain is not broken by the letting-go of hands. It is broken by the overbearing of one cycle by the other. David, when he lay with a woman, lay also with God; Solomon, when he lay with a woman, knew God and possessed Him and was possessed by Him. For in Solomon and in the Woman, the male clasped hands with the female.

But in the terrible moment when they should break free again, the male in the Jew was too weak, the female overbore him. He remained in the grip of the female. The force of inertia overpowered him, and he remained remembering. But very true had been David's vision, and very real Solomon's contact. So that the living thing was conserved, kept always alive and powerful, but restrained, restricted, partial.

For centuries, the Jew knew God as David had perceived Him, as Solomon had known Him. It was the God of the body, the rudimentary God of physical laws and physical functions. The Jew lived on in physical contact with God. Each of his physical functions he shared with God; he kept his body always like the body of a bride ready to serve the bridegroom. He had become the servant of his God, the female, passive. The female in him predominated, held him passive, set utter bounds to his movement, to his roving, kept his mind as a slave to guard intact the state of sensation wherein he found himself. Which persisted century after century, the secret, scrupulous voluptuousness of the Jew, become almost self-voluptuousness, engaged in the consciousness of his own physique, or in the extracted existence of his own physique. His own physique included the woman, naturally, since the man's body included the woman's, the woman's the man's. His religion had become a physical morality, deep and fundamental, but entirely of one sort. Its living element was this scrupulous physical voluptuousness, wonderful and satisfying in a large measure.

The conscious element was a resistance to the male or active principle. Being female, occupied in self-feeling, in realization of the age, in submission to sensation, the Jewish temper was antagonistic to the active male principle, which would deny the age and refuse sensation, seeking ever to make transformation, desiring to be an instrument of change, to register relationships. So this race recognized only male sins: it conceived only sins of commission, sins of change, of transformation. In the whole of the Ten Commandments, it is the female who speaks. It is natural to the male to make the male God a God of benevolence and mercy, susceptible to pity. Such is the male conception of God. It was the female spirit which conceived the saying: 'For I, the Lord thy God, am a jealous God, visiting the iniquities of the fathers upon the children unto the third and fourth generation of them that hate me, and showing mercy unto thousands of them that love me.'

It was a female conception. For is not man the child of woman? Does she not see in him her body, even more vividly than in her own? Man is more her body to her even than her own body. For the whole of flesh is hers. Woman knows that she is the fountain of all flesh. And her pride is that the body of man is of her issue. She can see the man as the One Being, for she knows he is of her issue.

It were a male conception to see God with a manifold Being, even though He be One God. For man is ever keenly aware of the multiplicity of things, and their diversity. But woman, issuing from the other end of infinity, coming forth as the flesh, manifest in sensation, is obsessed by the oneness of things, the One Being, undifferentiated. Man, on the other hand, coming forth as the desire to single out one thing from another, to reduce each thing to its intrinsic self by process of elimination, cannot but be possessed by the infinite diversity and contrariety in life, by a passionate sense of isolation, and a poignant yearning to be at one.

That is the fundamental of female conception: that there is but One Being: this Being necessarily female. Whereas man conceives a manifold Being, the supreme of which is male. And owing to the complete Monism of the female, which is essentially static, self-sufficient, the expression of God has been left always to the male, so that the supreme God is forever He.

Nevertheless, in the God of the Ancient Jew, the female has triumphed. That which was born of Woman, that is indeed the God of the Old Testament. So utterly is he born of Woman that he scarcely needs to consider Woman: she is there unuttered.

And the Jewish race, continued in this Monism, stable, circumscribed, utterly unadventurous, utterly self-preservative, yet very deeply living, until the present century.

But Christ rose from the suppressed male spirit of Judea, and uttered a new commandment: Thou shalt love thy neighbour as thyself. He repudiated Woman: 'Who is my mother?' He lived the male life utterly apart from woman.

'Thou shalt love thy neighbour as thyself' – that is the great utterance against Monism, and the compromise with Monism. It does not say 'Thou shalt love thy neighbour because he is thyself,' as the ancient Jew would have said. It commands 'Thou shalt recognize thy neighbour's distinction from thyself, and allow his separate being, because he also is of God, even though he be almost a contradiction to thyself.'

Such is the cry of anguish of Christianity: that man is separate from his brother, separate, maybe, even, in his measure, inimical to him. This the Jew had to learn. The old Jewish creed of identity, that Eve was identical with Adam, and all men children of one single parent, and therefore, in the absolute, identical, this must be destroyed.

Cunning and according to female suggestion is the story of the Creation: that Eve was born from the single body of Adam, without intervention of sex, both issuing from one flesh, as a child at birth seems to issue from one flesh of its mother. And the birth of Jesus is the retaliation to this: a child is born, not to the flesh, but to the spirit: and you, Woman, shall conceive, not to the body, but to the Word. 'In the beginning was the Word,' says the New Testament.

The great assertion of the Male was the New Testament, and, in its beauty, the Union of Male and Female. Christ was born of Woman, begotten by the Holy Spirit. This was why Christ should be called the Son of Man. For He was born of Woman. He was born to the Spirit, the Word, the Man, the Male.

And the assertion entailed the sacrifice of the Son of Woman. The body of Christ must be destroyed, that of Him which was Woman must be put to death, to testify that He was Spirit, that He was Male, that He was Man, without any womanly part.

So the other great camp was made. In the creation, Man was

driven forth from Paradise to labour for his body and for the woman. All was lost for the knowledge of the flesh. Out of the innocence and Nirvana of Paradise came, with the Fall, the consciousness of the flesh, the body of man and woman came into very being.

This was the first great movement of Man: the movement into the conscious possession of a body. And this consciousness of the body came through woman. And this knowledge, this possession, this enjoyment, was jealously guarded. In spite of all criticism and attack, Job remained true to this knowledge, to the utter belief in his body, in the God of his body. Though the Woman herself turned tempter, he remained true to it.

The senses, sensation, sensuousness, these things which are incontrovertibly Me, these are my God, these belong to God, said Job. And he persisted, and he was right. They issue from God on the female side.

But Christ came with His contradiction: That which is Not-Me, that is God. All is God, except that which I know immediately as Myself. First I must lose Myself, then I find God. Ye must be born again.

Unto what must man be born again? Unto knowledge of his own separate existence, as in Woman he is conscious of his own incorporate existence. Man must be born unto knowledge of his own distinct identity, as in woman he was born to knowledge of his identification with the Whole. Man must be born to the knowledge, that in the whole being he is nothing, as he was born to know that in the whole being he was all. He must be born to the knowledge that other things exist beside himself, and utterly apart from all, and before he can exist himself as a separate identity, he must allow and recognize their distinct existence. Whereas previously, on the more female Jewish side, it had been said: 'All that exists is as Me. We are all one family, out of one God, having one being.'

With Christ ended the Monism of the Jew. God, the One God, became a Trinity, three-fold. He was the Father, the All-containing; He was the Son, the Word, the Changer, the Separator; and He was the Spirit, the Comforter, the Reconciliator between the Two.

And according to its conditions, Christianity has, since Christ, worshipped the Father or the Son, the one more than the other. Out of an over-female race came the male utterance of Christ. Throughout Europe, the suppressed, inadequate male desire, both in men and women, stretched to the idea of Christ, as a woman should stretch out her hands to a man. But Greece, in whom the female was overridden and neglected, became silent. So through the Middle Ages went on in Europe this fight against the body, against the senses, against this continual triumph of the senses. The worship of Europe, predominantly female, all through the medieval period, was to the male, to the incorporeal Christ, as a bridegroom, whilst the art produced was the collective, stupendous, emotional gesture of the Cathedrals, where a blind, collective impulse rose into concrete form. It was the profound, sensuous desire and gratitude which produced an art of architecture, whose essence is in utter stability, of movement resolved and centralized, of absolute movement, that has no relationship with any other form, that admits the existence of no other form, but is conclusive, propounding in its sum the One Being of All.

There was, however, in the Cathedrals, already the denial of the Monism which the Whole uttered. All the little figures, the gargoyles, the imps, the human faces, whilst subordinated within the Great Conclusion of the Whole, still, from their obscurity, jeered their mockery of the Absolute, and declared for multiplicity, polygeny. But all medieval art has the static, architectural, absolute quality, in the main, even whilst in detail it is differentiated and distinct. Such is Dürer, for example.

When his art succeeds, it conveys the sense of Absolute Movement, movement proper only to the given form, and not relative to other movements. It portrays the Object, with its Movement content, and not the movement which contains in one of its moments the Object.

It is only when the Greek stimulus is received, with its addition of male influence, its addition of relative movement, its revelation of movement driving the object, the highest revelation which had yet been made, that medieval art became complete Renaissance art, that there was the union and fusion of the male and female spirits, creating a perfect expression for the time being.

During the medieval times, the God had been Christ on the Cross, the Body Crucified, the flesh destroyed, the Virgin Chastity combating Desire. Such had been the God of the Aspiration. But the God of Knowledge, of that which they acknowledged as themselves, had been the Father, the God of the Ancient Jew.

But now, with the Renaissance, the God of Aspiration became in accord with the God of Knowledge, and there was a great outburst of joy, and the theme was not Christ Crucified, but Christ born of Woman, the Infant Saviour and the Virgin; or of the Annunciation, the Spirit embracing the flesh in pure embrace.

This was the perfect union of male and female, in this the hands met and clasped, and never was such a manifestation of Joy. This Joy reached its highest utterance perhaps in Botticelli, as in his *Nativity of the Saviour*, in our National Gallery. Still there is the architectural composition, but what an outburst of movement from the source of motion. The Infant Christ is a centre, a radiating spark of movement, the Virgin is bowed in Absolute Movement, the earthly father, Joseph, is folded up, like a clod or a boulder, obliterated, whilst the Angels fly round in ecstasy, embracing and linking hands.

The bodily father is almost obliterated. As balance to the

Virgin Mother he is there, presented, but silenced, only the movement of his loin conveyed. He is not the male. The male is the radiant infant, over which the mother leans. They two are the ecstatic centre, the complete origin, the force which is both centrifugal and centripetal.

This is the joyous utterance of the Renaissance, to which we listen for ever. Perhaps there is a melancholy in Botticelli, a pain of Woman mated to the Spirit, a nakedness of the Aphrodite issued exposed to the clear elements, to the fleshlessness of the male. But still it is joy transparent over pain. It is the utterance of complete, perfect religious art, unwilling, perhaps, when the true male and the female meet. In the Song of Solomon, the female was preponderant, the male was impure, not single. But here the heart is satisfied for the moment, there is a moment of perfect being.

And it seems to be so in other religions: the most perfect moment centres round the mother and the male child, whilst the physical male is deified separately, as a bull, perhaps.

After Botticelli came Correggio. In him the development from gesture to articulate expression was continued, unconsciously, the movement from the symbolic to the representation went on in him, from the object to the animate creature. The Virgin and Child are no longer symbolic, in Correggio: they no longer belong to religious art, but are distinctly secular. The effort is to render the living person, the individual perceived, and not the great aspiration, or an idea. Art now passes from the naïve, intuitive stage to the state of knowledge. The female impulse, to feel and to live in feeling, is now embraced by the male impulse – to know, and almost carried off by knowledge. But not yet. Still Correggio is unconscious, in his art; he is in that state of elation which represents the marriage of male and female, with the pride of the male perhaps predominant. In the *Madonna with the Basket*, of the National Gallery, the Madonna is most thoroughly a wife, the child is most triumphantly a man's child. The Father is the origin. He is seen labouring in the distance, the true support of this mother and child. There is no Virgin worship, none of the mystery of woman. The artist has reached to a sufficiency of knowledge. He knows his woman. What he is now concerned with is not her great female mystery, but her individual character. The picture has become almost lyrical – it is the woman as known by the man, it is the woman as he has experienced her. But still she is also unknown, also she is the mystery. But Correggio's chief business is to portray the woman of his own experience and knowledge, rather than the woman of his aspiration and fear. The artist is now concerned with his own experience rather than with his own desire. The female is now more or less within the power and reach of the male. But still she is there, to centralize and control his movement, still the two react and are not resolved. But for the man, the woman is henceforth part of a stream of movement, she is herself a stream of movement, carried along with himself. He sees everything as motion, retarded perhaps by the flesh, or by the stable being of this life in the body. But still man is held and pivoted by the object, even if he tend to wear down the pivot to a nothingness.

Thus Correggio leads on to the whole of modern art, where the male still wrestles with the female, in unconscious struggle, but where he gains ever gradually over her, reducing her to nothing. Ever there is more and more vibration, movement, and less and less stability, centralization. Ever man is more and more occupied with his own experience, with his own overpowering of resistance, ever less and less aware of any resistance in the object, less and less aware of any stability, less and less aware of anything unknown, more and more preoccupied with that which he knows, till his knowledge tends to become an abstraction, because it is limited by no unknown.

It is the contradiction of Dürer, as the Parthenon Frieze was the contradiction of Babylon and Egypt. To Dürer woman did not exist; even as to a child at the breast, woman does not exist separately. She is the overwhelming condition of life. She was to Dürer that which possessed him, and not that which he possessed. Her being overpowered him, he could only see in her terms, in terms of stability and of stable, incontrovertible being. He is overpowered by the vast assurance at whose breasts he is suckled, and, as if astounded, he grasps at the unknown. He knows that he rests within some great stability, and, marvelling at his own power for movement, touches the objects of this stability, becomes familiar with them. It is a question of the starting-point. Dürer starts with a sense of that which he does not know and would discover; Correggio with the sense of that which he has known, and would re-create.

And in the Renaissance, after Botticelli, the motion begins to divide in these two directions. The hands no longer clasp in perfect union, but one clasp overbears the other. Botticelli develops to Correggio and to Andrea del Sarto, develops forward to Rembrandt, and Rembrandt to the Impressionists, to the male extreme of motion. But Botticelli, on the other hand, becomes Raphael, Raphael and Michelangelo.

In Raphael we see the stable, architectural developing out further, and becoming the geometric: the denial or refusal of all movement. In the *Madonna degli Ansidei* the child is drooping, the mother stereotyped, the picture geometric, static, abstract. When there is any union of male and female, there is no goal of abstraction: the abstract is used in place, as a means of a real union. The goal of the male impulse is the announcement of motion, endless motion, endless diversity, endless change. The goal of the female impulse is the announcement of infinite oneness, of infinite stability. When the two are working in combination, as they must in life, there is, as it were, a dual motion, centrifugal for the male, fleeing abroad, away from the centre, outward to infinite vibration, and centripetal for the female, fleeing in to the eternal centre of rest. A combination of the two movements produces a sum of motion and stability at once, satisfying. But in life there tends always to be more of one than the other. The Cathedrals, Fra Angelico, frighten us or [bore] us with their final annunciation of centrality and stability. We want to escape. The influence is too female for us.

In Botticelli, the architecture remains, but there is the wonderful movement outwards, the joyous, if still clumsy, escape from the centre. His religious pictures tend to be stereotyped, resigned. The Primavera herself is static, melancholy, a stability become almost a negation. It is as if the female, instead of being the great, unknown Positive, towards which all must flow, became the great Negative, the centre which denied all motion. And the Aphrodite stands there not as a force, to draw all things unto her, but as the naked, almost unwilling pivot, as the keystone which endured all thrust and remained static. But still there is the joy, the great motion around her, sky and sea, all the elements and living, joyful forces.

Raphael, however, seeks and finds nothing there. He goes to the centre to ask: 'What is this mystery we are all pivoted upon?' To Fra Angelico it was the unknown Omnipotent. It was a goal, to which man travelled inevitably. It was the desired, the end of the long horizontal journey. But to Raphael it was the negation. Still he is a seeker, an aspirant, still his art is religious art. But the Virgin, the essential female, was to him a negation, a neutrality. Such must have been his vivid experience. But still he seeks her. Still he desires the stability, the positive keystone which grasps the arch together, not the negative keystone neutralizing the thrust, itself a neutrality. And reacting upon his own desire, the male reacting upon itself, he creates the Abstraction, the geometric conception of life. The fundament of all is the geometry of all. Which is the Plato conception. And the desire is to formulate the complete geometry.

So Raphael, knowing that his desire reaches out beyond the range of possible experience, sensible that he will not find satisfaction in any one woman, sensible that the female impulse does not, or cannot unite in him with the male impulse sufficiently to create a stability, an eternal moment of truth for him, of realization, closes his eyes and his mind upon experience, and abstracting himself, reacting upon himself, produces the geometric conception of the fundamental truth, departs from religion, from any God idea, and becomes philosophic.

Raphael is the real end of Renaissance in Italy; almost he is the real end of Italy, as Plato was the real end of Greece. When the God-idea passes into the philosophic or geometric idea, then there is a sign that the male impulse has thrown the female impulse, and has recoiled upon itself, has become abstract, asexual.

Michelangelo, however, too physically passionate, containing too much of the female in his body ever to reach the geometric abstraction, unable to abstract himself, and at the same time, like Raphael, unable to find any woman who in her being should resist him and reserve still some unknown from him, strives to obtain his own physical satisfaction in his art. He is obsessed by the desire of the body. And he must react upon himself to produce his own bodily satisfaction, aware that he can never obtain it through woman. He must seek the moment, the consummation, the keystone, the pivot, in his own flesh. For his own body is both male and female.

Raphael and Michelangelo are men of different nature placed in the same position and resolving the same question in their several ways. Socrates and Plato are a parallel pair, and, in another degree, Tolstoi and Turgeniev, and, perhaps, St Paul and St John the Evangelist, and, perhaps, Shakespeare and Shelley.

The body it is which attaches us directly to the female. Sex, as we call it, is only the point where the dual stream begins to divide, where it is nearly together, almost one. An infant is of no very determinate sex: that is, it is of both. Only at adolescence is there a real differentiation, the one is singled out to predominate. In what we call happy natures, in the lazy, contented people, there is a fairly equable balance of sex. There is sufficient of the female in the body of such a man as to leave him fairly free. He does not suffer the torture of desire of a more male being. It is obvious even from the physique of such a man that in him there is a proper proportion between male and female, so that he can be easy, balanced, and without excess. The Greek sculptors of the "best" period, Phidias and then Sophocles, Alcibiades, then Horace, must have been fairly well-balanced men, not passionate to any excess, tending to voluptuousness rather than to passion. So also Victor Hugo and Schiller and Tennyson. The real voluptuary is a man who is female as well as male, and who lives according to the female side of his nature, like Lord Byron.

The pure male is himself almost an abstraction, almost bodiless, like Shelley or Edmund Spenser. But, as we know humanity, this condition comes of an omission of some vital part. In the ordinary sense, Shelley never lived. He transcended life. But we do not want to transcend life, since we are of life.

Why should Shelley say of the skylark:

'Hail to thee, blithe Spirit! – bird thou never wert! –'? Why should he insist on the bodilessness of beauty, when we cannot know of any save embodied beauty? Who would wish that the skylark were not a bird, but a spirit? If the whistling skylark were a spirit, then we should all wish to be spirits. Which were impious and flippant.

I can think of no being in the world so transcendently male as Shelley. He is phenomenal. The rest of us have bodies which contain the male and the female. If we were so singled out as

49

Shelley, we should not belong to life, as he did not belong to life. But it were impious to wish to be like the angels. So long as mankind exists it must exist in the body, and so long must each body pertain both to the male and the female.

In the degree of pure maleness below Shelley are Plato and Raphael and Wordsworth, then Goethe and Milton and Dante, then Michelangelo, then Shakespeare, then Tolstoi, then St Paul.

A man who is well balanced between male and female, in his own nature, is, as a rule, happy, easy to mate, easy to satisfy, and content to exist. It is only a disproportion, or a dissatisfaction, which makes the man struggle into articulation. And the articulation is of two sorts, the cry of desire or the cry of realization, the cry of satisfaction, the effort to prolong the sense of satisfaction, to prolong the moment of consummation.

A bird in spring sings with the dawn, ringing out from the moment of consummation in wider and wider circles. Dürer, Fra Angelico, Botticelli, all sing of the moment of consummation, some of them still marvelling and lost in the wonder at the other being, Botticelli poignant with distinct memory. Raphael too sings of the moment of consummation. But he was not lost in the moment, only sufficiently lost to know what it was. In the moment, he was not completely consummated. He must strive to complete his satisfaction from himself. So, whilst making his great acknowledgment to the Woman, he must add to her to make her whole, he must give her his completion. So he rings her round with pure geometry, till she becomes herself almost of the geometric figure, an abstraction. The picture becomes a great ellipse crossed by a dark column. This is the *Madonna degli Ansidei*. The Madonna herself is almost insignificant. She and the child are contained within the shaft thrust across the ellipse.

This column must always stand for the male aspiration, the arch or ellipse for the female completeness containing this aspiration. And the whole picture is a geometric symbol of the consummation of life.

What we call the Truth is, in actual experience, that momentary state when in living the union between the male and the female is consummated. This consummation may be also physical, between the male body and the female body. But it may be only spiritual, between the male and female spirit.

And the symbol by which Raphael expresses this moment of consummation is by a dark, strong shaft or column leaping up into, and almost transgressing a faint, radiant, inclusive ellipse.

To express the same moment Botticelli uses no symbol, but builds up a complicated system of circles, of movements wheeling in their horizontal plane about their fixed centres, the whole builded up dome-shape, and then the dome surpassed by another singing cycle in the open air above.

This is Botticelli always: different cycles of joy, different moments of embrace, different forms of dancing round, all contained in one picture, without solution. He has not solved it yet.

And Raphael, in reaching the pure symbolic solution, has surpassed art and become almost mathematics. Since the business of art is never to solve, but only to declare.

There is no such thing as solution. Nietzsche talks about the *Ewige Wiederkehr*. It is like Botticelli singing cycles. But each cycle is different. There is no real recurrence.

And to single out one cycle, one moment, and to exclude from this moment all context, and to make this moment timeless, this is what Raphael does, and what Plato does. So that their absolute Truth, their geometric Truth, is only true in timelessness.

Michelangelo, on the other hand, seeks for no absolute Truth. His desire is to realize in his body, in his feeling, the moment-consummation which is for Man the perfect truth-experience. But he knows of no embrace. For him, personally, woman does not exist. For Botticelli she existed as the Virgin-Mother, and as the Primavera, and as Aphrodite. She existed as the pure origin of life on the female side, as the bringer of light and delight, and as the passionately Desired of every man, as the Known and Unknown in one: to Raphael she existed either as a minor part of his experience, having nothing to do with his aspiration, or else his aspiration merely used her as a statement included within the Great Abstraction.

To Michelangelo the female scarcely existed outside his own physique. There he knew of her and knew the desire of her. But Raphael, in his passion to be self-complete, roused his desire for consummation to a white-hot pitch, so that he became incandescent, reacting on himself, consuming his own flesh and his own bodily life, to reach the pitch of perfect abstraction, the resisting body holding back the raging stream of outward force, till the two formed a stable incandescence, a luminous geometric conception of permanence and inviolability. Meanwhile his body burned away, overpowered, in this state of incandescence.

Michelangelo's will was different. The body in him, that which knew of the female and therefore was the female, was stronger and more insistent. His desire for consummation was desire for the satisfying moment when the male and female spirits touch in closest embrace, vivifying each other, not one destroying the other, but still are two. He knew that for Man consummation is a temporal state. The pure male spirit must ever conceive of timelessness, the pure female of the moment. And Michelangelo, more mixed than Raphael, must always rage within the limits of time and of temporal forms. So he reacted upon himself, sought the female in himself, aggrandized it, and so reached a wonderful momentary stability of flesh exaggerated till it became tenuous, but filled and balanced by the outward-pressing force. And he reached his consummation in that way, reached the perfect moment, when he realized and revealed his figures in all their marvellous equilibrium. The

Jewish tradition, with its great physical God, source of male and female, attracted him. By turning towards the female goal, of utter stability and permanence in Time, he arrived at his consummation. But only by reacting on himself, by withdrawing his own mobility. Thus he made his great figures, the Moses, static and looming, announcing, like the Jewish God, the magnificence and eternality of the physical law; the David, young, but with too much body for a young figure, the physique exaggerated, the clear, outward-leaping, essential spirit of the young man smothered over, the real maleness cloaked, so that the statue is almost a falsity. Then the slaves, heaving in body, fastened in bondage that refuses them movement; the motionless Madonna, no Virgin but Woman in the flesh, not the pure female conception, but the spouse of man, the mother of bodily children. The men are not male, nor the women female, to any degree.

The Adam can scarcely stir into life. That large body of almost transparent, tenuous texture is not established enough for motion. It is not that it is too ponderous: it is too unsubstantial, unreal. It is not motion, life, he craves, but body. Give him but a firm, concentrated physique. That is the cry of all Michelangelo's pictures.

But, powerful male as he was, he satisfies his desire by insisting upon and exaggerating the body in him, he reaches the point of consummation in the most marvellous equilibrium which his figures show. To attain this equilibrium he must exaggerate and exaggerate and exaggerate the flesh, make it ever more tenuous, keeping it really in true ratio. And then comes the moment, the perfect stable poise, the perfect balance between object and movement, the perfect combination of male and female in one figure.

It is wonderful, and peaceful, this equilibrium, once reached. But it is reached through anguish and self-battle and self-repression, therefore it is sad. Always, Michelangelo's pictures are full of joy, of self-acceptance and self-proclamation. Michelangelo fought and arrested the mobile male in him; Raphael was proud in the male he was, and gave himself utter liberty, at the female expense.

And it seems as though Italy had ever since the Renaissance been possessed by the Raphaelesque conception of the ultimate geometric basis of life, the geometric essentiality of all things. There is in the Italian, at the very bottom of all, the fundamental, geometric conception of absolute static combination. There is the shaft enclosed in the ellipse, as a permanent symbol. There exists no shaft, no ellipse separately, but only the whole complete thing; there is neither male nor female, but an absolute interlocking of the two in one, an absolute combination, so that each is gone in the complete identity. There is only the geometric abstraction of the moment of consummation, a moment made timeless. And this conception of a long, clinched, timeless embrace, this over-whelming conception of timeless consummation, of which there is no beginning nor end, from which there is no escape, has arrested the Italian race for three centuries. It is the source of its indifference and its fatalism and its positive abandon, and of its utter incapacity to be sceptical, in the Russian sense.

This conception contains also, naturally, as part of the same idea, Aphrodite-worship and Phallic-worship. But these are sub-ordinate, and belong to a sort of initiatory period. The real conception, for the individual, is marriage, inviolable marriage, which always was and always has been, no matter what appar-ent aberrations there may or may not be. And the manifestation of divinity is the child. In marriage, in utter, interlocked mar-riage, man and woman cease to be two beings and become one, one and one only, not two in one as with us, but absolute One, a geometric absolute, timeless, the Absolute, the Divine. And the child, as issue of this divine and timeless state, is hailed with love and joy.

But the Italian is now beginning to withdraw from his clinched and timeless embrace, from his geometric abstraction, into the northern conception of himself and the woman as two separate identities, which meet, combine, but always must withdraw again.

So that the Futurist Boccioni now makes his sculpture, *Development of a Bottle through Space*, try to express the withdrawal, and at the same time he must adhere to the conception of this same interlocked state of marriage between centripetal and centrifugal forces, the geometric abstraction of the bottle. But he can neither do one thing nor the other. He wants to re-state the real abstraction. And at the same time he has an unsatisfied desire to satisfy. He must insist on the centrifugal force, and so destroy at once his abstraction. He must insist on the male spirit of motion outwards, because, during three static centuries, there has necessarily come to pass a preponderance of the female in the race, so that the Italian is rather more female than male now, as is the whole Latin race rather voluptuous than passionate, too much aware of their utter lockedness male with female, and too hopeless, as males, to act, to be passionate. So that when I look at Boccioni's sculpture, and see him trying to state the timeless abstract being of a bottle, the pure geometric abstraction of the bottle, I am fascinated. But then, when I see him driven by his desire for the male complement into portraying motion, simple motion, trying to give expression to the bottle in terms of mechanics, I am confused. It is for science to explain the bottle in terms of force and motion. Geometry, pure mathematics, is very near to art, and the vivid attempt to render the bottle as a pure geometric abstraction might give rise to a work of art, because of the resistance of the medium, the stone. But a representation in stone of the lines of force which create that state of rest called a bottle, that is a model in mechanics.

And the two representations require two different states of

mind in the appreciator, so that the result is almost nothingness, mere confusion. And the portraying of a state of mind is impossible. There can only be made scientific diagrams of states of mind. A state of mind is a resultant between an attack and a resistance. And how can one produce a resultant without first causing the collision of the originating forces?

The attitude of the Futurists is the scientific attitude, as the attitude of Italy is mainly scientific. It is the forgetting of the old, perfect Abstraction, it is the departure of the male from the female, it is the act of withdrawal: the denying of consummation and the starting afresh, the learning of the alphabet.

CHAPTER 8
The Light of the World

The climax that was reached in Italy with Raphael has never been reached in like manner in England. There has never been, in England, the great embrace, the surprising consummation, which Botticelli recorded and which Raphael fixed in a perfect Abstraction.

Correggio, Andrea del Sarto, both men of less force than those other supreme three, continued the direct line of development, turning no curve. They still found women whom they could not exhaust: in them, the male still reacted upon the incontrovertible female. But ever there was a tendency to greater movement, to a closer characterization, a tendency to individualize the human being, and to represent him as being embedded in some common, divine matrix.

Till after the Renaissance, supreme God had always been God the Father. The Church moved and had its being in Almighty God, Christ was only the distant, incandescent gleam towards which humanity aspired, but which it did not know.

Raphael and Michelangelo were both servants of the Father, of the Eternal Law, of the Prime Being. Raphael, faced with the question of Not-Being, when it was forced upon him that he would never accomplish his own being in the flesh, that he would never know completeness, the momentary consummation, in the body, accomplished the Geometrical Abstraction, which is the abstraction from the Law, which is the Father.

There was, however, Christ's great assertion of Not-Being, of No-Consummation, of life after death, to reckon with. It was after the Renaissance, Christianity began to exist. It had not existed before.

In God the Father we are all one body, one flesh. But in Christ we abjure the flesh, there is no flesh. A man must lose his life to save it. All the natural desires of the body, these a man must be able to deny, before he can live. And then, when he lives, he lives, he shall live in the knowledge that he is himself, so that he can always say: 'I am I.'

In the Father we are one flesh, in Christ we are crucified, and rise again, and are One with Him in Spirit. It is the difference between Law and Love. Each man shall live according to the Law, which changeth not, says the old religion. Each man shall live according to Love, which shall save us from death and from the Law, says the new religion.

But what is Love? What is the deepest desire Man has yet known? It is always for this consummation, this momentary contact or union of male with female, of spirit with spirit and flesh with flesh, when each is complete in itself and rejoices in its own being, when each is in himself or in herself complete and single and essential. And love is the great aspiration towards this complete consummation and this joy; it is the aspiration of each man that all men, that all life, shall know it and rejoice. Since, until all men shall know it, no man shall fully know it. Since, by the Law, we are all one flesh. So that Love is only a closer vision of the Law, a more comprehensive interpretation: 'Think not I come to destroy the Law, or the Prophets: I come not to destroy, but to fulfil. For verily I say unto you, till heaven and earth pass, one jot or one tittle shall in no wise pass from the Law, till all be fulfilled.'

In Christ I must save my soul through love, I must lose my life, and thereby find it. The Law bids me preserve my life to the Glory of God. But Love bids me lose my life to the Glory of God. In Christ, when I shall have overcome every desire I know in myself, so that I adhere to nothing, but am loosed and set free and single, then, being without fear, and having nothing that I can lose, I shall know what I am, I, transcendent, intrinsic, eternal.

The Christian commandment: 'Thou shalt love thy neighbour as thyself' is a more indirect and moving, a more emotional form of the Greek commandment 'Know thyself.' This is what Christianity says, indirectly: 'Know thyself, and each man shall thereby know himself.'

Now in the Law, no man shall know himself, save in the Law. And the Law is the immediate law of the body. And the necessity of each man to know himself, to achieve his own consummation, shall be satisfied and fulfilled in the body. God, Almighty God, is the father, and in fatherhood man draws nearest to him. In the act of love, in the act of begetting, Man is with God and of God. Such is the Law. And there shall be no other God devised. That is the great obstructive commandment.

This is the old religious leap down, absolutely, even if not in direct statement. It is the Law. But through Christ it was at last declared that in the physical act of love, in the begetting of children, man does not necessarily know himself, nor become Godlike, nor satisfy his deep, innate desire to BE. The physical act of love may be a complete disappointment, a nothing, and fatherhood may be the least significant attribute to a man. And physical love may fail utterly, may prove a sterility, a nothingness. Is a man then duped, and is his deepest desire a joke played on him?

There is a law, beyond the known law, there is a new Commandment. There is love. A man shall find his consummation the crucifixion of the body and the resurrection of the spirit.

Christ, the Bridegroom, or the Bride, as may be, awaits the desiring soul that shall seek Him, and in Him shall all men find their consummation, after their new birth. It is the New Law; the old Law is revoked.

'This is my Body, take, and eat,' says Christ, in the Communion, the ritual representing the Consummation. 'Come unto Me all ye that labour and are heavy-laden, and I will give you rest.'

For each man there is the bride, for each woman the bridegroom, for all, the Mystic Marriage. It is the New Law. In the mystic embrace of Christ each man shall find fulfilment and relief, each man shall become himself, a male individual, tried, proved, completed, and satisfied. In the mystic embrace of Christ each man shall say, 'I am myself, and Christ is Christ'; each woman shall be proud and satisfied, saying, 'It is enough.'

So, by the New Law, man shall satisfy this his deepest desire. 'In the body ye must die, even as I died, on the cross,' says Christ, 'that ye may have everlasting life.' But this is a real contradiction of the Old Law, which says, 'In the life of the body we are one with the Father.' The Old Law bids us live: it is the old, original commandment, that we shall live in the Law, and not die. So that the new Christian preaching of Christ Crucified is indeed against the Law. 'And when ye are dead in the body, ye shall be one with the spirit, ye shall know the Bride, and be consummate in Her Embrace, in the Spirit,' continues the Christian Commandment.

It is a larger interpretation of the Law, but, also, it is a breach of the Law. For by the Law, Man shall in no wise injure or deny or desecrate his living body of flesh, which is of the Father. Therefore, though Christ gave the Holy Ghost, the Comforter;

though He bowed before the Father; though He said that no man should be forgiven the denial of the Holy Spirit, the Reconciler between the Father and the Son; yet did the Son deny the Father, must he deny the Father?

'Ye are my Spirit, in the Spirit ye know Me, and in marriage of the Spirit I am fulfilled of you,' said the Son.

And it is the Unforgivable Sin to declare that these two are contradictions one of the other, though contradictions they are. Between them is linked the Holy Spirit, as a reconciliation, and whoso shall speak hurtfully against the Holy Spirit shall find no forgiveness.

So Christ, up in arms against the Father, exculpated Himself and bowed to the Father. Yet man must insist either on one or on the other: either he must adhere to the Son or to the Father. And since the Renaissance, disappointed in the flesh, the northern races have sought the consummation through Love; and they have denied the Father.

The greatest and deepest human desire, for consummation, for Self-Knowledge, has sought a different satisfaction. In Love, in the act of Love, that which is mixed in me becomes pure, that which is female in me is given to the female, that which is male in her draws into me, I am complete, I am pure male, she is pure female; we rejoice in contact perfect and naked and clear, singled out unto ourselves, and given the surpassing freedom. No longer we see through a glass, darkly. For she is she, and I am I, and, clasped together with her, I know how perfectly she is not me, how perfectly I am not her, how utterly we are two, the light and the darkness, and how infinitely and eternally not-to-be-comprehended by either of us is the surpassing One we make. Yet of this One, this incomprehensible, we have an inkling that satisfies us.

And through Christ Jesus, I know that I shall find my Bride, when I have overcome the impurity of the flesh. When the flesh in me is put away, I shall embrace the Bride, and I shall know as I am known.

But why the Schism? Why shall the Father say 'Thou shalt have no other God before Me'? Why is the Lord our God a jealous God? Why, when the body fails me, must I still adhere to the Law, and give it praise as the perfect Abstraction, like Raphael, announce it as the Absolute? Why must I be imprisoned within the flesh, like Michelangelo, till I must stop the voice of my crying out, and be satisfied with a little where I wanted completeness?

And why, on the other hand, must I lose my life to save it? Why must I die, before I can be born again? Can I not be born again, save out of my own ashes, save in resurrection from the dead? Why must I deny the Father, to love the Son? Why are they not One God to me, as we always protest they are?

It is time that the schism ended, that man ceased to oppose the Father to the Son, the Son to the Father. It is time that the Protestant Church, the Church of the Son, should be one again with the Roman Catholic Church, the Church of the Father. It is time that man shall cease, first to live in the flesh, with joy, and then, unsatisfied, to renounce and to mortify the flesh, declaring that the Spirit alone exists, that Christ He is God.

If a man find incomplete satisfaction in the body, why therefore shall he renounce the body and say it is of the devil? And why, at the start, shall a man say, 'The body, that is all, and the consummation, that is complete in the flesh, for me.'

Must it always be that a man set out with a worship of passion and a blindness to love, and that he end with a stern commandment to love and a renunciation of passion?

Does not a youth now know that he desires the body as the *via media*, that consummation is consummation of body and spirit, both?

How can a man say, 'I am this body,' when he will desire

beyond the body tomorrow? And how can a man say, 'I am this spirit,' when his own mouth gives lie to the words it forms?

Why is a race, like the Italian race, fundamentally melancholy, save that it has circumscribed its consummation within the body? And the Jewish race, for the same reason, has become now almost hollow, with a pit of emptiness and misery in their eyes.

And why is the English race neutral, indifferent, like a thing that eschews life, save that it has said so insistently: 'I am this spirit. This body, it is not me, it is unworthy'? The body at last begins to wilt and become corrupt. But before it submits, half the life of the English race must be a lie. The life of the body, denied by the professed adherence to the spirit, must be something disowned, corrupt, ugly.

Why should the worship of the Son entail the denial of the Father?

Since the Renaissance, northern humanity has sought for consummation in the spirit, it has sought for the female apart from woman. 'I am I, and the Spirit is the Spirit; in the Spirit I am myself,' and this has been the utterance of our art since Raphael.

There has been the ever-developing dissolution of form, the dissolving of the solid body within the spirit. He began to break the clear outline of the object, to seek for further marriage, not only between body and body, not the perfect, stable union of body with body, not the utter completeness and accomplishment of architectural form, with its recurrent cycles, but the marriage between body and spirit, or between spirit and spirit.

It is no longer the Catholic exultation 'God is God,' but the Christian annunciation, 'Light is come into the world.' No longer has a man only to obey, but he has to die and be born again; he has to close his eyes upon his own immediate desires, and in the darkness receive the perfect light. He has to know himself in the spirit, he has to follow Christ to the Cross, and rise again in the light of the life.

And, in this light of life, he will see his Bride, he will embrace his complement and his fulfilment, and achieve his consummation. 'It is the spirit that quickeneth; the flesh forgetteth nothing; the words I speak unto you, they are the spirit, and they are life.'

And though in the Gospel, according to John particularly, Jesus constantly asserts that the Father has sent Him, and that He is of the Father, yet there is always the spirit of antagonism to the Father.

'And it came to pass, as He spake these things, a certain woman of the company lifted up her voice and said unto Him: "Blessed is the womb that bare thee, and the paps thou hast sucked."

'But He said, Yea, rather, blessed are they that hear the word of God, and keep it.'

And the woman who heard this knew that she was denied of the honour of her womb, and that the blessing of her breasts was taken away.

Again He said: 'And there be those that were born eunuchs, and there be those that were made eunuchs by men, and there be eunuchs which have made themselves eunuchs for the kingdom of heaven's sake. He that is able to receive it, let him receive it.' But before the Father a eunuch is blemished, even a childless man is without honour.

So that the spirit of Jesus is antagonistic to the spirit of the Father. And St John enhances this antagonism. But in St John there is the constant insistence on the Oneness of Father and Son, and on the Holy Spirit.

Since the Renaissance there has been the striving for the Light, and the escape from the Flesh, from the Body, the Object. And sometimes there has been the antagonism to the Father, sometimes reconciliation with Him. In painting, the Spirit, the Word, the Love, all that was represented by John, has appeared as light. Light is the constant symbol of Christ in the New Testament. It is light, actual sunlight or the luminous quality of day, which has infused more and more into the defined body, fusing away the outline, absolving the concrete reality, making a marriage, an embrace between the two things, light and object.

In Rembrandt there is the first great evidence of this, the new exposition of the commandment 'Know thyself.' It is more than the 'Hail, holy Light!' of Milton. It is the declaration that light is our medium of existence, that where the light falls upon our darkness, there we *are*: that I am but the point where light and darkness meet and break upon one another.

There is now a new conception of life, an utterly new conception, of duality, of two-fold existence, light and darkness, object and spirit two-fold, and almost inimical.

The old desire, for movement about a centre of rest, for stability, is gone, and in its place rises the desire for pure ambience, pure spirit of change, free from all laws and conditions of being.

Henceforward there are two things, and not one. But there is journeying towards the one thing again. There is no longer the One God Who contains us all, and in Whom we live and move and have our being, and to Whom belongs each one of our movements. I am no longer a child of the Father, brother of all men. I am no longer part of the great body of God, as all men are part of it. I am no longer consummate in the body of God, identified with it and divine in the act of marriage.

The conception has utterly changed. There is the Spirit, and there is Myself. I exist in contact with the Spirit, but I am not the Spirit. I am other, I am Myself. Now I am become a man, I am no more a child of the Father. I am a man. And there are many men. And the Father has lost his importance. We are multiple, manifold men, we own only one Hope, one Desire, one Bride, one Spirit.

At last man insists upon his own separate Self, insists that he has a distinct, inconquerable being which stands apart even from Spirit, which exists other than the Spirit, and which seeks marriage with the Spirit.

And he must study himself and marvel over himself in the light of the Spirit, he must become lyrical: but he must glorify the Spirit, above all. Since that is the Bride. So Rembrandt paints his own portrait again and again, sees it again and again within the light.

He has no hatred of the flesh. That he was not completed in the flesh, even in the marriage of the body, is inevitable. But he is married in the flesh, and his wife is with him in the body, he loves his body, which she gave him complete, and he loves her body, which is not himself, but which he has known. He has known and rejoiced in the earthly bride, he will adhere to her always. But there is the Spirit beyond her: there is his desire which transcends her, there is the Bride still he craves for and courts. And he knows, this is the Spirit, it is not the body. And he paints it as the light. And he paints himself within the light. For he has a deep desire to know himself in the embrace of the spirit. For he does not know himself, he is never consummated.

In the Old Law, fulfilled in him, he is not appeased, he must transcend the Law. The Woman is embraced, caught up, and carried forward, the male spirit, passing on half satisfied, must seek a new bride, a further consummation. For there is no bride on earth for him.

To Dürer, the whole earth was as a bride, unknown and un-accomplished, offering satisfaction to him. And he sought out the earth endlessly, as a man seeks to know a bride who sur-passes him. It was all: the Bride.

But to Rembrandt the bride was not to be found, he must react upon himself, he must seek in himself for his own consummation. There was the Light, the Spirit, the Bridegroom. But when Rembrandt sought the complete Bride, sought for his own consummation, he knew it was not to be found, he knew she did not exist in the concrete. He knew, as Michelangelo knew, that there was not on the earth a woman to satisfy him, to be his mate. He must seek for the Bride beyond the physical woman; he must seek for the great female principle in an abstraction.

But the abstraction was not the geometric abstraction, created from knowledge, a state of Absolute Remembering, making Absolute of the Consummation which had been, as in Raphael. It was the desired Unknown, the goodly Unknown, the Spirit, the Light. And with this Light Rembrandt must seek even the marriage of the body. Everything he did approximates to the Consummation, but never can realize it. He paints always faith, belief, hope; never Raphael's terrible, dead certainty.

To Dürer, every moment of his existence was occupied. He existed within the embrace of the Bride, which embrace he could never fathom nor exhaust.

Raphael knew and outraged the Bride, but he harked back, obsessed by the consummation which had been.

To Rembrandt, woman was only the first acquaintance with the Bride. Of woman he obtained and expected no complete satisfaction. He knew he must go on, beyond the woman. But though the flesh could not find its consummation, still he did not deny the flesh. He was an artist, and in his art no artist ever could blaspheme the Holy Spirit, the Reconciler. Only a dogmatist could do that. Rembrandt did not deny the flesh, as so many artists try to do. He went on from her to the fuller knowledge of the Bride, in true progression. Which makes the wonderful beauty of Rembrandt.

But, like Michelangelo, owning the flesh, and a northern Christian being bent on personal salvation, personal consummation in the flesh, such as a Christian feels with us when he receives the Sacrament and hears the words 'This is My Body, take, and eat,' Rembrandt craved to marry the flesh and the Spirit, to achieve consummation in the flesh through marriage with the Spirit.

Which is the great northern confusion. For the flesh is of the flesh, and the Spirit of the Spirit, and they are two, even as the Father and the Son are two, and not One.

Raphael conceived the two as One, thereby revoking Time. Michelangelo would have created the bridal Flesh, to satisfy himself. Rembrandt would have married his own flesh to the Spirit, taken the consummate Kiss of the Light upon his fleshly face.

Which is a confusion. For the Father cannot know the Son, nor the Son the Father. So, in Rembrandt, the marriage is always imperfect, the embrace is never close nor consummate, as it is in Botticelli or in Raphael, or in Michelangelo. There is an eternal non-marriage betwixt flesh and spirit. They are two; they are never Two-in-One. So that in Rembrandt there is never complete marriage betwixt the Light and the Body. They are contiguous, never.

This has been the confusion and the error of the northern countries, but particularly of Germany, this desire to have the spirit mate with the flesh, the flesh with the spirit. Spirit can mate with spirit, and flesh with flesh, and the two matings can take place separately, flesh with flesh, or spirit with spirit. But to try to mate flesh with spirit makes confusion.

The bride I mate with my body may or may not be the Bride in whom I find my consummation. It may be that, at times, the great female principle does not abide abundantly in woman: that, at certain periods, woman, in the body, is not the supreme representative of the Bride. It may be the Bride is hidden from Man, as the Light, or as the Darkness, which he can never know in the flesh.

It may be, in the same way, that the great male principle is only weakly evidenced in man during certain periods, that the Bridegroom be hidden away from woman, for a century or centuries, and that she can only find Him as the voice, or the Wind. So I think it was with her during the medieval period; that the greatest women of the period knew that the Bridegroom did not exist for them in the body, but as the Christ, the Spirit.

And, in times of the absence of the bridegroom from the body, then woman in the body must either die in the body, or mating in the body, she must mate with the Bridegroom in the Spirit, in a separate marriage. She cannot mate her body with the Spirit, nor mate her spirit with the Body. That is confusion. Let her mate the man in body, and her spirit with the Spirit, in a separate marriage. But let her not try to mate her spirit with the body of the man, that does not mate her Spirit.

The effort to mate spirit with body, body with spirit, is the crying confusion and pain of our times.

Rembrandt made the first effort. But art has developed to a clarity since then. It reached its climax in our own Turner. He did not seek to mate body with spirit. He mated his body easily, he did not deny it. But what he sought was the mating of the Spirit. Ever, he sought the consummation in the Spirit, and he reached it at last. Ever, he sought the Light, to make the light transfuse the body, till the body was carried away, a mere bloodstain, became a ruddy stain of red sunlight within white sunlight. This was perfect consummation in Turner, when, the body gone, the ruddy light meets the crystal light in a perfect fusion, the utter dawn, the utter golden sunset, the extreme of all life, where all is One, One-Being, a perfect glowing Oneness.

Like Raphael, it becomes an abstraction. But this, in Turner, is the abstraction from the spiritual marriage and consummation, the final transcending of all the Law, the achieving of what is to us almost a nullity. If Turner had ever painted his last picture, it would have been a white, incandescent surface, the same whiteness when he finished as when he began, proceeding from nullity to nullity, through all the range of colour.

Turner is perfect. Such a picture as his *Norham Castle, Sunrise*, where only the faintest shadow of life stains the light, is the last word that can be uttered, before the blazing and timeless silence.

He sought, and he found, perfect marriage in the spirit. It was apart from woman. His Bride was the Light. Or he was the bride himself, and the Light – the Bridegroom. Be that as it may, he became one and consummate with the Light, and gave us the consummate revelation.

Corot, also, nearer to the Latin tradition of utter consummation in the body, made a wonderful marriage in the spirit between light and darkness, just tinctured with life. But he contained more of the two consummations together, the marriage in the body, represented in geometric form, and the marriage in the spirit, represented by shimmering transfusion and infusion of light through darkness.

But Turner is the crisis in this effort: he achieves pure light, pure and singing. In him the consummation is perfect, the perfect marriage in the spirit.

In the body his marriage was other. He never attempted to mingle the two. The marriage in the body, with the woman, was apart from, completed away from the marriage in the Spirit, with the Bride, the Light.

But I cannot look at a later Turner picture without abstracting myself, without denying that I have limbs, knees and thighs and breast. If I look at the *Norham Castle*, and remember my own knees and my own breast, then the picture is a nothing to me. I must not know. And if I look at Raphael's *Madonna degli Ansidei*, I am cut off from my future, from aspiration. The gate is shut upon me, I can go no further. The thought of Turner's *Sunrise* becomes magic and fascinating, it gives the lie to this completed symbol. I know I am the other thing as well.

So that, whenever art or any expression becomes perfect, it becomes a lie. For it is only perfect by reason of abstraction from that context by which and in which it exists as truth.

So Turner is a lie, and Raphael is a lie, and the marriage in the spirit is a lie, and the marriage in the body is a lie, each is a lie without the other. Since each excludes the other in these instances, they are both lies. If they were brought together, and reconciled, then there were a jubilee. But where is the Holy Spirit that shall reconcile Raphael and Turner?

There must be marriage of body in body, and of spirit in spirit, and Two-in-One. And the marriage in the body must not deny the marriage in the spirit, for that is blasphemy against the Holy Ghost; and the marriage in the spirit shall not deny the marriage in the body, for that is blasphemy against the Holy Ghost. But the two must be for ever reconciled, even if they must exist on occasions apart one from the other.

For in Botticelli the dual marriage is perfect, or almost perfect, body and spirit reconciled, or almost reconciled, in a perfect dual consummation. And in all art there is testimony to the wonderful dual marriage, the true consummation. But in Raphael, the marriage in the spirit is left out so much that it is almost denied, so that the picture is almost a lie, almost a blasphemy. And in Turner, the marriage in the body is almost denied in the same way, so that his picture is almost a blasphemy. But neither in Raphael nor in Turner is the denial positive: it is only an over-affirmation of the one at the expense of the other.

But in some men, in some small men, like bishops, the denial of marriage in the body is positive and blasphemous, a sin against the Holy Ghost. And in some men, like Prussian army officers, the denial of marriage in the spirit is an equal blasphemy. But which of the two is a greater sinner, working better for the destruction of his fellow-man, that is for the One God to judge.

WHISTLING OF BIRDS (1917)

The frost held for many weeks, until the birds were dying rapidly. Everywhere in the fields and under the hedges lay the ragged remains of lapwings, starlings, thrushes, redwings, innumerable ragged bloody cloaks of birds, whence the flesh was eaten by invisible beasts of prey.

Then, quite suddenly, one morning, the change came. The wind went to the south, came off the sea warm and soothing. In the afternoon there were little gleams of sunshine, and the doves began, without interval, slowly and awkwardly to coo. The doves were cooing, though with a laboured sound, as if they were still winter-stunned. Nevertheless, all the afternoon they continued their noise, in the mild air before the frost had thawed off the road. At evening the wind blew gently, still gathering a bruising quality of frost from the hard earth. Then, in the yellow-gleamy sunset, wild birds began to whistle faintly in the blackthorn thickets of the stream-bottom.

It was startling and almost frightening after the heavy silence of frost. How could they sing at once, when the ground was thickly strewn with the torn carcasses of birds? Yet out of the evening came the uncertain, silvery sounds that made one's soul start alert, almost with fear. How could the little silver bugles sound the rally so swiftly, in the soft air, when the earth was yet bound? Yet the birds continued their whistling, rather dimly and brokenly, but throwing the threads of silver, germinating noise into the air.

It was almost a pain to realize, so swiftly, the new world. *Le monde est mort. Vive le monde*! But the birds omitted even the first part of the announcement, their cry was only a faint, blind, fecund *vive*!

There is another world. The winter is gone. There is a new world of spring. The voice of the turtle is heard in the land. But the flesh shrinks from so sudden a transition. Surely the call is premature while the clods are still frozen, and the ground is littered with the remains of wings! Yet we have no choice. In the bottoms of impenetrable blackthorn, each evening and morning now, out flickers a whistling of birds.

Where does it come from, the song? After so long a cruelty, how can they make it up so quickly? But it bubbles through them, they are like little well-heads, little fountain-heads whence the spring trickles and bubbles forth. It is not of their own doing. In their throats the new life distils itself into sound. It is the rising of silvery sap of a new summer, gurgling itself forth.

All the time, whilst the earth lay choked and killed and winter mortified, the deep undersprings were quiet. They only wait for the ponderous encumbrance of the old order to give way, yield in the thaw, and there they are, a silver realm at once. Under the surge of ruin, unmitigated winter, lies the silver potentiality of all blossom. One day the black tide must spend itself and fade back. Then all-suddenly appears the crocus, hovering triumphant in the rear, and we know the order has changed, there is a new regime, sound of a new *vive! vive!*

It is no use any more to look at the torn remnants of birds that lie exposed. It is no longer any use remembering the sullen thunder of frost and the intolerable pressure of cold upon us. For whether we will or not, they are gone. The choice is not ours. We may remain wintry and destructive for a little longer, if we wish it, but the winter is gone out of us, and willy-nilly our hearts sing a little at sunset.

Even whilst we stare at the ragged horror of the birds scattered broadcast, part-eaten, the soft, uneven cooing of the pigeon ripples from the outhouses, and there is a faint silver whistling in the bushes come twilight. No matter, we stand and stare at the torn and unsightly ruins of life, we watch the weary, mutilated columns of winter retreating under our eyes. Yet in our ears are the silver vivid bugles of a new creation advancing on us from behind, we hear the rolling of the soft and happy drums of the doves.

We may not choose the world. We have hardly any choice for ourselves. We follow with our eyes the bloody and horrid line of march of extreme winter, as it passes away. But we cannot hold back the spring. We cannot make the birds silent, prevent the bubbling of the wood-pigeons. We cannot stay the fine world of silver-fecund creation from gathering itself and taking place upon us. Whether we will or no, the daphne tree will soon be giving off perfume, the lambs dancing on two feet, the celandines will twinkle all over the ground, there will be a new heaven and new earth.

For it is in us, as well as without us. Those who can may follow the columns of winter in their retreat from the earth. Some of us, we have no choice, the spring is within us, the silver fountain begins to bubble under our breast, there is gladness in spite of ourselves. And on the instant we accept the gladness! The first day of change, out whistles an unusual, interrupted pæan, a fragment that will augment itself imperceptibly. And this in spite of the extreme bitterness of the suffering, in spite of the myriads of torn dead.

Such a long, long winter, and the frost only broke yesterday.

Yet it seems, already, we cannot remember it. It is strangely remote, like a far-off darkness. It is as unreal as a dream in the night. This is the morning of reality, when we are ourselves. This is natural and real, the glimmering of a new creation that stirs in us and about us. We know there was winter, long, fearful. We know the earth was strangled and mortified, we know the body of life was torn and scattered broadcast. But what is this retrospective knowledge? It is something extraneous to us, extraneous to this that we are now. And what we are, and what, it seems, we always have been, is this quickening lovely silver plasm of pure creativity. All the mortification and tearing, ah yes, it was upon us, encompassing us. It was like a storm or a mist or a falling from a height. It was estrangled upon us, like bats in our hair, driving us mad. But it was never really our innermost self. Within, we were always apart, we were this, this limpid fountain of silver, then quiescent, rising and breaking now into the flowering.

It is strange, the utter incompatibility of death with life. Whilst there is death, life is not to be found. It is all death, one overwhelming flood. And then a new tide rises, and it is all life, a fountain of silvery blissfulness. It is one or the other. We are for life, or we are for death, one or the other, but never in our essence both at once.

Death takes us, and all is torn redness, passing into darkness. Life rises, and we are faint fine jets of silver running out to blossom. All is incompatible with all. There is the silver-speckled, incandescent-lovely thrush, whistling pipingly his first song in the blackthorn thicket. How is he to be connected with the bloody, feathered unsightliness of the thrush-remnants just outside the bushes? There is no connexion. They are not to be referred the one to the other. Where one is, the other is not. In the kingdom of death the silvery song is not. But where there is life, there is no death. No death whatever, only silvery gladness, perfect, the otherworld.

The blackbird cannot stop his song, neither can the pigeon. It takes place in him, even though all his race was yesterday destroyed. He cannot mourn, or be silent, or adhere to the dead. Of the dead he is not, since life has kept him. The dead must bury their dead. Life has now taken hold on him and tossed him into the new ether of a new firmament, where he bursts into song as if he were combustible. What is the past, those others, now he is tossed clean into the new, across the untranslatable difference?

In his song is heard the first brokenness and uncertainty of the transition. The transit from the grip of death into new being is a death from death, in its sheer metempsychosis a dizzy agony. But only for a second, the moment of trajectory, the passage from one state to the other, from the grip of death to the liberty of newness. In a moment he is a kingdom of wonder, singing at the centre of a new creation.

The bird did not hang back. He did not cling to his death and his dead. There is no death, and the dead have buried their dead. Tossed into the chasm between two worlds, he lifted his wings in dread, and found himself carried on the impulse.

We are lifted to be cast away into the new beginning. Under our hearts the fountain surges, to toss us forth. Who can thwart the impulse that comes upon us? It comes from the unknown upon us, and it behoves us to pass delicately and exquisitely upon the subtle new wind from heaven, conveyed like birds in unreasoning migrations from death to life.

POETRY OF THE PRESENT (1919)

It seems when we hear a skylark singing as if sound were running into the future, running so fast and utterly without consideration, straight on into futurity. And when we hear a nightingale, we hear the pause and the rich, piercing rhythm of recollection, the perfected past. The lark may sound sad, but with the lovely lapsing sadness that is almost a swoon of hope. The nightingale's triumph is a pæan, but a death-pæan.

So it is with poetry. Poetry is, as a rule, either the voice of the far future, exquisite and ethereal, or it is the voice of the past, rich, magnificent. When the Greeks heard the *Iliad* and the *Odyssey*, they heard their own past calling in their hearts, as men far inland sometimes hear the sea and fall weak with powerful, wonderful regret, nostalgia; or else their own future rippled its time-beats through their blood, as they followed the painful, glamorous progress of the Ithacan. This was Homer to the Greeks: their Past, splendid with battles won and death achieved, and their Future, the magic wandering of Ulysses through the unknown.

With us it is the same. Our birds sing on the horizons. They sing out of the blue, beyond us, or out of the quenched night. They sing at dawn and sunset. Only the poor, shrill, tame canaries whistle while we talk. The wild birds begin before we are awake, or as we drop into dimness, out of waking. Our poets sit by the gateways, some by the east, some by the west. As we arrive and as we go out our hearts surge with response. But whilst we are in the midst of life, we do not hear them.

The poetry of the beginning and the poetry of the end must have that exquisite finality, perfection which belongs to all that is far off. It is in the realm of all that is perfect. It is of the nature of all that is complete and consummate. This completeness, this consummateness, the finality and the perfection are conveyed in exquisite form: the perfect symmetry, the rhythm which returns upon itself like a dance where the hands link and loosen and link for the supreme moment of the end. Perfected bygone moments, perfected moments in the glimmering futurity, these are the treasured gem-like lyrics of Shelley and Keats.

But there is another kind of poetry: the poetry of that which is at hand: the immediate present. In the immediate present there is no perfection, no consummation, nothing finished. The strands are all flying, quivering, intermingling into the web, the waters are shaking the moon. There is no round, consummate moon on the face of running water, nor on the face of the unfinished tide. There are no gems of the living plasm. The living plasm vibrates unspeakably, it inhales the future, it exhales the past, it is the quick of both, and yet it is neither. There is no plasmic finality, nothing crystal, permanent. If we try to fix the living tissue, as the biologists fix it with formation, we have only a hardened bit of the past, the bygone life under our observation.

Life, the ever-present, knows no finality, no finished crystal-lization. The perfect rose is only a running flame, emerging and flowing off, and never in any sense at rest, static, finished. Herein lies its transcendent loveliness. The whole tide of all life and all time suddenly heaves, and appears before us as an appar-ition, a revelation. We look at the very white quick of nascent creation. A waterlily heaves herself from the flood, looks around, gleams, and is gone. We have seen the incarnation, the quick of the ever-swirling flood. We have seen the invisible. We have seen, we have touched, we have partaken of the very substance of creative change, creative mutation. If you tell me about the lotus, tell me of nothing changeless or eternal. Tell me of the mystery of the inexhaustible, forever-unfolding creative spark. Tell me of the incarnate disclosure of the flux, mutation in blossom, laughter and decay perfectly open in their transit, nude in their movement before us.

Let me feel the mud and the heavens in my lotus. Let me feel the heavy, silting, sucking mud, the spinning of sky winds. Let me feel them both in purest contact, the nakedness of sucking weight, nakedly passing radiance. Give me nothing fixed, set, static. Don't give me the infinite or the eternal: nothing of infinity, nothing of eternity. Give me the still, white seething, the incandescence and the coldness of the incarnate moment: the moment, the quick of all change and haste and opposition: the moment, the immediate present, the Now. The immediate moment is not a drop of water running downstream. It is the source and issue, the bubbling up of the stream. Here, in this very instant moment, up bubbles the stream of time, out of the wells of futurity, flowing on to the oceans of the past. The source, the issue, the creative quick.

There is poetry of this immediate present, instant poetry, as well as poetry of the infinite past and the infinite future. The seething poetry of the incarnate Now is supreme, beyond even the everlasting gems of the before and after. In its quivering momentaneity it surpasses the crystalline, pearl-hard jewels, the poems of the eternities. Do not ask for the qualities of the unfading timeless gems. Ask for the whiteness which is the seethe of mud, ask for that incipient putrescence which is the skies falling, ask for the never-pausing, never-ceasing life itself. There must be mutation, swifter than iridescence, haste, not rest, come-and-go, not fixity, inconclusiveness, immediacy, the quality of life itself, without denouement or close. There must be the rapid momentaneous association of things which meet and pass on the for ever incalculable journey of creation: everything left in its own rapid, fluid relationship with the rest of things.

This is the unrestful, ungraspable poetry of the sheer present, poetry whose very permanency lies in its wind-like transit. Whitman's is the best poetry of this kind. Without beginning and without end, without any base and pediment, it sweeps past for ever, like a wind that is for ever in passage, and unchainable. Whitman truly looked before and after. But he did not sigh for what is not. The clue to all his utterance lies in the sheer appreciation of the instant moment, life surging itself into utterance at its very well-head. Eternity is only an abstraction from the actual present. Infinity is only a great reservoir of recollection, or a reservoir of aspiration: man-made. The quivering nimble hour of the present, this is the quick of Time. This is the immanence. The quick of the universe is the *pulsating, carnal self*, mysterious and palpable. So it is always.

Because Whitman put this into his poetry, we fear him and respect him so profoundly. We should not fear him if he sang only of the 'old unhappy far-off things,' or of the 'wings of the morning.' It is because his heart beats with the urgent, insurgent Now, which is even upon us all, that we dread him. He is so near the quick.

From the foregoing it is obvious that the poetry of the instant present cannot have the same body or the same motion as the poetry of the before and after. It can never submit to the same conditions. It is never finished. There is no rhythm which returns upon itself, no serpent of eternity with its tail in its own mouth. There is no static perfection, none of that finality which we find so satisfying because we are so frightened.

Much has been written about free verse. But all that can be said, first and last, is that free verse is, or should be direct utterance from the instant, whole man. It is the soul and the mind and body surging at once, nothing left out. They speak all together. There is some confusion, some discord. But the confusion and the discord only belong to the reality, as noise belongs to the plunge of water. It is no use inventing fancy laws for free verse, no use drawing a melodic line which all the feet must toe. Free verse toes no melodic line, no matter what drill-sergeant. Whitman pruned away his clichés – perhaps his clichés of rhythm as well as of phrase. And this is about all we can do, deliberately, with free verse. We can get rid of the stereotyped movements and the old hackneyed associations of sound or sense. We can break down those artificial conduits and canals through which we do so love to force our utterance. We can break the stiff neck of habit. We can be in ourselves spontaneous and flexible as flame, we can see that utterance rushes out without artificial form or artificial smoothness. But we cannot positively prescribe any motion, any rhythm. All the laws we invent or discover – it amounts to pretty much the same – will fail to apply to free verse. They will only apply to some form of restricted, limited unfree verse.

All we can say is that free verse does *not* have the same nature as restricted verse. It is not of the nature of reminiscence. It is not the past which we treasure in its perfection between our hands. Neither is it the crystal of the perfect future, into which we gaze. Its tide is neither the full, yearning flow of aspiration, nor the sweet, poignant ebb of remembrance and regret. The past and the future are the two great bournes of human emotion, the two great homes of the human days, the two eternities. They are both conclusive, final. Their beauty is the beauty of the goal, finished, perfected. Finished beauty and measured symmetry belong to the stable, unchanging eternities.

But in free verse we look for the insurgent naked throb of the instant moment. To break the lovely form of metrical verse, and to dish up the fragments as a new substance, called *vers libre*, this is what most of the free-versifiers accomplish. They do not know that free verse has its own *nature*, that it is neither star nor pearl, but instantaneous like plasm. It has no goal in either eternity. It has no finish. It has no satisfying stability, satisfying to those who like the immutable. None of this. It is the instant; the quick; the very jetting source of all will-be and has-been. The utterance is like a spasm, naked contact with all influences at once. It does not want to get anywhere. It just takes place.

For such utterance any externally applied law would be mere shackles and death. The law must come new each time from within. The bird is on the wing in the winds, flexible to every breath, a living spark in the storm, its very flickering depending upon its supreme mutability and power of change. Whence such a bird came: whither it goes: from what solid earth it rose up, and upon what solid earth it will close its wings and settle, this is not the question. This is a question of before and after. Now, *now*, the bird is on the wing in the winds.

Such is the rare new poetry. One realm we have never conquered: the pure present. One great mystery of time is terra incognita to us: the instant. The most superb mystery we have hardly recognized: the immediate, instant self. The quick of all time is the instant. The quick of all the universe, of all creation, is the incarnate, carnal self. Poetry gave us the clue: free verse: Whitman. Now we know.

The ideal – what is the ideal? A figment. An abstraction. A static abstraction, abstracted from life. It is a fragment of the before or the after. It is a crystallized aspiration, or a crystallized remembrance: crystallized, set, finished. It is a thing set apart, in the great storehouse of eternity, the storehouse of finished things.

We do not speak of things crystallized and set apart. We speak of the instant, the immediate self, the very plasm of the self. We speak also of free verse.

All this should have come as a preface to *Look! We Have Come Through!* But is it not better to publish a preface long after the book it belongs to has appeared? For then the reader will have had his fair chance with the book, alone.

MEMOIR OF MAURICE MAGNUS (1921–22)

On a dark, wet, wintry evening in November, 1919, I arrived in Florence, having just got back to Italy for the first time since 1914. My wife was in Germany, gone to see her mother, also for the first time since that fatal year 1914. We were poor; who was going to bother to publish me and to pay for my writings, in 1918 and 1919? I landed in Italy with nine pounds in my pocket and about twelve pounds lying in the bank in London. Nothing more. My wife, I hoped, would arrive in Florence with two or three pounds remaining. We should have to go very softly, if we were to house ourselves in Italy for the winter. But after the desperate weariness of the war, one could not bother.

So I had written to N— D— to get me a cheap room somewhere in Florence, and to leave a note at Cook's. I deposited my bit of luggage at the station, and walked to Cook's in the Via Tornabuoni. Florence was strange to me: seemed grim and dark and rather awful on the cold November evening. There was a note from D—, who has never left me in the lurch. I went down the Lung 'Arno to the address he gave.

I had just passed the end of the Ponte Vecchio, and was watching the first lights of evening and the last light of day on the swollen river as I walked, when I heard D—'s voice:

'Isn't that Lawrence? Why of course it is, of course it is, beard and all! Well, how are you, eh? You got my note? Well now, my dear boy, you just go on to the Cavelotti – straight ahead,

83

D. H. LAWRENCE

straight ahead – you've got the number. There's a room for you there. We shall be there in half an hour. Oh, let me introduce you to M—'

I had unconsciously seen the two men approaching, D— tall and portly, the other man rather short and strutting. They were both buttoned up in their overcoats, and both had rather curly little hats. But D— was decidedly shabby and a gentleman, with his wicked red face and tufted eyebrows. The other man was almost smart, all in grey, and he looked at first sight like an actor-manager, common. There was a touch of down-on-his-luck about him too. He looked at me, buttoned up in my old thick overcoat, and with my beard bushy and raggy because of my horror of entering a strange barber's shop, and he greeted me in a rather fastidious voice, and a little patronizingly. I forgot to say I was carrying a small hand-bag. But I realized at once that I ought, in this little grey-sparrow man's eyes – he stuck his front out tubbily, like a bird, and his legs seemed to perch behind him, as a bird's do – I ought to be in a cab. But I wasn't. He eyed me in that shrewd and rather impertinent way of the world of actor-managers: cosmopolitan, knocking shabbily round the world.

He looked a man of about forty, spruce and youngish in his deportment, very pink-faced, and very clean, very natty, very alert, like a sparrow painted to resemble a tom-tit. He was just the kind of man I had never met: little smart man of the shabby world, very much on the spot, don't you know.

'How much does it cost?' I asked D—, meaning the room.

'Oh, my dear fellow, a trifle. Ten francs a day. Third rate, tenth rate, but not bad at the price. Pension terms of course – everything included – except wine.'

'Oh no, not at all bad for the money,' said M—. 'Well now, shall we be moving? You want the post office, D—?' His voice was precise and a little mincing, and it had an odd high squeak.

'I do,' said D—.

'Well then come down here –' M— turned to a dark little alley.

'Not at all,' said D—. 'We turn down by the bridge.'

'This is quicker,' said M—. He had a twang rather than an accent in his speech – not definitely American.

He knew all the short cuts of Florence. Afterwards I found that he knew all the short cuts in all the big towns of Europe.

I went on to the Cavelotti and waited in an awful plush and gilt drawing-room, and was given at last a cup of weird muddy brown slush called tea, and a bit of weird brown mush called jam on some bits of bread. Then I was taken to my room. It was far off, on the third floor of the big, ancient, deserted Florentine house. There I had a big and lonely, stone-comfortless room looking on to the river. Fortunately it was not very cold inside, and I didn't care. The adventure of being back in Florence again after the years of war made one indifferent.

After an hour or so someone tapped. It was D— coming in with his grandiose air – now a bit shabby, but still very courtly.

'Why here you are – miles and miles from human habitation! I *told* her to put you on the second floor, where we are. What does she mean by it? Ring that bell. Ring it.'

'No,' said I, 'I'm all right here.'

'What!' cried D—. 'In this Spitzbergen! Where's that bell?'

'Don't ring it,' said I, who have a horror of chambermaids and explanations.

'Not ring it! Well you're a man, you are! Come on then. Come on down to my room. Come on. Have you had some tea – filthy muck they call tea here? I never drink it.'

I went down to D—'s room on the lower floor. It was a lit-tered mass of books and typewriter and papers: D— was just finishing his novel. M— was resting on the bed, in his shirt sleeves: a tubby, fresh-faced little man in a suit of grey, faced cloth bound at the edges with grey silk braid. He had light blue eyes, tired underneath, and crisp, curly, dark brown hair just grey at the temples. But everything was neat and even finicking about his person.

'Sit down! Sit down!' said D—, wheeling up a chair. 'Have a whisky?'

'Whisky!' said I.

'Twenty-four francs a bottle – and a find at that,' moaned D—. I must tell that the exchange was then about forty-five lire to the pound.

'Oh N—,' said M—, 'I didn't tell you. I was offered a bottle of 1913 Black and White for twenty-eight lire.'

'Did you buy it?'

'No. It's your turn to buy a bottle.'

'Twenty-eight francs – my dear fellow!' said D—, cocking up his eyebrows. 'I shall have to starve myself to do it.'

'Oh no you won't, you'll eat here just the same,' said M—.

'Yes, and I'm starved to death. Starved to death by the muck – the absolute muck they call food here. I can't face twenty-eight francs, my dear chap – can't be done, on my honour.'

'Well look here, N—. We'll both buy a bottle. And you can get the one at twenty-two, and I'll buy the one at twenty-eight.'

So it always was, M— indulged D—, and spoilt him in every way. And of course D— wasn't grateful. *Au contraire!* And M—'s pale blue smallish round eyes, in his cockatoo-pink face, would harden to indignation occasionally.

The room was dreadful. D— never opened the windows: didn't believe in opening windows. He believed that a certain amount of nitrogen – I should say a great amount – is beneficial. The queer smell of a bedroom which is slept in, worked in, lived in, smoked in, and in which men drink their whiskies, was something new to me. But I didn't care. One had got away from the war.

We drank our whiskies before dinner. M— was rather yellow under the eyes, and irritable; even his pink fattish face went yellowish.

'Look here,' said D—. 'Didn't you say there was a turkey for dinner? What? Have you been to the kitchen to see what they're doing to it?'

'Yes,' said M— testily. 'I forced them to prepare it to roast.'

'With chestnuts – stuffed with chestnuts?' said D—.

'They *said* so,' said M—.

'Oh, but go down and see that they're doing it. Yes, you've got to keep your eye on them, got to. The most awful howlers if you don't. You go now and see what they're up to.' D— used his most irresistible grand manner.

'It's too late,' persisted M—, testy.

'It's *never* too late. You just run down and absolutely prevent them from boiling that bird in the old soup-water,' said D—. 'If you need force, fetch me.'

M— went. He was a great epicure, and knew how things should be cooked. But of course his irruptions into the kitchen roused considerable resentment, and he was getting quaky. However, he went. He came back to say the turkey was being roasted, but without chestnuts.

'What did I tell you! What did I tell you!' cried D—. 'They are absolute —! If you don't hold them by the neck while they peel the chestnuts, they'll stuff the bird with old boots, to save themselves trouble. Of course you should have gone down sooner, M—.'

Dinner was always late, so the whisky was usually two whiskies. Then we went down, and were merry in spite of all things. That is, D— always grumbled about the food. There was one unfortunate youth who was boots and porter and waiter and all. He brought the big dish to D—, and D— always poked and pushed among the portions, and grumbled frantically, sotto voce, in Italian to the youth Beppo, getting into a nervous frenzy. Then M— called the waiter to himself, picked the nicest bits off the dish and gave them to D—, then helped himself.

The food was not good, but with D— it was an obsession. With the waiter he was terrible – 'Cos' è? Zuppa? Grazie. No niente per me. *No – No!* – Quest' acqua sporca non bevo io. I don't drink this dirty water. What – What's that in it – a piece of dish clout? Oh holy Dio, I can't eat another thing this evening –'

And he yelled for more bread – bread being war rations and very limited in supply – so M— in nervous distress gave him his piece, and D— threw the crumb part on the floor, anywhere, and called for another litre. We always drank heavy dark red wine at three francs a litre. D— drank two-thirds, M— drank least. He loved his liquors, and did not care for wine. We were noisy and unabashed at table. The old Danish ladies at the other end of the room, and the rather impecunious young Duca and family not far off were not supposed to understand English. The Italians rather liked the noise, and the young signorina with the high-up yellow hair eyed us with profound interest. On we sailed, gay and noisy, D— telling witty anecdotes and grumbling wildly and only half whimsically about the food. We sat on till most people had finished – then went up to more whisky – one more perhaps – in M—'s room.

When I came down in the morning I was called into M—'s room. He was like a little pontiff in a blue kimono-shaped dressing-gown with a broad border of reddish purple: the blue was a soft mid-blue, the material a dull silk. So he minced about, in demi-toilette. His room was very clean and neat, and slightly perfumed with essences. On his dressing-table stood many cut glass bottles and silver-topped bottles with essences and pomades and powders, and heaven knows what. A very elegant little prayer book lay by his bed – and a life of St Benedict. For M— was a Roman Catholic convert. All he had was expensive and finicking: thick leather silver-studded suit-cases standing near the wall, trouser-stretcher all nice, hair-brushes and clothes-brush with old ivory backs. I wondered over him and his niceties and little pomposities. He was a new bird to me.

For he wasn't at all just the common person he looked. He was queer and sensitive as a woman with D—, and patient and fastidious. And yet he *was* common, his very accent was common, and D— despised him.

And M— rather despised me because I did not spend money. I paid for a third of the wine we drank at dinner, and bought the third bottle of whisky we had during M—'s stay. After all, he only stayed three days. But I would not spend for myself. I had no money to spend, since I knew I must live and my wife must live.

'Oh,' said M—. 'Why, that's the very time to spend money, when you've got none. If you've got none, why try to save it? That's been my philosophy all my life; when you've got no money, you may just as well spend it. If you've got a good deal, that's the time to look after it.' Then he laughed his queer little laugh, rather squeaky. These were his exact words.

'Precisely,' said D—. 'Spend when you've nothing to spend, my boy. Spent *hard* then.'

'No,' said I. 'If I can help it, I will never let myself be penniless while I live. I mistrust the world too much.'

'But if you're going to live in fear of the world,' said M—, 'what's the good of living at all? Might as well die.'

I think I give his words almost verbatim. He had a certain impatience of me and of my presence. Yet we had some jolly times – mostly in one or other of their bedrooms, drinking a whisky and talking. We drank a bottle a day – I had very little, preferring the wine at lunch and dinner, which seemed delicious after the war famine. D— would bring up the remains of the second litre in the evening, to go on with before the coffee came.

I arrived in Florence on the Wednesday or Thursday evening; I think Thursday. M— was due to leave for Rome on the Saturday. I asked D— who M— was. 'Oh, you never know what he's at. He was manager for Isadora Duncan for a long time – knows all the capitals of Europe: St Petersburg, Moscow, Tiflis, Constantinople, Berlin, Paris – knows them as you and I know Florence. He's been mostly in that line – theatrical. Then a journalist. He edited the *Roman Review* till the war killed it. Oh, a many-sided sort of fellow.'

'But how do you know him?' said I.

'I met him in Capri years and years ago – oh, sixteen years ago – and clean forgot all about him till somebody came to me one day in Rome and said: You're N— D—. *I* didn't know who he was. But he'd never forgotten me. Seems to be smitten by me, somehow or other. All the better for me, ha-ha! – if he *likes* to run round for me. My dear fellow, I wouldn't prevent him, if it amuses him. Not for worlds.'

And that was how it was. M— ran D—'s errands, forced the other man to go to the tailor, to the dentist, and was almost a guardian angel to him.

'Look here!' cried D—. '*I can't* go to that damned tailor. Let the thing wait, I can't go.'

'Oh yes. Now look here N—, if you don't get it done now while I'm here you'll never get it done. I made the appointment for three o'clock –'

'To hell with you! Details! Details! I can't stand it, I tell you.'

D— chafed and kicked, but went.

'A little fussy fellow,' he said. 'Oh yes, fussing about like a woman. Fussy, you know, fussy. I *can't stand* these fussy –' And D— went off into improprieties.

Well, M— ran round and arranged D—'s affairs and settled his little bills, and was so benevolent, and so impatient and nettled at the ungrateful way in which the benevolence was accepted. And D— despised him all the time as a little busybody and an inferior. And I there between them just wondered. It seemed to me M— would get very irritable and nervous at mid-day and before dinner, yellow round the eyes and played out. He wanted his whisky. He was tired after running round on a thousand errands and quests which I never understood. He always took his morning coffee at dawn, and was out to early Mass and pushing his affairs before eight o'clock in the morning. But what his affairs were I still do not know. Mass is all I am certain of.

However, it was his birthday on the Sunday, and D— would not let him go. He had once said he would give a dinner for his birthday, and this he was not allowed to forget. It seemed to me M— rather wanted to get out of it. But D— was determined to have that dinner.

'You aren't going before you've given us that hare, don't you imagine it, my boy. I've got the smell of that hare in my imagination, and I've damned well got to set my teeth in it. Don't you imagine you're going without having produced that hare.'

So poor M—, rather a victim, had to consent. We discussed what we should eat. It was decided the hare should have truffles, and a dish of champignons, and cauliflower, and zabaioni – and I forget what else. It was to be on Saturday evening. And M— would leave on Sunday for Rome.

Early on the Saturday morning he went out, with the first daylight, to the old market, to get the hare and the mushrooms. He went himself because he was a connoisseur.

On the Saturday afternoon D— took me wandering round to buy a birthday present.

'I shall have to buy him something – have to – have to –' he said fretfully. He only wanted to spend about five francs. We trailed over the Ponte Vecchio, looking at the jewellers' booths there. It was before the foreigners had come back, and things were still rather dusty and almost at pre-war prices. But we could see nothing for five francs except the little saint-medals. D— wanted to buy one of those. It seemed to me infra dig. So at last coming down to the Mercato Nuovo we saw little bowls of Volterra marble, a natural amber colour, for four francs.

'Look, buy one of those,' I said to D—, 'and he can put his pins or studs or any trifle in, as he needs.'

So we went in and bought one of the little bowls of Volterra marble.

M— seemed so touched and pleased with the gift.

'Thank you a thousand times, N—,' he said. 'That's charming! That's exactly what I want.'

The dinner was quite a success, and, poorly fed as we were at the pension, we stuffed ourselves tight on the mushrooms and the hare and the zabaioni, and drank ourselves tight with the good red wine which swung in its straw flask in the silver swing on the table. A flask has two and a quarter litres. We were four persons, and we drank almost two flasks. D— made the waiter measure the remaining half-litre and take it off the bill. But good, good food, and cost about twelve francs a head the whole dinner.

Well, next day was nothing but bags and suit-cases in M—'s room, and the misery of departure with luggage. He went on the midnight train to Rome: first-class.

'I always travel first-class,' he said, 'and I always shall, while I can buy the ticket. Why should I go second? It's beastly enough to travel at all.'

'My dear fellow, I came up third the last time I came from Rome,' said D—. 'Oh, not bad, not bad. Damned fatiguing journey anyhow.'

So the little outsider was gone, and I was rather glad. I don't think he liked me. Yet one day he said to me at table:

'How lovely your hair is – such a lovely colour! What do you dye it with?'

I laughed, thinking he was laughing too. But no, he meant it.

'It's got no particular colour at all,' I said, 'so I couldn't dye it that!'

'It's a lovely colour,' he said. And I think he didn't believe me, that I didn't dye it. It puzzled me, and it puzzles me still.

But he was gone. D— moved into M—'s room, and asked me to come down to the room he himself was vacating. But I preferred to stay upstairs.

M— was a fervent Catholic, taking the religion, alas, rather unctuously. He had entered the Church only a few years before. But he had a bishop for a god-father, and seemed to be very intimate with the upper clergy. He was very pleased and proud because he was a constant guest at the famous old monastery south of Rome. He talked of becoming a monk; a monk in that aristocratic and well-bred order. But he had not even begun his theological studies: or any studies of any sort. And D— said he only chose the Benedictines because they lived better than any of the others.

But I had said to M— that when my wife came and we moved south, I would like to visit the monastery some time, if I might. 'Certainly,' he said. 'Come when I am there. I shall be there in about a month's time. Do come! Do be sure and come. It's a wonderful place – oh, wonderful. It will make a great impression on you. Do come. Do come. And I will tell Don Bernardo, who is my *greatest* friend, and who is guest-master, about you. So that if you wish to go when I am not there, write to Don Bernardo. But do come when I am there.'

My wife and I were due to go into the mountains south of Rome, and stay there some months. Then I was to visit the big, noble monastery that stands on a bluff hill like a fortress crowning a great precipice, above the little town and the plain between the mountains. But it was so icy cold and snowy among the mountains, it was unbearable. We fled south again, to Naples, and to Capri. Passing, I saw the monastery crouching there above, world-famous, but it was impossible to call then.

I wrote and told M— of my move. In Capri I had an answer from him. It had a wistful tone – and I don't know what made me think that he was in trouble, in monetary difficulty. But I felt it acutely – a kind of appeal. Yet he said nothing direct. And he wrote from an expensive hotel in Anzio, on the sea near Rome.

At the moment I had just received twenty pounds unexpected and joyful from America – a gift too. I hesitated for some time, because I felt unsure. Yet the curious appeal came out of the letter, though nothing was said. And I felt also I owed M— that dinner, and I didn't want to owe him anything, since he despised me a little for being careful. So partly out of revenge, perhaps, and partly because I felt the strange wistfulness of him appealing to me, I sent him five pounds, saying perhaps I was mistaken in imagining him very hard up, but if so, he wasn't to be offended.

It is strange to me even now, how I knew he was appealing to me. Because it was all as vague as I say. Yet I felt it so strongly. He replied: 'Your cheque has saved my life. Since I last saw you I have fallen down an abyss. But I will tell you when I see you. I shall be at the monastery in three days. Do come – and come alone.' I have forgotten to say that he was a rabid woman-hater.

This was just after Christmas. I thought his 'saved my life' and 'fallen down an abyss' was just the American touch of 'very, very –.' I wondered what on earth the abyss could be, and I decided it must be that he had lost his money or his hopes. It seemed to me that some of his old buoyant assurance came out again in this letter. But he was now very friendly, urging me to come to the monastery, and treating me with a curious little tenderness and protectiveness. He had a queer delicacy of his own, varying with a bounce and a commonness. He was a common little bounder. And then he had this curious delicacy and tenderness and wistfulness.

I put off going north. I had another letter urging me – and it seemed to me that, rather assuredly, he was expecting more money. Rather cockily, as if he had a right to it. And that made me not want to give him any. Besides, as my wife said, what right had I to give away the little money we had, and we there stranded in the south of Italy with no resources if once we were spent up. And I have always been determined *never* to come to my last shilling – if I have to reduce my spending almost to nothingness. I have always been determined to keep a few pounds between me and the world.

I did not send any money. But I wanted to go to the monastery, so wrote and said I would come for two days. I always remember getting up in the black dark of the January morning, and making a little coffee on the spirit-lamp, and watching the clock, the big-faced, blue old clock on the campanile in the piazza in Capri, to see I wasn't late. The electric light in the piazza lit up the face of the campanile. And we were then a stone's throw away, high in the Palazzo Ferraro, opposite the bubbly roof of the little duomo. Strange dark winter morning, with the open sea beyond the roofs, seen through the side window, and the thin line of the lights of Naples twinkling far, far off.

At ten minutes to six I went down the smelly dark stone stairs of the old palazzo, out into the street. A few people were already hastening up the street to the terrace that looks over the sea to the bay of Naples. It was dark and cold. We slid down in the funicular to the shore, then in little boats were rowed out over the dark sea to the steamer that lay there showing her lights and hooting.

It was three long hours across the sea to Naples, with dawn coming slowly in the east, beyond Ischia, and flushing into lovely colour as our steamer pottered along the peninsula, calling at Massa and Sorrento and Piano. I always loved hanging over the side and watching the people come out in boats from the little places of the shore, that rose steep and beautiful. I love the movement of these watery Neapolitan people, and the naïve trustful way they clamber in and out the boats, and their softness, and their dark eyes. But when the steamer leaves the peninsula and begins to make away round Vesuvius to Naples, one is already tired, and cold, cold, cold in the wind that comes piercing from the snowcrests away there along Italy. Cold, and reduced to a kind of stony apathy by the time we come to the mole in Naples, at ten o'clock – or twenty past ten.

We were rather late, and I missed the train. I had to wait till two o'clock. And Naples is a hopeless town to spend three hours in. However, time passes. I remember I was calculating in my mind whether they had given me the right change at the ticket-window. They hadn't – and I hadn't counted in time. Thinking of this, I got in the Rome train. I had been there ten minutes when I heard a trumpet blow.

'Is this the Rome train?' I asked my fellow-traveller.

'Si.'

'The express?'

'No, it is the slow train.'

'It leaves?'

'At ten past two.'

I almost jumped through the window. I flew down the platform.

'The diretto!' I cried to a porter.

'Parte! Eccolo là!' he said, pointing to a big train moving inevitably away.

I flew with wild feet across the various railway lines and seized the end of the train as it travelled. I had caught it. Perhaps if I had missed it fate would have been different. So I sat still for about three hours. Then I had arrived.

There is a long drive up the hill from the station to the

monastery. The driver talked to me. It was evident he bore the monks no good will.

'Formerly,' he said, 'if you went up to the monastery you got a glass of wine and a plate of macaroni. But now they kick you out of the door.'

'Do they?' I said. 'It is hard to believe.'

'They kick you out of the gate,' he vociferated.

We twisted up and up the wild hillside, past the old castle of the town, past the last villa, between trees and rocks. We saw no one. The whole hill belongs to the monastery. At last at twilight we turned the corner of the oak wood and saw the monastery like a huge square fortress-palace of the sixteenth century crowning the near distance. Yes, and there was M— just stepping through the huge old gateway and hastening down the slope to where the carriage must stop. He was bare-headed, and walking with his perky, busy little stride, seemed very much at home in the place. He looked up to me with a tender, intimate look as I got down from the carriage. Then he took my hand.

'So *very* glad to see you,' he said. 'I'm so *pleased* you've come.'

And he looked into my eyes with that wistful, watchful tenderness rather like a woman who isn't quite sure of her lover. He had a certain charm in his manner; and an odd pompous touch with it at this moment, welcoming his guest at the gate of the vast monastery which reared above us from its buttresses in the rock, was rather becoming. His face was still pink, his eyes pale blue and sharp, but he looked greyer at the temples.

'Give me your bag,' he said. 'Yes do – and come along. Don Bernardo is just at Evensong, but he'll be here in a little while. Well now, tell me all the news.'

'Wait,' I said. 'Lend me five francs to finish paying the driver – he has no change.'

'Certainly, certainly,' he said, giving the five francs.

I had no news – so asked him his.

'Oh, I have none either,' he said. 'Very short of money, that of course is *no* news.' And he laughed his little laugh. 'I'm so glad to be here,' he continued. 'The peace, and the rhythm of the life is so *beautiful*! I'm sure you'll love it.'

We went up the slope under the big, tunnel-like entrance and were in the grassy courtyard, with the arched walk on the far sides, and one or two trees. It was like a grassy cloister, but still busy. Black monks were standing chatting, an old peasant was just driving two sheep from the cloister grass, and an old monk was darting into the little post-office which one recognized by the shield with the national arms over the doorway. From under the far arches came an old peasant carrying a two-handed saw.

And there was Don Bernardo, a tall monk in a black, well-shaped gown, young, good-looking, gentle, hastening forward with a quick smile. He was about my age, and his manner seemed fresh and subdued, as if he were still a student. One felt one was at college with one's college mates.

We went up the narrow stair and into the long, old, naked white corridor, high and arched. Don Bernardo had got the key of my room: two keys, one for the dark antechamber, one for the bedroom. A charming and elegant bedroom, with an engraving of English landscape, and outside the net curtain a balcony looking down on the garden, a narrow strip beneath the walls, and beyond, the clustered buildings of the farm, and the oak woods and arable fields of the hill summit: and beyond again, the gulf where the world's valley was, and all the mountains that stand in Italy on the plains as if God had just put them down ready made. The sun had already sunk, the snow on the mountains was full of a rosy glow, the valleys were full of shadow. One heard, far below, the trains shunting, the world clinking in the cold air.

'Isn't it wonderful! Ah, the most wonderful place on earth!'

said M—. 'What now could you wish better than to end your days here? The peace, the beauty, the eternity of it.' He paused and sighed. Then he put his hand on Don Bernardo's arm and smiled at him with that odd, rather wistful smirking tenderness that made him such a quaint creature in my eyes.

'But I'm going to enter the order. You're going to let me be a monk and be one of you, aren't you, Don Bernardo?'

'We will see,' smiled Don Bernardo. 'When you have begun your studies.'

'It will take me two years,' said M—. 'I shall have to go to the college in Rome. When I have got the money for the fees –' He talked away, like a boy planning a new rôle.

'But I'm sure Lawrence would like to drink a cup of tea,' said Don Bernardo. He spoke English as if it were his native language. 'Shall I tell them to make it in the kitchen, or shall we go to your room?'

'Oh, we'll go to my room. How thoughtless of me! Do forgive me, won't you?' said M—, laying his hand gently on my arm. 'I'm so awfully sorry, you know. But we get so excited and enchanted when we talk of the monastery. But come along, come along, it will be ready in a moment on the spirit-lamp.'

We went down to the end of the high, white, naked corridor. M— had a quite sumptuous room, with a curtained bed in one part, and under the window his writing-desk with papers and photographs, and nearby a sofa and an easy table, making a little sitting-room, while the bed and toilet things, pomades and bottles were all in the distance, in the shadow. Night was fallen. From the window one saw the world far below, like a pool the flat plain, a deep pool of darkness with little twinkling lights, and rows and bunches of light that were the railway station.

I drank my tea, M— drank a little liqueur, Don Bernardo in his black winter robe sat and talked with us. At least he did very little talking. But he listened and smiled and put in a word or two as we talked, seated round the table on which stood the green-shaded electric lamp.

The monastery was cold as the tomb. Couched there on the top of its hill, it is not much below the winter snow-line. Now by the end of January all the summer heat is soaked out of the vast, ponderous stone walls, and they become masses of coldness cloaking around. There is no heating apparatus whatsoever – none. Save the fire in the kitchen, for cooking, nothing. Dead, silent, stone cold everywhere.

At seven we went down to dinner. Capri in the daytime was hot, so I had brought only a thin old dust-coat. M— therefore made me wear a big coat of his own, a coat made of thick, smooth black cloth, and lined with black sealskin, and having a collar of silky black sealskin. I can still remember the feel of the silky fur. It was queer to have him helping me solicitously into this coat, and buttoning it at the throat for me.

'Yes, it's a beautiful coat. Of course!' he said. 'I hope you find it warm.'

'Wonderful,' said I. 'I feel as warm as a millionaire.'

'I'm so glad you do,' he laughed.

'You don't mind my wearing your grand coat?' I said.

'Of course not! Of course not! It's a pleasure to me if it will keep you warm. We don't want to die of cold in the monastery, do we? That's one of the mortifications we will do our best to avoid. What? Don't you think? Yes, I think this coldness is going almost too far. I had that coat made in New York fifteen years ago. Of course in Italy –' he said It'ly – 'I've never worn it, so it is as good as new. And it's a beautiful coat, fur and cloth of the very best. *And* the tailor.' He laughed a little, self-approving laugh. He liked to give the impression that he dealt with the *best* shops, don't you know, and stayed in the *best* hotels, etc. I grinned inside the coat, detesting best hotels, best shops, and best overcoats. So off we went, he in his grey overcoat and I in my sealskin millionaire monster, down the dim corridor to the guests' refectory. It was a bare room with a long white table. M— and I sat at the near end. Further down was another man, perhaps the father of one of the boy students. There is a college attached to the monastery.

We sat in the icy room, muffled up in our overcoats. A lay-brother with a bulging forehead and queer, fixed eyes waited on us. He might easily have come from an old Italian picture. One of the adoring peasants. The food was abundant – but alas, it had got cold in the long cold transit from the kitchen. And it was roughly cooked, even if it was quite wholesome. Poor M— did not eat much, but nervously nibbled his bread. I could tell the meals were a trial to him. He could not bear the cold food in that icy, empty refectory. And his phthisickiness offended the lay brothers. I could see that his little pomposities and his 'superior' behaviour and his long stay made them have that old monastic grudge against him, silent but very obstinate and effectual – the same now as six hundred years ago. We had a decanter of good red wine – but he did not care for much wine. He was glad to be peeling the cold orange which was dessert.

After dinner he took me down to see the church, creeping like two thieves down the dimness of the great, prison-cold white corridors, on the cold flag floors. Stone cold: the monks must have invented the term. These monks were at Compline. So we went by our two secret little selves into the tall dense nearly-darkness of the church. M—, knowing his way about here as in the cities, led me, poor wondering worldling, by the arm through the gulfs of the tomb-like place. He found the electric light switches inside the church, and stealthily made me a light as we went. We looked at the lily marble of the great floor, at the pillars, at the Benvenuto Cellini casket, at the really lovely pillars and slabs of different coloured marbles, all coloured marbles, yellow and grey and rose and green and lily white, veined and mottled and splashed: lovely, lovely stones – And Benvenuto had used pieces of lapis lazuli, blue as cornflowers. Yes, yes, all very rich and wonderful.

We tiptoed about the dark church stealthily, from altar to altar, and M— whispered ecstasies in my ear. Each time we passed before an altar, whether the high altar or the side chapels, he did a wonderful reverence, which he must have practised for hours, bowing waxily down and sinking till his one knee touched the pavement, then rising like a flower that rises and unfolds again, till he had skipped to my side and was playing cicerone once more. Always in his grey overcoat, and in whispers: me in the big black overcoat, millionairish. So we crept into the chancel and examined all the queer fat babies of the choir stalls, carved in wood and rolling on their little backs between monk's place and monk's place – queer things for the chanting monks to have between them, these shiny, polished, dark brown fat babies, all different, and all jolly and lusty. We looked at everything in the church – and then at everything in the ancient room at the side where surplices hang and monks can wash their hands.

Then we went down to the crypt, where the modern mosaics glow in wonderful colours, and sometimes in fascinating little fantastic trees and birds. But it was rather like a scene in the theatre, with M— for the wizard and myself a sort of Parsifal in the New York coat. He switched on the lights, the gold mosaic of the vaulting glittered and bowed, the blue mosaic glowed out, the holy of holies gleamed theatrically, the stiff mosaic figures posed around us. To tell the truth I was glad to get back to the normal human room and sit on a sofa huddled in my overcoat, and look at photographs which M— showed me: photographs of everywhere in Europe. Then he showed me a wonderful photograph of a picture of a lovely lady – asked me what I thought of it, and seemed to expect me to be struck to bits by the beauty. His almost sanctimonious expectation made me tell the truth, that I thought it just a bit cheap, trivial. And then he said, dramatic:

'That's my mother.'

It looked so unlike anybody's mother, much less M—'s, that I was startled. I realized that she was his great stunt, and that I had put my foot in it. So I just held my tongue. Then I said, for I felt he was going to be silent forever:

'There are so few portraits, unless by the really great artists, that aren't a bit cheap. She must have been a beautiful woman.'

'Yes, she *was*,' he said curtly. And we dropped the subject.

He locked all his drawers *very* carefully, and kept the keys on a chain. He seemed to give the impression that he had a great many secrets, perhaps dangerous ones, locked up in the drawers of his writing-table there. And I always wonder what the secrets can be, that are able to be kept so tight under lock and key.

Don Bernardo tapped and entered. We all sat round and sipped a funny liqueur which I didn't like. M— lamented that the bottle was finished. I asked him to order another and let me pay for it. So he said he would tell the postman to bring it up next day from the town. Don Bernardo sipped his tiny glass with the rest of us, and he told me, briefly, his story – and we talked politics till nearly midnight. Then I came out of the black overcoat and we went to bed.

In the morning a fat, smiling, nice old lay-brother brought me my water. It was a sunny day. I looked down on the farm cluster and the brown fields and the sere oak woods of the hill-crown, and the rocks and bushes savagely bordering it round. Beyond, the mountains with their snow were blue-glistery with sunshine, and seemed quite near, but across a sort of gulf. All was still and sunny. And the poignant grip of the past, the grandiose, violent past of the Middle Ages, when blood was strong and unquenched and life was flamboyant with splendours and horrible miseries, took hold of me till I could hardly bear it. It was really agony to me to be in the monastery and to see the old farm and the bullocks slowly working in the fields below, and the black pigs rooting among weeds, and to see a monk sitting on a parapet in the sun, and an old, old man in skin sandals and white bunched, swathed legs come driving an ass slowly to the monastery gate, slowly, with all that lingering nonchalance and wildness of the Middle Ages, and yet to know that I was myself, child of the present. It was so strange from M—'s window to look down on the plain and see the white road going straight past a mountain that stood like a loaf of sugar, the river meandering in loops, and the railway with glistening lines making a long black swoop across the flat and into the hills. To see trains come steaming, with white smoke flying. To see the station like a little harbour where trucks like shipping stood anchored in rows in the black bay of railway. To see trains stop in the station and tiny people swarming like flies! To see all this from the monastery, where the Middle Ages live on in a sort of agony, like Tithonus, and cannot die, this was almost a violation to my soul, made almost a wound.

Immediately after coffee we went down to Mass. It was celebrated in a small crypt chapel underground, because that was warmer. The twenty or so monks sat in their stalls, one monk officiating at the altar. It was quiet and simple, the monks sang sweetly and well, there was no organ. It seemed soon to pass by. M— and I sat near the door. He was very devoted and scrupulous in his going up and down. I was an outsider. But it was pleasant – not too sacred. One felt the monks were very human in their likes and their jealousies. It was rather like a group of dons in the dons' room at Cambridge, a cluster of professors in any college. But during Mass they, of course, just sang their responses. Only I could tell some watched the officiating monk rather with ridicule – he was one of the ultra-punctilious sort, just like a don. And some boomed their responses with a grain of defiance against some brother monk who had earned dislike. It was human, and more like a university than anything. We went to Mass every morning, but I did not go to Evensong.

After Mass M— took me round and showed me everything of the vast monastery. We went into the Bramante Courtyard, all stone, with its great well in the centre, and the colonnades of arches going round, full of sunshine, gay and Renaissance, a little bit ornate but still so jolly and gay, sunny pale stone waiting for the lively people, with the great flight of pale steps sweeping up to the doors of the church, waiting for gentlemen in scarlet trunk-hose, slender red legs, and ladies in brocade gowns, and page-boys with fluffed, golden hair. Splendid, sunny, gay Bramante Courtyard of lively stone. But empty. Empty of life. The gay red-legged gentry dead forever. And when pilgrimages do come and throng in, it is horrible artisan excursions from the great town, and the sordidness of industrialism.

We climbed the little watchtower that is now an observatory, and saw the vague and unshaven Don Giovanni among all his dust and instruments. M— was very familiar and friendly, chattering in his quaint Italian, which was more wrong than any Italian I have ever heard spoken; very familiar and friendly, and a tiny bit deferential to the monks, and yet, and yet – rather patronizing. His little pomposity and patronizing tone coloured even his deferential yearning to be admitted to the monastery. The monks were rather brief with him. They no doubt have their likes and dislikes greatly intensified by the monastic life.

We stood on the summit of the tower and looked at the world below: the town, the castle, the white roads coming straight as judgment out of the mountains north, from Rome, and piercing into the mountains south, toward Naples, traversing the flat, flat plain. Roads, railway, river, streams, a world in accurate and lively detail, with mountains sticking up abruptly and rockily, as the old painters painted it. I think there is no way of painting

Italian landscape except that way – that started with Lorenzetti and ended with the sixteenth century.

We looked at the ancient cell away under the monastery, where all the sanctity started. We looked at the big library that belongs to the State, and at the smaller library that belongs still to the abbot, I was tired, cold, and sick among the books and illuminations. I could not bear it any more. I felt I must be outside, in the sun, and see the world below, and the way out.

That evening I said to M—:

'And what was the abyss, then?'

'Oh well, you know,' he said, 'it was a cheque which I made out at Anzio. There should have been money to meet it, in my bank in New York. But it appears the money had never been paid in by the people that owed it me. So there was I in a very nasty hole, an unmet cheque, and no money at all in Italy. I really had to escape here. It is an *absolute* secret that I am here, and it must be, till I can get this business settled. Of course I've written to America about it. But as you see, I'm in a very nasty hole. That five francs I gave you for the driver was the last penny I had in the world: absolutely the last penny. I haven't even anything to buy a cigarette or a stamp.' And he laughed chirpily, as if it were a joke. But he didn't really think it a joke. Nor was it a joke.

I had come with only two hundred lire in my pocket, as I was waiting to change some money at the bank. Of this two hundred I had one hundred left or one hundred and twenty-five. I should need a hundred to get home. I could only give M— the twenty-five, for the bottle of drink. He was rather crestfallen. But I didn't want to give him money this time: because he expected it.

However, we talked about his plans: how he was to earn something. He told me what he had written. And I cast over in my mind where he might get something published in London, wrote a couple of letters on his account, told him where I thought he had best send his material. There wasn't a great deal of hope, for his smaller journalistic articles seemed to me very self-conscious and poor. He had one about the monastery, which I thought he might sell because of the photographs.

That evening he first showed me the Legion manuscript. He had got it rather raggedly typed out. He had a typewriter, but felt he ought to have somebody to do his typing for him, as he hated it and did it unwillingly. That evening and when I went to bed and when I woke in the morning I read this manuscript. It did not seem very good – vague and diffuse where it shouldn't have been – lacking in sharp detail and definite event. And yet there was something in it that made me want it done properly. So we talked about it, and discussed it carefully, and he unwillingly promised to tackle it again. He was curious, always talking about his work, even always working, but never *properly* doing anything.

We walked out in the afternoon through the woods and across the rocky bit of moorland which covers most of the hill-top. We were going to the ruined convent which lies on the other brow of the monastery hill, abandoned and sad among the rocks and heath and thorny bushes. It was sunny and warm. A barefoot little boy was tending a cow and three goats and a pony, a barefoot little girl had five geese in charge. We came to the convent and looked in. The further part of the courtyard was still entire, the place was a sort of farm, two rooms occupied by a peasant-farmer. We climbed about the ruins. Some creature was crying – crying, crying, crying with a strange, inhuman persistence, leaving off and crying again. We listened and listened – the sharp, poignant crying. Almost it might have been a sharp-voiced baby. We scrambled about, looking. And at last outside a little cave-like place found a blind black puppy crawling miserably on the floor, unable to walk, and crying incessantly. We put it back in the little cave-like shed, and went away. The place was deserted save for the crying puppy.

On the road outside however was a man, a peasant, just drawing up to the arched convent gateway with an ass under a load of brushwood. He was thin and black and dirty. He took off his hat, and we told him of the puppy. He said the bitch-mother had gone off with his son with the sheep. Yes, she had been gone all day. Yes, she would be back at sunset. No, the puppy had not drunk all day. Yes, the little beast cried, but the mother would come back to him.

They were the old-world peasants still about the monastery, with the hard, small bony heads and deep-lined faces and utterly blank minds, crying their speech as crows cry, and living their lives as lizards among the rocks, blindly going on with the little job in hand, the present moment, cut off from all past and future, and having no idea and no sustained emotion, only that eternal will-to-live which makes a tortoise wake up once more in spring, and makes a grasshopper whistle on in the moonlight nights even of November. Only these peasants don't whistle much. The whistlers go to America. It is the hard, static, unhoping souls that persist in the old life. And still they stand back, as one passes them in the corridors of the great monastery, they press themselves back against the whitewashed walls of the still place, and drop their heads, as if some mystery were passing by, some God-mystery, the higher beings, which they must not look closely upon. So also this old peasant – he was not old, but deep-lined like a gnarled bough. He stood with his hat down in his hands as we spoke to him and answered the short, hard, insentient answers, as a tree might speak.

'The monks keep their peasants humble,' I said to M—.

'Of course!' he said. 'Don't you think they are quite right? Don't you think they should be humble?' And he bridled like a little turkey-cock on his hind legs.

'Well,' I said, 'if there's any occasion for humility, I do.'

'Don't you think there is occasion?' he cried. 'If there's one thing worse than another, it's this *equality* that has come into the world. Do you believe in it yourself?'

'No,' I said. 'I don't believe in equality. But the problem is, wherein does superiority lie.'

'Oh,' chirped M— complacently. 'It lies in many things. It lies in birth and in upbringing and so on, but it is chiefly in *mind*. Don't you think? Of course I don't mean that the physical qualities aren't *charming*. They are, and nobody appreciates them more than I do. Some of the peasants are *beautiful* creatures, perfectly beautiful. But that passes. And the mind endures.'

I did not answer. M— was not a man one talked far with. But I thought to myself, I *could* not accept M—'s superiority to the peasant. If I had really to live always under the same roof with either one of them, I would have chosen the peasant. If I had had to choose, I would have chosen the peasant. Not because the peasant was wonderful and stored with mystic qualities. No, I don't give much for the wonderful mystic qualities in peasants. Money is their mystery of mysteries, absolutely. No, if I chose the peasant it would be for what he *lacked* rather than for what he had. He lacked that complacent mentality that M— was so proud of, he lacked all the trivial trash of glib talk and more glib thought, all the conceit of our shallow consciousness. For his mindlessness I would have chosen the peasant: and for his strong blood-presence. M— wearied me with his facility and his readiness to rush into speech, and for the exhaustive nature of his presence. As if he had no strong blood in him to sustain him, only this modern parasitic lymph which cries for sympathy all the time.

'Don't you think yourself that you are superior to that peasant?' he asked me, rather ironically. He half expected me to say no.

'Yes, I do,' I replied. 'But I think most middle-class, most so-called educated people are inferior to the peasant. I do that.'

'Of course,' said M— readily. 'In their *hypocrisy* –' He was great against hypocrisy – especially the English sort.

'And if I think myself superior to the peasant, it is only that I feel myself like the growing tip, or one of the growing tips of the tree, and him like a piece of the hard, fixed tissue of the branch or trunk. We're part of the same tree: and it's the same sap,' said I.

'Why, exactly! Exactly!' cried M—. 'Of course! The Church would teach the same doctrine. We are all one in Christ – but between our souls and our duties there are great differences.'

It is terrible to be agreed with, especially by a man like M—. All that one says, and means, turns to nothing.

'Yes,' I persisted. 'But it seems to me the so-called culture, education, the so-called leaders and leading-classes today, are only parasites – like a great flourishing bush of parasitic consciousness flourishing on top of the tree of life, and sapping it. The consciousness of today doesn't rise from the roots. It is just parasitic in the veins of life. And the middle and upper classes are just parasitic upon the body of life which still remains in the lower classes.'

'What!' said M— acidly. 'Do you believe in the democratic lower classes?'

'Not a bit,' said I.

'I should think not, indeed!' he cried complacently.

'No, I don't believe the lower classes can ever make life whole again, till they *do* become humble, like the old peasants, and yield themselves to real leaders. But not to great negators like Lloyd George or Lenin or Briand.'

'Of course! of course!' he cried. 'What you need is the Church in power again. The Church has a place for everybody.'

'You don't think the Church belongs to the past?' I asked.

'Indeed I don't, or I shouldn't be here. No,' he said sententiously, 'the Church is eternal. It puts people in their proper place. It puts women down into *their* proper place, which is the first thing to be done –'

He had a great dislike of women, and was very acid about them. Not because of their sins, but because of their virtues: their economies, their philanthropies, their spiritualities. Oh, how he loathed women. He had been married, but the marriage had not been a success. He smarted still. Perhaps his wife had despised him, and he had not *quite* been able to defeat her contempt.

So, he loathed women, and wished for a world of men. 'They talk about love between men and women,' he said. 'Why it's all a *fraud*. The woman is just taking all and giving nothing, and feeling sanctified about it. All she tries to do is to thwart a man in whatever he is doing. No, I have found my life in my *friendships*. Physical relationships are very attractive, of course, and one tries to keep them as decent and all that as one can. But one knows they will pass and be finished. But one's *mental* friendships last for ever.'

'With me, on the contrary,' said I. 'If there is no profound blood-sympathy, I know the mental friendship is trash. If there is real, deep blood response, I will stick to that if I have to betray all the mental sympathies I ever made, or all the lasting spiritual loves I ever felt.'

He looked at me, and his face seemed to fall. Round the eyes he was yellow and tired and nervous. He watched me for some time.

'Oh!' he said, in a queer tone, rather cold. 'Well, my experience has been the opposite.'

We were silent for some time.

'And you,' I said, 'even if you do manage to do all your studies and enter the monastery, do you think you will be satisfied?'

'If I can be so fortunate, I do really,' he said. 'Do you doubt it?'

'Yes,' I said. 'Your nature is worldly, more worldly than mine. Yet I should die if I had to stay up here.'

'Why?' he asked, curiously.

'Oh, I don't know. The past, the past. The beautiful, the wonderful past, it seems to prey on my heart, I can't bear it.'

He watched me closely.

'Really!' he said stoutly. 'Do you feel like that? But don't you think it is a far preferable life up here than down there? Don't you think the past is far preferable to the future, with all this *socialismo* and these *communisti* and so on?'

We were seated, in the sunny afternoon, on the wild hill-top high above the world. Across the stretch of pale, dry, standing thistles that peopled the waste ground, and beyond the rocks was the ruined convent. Rocks rose behind us, the summit. Away on the left were the woods which hid us from the great monastery. This was the mountain top, the last foothold of the old world. Below we could see the plain, the straight white road, straight as a thought, and the more flexible black railway with the railway station. There swarmed the *ferrovieri* like ants. There was democracy, industrialism, socialism, the red flag of the communists and the red, white and green tricolor of the fascisti. That was another world. And how bitter, how barren a world! Barren like the black cinder-track of the railway, with its two steel lines.

And here above, sitting with the little stretch of pale, dry thistles around us, our back to a warm rock, we were in the Middle Ages. Both worlds were agony to me. But here, on the mountain top was worst: the past, the poignancy of the not-quite-dead past.

'I think one's got to go through with the life down there – get somewhere beyond it. One can't go back,' I said to him.

'But do you call the monastery going back?' he said. 'I don't. The peace, the eternity, the concern with things that matter. I consider it the happiest fate that could happen to me. Of course it means putting physical things aside. But when you've done that – why, it seems to me perfect.'

'No,' I said. 'You're too worldly.'

'But the monastery is worldly too. We're not Trappists. Why the monastery is one of the centres of the world – one of the most active centres.'

'Maybe. But that impersonal activity, with the blood suppressed and going sour – no, it's too late. It is too abstract – political maybe –'

'I'm sorry you think so,' he said, rising. 'I don't.'

'Well,' I said. 'You'll never be a monk here, M——. You see if you are.'

'You don't think I shall?' he replied, turning to me. And there was a catch of relief in his voice. Really, the monastic state must have been like going to prison for him.

'You haven't a vocation,' I said.

'I may not *seem* to have, but I hope I actually have.'

'You haven't.'

'Of course, if you're so sure,' he laughed, putting his hand on my arm.

He seemed to understand so much, round about the questions that trouble one deepest. But the quick of the question he never felt. He had no real middle, no real centre bit to him. Yet, round and round about all the questions, he was so intelligent and sensitive.

We went slowly back. The peaks of those Italian mountains in the sunset, the extinguishing twinkle of the plain away below, as the sun declined and grew yellow; the intensely powerful mediæval spirit lingering on this wild hill summit, all the wonder of the mediæval past; and then the huge mossy stones in the wintry wood, that was once a sacred grove; the ancient path through the wood, that led from temple to temple on the hill summit, before Christ was born; and then the great Cyclopean wall one passes at the bend of the road, built even before the pagan temples; all this overcame me so powerfully this afternoon, that I was almost speechless. That hill-top must have been one of man's intense sacred places for three thousand years. And men die generation after generation, races die, but the new cult finds root in the old sacred place, and the quick spot of earth dies very slowly. Yet at last it too dies. But this quick spot is still not quite dead. The great monastery couchant there, half empty, but also not quite dead. And M— and I walking across as the sun set yellow and the cold of the snow came into the air, back home to the monastery! And I feeling as if my heart had once more broken: I don't know why. And he feeling his fear of life, that haunted him, and his fear of his own self and its consequences, that never left him for long. And he seemed to walk close to me, very close. And we had neither of us anything more to say.

Don Bernardo was looking for us as we came up under the archway, he hatless in the cold evening, his black dress swinging voluminous. There were letters for M—. There was a small cheque for him from America – about fifty dollars – from some newspaper in the Middle West that had printed one of his articles. He had to talk with Don Bernardo about this.

I decided to go back the next day. I could not stay any longer. M— was very disappointed, and begged me to remain. 'I thought you would stay a week at least,' he said. 'Do stay over Sunday. Oh do!' But I couldn't, I didn't want to. I could see that his days were a torture to him – the long, cold days in that vast quiet building, with the strange and exhausting silence in the air, and the sense of the past preying on one, and the sense of the silent, suppressed scheming struggle of life going on still in the sacred place.

It was a cloudy morning. In the green courtyard the big Don Anselmo had just caught the little Don Lorenzo round the waist and was swinging him over a bush, like lads before school. The Prior was just hurrying somewhere, following his long fine nose. He bade me good-bye; pleasant, warm, jolly, with a touch of wistfulness in his deafness. I parted with real regret from Don Bernardo.

M— was coming with me down the hill – not down the carriage road, but down the wide old paved path that swoops so wonderfully from the top of the hill to the bottom. It feels thousands of years old. M— was quiet and friendly. We met Don Vincenzo, he who has the care of the land and crops, coming slowly, slowly uphill in his black cassock, treading slowly with his great thick boots. He was reading a little book. He saluted us as we passed. Lower down a strapping girl was watching three merino sheep among the bushes. One sheep came on its exquisite slender legs to smell of me, with that insatiable curiosity of a pecora. Her nose was silken and elegant as she reached it to sniff at me, and the yearning, wondering, inquisitive look in her eyes, made me realize that the Lamb of God must have been such a sheep as this.

M— was miserable at my going. Not so much at my going, as at being left alone up there. We came to the foot of the hill, on to the town highroad. So we went into a little cave of a wine-kitchen to drink a glass of wine. M— chatted a little with the young woman. He chatted with everybody. She eyed us closely – and asked if we were from the monastery. We said we were. She seemed to have a little lurking antagonism round her nose, at the mention of the monastery. M— paid for the wine – a franc. So we went out on the highroad, to part.

'Look,' I said. 'I can only give you twenty lire, because I shall need the rest for the journey –'

But he wouldn't take them. He looked at me wistfully. Then I went on down to the station, he turned away uphill. It was market in the town, and there were clusters of bullocks, and women cooking a little meal at a brazier under the trees, and goods spread out on the floor to sell, and sacks of beans and corn standing open, clustered round the trunks of the mulberry trees, and wagons with their shafts on the ground. The old peasants in their brown homespun frieze and skin sandals were watching for the world. And there again was the Middle Ages.

It began to rain, however. Suddenly it began to pour with rain, and my coat was wet through, and my trouser-legs. The train from Rome was late – I hoped not very late, or I should miss the boat. She came at last: and was full. I had to stand in the corridor. Then the man came to say dinner was served, so I luckily got a place and had my meal too. Sitting there in the dining-car, among the fat Neapolitans eating their macaroni, with the big glass windows steamed opaque and the rain beating outside, I let myself be carried away, away from the monastery, away from M—, away from everything.

At Naples there was a bit of sunshine again, and I had time to go on foot to the Immacolatella, where the little steamer lay. There on the steamer I sat in a bit of sunshine, and felt that again the world had come to an end for me, and again my heart was broken. The steamer seemed to be making its way away from the old world, that had come to another end in me.

It was after this I decided to go to Sicily. In February, only a few days after my return from the monastery, I was on the steamer for Palermo, and at dawn looking out on the wonderful coast of Sicily. Sicily, tall, forever rising up to her gem-like summits, all golden in dawn, and always glamorous, always hovering as if inaccessible, and yet so near, so distinct. Sicily unknown to me, and amethystine-glamorous in the Mediterranean dawn: like the dawn of our day, the wonder-morning of our epoch.

I had various letters from M—. He had told me to go to Girgenti. But I arrived in Girgenti when there was a strike of sulphur-miners, and they threw stones. So I did not want to live in Girgenti. M— hated Taormina – he had been everywhere, tried everywhere, and was not, I found, in any good odour in most places. He wrote however saying he hoped I would like it. And later he sent the Legion manuscript. I thought it was good, and told him so. It was offered to publishers in London, but rejected.

In early April I went with my wife to Syracuse for a few days: lovely, lovely days, with the purple anemones blowing in the Sicilian fields, and Adonis-blood red on the little ledges, and the corn rising strong and green in the magical, malarial places, and Etna flowing now to the northward, still with her crown of snow. The lovely, lovely journey from Catania to Syracuse, in spring, winding round the blueness of that sea, where the tall pink asphodel was dying, and the yellow asphodel like a lily showing her silk. Lovely, lovely Sicily, the dawn place, Europe's dawn, with Odysseus pushing his ship out of the shadows into the blue. Whatever had died for me, Sicily had then not died: dawn-lovely Sicily, and the Ionian sea.

We came back, and the world was lovely: our own house above the almond trees, and the sea in the cove below. Calabria glimmering like a changing opal away to the left, across the blue, bright straits and all the great blueness of the lovely dawn-sea in front, where the sun rose with a splendour like trumpets every morning, and me rejoicing like a madness in this dawn, day-dawn, life-dawn, the dawn which is Greece, which is me.

Well, into this lyricism suddenly crept the serpent. It was a lovely morning, still early. I heard a noise on the stairs from the lower terrace, and went to look. M— on the stairs, looking up at me with a frightened face.

'Why!' I said. 'Is it you?'

'Yes,' he replied. 'A terrible thing has happened.'

He waited on the stairs, and I went down. Rather unwillingly, because I detest terrible things, and the people to whom they happen. So we leaned on the creeper-covered rail of the terrace, under festoons of creamy bignonia flowers, and looked at the pale blue, ethereal sea.

'When did you get back?' said he.

'Last evening.'

'Oh! I came before. The contadini said they thought you would come yesterday evening. I've been here several days.'

'Where are you staying?'

'At the San Domenico.'

The San Domenico being then the most expensive hotel here, I thought he must have money. But I knew he wanted something of me.

'And are you staying some time?'

He paused a moment, and looked round cautiously.

'Is your wife there?' he asked, sotto voce.

'Yes, she's upstairs.'

'Is there anyone who can hear?'

'No – only old Grazia down below, and she can't understand anyhow.'

'Well,' he said, stammering. 'Let me tell you what's happened. I had to escape from the monastery. Don Bernardo had a telephone message from the town below, that the carabinieri were looking for an Americano – my name – Of course you can guess how I felt, up there! Awful! Well – ! I had to fly at a moment's notice. I just put two shirts in a handbag and went. I slipped down a path – or rather, it isn't a path – down the back of the hill. Ten minutes after Don Bernardo had the message I was running down the hill.'

'But what did they want you for?' I asked dismayed.

'Well,' he faltered. 'I told you about the cheque at Anzio, didn't I? Well it seems the hotel people applied to the police. Anyhow,' he added hastily, 'I couldn't let myself be arrested up there, could I? So awful for the monastery!'

'Did they know then that you were in trouble?' I asked.

'Don Bernardo knew I had no money,' he said. 'Of course he had to know. Yes – he knew I was in *difficulty*. But, of course, he didn't know – well – *everything*.' He laughed a little, comical laugh over the *everything*, as if he was just a little bit naughtily proud of it: most ruefully also.

'No,' he continued, 'that's what I'm most afraid of – that they'll find out everything at the monastery. Of course it's *dreadful* – the Americano, been staying there for months, and everything so nice and –, well you know how they are, they imagine every American is a millionaire, if not a multi-millionaire. And suddenly to be wanted by the police! Of course it's *dreadful*! Anything rather than a scandal at the monastery – anything. Oh, how awful it was! I can tell you, in that quarter of an hour, I sweated blood. Don Bernardo lent me two hundred lire of the monastery money – which he'd no business to do. And I escaped down the back of the hill, I walked to the next station up the line, and took the next train – the slow train – a few stations up towards Rome. And there I changed and caught the diretto for Sicily. I came straight to you – Of course I was in *agony*: imagine it! I spent most of the time as far as Naples in the lavatory.' He laughed his little jerky laugh.

'What class did you travel?'

'Second. All through the night. I arrived more dead than alive, not having had a meal for two days – only some sandwich stuff I bought on the platform.'

'When did you come then?'

'I arrived on Saturday evening. I came out here on Sunday morning, and they told me you were away. Of course, imagine what it's like! I'm in torture every minute, in torture, of course. Why just imagine!' And he laughed his little laugh.

'But how much money have you got?'

'Oh – I've just got twenty-five francs and five soldi.' He laughed as if it was rather a naughty joke.

'But,' I said, 'if you've got no money, why do you go to the San Domenico? How much do you pay there?'

'Fifty lire a day. Of course it's *ruinous* –'

'But at the Bristol you only pay twenty-five – and at Fichera's only twenty.'

'Yes, I know you do,' he said. 'But I stayed at the Bristol once, and I loathed the place. Such an offensive manager. And I couldn't touch the food at Fichera's.'

'But who's going to pay for the San Domenico, then?' I asked.

'Well, I thought,' he said, 'you know all those manuscripts of mine? Well, you think they're some good, don't you? Well, I thought if I made them over to you, and you did what you could with them and just kept me going till I can get a new start – or till I can get away –'

I looked across the sea: the lovely morning-blue sea towards Greece.

'Where do you want to get away to?' I said.

'To Egypt. I know a man in Alexandria who owns news-papers there. I'm sure if I could get over there he'd give me an editorship or something. And of course money will come. I've written to —, who was my *greatest* friend, in London. He will send me something –'

'And what else do you expect?'

'Oh, my article on the monastery was accepted by *Land and Water* – thanks to you and your kindness, of course. I thought if I might stay very quietly with you, for a time, and write some things I'm wanting to do, and collect a little money – and then get away to Egypt –'

He looked up into my face, as if he were trying all he could on me. First thing I knew was that I could not have him in the house with me: and even if I could have done it, my wife never could.

'You've got a lovely place here, perfectly beautiful,' he said.

'Of course, if it had to be Taormina, you've chosen far the best place here. I like this side so much better than the Etna side. Etna always there and people raving about it gets on my nerves. And a *charming* house, *charming.*'

He looked round the loggia and along the other terrace.

'Is it all yours?' he said.

'We don't use the ground floor. Come in here.'

So we went into the salotta.

'Oh, what a beautiful room,' he cried. 'But perfectly palatial. Charming! Charming! *Much* the nicest house in Taormina.'

'No,' I said, 'as a house it isn't very grand, though I like it for myself. It's just what I want. And I love the situation. But I'll go and tell my wife you are here.'

'Will you?' he said, bridling nervously. 'Of course I've never met your wife.' And he laughed the nervous, naughty, jokey little laugh.

I left him, and ran upstairs to the kitchen. There was my wife, with wide eyes. She had been listening to catch the conversation. But M—'s voice was too hushed.

'M—!' said I softly. 'The carabinieri wanted to arrest him at the monastery, so he has escaped here, and wants me to be responsible for him.'

'Arrest him what for?'

'Debts, I suppose. Will you come down and speak to him?'

M— of course was very charming with my wife. He kissed her hand humbly, in the correct German fashion, and spoke with an air of reverence that infallibly gets a woman.

'Such a beautiful place you have here,' he said, glancing through the open doors of the room, at the sea beyond. 'So clever of you to find it.'

'Lawrence found it,' said she. 'Well, and you are in all kinds of difficulty!'

'Yes, isn't it terrible!' he said, laughing as if it were a

joke – rather a wry joke. 'I felt dreadful at the monastery. So dreadful for them, if there was any sort of scandal. And after I'd been so well received there – and so much the Signor Americano – Dreadful, don't you think?' He laughed again, like a naughty boy.

We had an engagement to lunch that morning. My wife was dressed, so I went to get ready. Then we told M— we must go out, and he accompanied us to the village. I gave him just the hundred francs I had in my pocket, and he said could he come and see me that evening? I asked him to come next morning.

'You're so awfully kind,' he said, simpering a little.

But by this time I wasn't feeling kind.

'He's quite nice,' said my wife. 'But he's rather an impossible little person. And you'll see, he'll be a nuisance. Whatever do you pick up such dreadful people for?'

'Nay,' I said. 'You can't accuse me of picking up dreadful people. He's the first. And even he isn't dreadful.'

The next morning came a letter from Don Bernardo addressed to me, but only enclosing a letter to M—. So he was using my address. At ten o'clock he punctually appeared: slipping in as if to avoid notice. My wife would not see him, so I took him out on the terrace again.

'Isn't it beautiful here!' he said. 'Oh, so beautiful! If only I had peace of mind. Of course I sweat blood every time anybody comes through the door. You are splendidly private out here.'

'Yes,' I said. 'But M—, there isn't a room for you in the house. There isn't a spare room anyway. You'd better think of getting something cheaper in the village.'

'But what can I get?' he snapped.

That rather took my breath away. Myself, I had never been near the San Domenico hotel. I knew I simply could not afford it.

'What made you go to the San Domenico in the first place?' I said. 'The most expensive hotel in the place!'

'Oh, I'd stayed there for two months, and they knew me, and I knew they'd ask no questions. I knew they wouldn't ask for a deposit or anything.'

'But nobody dreams of asking for a deposit,' I said.

'Anyhow I shan't take my meals there. I shall just take coffee in the morning. I've had to eat there so far, because I was starved to death, and had no money to go out. But I had two meals in that little restaurant yesterday; disgusting food.'

'And how much did that cost?'

'Oh fourteen francs and fifteen francs, with a quarter of wine – and such a poor meal!'

Now I was annoyed, knowing that I myself should have bought bread and cheese for one franc, and eaten it in my room. But also I realized that the modern creed says, if you sponge, sponge thoroughly: and also that every man has a 'right to live,' and that if he can manage to live well, no matter at whose expense, all credit to him. This is the kind of talk one accepts in one's slipshod moments; now it was actually tried on me, I didn't like it at all.

'But who's going to pay your bill at the San Domenico?' I said.

'I thought you'd advance me the money on those manuscripts.'

'It's no good talking about the money on the manuscripts,' I said. 'I should have to give it to you. And as a matter of fact, I've got just sixty pounds in the bank in England, and about fifteen hundred lire here. My wife and I have got to live on that. We don't spend as much in a week as you spend in three days at the San Domenico. It's no good your thinking I can advance money on the manuscripts. I can't. If I was rich, I'd give you money. But I've got no money, and never have had any. Have you nobody you can go to?'

'I'm waiting to hear from ——. When I go back into the village,

I'll telegraph to him,' replied M—, a little crestfallen. 'Of course I'm in torture night and day, or I wouldn't appeal to you like this. I know it's unpleasant for you –' and he put his hand on my arm and looked up beseechingly. 'But what am I to do?'

'You must get out of the San Domenico,' I said. 'That's the first thing.'

'Yes,' he said, a little piqued now. 'I know it is. I'm going to ask Pancrazio Melenga to let me have a room in his house. He knows me quite well – he's an awfully nice fellow. He'll do *anything* for me – *anything*. I was just going there yesterday afternoon when you were coming from Timeo. He was out, so I left word with his wife, who is a charming little person. If he has a room to spare, I know he will let me have it. And he's a *splendid* cook – splendid. By far the nicest food in Taormina.'

'Well,' I said. 'If you settle with Melenga, I will pay your bill at the San Domenico, but I can't do any more. I simply can't.'

'But what am I to *do*?' he snapped.

'I don't know,' I said. 'You must think.'

'I came here,' he said, 'thinking you would help me. What am I to do, if you won't? I shouldn't have come to Taormina at all, save for you. Don't be unkind to me – don't speak so coldly to me –' He put his hand on my arm, and looked up at me with tears swimming in his eyes. Then he turned aside his face, overcome with tears. I looked away at the Ionian sea, feeling my blood turn to ice and the sea go black. I loathe scenes such as this.

'Did you telegraph to —?' I said.

'Yes. I have no answer yet. I hope you don't mind – I gave your address for a reply.'

'Oh,' I said. 'There's a letter for you from Don Bernardo.'

He went pale. I was angry at his having used my address in this manner.

'Nothing further has happened at the monastery,' he said.

'They rang up from the Questura, from the police station, and Don Bernardo answered that the Americano had left for Rome. Of course I did take the train for Rome. And Don Bernardo wanted me to go to Rome. He advised me to do so. I didn't tell him I was here till I had got here. He thought I should have had more resources in Rome, and of course I should. I should certainly have gone there, if it hadn't been for *you here –*'

Well, I was getting tired and angry. I would not give him any more money at the moment. I promised, if he would leave the hotel I would pay his bill, but he must leave it at once. He went off to settle with Melenga. He asked again if he could come in the afternoon: I said I was going out.

He came nevertheless while I was out. This time my wife found him on the stairs. She was for hating him, of course. So she stood immovable on the top stair, and he stood two stairs lower, and he kissed her hand in utter humility. And he pleaded with her, and as he looked up to her on the stairs the tears ran down his face and he trembled with distress. And her spine crept up and down with distaste and discomfort. But he broke into a few phrases of touching German, and I know he broke down her reserve and she promised him all he wanted. This part she would never confess, though. Only she was shivering with revulsion and excitement and even a sense of power, when I came home.

That was why M— appeared more impertinent than ever, next morning. He had arranged to go to Melenga's house the following day, and to pay ten francs a day for his room, his meals extra. So that was something. He made a long tale about not eating any of his meals in the hotel now, but pretending he was invited out, and eating in the little restaurants where the food was so bad. And he had now only fifteen lire left in his pocket. But I was cold, and wouldn't give him any more. I said I would give him money next day, for his bill.

He had now another request, and a new tone.

'Won't you do *one more* thing for me?' he said. 'Oh do! Do do this one thing for me. I want you to go to the monastery and bring away my important papers and some clothes and my important trinkets. I have made a list of the things here – and where you'll find them in my writing-table and in the chest of drawers. I don't think you'll have any trouble. Don Bernardo has the keys. He will open everything for you. And I beg you, *in the name of God*, don't let anybody else see the things. Not even Don Bernardo. Don't, whatever you do, let him see the papers and manuscripts you are bringing. If he sees them, there's an end to me at the monastery. I can *never* go back there. I am ruined in their eyes for ever. As it is – although Don Bernardo is the best person in the world and my dearest friend, still – you know what people are – especially monks. A little curious, don't you know, a little inquisitive. Well, let us hope for the best as far as that goes. But you will do this for me, won't you? I shall be so eternally grateful.'

Now a journey to the monastery meant a terrible twenty hours in the train each way – all that awful journey through Calabria to Naples and northwards. It meant mixing myself up in this man's affairs. It meant appearing as his accomplice at the monastery. It meant travelling with all his 'compromising' papers and his valuables. And all this time, I never knew what mischiefs he had really been up to, and I didn't trust him, not for one single second. He would tell me nothing save that Anzio hotel cheque. I knew that wasn't all, by any means. So I mistrusted him. And with a feeling of utter mistrust goes a feeling of contempt and dislike – And finally, it would have cost me at least ten pounds sterling, which I simply did not want to spend in waste.

'I don't want to do that,' I said.

'Why not?' he asked, sharp, looking green. He had planned it all out.

'No, I don't want to.'

'Oh, but I *can't* remain here as I am. I've got no *clothes* – I've got nothing to *wear*. I *must* have my things from the monastery. What can I do? What can I do? I came to you, if it hadn't been for you I should have gone to Rome. I came to you – Oh yes, you *will* go. You *will* go, won't you? You *will* go to the monastery for my things?' And again he put his hand on my arm, and the tears began to fall from his upturned eyes. I turned my head aside. Never had the Ionian sea looked so sickening to me.

'I don't *want* to,' said I.

'But you *will*! You will! You *will* go to the monastery for me, won't you? Everything else is no good if you won't. I've nothing to wear. I haven't got my manuscripts to work on, I can't do the things I am doing. Here I live in a sweat of anxiety. I try to work, and I can't settle. I can't do anything. It's dreadful. I shan't have a minute's peace till I have got those things from the monastery, till I know they can't get at my private papers. You will do this for me! You will, won't you? Please do! Oh please do!' And again tears.

And I with my bowels full of bitterness, loathing the thought of that journey there and back, on such an errand. Yet not quite sure that I ought to refuse. And he pleaded and struggled, and tried to bully me with tears and entreaty and reproach, to do his will. And I couldn't quite refuse. But neither could I agree.

At last I said:

'I don't want to go, and I tell you. I won't promise to go. And I won't say that I will not go. I won't say until tomorrow. Tomorrow I will tell you. Don't come to the house. I will be in the Corso at ten o'clock.'

'I didn't doubt for a minute you would do this for me,' he said. 'Otherwise I should never have come to Taormina.' As if he had done me an honour in coming to Taormina; and as if I had betrayed *him*.

'Well,' I said. 'If you make these messes you'll have to get out of them yourself. I don't know why you are *in* such a mess.'

'Any man may make a mistake,' he said sharply, as if correcting me.

'Yes, a *mistake!*' said I. 'If it's a question of a mistake.'

So once more he went, humbly, beseechingly, and yet, one could not help but feel, with all that terrible insolence of the humble. It is the humble, the wistful, the would-be-loving souls today who bully us with their charity-demanding insolence. They just make up their minds, these needful sympathetic souls, that one is there to do their will. Very good.

I decided in the day I would *not* go. Without reasoning it out, I knew I *really* didn't want to go. I plainly didn't want it. So I wouldn't go.

The morning came again hot and lovely. I set off to the village. But there was M— watching for me on the path beyond the valley. He came forward and took my hand warmly, clingingly. I turned back, to remain in the country. We talked for a minute of his leaving the hotel – he was going that afternoon, he had asked for his bill. But he was waiting for the other answer.

'And I have decided,' I said, 'I won't go to the monastery.'

'You won't.' He looked at me. I saw how yellow he was round the eyes, and yellow under his reddish skin.

'No,' I said.

And it was final. He knew it. We went some way in silence. I turned in at the garden gate. It was a lovely, lovely morning of hot sun. Butterflies were flapping over the rosemary hedges and over a few little red poppies, the young vines smelt sweet in flower, very sweet, the corn was tall and green, and there were still some wild, rose-red gladiolus flowers among the watery green of the wheat. M— had accepted my refusal. I expected him to be angry. But no, he seemed quieter, wistfuller, and he seemed almost to love me for having refused him. I stood at a bend in the path. The sea was heavenly blue, rising up beyond the vines and olive leaves, lustrous pale lacquer blue, rising up beyond the vines and olive leaves, lustrous pale lacquer blue as only the Ionian sea can be. Away at the brook below the women were washing, and one could hear the chock-chock-chock of linen beaten against the stones. I felt M— then an intolerable weight and like a clot of dirt over everything.

'May I come in?' he said to me.

'No,' I said. 'Don't come to the house. My wife doesn't want it.'

Even that he accepted without any offence, and seemed only to like me better for it. That was a puzzle to me. I told him I would leave a letter and a cheque for him at the bank in the Corso that afternoon.

I did so, writing a cheque for a few pounds, enough to cover his bill and leave a hundred lire or so over, and a letter to say I could *not* do any more, and I didn't want to see him any more.

So, there was an end of it for a moment. Yet I felt him looming in the village, waiting. I had rashly said I would go to tea with him to the villa of one of the Englishmen resident here, whose acquaintance I had not made. Alas, M— kept me to the promise. As I came home he appealed to me again. He was rather insolent. What good to him, he said, were the few pounds I had given him? He had got a hundred and fifty lire left. What good was that? I realized it really was not a solution, and said nothing. Then he spoke of his plans for getting to Egypt. The fare, he had found out, was thirty-five pounds. And where were thirty-five pounds coming from? Not from me.

I spent a week avoiding him, wondering what on earth the poor devil was doing, and yet *determined* he should not be a parasite on me. If I could have given him fifty pounds and sent him to Egypt to be a parasite on somebody else, I would have done so. Which is what we call charity. However, I couldn't.

My wife chafed, crying: 'What have you done! We shall have

him on our hands all our life. We can't let him starve. It is degrading, degrading, to have him hanging on to us.'

'Yes,' I said. 'He must starve or work or something. I am not God who is responsible for him.'

M— was determined not to lose his status as a gentleman. In a way I sympathized with him. He would never be out at elbows. That is your modern rogue. He will not degenerate outwardly. Certain standards of a gentleman he *would* keep up: he would be well-dressed, he would be lavish with borrowed money, he would be as far as possible honourable in his small transactions of daily life. Well, very good. I sympathized with him to a certain degree. If he could find his own way out, well and good. Myself, I was not his way out.

Ten days passed. It was hot and I was going about the terrace in pyjamas and a big old straw hat, when suddenly, a Sicilian, handsome, in the prime of life, and in his best black suit, smiling at me and taking off his hat!

And could he speak to me. I threw away my straw hat, and we went into the salotta. He handed me a note.

'Il Signor M— mi ha dato questa lettera per Lei!' he began, and I knew what was coming. Melenga had been a waiter in good hotels, had saved money, built himself a fine house which he let to foreigners. He was a pleasant fellow, and at his best now, because he was in a rage. I must repeat M—'s letter from memory – 'Dear Lawrence, would you do me another kindness. *Land and Water* sent a cheque for seven guineas for the article on the monastery, and Don Bernardo forwarded this to me under Melenga's name. But unfortunately he made a mistake, and put Orazio instead of Pancrazio, so the post office would not deliver the letter, and have returned it to the monastery. This morning Melenga insulted me, and I cannot stay in his house another minute. Will you be so kind as to advance me these seven guineas, and I shall leave Taormina at once, for Malta.'

I asked Melenga what had happened, and read him the letter. He was handsome in his rage, lifting his brows and suddenly smiling:

'Ma senta, Signore! Signor M— has been in my house for ten days, and lived well, and eaten well, and drunk well, and I have not seen a single penny of his money. I go out in the morning and buy all the things, all he wants, and my wife cooks it, and he is very pleased, very pleased, has never eaten such good food in his life, and everything is splendid, splendid. And he never pays a penny. Not a penny. Says he is waiting for money from England, from America, from India. But the money never comes. And I am a poor man, Signore, I have a wife and child to keep. I have already spent three hundred lire for this Signor M—, and I never see a penny of it back. And he says the money is coming, it is coming – But when? He never says he has got no money. He says he is expecting. Tomorrow – always tomorrow. It will come tonight, it will come tomorrow. This makes me in a rage. Till at last this morning I said to him I would bring nothing in, and he shouldn't have not so much as a drop of coffee in my house until he paid for it. It displeases me, Signore, to say such a thing. I have known Signor M— for many years, and he has always had money, and always been pleasant, molto bravo, and also generous with his money. Si, lo so! And my wife, poverina, she cries and says if the man has no money he must eat. But he doesn't say he has no money. He says always it is coming, it is coming, today, tomorrow, today, tomorrow. E non viene mai niente. And this enrages me, Signore. So I said that to him this morning. And he said he wouldn't stay in my house, and that I had insulted him, and he sends me this letter to you, Signore, and says you will send him the money. Ecco come!'

Between his rage he smiled at me. One thing however I could see: he was not going to lose his money, M— or no M—.

'Is it true that a letter came which the post would not deliver?' I asked him.

'Si signore, e vero. It came yesterday, addressed to me. And why, signore, why do his letters come addressed in my name? Why? Unless he has done something – ?'

He looked at me enquiringly. I felt already mixed up in shady affairs.

'Yes,' I said, 'there is something. But I don't know exactly what. I don't ask, because I don't want to know in these affairs. It is better not to know.'

'Gia! Gia! Molto meglio, signore. There will be something. There will be something happened that he had to escape from that monastery. And it will be some affair of the police.'

'Yes, I think so,' said I. 'Money and the police. Probably debts. I don't ask. He is only an acquaintance of mine, not a friend.'

'Sure it will be an affair of the police,' he said with a grimace. 'If not, why does he use my name! Why don't his letters come in his own name? Do you believe, signore, that he has any money? Do you think this money will come?'

'I'm sure he's *got* no money,' I said. 'Whether anybody will send him any I don't know.'

The man watched me attentively.

'He's got nothing?' he said.

'No. At the present he's got nothing.'

Then Pancrazio exploded on the sofa.

'Allora! Well then! Well then, why does he come to my house, why does he come and take a room in my house, and ask me to buy food, good food as for a gentleman who can pay, and a flask of wine, and everything, if he has no money? If he has no money, why does he come to Taormina? It is many years that he has

been in Italy – ten years, fifteen years. And he has no money.
Where has he had his money from before? Where?'

'From his writing, I suppose.'

'Well then why doesn't he get money for his writing now?
He writes. He writes, he works, he says it is for the big newspapers.'

'It is difficult to sell things.'

'Heh! then why doesn't he live on what he made before? He
hasn't a soldo. He hasn't a penny – But how! How did he pay his
bill at the San Domenico?'

'I had to lend him the money for that. He really hadn't a
penny.'

'You! You! Well then, he has been in Italy all these years. How
is it he has nobody that he can ask for a hundred lire or two?
Why does he come to you? Why? Why has he nobody in Rome,
in Florence, anywhere?'

'I wonder that myself.'

'Siccuro! He's been all these years here. And why doesn't he
speak proper Italian? After all these years, and speaks all upside-
down, it isn't Italian, an ugly confusion. Why? Why? He passes
for a signore, for a man of education. And he comes to take the
bread out of my mouth. And I have a wife and child, I am a poor
man, I have nothing to eat myself if everything goes to a mezzo-
signore like him. Nothing! He owes me now three hundred lire.
But he will not leave my house, he will not leave Taormina till
he has paid. I will go to the Prefettura, I will go to the Questura,
to the police. I will not be swindled by such a mezzo-signore.
What does he want to do? If he has no money, what does he
want to do?'

'To go to Egypt where he says he can earn some,' I replied
briefly. But I was feeling bitter in the mouth. When the man
called M— a mezzo-signore, a half-gentleman, it was so true.
And at the same time it was so cruel, and so rude. And

Melenga – there I sat in my pyjamas and sandals – probably he would be calling me also a mezzo-signore, or a quarto-signore even. He was a Sicilian who feels he is being done out of his money – and that is saying everything.

'To Egypt! And who will pay for him to go? Who will give him money? But he must pay me first. He must pay me first.'

'He says,' I said, 'that in the letter which went back to the monastery there was a cheque for seven pounds – some six hundred lire – and he asks me to send him this money, and when the letter is returned again I shall have the cheque that is in it.'

Melenga watched me.

'Six hundred lire –' he said.

'Yes.'

'Oh well then. If he pays me, he can stay –' he said; he almost added: 'till the six hundred is finished.' But he left it unspoken.

'But am I going to send the money? Am I sure that what he says is true?'

'I think it is true. I think it is true,' said he. 'The letter *did* come.'

I thought for a while.

'First,' I said, 'I will write and ask him if it is quite true, and to give me a guarantee.'

'Very well,' said Melenga.

I wrote to M—, saying that if he could assure me that what he said about the seven guineas was quite correct, and if he would give me a note to the editor of *Land and Water*, saying that the cheque was to be paid to me, I would send the seven guineas.

Melenga was back in another half-hour. He brought a note which began:

'Dear Lawrence, I seem to be living in an atmosphere of suspicion. First Melenga this morning, and now you –' Those are the exact opening words. He went on to say that of course his word was true, and he enclosed a note to the editor, saying the seven guineas were to be transferred to me. He asked me please to send the money, as he could not stay another night at Melenga's house, but would leave for Catania, where, by the sale of some trinkets, he hoped to make some money and to see once more about a passage to Egypt. He had been to Catania once already – travelling *third class*! – but had failed to find any cargo boat that would take him to Alexandria. He would get away now to Malta. His things were being sent down to Syracuse from the monastery.

I wrote and said I hoped he would get safely away, and enclosed the cheque.

'This will be for six hundred lire,' said Melenga.

'Yes,' said I.

'Eh, va bene! If he pays the three hundred lire, he can stop in my house for thirty lire a day.'

'He says he won't sleep in your house again.'

'Ma! Let us see. If he likes to stay. He has always been a bravo signore. I have always liked him quite well. If he wishes to stay and pay me thirty lire a day –'

The man smiled at me rather greenly.

'I'm afraid he is offended,' said I.

'Eh, va bene! Ma senta, Signore. When he was here before – you know I have this house of mine to let. And you know the English signorina goes away in the summer. Oh, very well. Says M—, he writes for a newspaper, he owns a newspaper, I don't know what, in Rome. He will put in an advertisement advertising my villa. And so I shall get somebody to take it. Very well. And he put in the advertisement. He sent me the paper and I saw it there. But no one came to take my villa. Va bene! But after a year, in the January, that is, came a bill for me for twenty-two lire to pay for it. Yes, I had to pay the twenty-two lire, for nothing – for the advertisement which Signore M— put in the paper.'

'Bah!' said I.

He shook hands with me and left. The next day he came after me in the street and said that M— had departed the previous evening for Catania. As a matter of fact the post brought me a note of thanks from Catania. M— was never indecent, and one could never dismiss him just as a scoundrel. He was not. He was one of these modern parasites who just assume their right to live and live well, leaving the payment to anybody who can, will, or must pay. The end is inevitably swindling.

There came also a letter from Rome, addressed to me. I opened it unthinking. It was for M—, from an Italian lawyer, stating that enquiry had been made about the writ against M—, and that it was for *qualche affaro di truffa*, some affair of swindling: that the lawyer had seen this, that and the other person, but nothing could be done. He regretted, etc., etc. I forwarded this letter to M— at Syracuse, and hoped to God it was ended. Ah, I breathed free now he had gone.

But no. A friend who was with us dearly wanted to go to Malta. It is only about eighteen hours' journey from Taormina – easier than going to Naples. So our friend invited us to take the trip with her, as her guests. This was rather jolly. I calculated that M—, who had been gone a week or so, would easily have got to Malta. I had had a friendly letter from him from Syracuse, thanking me for the one I had forwarded, and enclosing an I.O.U. for the various sums of money he had had.

So, on a hot, hot Thursday, we were sitting in the train again running south, the four and a half hours' journey to Syracuse. And M— dwindled now into the past. If we should see him! But no, it was impossible. After all the wretchedness of that affair we were in holiday spirits.

The train ran into Syracuse station. We sat on, to go the few yards further into the port. A tout climbed on the foot-board: were we going to Malta? Well, we couldn't. There was a strike of the steamers, we couldn't go. When would the steamer go? Who knows? Perhaps tomorrow.

We got down crestfallen. What should we do? There stood the express train about to start off back northwards. We could be home again that evening. But no, it would be too much of a fiasco. We let the train go, and trailed off into the town, to the Grand Hotel, which is an old Italian place just opposite the port. It is rather a dreary hotel – and many bloodstains of squashed mosquitoes on the bedroom walls. Ah, vile mosquitoes!

However, nothing to be done. Syracuse port is fascinating too, a tiny port with the little Sicilian ships having the slanting eyes painted on the prow, to see the way, and a coal boat from Cardiff, and one American and two Scandinavian steamers – no more. But there were two torpedo boats in the harbour, and it was like a festa, a strange, lousy festa.

Beautiful the round harbour where the Athenian ships came. And wonderful, beyond, the long sinuous sky-line of the long flat-topped table-land hills which run along the southern coast, so different from the peaky, pointed, bunched effect of many-tipped Sicily in the north. The sun went down behind that lovely, sinuous sky-line, the harbour water was gold and red, the people promenaded in thick streams under the pomegranate trees and hibiscus trees. Arabs in white burnouses and fat Turks in red and black alpaca long coats strolled also – waiting for the steamer.

Next day it was very hot. We went to the consul and the steamer agency. There was real hope that the brute of a steamer might actually sail that night. So we stayed on, and wandered round the town on the island, the old solid town, and sat in the church looking at the grand Greek columns embedded there in the walls.

When I came in to lunch the porter said there was a letter for me. Impossible! said I. But he brought me a note. Yes. M—! He was staying at the other hotel along the front. 'Dear Lawrence, I saw you this morning, all three of you walking down the Via Nazionale, but you would not look at me. I have got my visés and everything ready. The strike of the steamboats has delayed me here. I am sweating blood. I have a last request to make of you. Can you let me have ninety lire, to make up what I need for my hotel bill? If I cannot have this I am lost. I hoped to find you at the hotel but the porter said you were out. I am at the Casa Politi, passing every half-hour in agony. If you can be so kind as to stretch your generosity to this last loan, of course I shall be eternally grateful. I can pay you back once I get to Malta –'

Well, here was a blow! The worst was that he thought I had cut him – a thing I wouldn't have done. So after luncheon behold me going through the terrific sun of that harbour front of Syracuse, an enormous and powerful sun, to the Casa Politi. The porter recognized me and looked enquiringly. M— was out, and I said I would call again at four o'clock.

It happened we were in the town eating ices at four, so I didn't get to his hotel till half-past. He was out – gone to look for me. So I left a note saying I had not seen him in the Via Nazionale, that I had called twice, and that I should be in the Grand Hotel in the evening.

When we came in at seven, M— in the hall, sitting the picture of misery and endurance. He took my hand in both his, and bowed to the women, who nodded and went upstairs. He and I went and sat in the empty lounge. Then he told me the trials he had had – how his luggage had come, and the station had charged him eighteen lire a day for deposit – how he had had to wait on at the hotel because of the ship – how he had tried to sell his trinkets, and had today parted with his opal sleevelinks – so that now he only wanted seventy, not ninety lire. I gave him a hundred note, and he looked into my eyes, his own eyes swimming with tears, and he said he was sweating blood.

Well, the steamer went that night. She was due to leave at ten. We went on board after dinner. We were going second class. And so, for once, was M—. It was only an eight hours' crossing, yet, in spite of all the blood he had sweated, he would not go third class. In a way I admired him for sticking to his principles. I should have gone third myself, out of shame of spending somebody else's money. He would not give way to such weakness. He knew that as far as the world goes, you're a first-class gentleman if you have a first-class ticket; if you have a third, no gentleman at all. It behoved him to be a gentleman. I understood his point, but the women were indignant. And I was just rather tired of him and his gentlemanliness.

It amused me very much to lean on the rail of the upper deck and watch the people coming on board – first going into the little customs house with their baggage, then scuffling up the gangway on board. The tall Arabs in their ghostly white woollen robes came carrying their sacks: they were going on to Tripoli. The fat Turk in his fez and long black alpaca coat with white drawers underneath came beaming up to the second class. There was a great row in the customs house: and then, simply running like a beetle with rage, there came on board a little Maltese or Greek fellow, followed by a tall lantern-jawed fellow: both seedy-looking scoundrels suckled in scoundrelism. They raved and nearly threw their arms away into the sea, talking wildly in some weird language with the fat Turk, who listened solemnly, away below on the deck. Then they rushed to somebody else. Of course, we were dying with curiosity. Thank heaven I heard men talking in Italian. It appears the two seedy fellows were trying to smuggle silver coin in small sacks and rolls out of the country. They were detected. But they declared they had a right to take it away, as it was foreign specie, English florins and half-crowns, and South American dollars and Spanish money. The customs-officers however detained the lot. The

little enraged beetle of a fellow ran back and forth from the ship
to the customs, from the customs to the ship, afraid to go without his money, afraid the ship would go without him.

At five minutes to ten, there came M—: very smart in his
little grey overcoat and grey curly hat, walking very smart and
erect and genteel, and followed by a porter with a barrow of luggage. They went into the customs, M— in his grey suède gloves
passing rapidly and smartly in, like the grandest gentleman on
earth, and with his grey suède hands throwing open his luggage
for inspection. From on board we could see the interior of the
little customs shed.

Yes, he was through. Brisk, smart, superb, like the grandest
little gentleman on earth, strutting because he was late, he
crossed the bit of flagged pavement and came up the gangway,
haughty as you can wish. The carabinieri were lounging by the
foot of the gangway, fooling with one another. The little gentleman passed them with his nose in the air, came quickly on
board, followed by his porter, and in a moment disappeared.
After about five minutes the porter reappeared – a red-haired
fellow, I knew him – he even saluted me from below, the brute.
But M— lay in hiding.

I trembled for him at every unusual stir. There on the quay
stood the English consul with his bull-dog, and various elegant
young officers with yellow on their uniforms, talking to elegant
young Italian ladies in black hats with stiff ospreys and bunchy
furs, and gangs of porters and hotel people and onlookers. Then
came a tramp-tramp-tramp of a squad of soldiers in red fezzes
and baggy grey trousers. Instead of coming on board they
camped on the quay. I wondered if all these had come for poor
M—. But apparently not.

So the time passed, till nearly midnight, when one of the elegant young lieutenants began to call the names of the soldiers:

and the soldiers answered: and one after another filed on board with their kit. So, they were on board, on their way to Africa.

Now somebody called out – and the visitors began to leave the boat. Barefooted sailors and a boy ran to raise the gangway. The last visitor or official with a bunch of papers stepped off the gangway. People on shore began to wave handkerchiefs. The red-fezzed soldiers leaned like so many flower-pots over the lower rail. There was a calling of farewells. The ship was fading into the harbour, the people on shore seemed smaller, under the lamp, in the deep night – without one's knowing why.

So, we passed out of the harbour, passed the glittering lights of Ortygia, past the two lighthouses, into the open Mediterranean. The noise of a ship in the open sea! It was a still night, with stars, only a bit chill. And the ship churned through the water.

Suddenly, like a *revenant*, appeared M— near us, leaning on the rail and looking back at the lights of Syracuse sinking already forlorn and little on the low darkness. I went to him.

'Well,' he said, with his little smirk of a laugh. 'Good-bye Italy!'

'Not a sad farewell either,' said I.

'No, my word, not this time,' he said. 'But what an awful long time we were starting! A brutta mezz'ora for me, indeed. Oh, my word, I begin to breathe free for the first time since I left the monastery! How awful it's been! But of course, in Malta, I shall be all right. Don Bernardo has written to his friends there. They'll have everything ready for me that I want, and I can pay you back the money you so kindly lent me.'

We talked for some time, leaning on the inner rail of the upper deck.

'Oh,' he said, 'there's Commander So-and-so, of the British fleet. He's stationed in Malta. I made his acquaintance in the hotel. I hope we're going to be great friends in Malta. I hope I shall have an opportunity to introduce you to him. Well, I suppose you will want to be joining your ladies. So long, then. Oh, for tomorrow morning! I never longed so hard to be in the British Empire –' He laughed, and strutted away.

In a few minutes we three, leaning on the rail of the second-class upper deck, saw our little friend large as life on the first-class deck, smoking a cigar and chatting in an absolutely first-class-ticket manner with the above mentioned Commander. He pointed us out to the Commander, and we felt the first-class passengers were looking across at us second-class passengers with pleasant interest. The women went behind a canvas heap to laugh, I hid my face under my hat-brim to grin and watch. Larger than any first-class ticketer leaned our little friend on the first-class rail, and whiffed at his cigar. So *dégagé* and so genteel he could be. Only I noticed he wilted a little when the officers of the ship came near.

He was still on the first-class deck when we went down to sleep. In the morning I came up soon after dawn. It was a lovely summer Mediterranean morning, with the sun rising up in a gorgeous golden rage, and the sea so blue, so fairy blue, as the Mediterranean is in summer. We were approaching quite near to a rocky, pale yellow island with some vineyards, rising magical out of the swift blue sea into the morning radiance. The rocks were almost as pale as butter, the islands were like golden shadows loitering in the midst of the Mediterranean, lonely among all the blue.

M— came up to my side.

'Isn't it lovely! Isn't it beautiful!' he said. 'I love approaching these islands in the early morning.' He had almost recovered his assurance, and the slight pomposity and patronizing tone I had first known in him. 'In two hours I shall be free! Imagine it! Oh what a beautiful feeling!' I looked at him in the morning light. His face was a good deal broken by his last month's experience, older looking, and dragged. Now that the excitement was nearing its end, the tiredness began to tell on him. He was yellowish round the eyes, and the whites of his round, rather impudent blue eyes were discoloured.

Malta was drawing near. We saw the white fringe of the sea upon the yellow rocks, and a white road looping on the yellow rocky hillside. I thought of St Paul, who must have been blown this way, must have struck the island from this side. Then we saw the heaped glitter of the square facets of houses, Valletta, splendid above the Mediterranean, and a tangle of shipping and Dreadnoughts and watch-towers in the beautiful, locked-in harbour.

We had to go down to have passports examined. The officials sat in the long saloon. It was a horrible squash and squeeze of the first- and second-class passengers. M— was a little ahead of me. I saw the American eagle on his passport. Yes, he passed all right. Once more he was free. As he passed away he turned and gave a condescending affable nod to me and to the Commander, who was just behind me.

The ship was lying in Valletta harbour. I saw M—, quite superb and brisk now, ordering a porter with his luggage into a boat. The great rocks rose above us, yellow and carved, cut straight by man. On top were all the houses. We got at last into a boat and were rowed ashore. Strange to be on British soil and to hear English. We got a carriage and drove up the steep high-road through the cutting in the rock, up to the town. There, in the big square we had coffee, sitting out of doors. A military band went by playing splendidly in the bright, hot morning. The Maltese lounged about, and watched. Splendid the band, and the soldiers! One felt the splendour of the British Empire, let the world say what it likes. But alas, as one stayed on even in Malta, one felt the old lion had gone foolish and amiable. Foolish and amiable, with the weak amiability of old age.

We stayed in the Great Britain Hotel. Of course one could not be in Valletta for twenty-four hours without meeting M—. There he was, in the Strada Reale, strutting in a smart white duck suit, with a white piqué cravat. But alas, he had no white shoes: they had got lost or stolen. He had to wear black boots with his summer finery.

He was staying in an hotel a little further down our street, and he begged me to call and see him, he begged me to come to lunch. I promised and went. We went into his bedroom, and he rang for more sodas.

'How wonderful it is to be here!' he said brightly. 'Don't you like it immensely? And oh, how wonderful to have a whisky and soda! Well now, say when.'

He finished one bottle of Black and White, and opened another. The waiter, a good-looking Maltese fellow, appeared with two syphons. M— was very much the signore with him, and at the same time very familiar: as I should imagine a rich Roman of the merchant class might have been with a pet slave. We had quite a nice lunch, and whisky and soda and a bottle of French wine. And M— was the charming and attentive host.

After lunch we talked again of manuscripts and publishers and how he might make money. I wrote one or two letters for him. He was anxious to get something under way. And yet the trouble of these arrangements was almost too much for his nerves. His face looked broken and old, but not like an old man, like an old boy, and he was really very irritable.

For my own part I was soon tired of Malta, and would gladly have left after three days. But there was the strike of steamers still, we had to wait on. M— professed to be enjoying himself hugely, making excursions every day, to St Paul's Bay and to the other islands. He had also made various friends or acquaintances. Particularly two young men, Maltese, who were friends of Don Bernardo. He introduced me to these two young men: one

Gabriel Mazzaiba and the other Salonia. They had small busi-nesses down on the wharf. Salonia asked M— to go for a drive in a motor-car round the island, and M— pressed me to go too. Which I did. And swiftly, on a Saturday afternoon, we dodged about in the car upon that dreadful island, first to some fearful and stony bay, arid, treeless, desert, a bit of stony desert by the sea, with unhappy villas and a sordid, scrap-iron front: then away inland up long and dusty roads, across a bone-dry, bone-bare, hideous landscape. True, there was ripening corn, but this was all of a colour with the dust-yellow, bone-bare island. Malta is all a pale, softish, yellowish rock, just like bathbrick: this goes into fathomless dust. And the island is stark as a corpse, no trees, no bushes even: a fearful landscape, cultivated, and weary with ages of weariness, and old weary houses here and there.

We went to the old capital in the centre of the island, and this is interesting. The town stands on a bluff of hill in the middle of the dreariness, looking at Valletta in the distance, and the sea. The houses are all pale yellow, and tall, and silent, as if forsaken. There is a cathedral, too, and a fortress outlook over the sun-blazed, sun-dried, disheartening island. Then we dashed off to another village and climbed a church-dome that rises like a tall blister on the plain, with houses round and corn beyond and dust that has no glamour, stale, weary, like bone-dust, and thorn hedges sometimes, and some tin-like prickly pears. In the dusk we came round by St Paul's Bay, back to Valletta.

The young men were very pleasant, very patriotic for Malta, very Catholic. We talked politics and a thousand things. M— was gently patronizing, and seemed, no doubt, to the two Maltese a very elegant and travelled and wonderful gentleman. They, who had never seen even a wood, thought how wonder-ful a forest must be, and M— talked to them of Russia and of Germany.

But I was glad to leave that bone-dry, hideous island.

M— begged me to stay longer: but not for worlds! He was establishing himself securely: was learning the Maltese language,
and cultivating a thorough acquaintance with the island. And
he was going to establish himself. Mazzaiba was exceedingly
kind to him, helping him in every way. In Rabato, the suburb of
the old town – a quiet, forlorn little yellow street – he found a
tiny house of two rooms and a tiny garden. This would cost five
pounds a year. Mazzaiba lent the furniture – and when I left, M—
was busily skipping back and forth from Rabato to Valletta,
arranging his little home, and very pleased with it. He was also
being very Maltese, and rather anti-British, as is essential, apparently, when one is not a Britisher and finds oneself in any part of
the British Empire. M— was very much the American gentleman.

Well, I was thankful to be home again and to know that he
was safely shut up in that beastly island. He wrote me letters,
saying how he loved it all, how he would go down to the sea –
five or six miles' walk – at dawn, and stay there all day, studying
Maltese and writing for the newspapers. The life was fascinating, the summer was blisteringly hot, and the Maltese were *most*
attractive, especially when they knew you were not British.
Such good-looking fellows, too, and do anything you want.
Wouldn't I come and spend a month? – I did not answer – felt I
had had enough. Came a postcard from M—: 'I haven't had a
letter from you, nor any news at all. I am afraid you are ill, and
feel so anxious. Do write –' But no, I didn't want to write.

During August and September and half October we were away
in the north. I forgot my little friend: hoped he was gone out of
my life. But I had that fatal sinking feeling that he *hadn't* really
gone out of it yet.

In the beginning of November a little letter from Don
Bernardo – did I know that M— had committed suicide in Malta?
Following that, a scrubby Maltese newspaper, posted by Salonia,

with a marked notice: 'The suicide of an American gentleman at Rabato. Yesterday the American M— M—, a well-built man in the prime of life, was found dead in his bed in his house at Rabato. By the bedside was a bottle containing poison. The deceased had evidently taken his life by swallowing prussic acid. Mr M— had been staying for some months on the island, studying the language and the conditions with a view to writing a book. It is understood that financial difficulties were the cause of this lamentable event.'

Then Mazzaiba wrote asking me what I knew of M—, and saying the latter had borrowed money which he, Mazzaiba, would like to recover. I replied at once, and then received the following letter from Salonia. 'Valletta, 20 November, 1920. My dear Mr Lawrence, some time back I mailed you our *Daily Malta Chronicle* which gave an account of the death of M—. I hope you have received same. As the statements therein given were very vague and not quite correct, please accept the latter part of this letter as a more correct version.

"The day before yesterday Mazzaiba received your letter which he gave me to read. As you may suppose we were very much astonished by its general purport. Mazzaiba will be writing to you in a few days, in the meantime I volunteered to give you the details you asked for.

'Mazzaiba and I have done all in our power to render M—'s stay here as easy and pleasant as possible from the time we first met him in your company at the Great Britain Hotel. [This is not correct. They were already quite friendly with M— before that motor-drive, when I saw these two Maltese for the first time.] He lived in an embarrassed mood since then, and though we helped him as best we could both morally and financially he never confided to us his troubles. To this very day we cannot but look on his coming here and his stay amongst us, to say the least of the way he left us, as a huge farce wrapped up in mystery, a painful experience unsolicited by either of us and a cause of grief unrequited except by our own personal sense of duty towards a stranger.

'Mazzaiba out of mere respect did not tell me of his commitments towards M— until about a month ago, and this he did in a most confidential and private manner merely to put me on my guard, thinking, and rightly, too, that M— would be falling on me next time for funds; Mazzaiba having already given him about £55 and would not possibly commit himself any further. Of course, we found him all along a perfect gentleman. Naturally, he hated the very idea that we or anybody else in Malta should look upon him in any other light. He never asked directly, though Mazzaiba (later myself) was always quick enough to interpret rightly what he meant and obliged him forthwith.

'At this stage, to save the situation, he made up a scheme that the three of us should exploit the commercial possibilities in Morocco. It very nearly materialized, everything was ready, I was to go with him to Morocco, Mazzaiba was to take charge of affairs here and to dispose of transactions we initiated there. Fortunately, for lack of the necessary funds the idea had to be dropped, and there it ended, thank God, after a great deal of trouble I had in trying to set it well on foot.

'Last July, the Police, according to our law, advised him that he was either to find a surety or to deposit a sum of money with them as otherwise at the expiration of his three months' stay he would be compelled to leave the place. Money he had none, so he asked Mazzaiba to stand as surety. Mazzaiba could not as he was already guarantor for his alien cousins who were here at the time. Mazzaiba (not M—) asked me and I complied, thinking that the responsibility was just moral and only exacted as a matter of form.

'When, as stated before, Mazzaiba told me that M— owed him £55 and that he owed his grocer and others at Notabile (the old town, of which Rabato is the suburb) over £10, I thought I might as well look up my guarantee and see if I was directly responsible for any debts he incurred here. The words of his declaration which I endorsed stated that "I hereby solemnly promise that I will not be a burden to the inhabitants of these islands, etc.," and deeming that unpaid debts to be more or less a burden, I decided to withdraw my guarantee, which I did on the 23rd ult. The reason I gave to the police was that he was outliving his income and that I did not intend to shoulder any financial responsibility in the matter. On the same day I wrote to him up at Notabile saying that for family reasons I was compelled to withdraw his surety. He took my letter in the sense implied and no way offended at my procedure.

'M—, in his resourceful way, knowing that he would with great difficulty find another guarantor, wrote at once to the police saying that he understood from Mr Salonia that he (S) had withdrawn his guarantee, but as he (M) would be leaving the island in about three weeks' time (still intending to exploit Morocco) he begged the Commissioner to allow him this period of grace, without demanding a new surety. In fact he asked me to find him a cheap passage to Gib. in an ingoing tramp steamer. The police did not reply to his letter at all, no doubt they had everything ready and well thought out. He was alarmed in not receiving an acknowledgment, and, knowing full well what he imminently expected at the hands of the Italian police, he decided to prepare for the last act of his drama.

'We had not seen him for three or four days when he came to Mazzaiba's office on Wednesday, 3rd inst., in the forenoon. He stayed there for some time talking on general subjects and looking somewhat more excited than usual. He went up to town alone at noon as Mazzaiba went to Singlea. I was not with them in the morning, but in the afternoon about 4.30, whilst I was talking to Mazzaiba in his office, M— again came in looking very excited, and, being closing time, we went up, the three of us, to town, and there left him in the company of a friend.

'On Thursday morning, 4th inst., at about 10 a.m., two detectives in plain clothes met him in a street at Notabile. One of them quite casually went up to him and said very civilly that the inspector of police wished to see him *re* a guarantee or something, and that he was to go with him to the police station. This was an excuse as the detective had about him a warrant for his arrest for frauding an hotel in Rome, and that he was to be extradited at the request of the authorities in Italy. M— replied that as he was in his sandals he would dress up and go with them immediately, and, accompanying him to his house at No. 1 Strada S. Pietro, they allowed him to enter. He locked the door behind him, leaving them outside.

'A few minutes later he opened his bedroom window and dropped a letter addressed to Don Bernardo which he asked a boy in the street to post for him, and immediately closed the window again. One of the detectives picked up the letter and we do not know to this day if same was posted at all. Some time elapsed and he did not come out. The detectives were by this time very uneasy and as another police official came up they decided to burst open the door. As the door did not give way they got a ladder and climbed over the roof, and there they found M— in his bedroom dying from poisoning, outstretched on his bed and a glass of water close by. A priest was immediately called in who had just time to administer Extreme Unction before he died at 11.45 a.m.

'At 8.0 a.m. the next day his body was admitted for examination at the Floriana Civil Hospital and death was certified to be from poisoning with hydrocyanic acid. His age was given as 44, being buried on his birthday (7th Novr.), with R. Catholic Rites at the expense of *His Friends in Malta.*

'Addenda: Contents of Don Bernardo's letter: –

' "I leave it to you and to Gabriel Mazzaiba to arrange my affairs. I cannot live any longer. Pray for me."

'Document found on his writing-table:

' "In case of my unexpected death inform American consul.

' "I want to be buried first class, my wife will pay.

' "My little personal belongings to be delivered to my wife. (Address.)

' "My best friend here, Gabriel Mazzaiba, inform him. (Address.)

' "My literary executor N— D—. (Address.)

' "All manuscripts and books for N—D . I leave my literary property to N— D— to whom half of the results are to accrue. The other half my debts are to be paid with:

' "Furniture etc. belong to Coleiro, Floriana.

' "Silver spoons etc. belong to Gabriel Mazzaiba. (Address.).''

'The American Consul is in charge of all his personal belongings. I am sure he will be pleased to give you any further details you may require. By the way, his wife refused to pay his burial expenses, but five of his friends in Malta undertook to give him a decent funeral. His mourners were: The consul, the vice-consul, Mr A., an American citizen, Gabriel Mazzaiba and myself.

'Please convey to Mrs Lawrence an expression of our sincere esteem and high regard and you will kindly accept equally our warmest respects, whilst soliciting any information you would care to pass on to us regarding the late M—. Believe me, My dear Mr Lawrence, etc.'

[Mrs M— refunded the burial expenses through the American consul about two months after her husband's death.]

When I had read this letter the world seemed to stand still for me. I knew that in my own soul I had said, 'Yes, he must die if he cannot find his own way.' But for all that, now I *realized* what it must have meant to be the hunted, desperate man: everything seemed to stand still. I could, by giving half my money, have saved his life. I had chosen not to save his life.

Now, after a year has gone by, I keep to my choice. I still would not save his life. I respect him for dying when he was cornered. And for this reason I feel still connected with him: still have this to discharge, to get his book published, and to give him his place, to present him just as he was as far as I knew him myself.

The worst thing I have against him, is that he abused the confidence, the kindness, and the generosity of unsuspecting people like Mazzaiba. He did not *want* to, perhaps. But he did it. And he leaves Mazzaiba swindled, distressed, confused, and feeling sold in the best part of himself. What next? What is one to feel towards one's strangers, after having known M—? It is this Judas treachery to *ask* for sympathy and for generosity, to take it when given – and then: 'Sorry, but anybody may make a mistake!' It is this betraying with a kiss which makes me still say: 'He should have died sooner.' No, I would not help to keep him alive, not if I had to choose again. I would let him go over into death. He shall and should die, and so should all his sort: and so they will. There are so many kiss-giving Judases. He was not a criminal: he was obviously well intentioned: but a Judas every time, selling the good feeling he had tried to arouse, and had aroused, for any handful of silver he could get. A little loving vampire!

Yesterday arrived the manuscript of the Legion, from Malta. It is exactly two years since I read it first in the monastery. Then I was moved and rather horrified. Now I am chiefly amused; because in my mind's eye is the figure of M— in the red trousers and the blue coat with lappets turned up, swinging like a little indignant pigeon across the drill yards and into the canteen of Bel-Abbès. He *is* so indignant, so righteously and morally indignant, and so funny. All the horrors of the actuality fade before the indignation, his little, tuppenny indignation.

Oh, M— is a prime hypocrite. *How* loudly he rails against the *Boches*! *How* great his enthusiasm for the pure, the spiritual Allied cause. Just so long as he is in Africa, and it suits his purpose! His scorn for the German tendencies of the German legionaries: even Count de R. secretly leans towards Germany. 'Blood is thicker than water,' says our hero glibly. Some blood, thank God. Apparently not his own. For according to all showing he was, by blood, pure German: father and mother: even Hohenzollern blood !!! Pure German! Even his speech, his *mother-tongue*, was German and not English! And then the little mongrel! !

But perhaps something happens to blood when once it has been taken to America.

And then, once he is in Valbonne, lo, a change! Where now is sacred France and the holy Allied Cause! Where is our hero's fervour? It is *worse than* Bel-Abbès! Yes, indeed, far less human, more hideously cold. One is driven by very rage to wonder if he was really a spy, a German spy whom Germany cast off because he was no good.

The little *gentleman*! God damn his white-blooded gentility. The legionaries must have been gentlemen, that they didn't kick him every day to the lavatory and back.

'You are a journalist?' said the colonel.

'No, a *littérateur*,' said M— perkily.

'That is something more?' said the Colonel.

Oh, I would have given a lot to have seen it and heard it. The *littérateur*! Well, I hope this book will establish his fame as such. I hope the editor, if it gets one, won't alter any more of the marvellously staggering sentences and the joyful French mistakes. The *littérateur*! – the impossible little pigeon!

But the Bel-Abbès part is alive and interesting. It should be read only by those who have the stomach. Ugly, foul – alas, it is no uglier and no fouler than the reality. M— himself was near

enough to being a scoundrel, thief, forger, etc., etc. – what lovely
strings of names he hurls at them! – to be able to appreciate his
company. He himself was such a liar, that he was not taken in.
But his conceit as a gentleman *keeping up appearances* gave him a
real standpoint from which to see the rest. The book is in its way
a real creation. But I would hate it to be published and taken at
its face value, with M— as a spiritual dove among vultures of
lust. Let us first put a pinch of salt on the tail of this dove. What
he did do in the way of vice, even in Bel-Abbès, I never chose to
ask him.

Yes, yes, he sings another note when he is planted right among
the sacred Allies, with never a German near. Then the gor-
geousness goes out of his indignation. He takes it off with the
red trousers. Now he is just a sordid little figure in filthy corduroys. There is no vice to purple his indignation, the little holy
liar. There is only sordidness and automatic, passionless, colour-
less awful mud. When all is said and done, mud, cold, hideous,
foul, engulfing mud, up to the waist, this is the final symbol of
the Great War. Hear some of the horrified young soldiers. They
dare hardly speak of it yet.

The Valbonne part is worse, really, than the Bel-Abbès part.
Passionless, barren, utterly, coldly foul and hopeless. The
ghastly emptiness, and the slow mud-vortex, the brink of it.

Well, now M— has gone himself. Yes, and he would be gone
in the common mud and dust himself, if it were not that the
blood still beats warm and hurt and kind in some few hearts.
M— 'hinted' at Mazzaiba for money, in Malta, and Mazzaiba
gave it to him, thinking him a man in distress. He thought him
a gentleman, and lovable, and in trouble! And Mazzaiba – it isn't
his real name, but there he is, real enough – still has this feeling
of grief for M—. So much so that now he has had the remains
taken from the public grave in Malta, and buried in his own, the
Mazzaiba grave, so that they shall not be lost. For my part, I

would have said that the sooner they mingled with the universal dust, the better. But one is glad to see a little genuine kindness and gentleness, even if it is wasted on the bones of that selfish little scamp of a M—. He despised his 'physical friendships –' though he didn't forgo them. So why should anyone rescue his physique from the public grave?

But there you are – there was his power: to arouse affection and a certain tenderness in the hearts of others, for himself. And on this he traded. One sees the trick working all the way through the Legion book. God knows how much warm kindness, generosity, was showered on him during the course of his forty-odd years. And selfish little scamp, he took it as a greedy boy takes cakes off a dish, quickly, to make the most of his opportunity while it lasted. And the cake once eaten: *buona sera*! He patted his own little paunch and felt virtuous. Merely physical feeling, you see! He had a way of saying 'physical' a sort of American way, as if it were spelt 'fisacal' – that made me want to kick him.

Not that he was mean, while he was about it. No, he would give very freely: even a little ostentatiously, always feeling that he was being a *liberal gentleman*. Ach, the liberality and the gentility he prided himself on! *Ecco!* And he gave a large tip, with a little winsome smile. But in his heart of hearts it was always himself he was thinking of, while he did it. Playing his rôle of the gentleman who was awfully *nice* to everybody: so long as they were nice to him, or so long as it served his advantage. Just private charity!

Well, poor devil, he is dead: which is all the better. He had his points, the courage of his own terrors, quick-wittedness, sensitiveness to certain things in his surroundings. I prefer him, scamp as he is, to the ordinary respectable person. He ran his risks: he *had* to be running risks with the police, apparently. And he poisoned himself rather than fall into their clutches.

I like him for that. And I like him for the sharp and quick way he made use of every one of his opportunities to get out of that beastly army. There I admire him: a courageous isolated little devil, facing his risks, and like a good rat, *determined* not to be trapped. I won't forgive him for trading on the generosity of others, and so dropping poison into the heart of all warm-blooded faith. But I am glad after all that Mazzaiba has rescued his bones from the public grave. I wouldn't have done it myself, because I don't forgive him his 'fisacal' impudence and parasitism. But I am glad Mazzaiba has done it. And, for my part, I will put his Legion book before the world if I can. Let him have his place in the world's consciousness.

Let him have his place, let his word be heard. He went through vile experiences: he looked them in the face, braved them through, and kept his manhood in spite of them. For manhood is a strange quality, to be found in human rats as well as in hot-blooded men. M— carried the human consciousness through circumstances which would have been too much for me. I would have died rather than be so humiliated, I could never have borne it. Other men, I know, went through worse things in the war. But then, horrors, like pain, are their own anæsthetic. Men lose their normal consciousness, and go through in a sort of delirium. The bit of Stendhal which Dos Passos quotes in front of *Three Soldiers* is frighteningly true. There are certain things which are so bitter, so horrible, that the contemporaries just cannot know them, cannot contemplate them. So it is with a great deal of the late war. It was so foul, and humanity in Europe fell suddenly into such ignominy and inhuman ghastliness, that we shall *never* fully realize what it was. We just cannot bear it. We haven't the soul-strength to contemplate it.

And yet, humanity can only finally conquer by realizing. It is human destiny, since Man fell into consciousness and self-consciousness, that we can only go forward step by step through realization, full, bitter, conscious realization. This is true of all the great terrors and agonies and anguishes of life: sex, and war, and even crime. When Flaubert in his story – it is so long since I read it – makes his saint have to kiss the leper, and naked clasp the leprous awful body against his own, that is what we must at last do. It is the great command *Know Thyself*. We've got to *know* what sex is, let the sentimentalists wiggle as they like. We've got to know the greatest and most shattering human passions, let the puritans squeal as they like for screens. And we've got to know humanity's criminal tendency, look straight at humanity's great deeds of crime against the soul. We have to fold this horrible leper against our naked warmth: because life and the throbbing blood and the believing soul are greater even than leprosy. Knowledge, true knowledge is like vaccination. It prevents the continuing of ghastly moral disease.

And so it is with the war. Humanity in Europe fell horribly into a hatred of the living soul, in the war. There is no gainsaying it. We all fell. Let us not try to wriggle out of it. We fell into hideous depravity of hating the human soul; a purulent small-pox of the spirit we had. It was shameful, shameful, shameful, in every country and in all of us. Some tried to resist, and some didn't. But we were all drowned in shame. A purulent small-pox of the vicious spirit, vicious against the deep soul that pulses in the blood.

We haven't got over it. The small-pox sores are running yet in the spirit of mankind. And we have got to take this putrid spirit to our bosom. There's nothing else for it. Take the foul rotten spirit of mankind, full of the running sores of the war, to our bosom, and cleanse it there. Cleanse it not with blind love: ah no, that won't help. But with bitter and wincing realization. We have to take the disease into our consciousness and let it go through our soul, like some virus. We have got to realize. And then we can surpass.

M— went where I could never go. He carried the human consciousness unbroken through circumstances I could not have borne. It is not heroism to rush on death. It is cowardice to accept a martyrdom today. That is the feeling one has at the end of Dos Passos' book. To let oneself be absolutely trapped? Never! I prefer M—. He drew himself out of the thing he loathed, despised, and feared. He fought it, for his own spirit and liberty. He fought it open-eyed. He went through. They were more publicly heroic, they won war medals. But the lonely terrified courage of the isolated spirit which grits its teeth and stares the horrors in the face and *will* not succumb to them, but fights its way through them, *knowing* that it must surpass them: this is the rarest courage. And this courage M— had: and the man in the Dos Passos book didn't *quite* have it. And so, though M— poisoned himself, and I would not wish him *not* to have poisoned himself: though as far as warm life goes, I don't forgive him; yet, as far as the eternal and unconquerable spirit of man goes, I am with him through eternity. I am grateful to him, he beat out for me boundaries of human experience which I could not have beaten out for myself. The *human* traitor he was. But he was not traitor to the spirit. In the great spirit of human consciousness he was a hero, little, quaking and heroic: a strange, quaking little star.

Even the dead ask only for *justice*: not for praise or exoneration. Who dares humiliate the dead with excuses for their living? I hope I may do M— justice; and I hope his restless spirit may be appeased. I do not try to forgive. The living blood knows no forgiving. Only the overweening spirit takes on itself to dole out forgiveness. But Justice is a sacred human right. The overweening spirit pretends to perch above justice. But I am a man, not a spirit, and men with blood that throbs and throbs and throbs can only live at length by being just, can only die in peace if they have justice. Forgiveness gives the whimpering dead no rest. Only deep, true justice.

There is M—'s manuscript then, like a map of the lower places of mankind's activities. There is the war: foul, foul, un-utterably foul. As foul as M— says. Let us make up our minds about it.

It is the only help: to realize, *fully*, and then make up our minds. The war was *foul*. As long as I am a man, I say it and assert it, and further I say, as long as I am a man such a war shall never occur again. It shall not, and it shall not. All modern militarism is foul. It shall go. A man I am, and above machines, and it shall go, forever, because I have found it vile, vile, too vile ever to experience again. Cannons shall go. Never again shall trenches be dug. They *shall* not, for I am a man, and such things are within the power of man, to break and make. I have said it, and as long as blood beats in my veins, I mean it. Blood beats in the veins of many men who mean it as well as I.

Man perhaps *must* fight. Mars, the great god of war, will be a god forever. Very well. Then if fight you must, fight you shall, and without engines, without machines. Fight if you like, as the Roman fought, with swords and spears, or like the Red Indian, with bows and arrows and knives and war paint. But never again shall you fight with the foul, base, fearful, monstrous machines of war which man invented for the last war. You shall not. The diabolic mechanisms are man's, and I am a man. Therefore they are mine. And I smash them into oblivion. With every means in my power, *except* the means of these machines, I smash them into oblivion. I am at war! I, a man, am at war! – with these foul machines and contrivances that men have conjured up. Men have conjured them up. I, a man, will conjure them down again. Won't I? – but I will! I am not one man, I am many, I am most.

So much for the war! So much for M—'s manuscript. Let it be read. It is not this that will do harm, but sloppy sentiment and cant. Take the bitterness and cleanse the blood.

Now would you believe it, that little scamp M— spent over a hundred pounds of borrowed money during his four months in Malta, when his expenses, he boasted to me, need not have been more than a pound a week, once he got into the little house in Notabile. That is, he spent at least seventy pounds too much. Heaven knows what he did with it, apart from 'guzzling.' And this hundred pounds must be paid back in Malta. Which it never will be, unless this manuscript pays it back. Pay the gentleman's last debts, if no others.

He had to be a gentleman. I didn't realize till after his death. I never suspected him of royal blood. But there you are, you never know where it will crop out. He was the grandson of an emperor. His mother was the illegitimate daughter of the German Kaiser: D— says, of the old Kaiser Wilhelm I, Don Bernardo says, of Kaiser Frederick Wilhelm, father of the present ex-Kaiser. She was born in Berlin on the 31 October, 1845: and her portrait, by Paul, now hangs in a gallery in Rome. Apparently there had been some injustice against her in Berlin – for she seems once to have been in the highest society there, and to have attended at court. Perhaps she was discreetly banished by Wilhelm II, hence M—'s hatred of that monarch. She lies buried in the Protestant Cemetery in Rome, where she died in 1912, with the words *Filia Regis* on her tomb. M— adored her, and she him. Part of his failings one can *certainly* ascribe to the fact that he was an only son, an adored son, in whose veins the mother imagined only royal blood. And she must have thought him so beautiful, poor thing! Ah well, they are both dead. Let us be just and wish them Lethe.

M— himself was born in New York, 7th November, 1876; so at least it says on his passport. He entered the Catholic Church in England in 1902. His father was a Mr L— M—, married to the mother in 1867.

So poor M— had Hohenzollern blood in his veins: close kin

to the ex-Kaiser William. Well, that itself excuses him a great deal: because of the cruel illusion of importance *manqué*, which it must have given him. He never breathed a word of this to me. Yet apparently it is accepted at the monastery, the great monastery which knows most European secrets of any political significance. And for myself, I believe it is true. And if he was a scamp and a treacherous little devil, he had also qualities of nerve and breeding undeniable. He faced his way through that Legion experience: royal nerves dragging themselves through the sewers, without giving way. But alas, for royal blood! Like most other blood, it has gradually gone white, during our spiritual era. Bunches of nerves! And whitish, slightly acid blood. And no bowels of deep compassion and kindliness. Only charity – a little more than kin, and less than kind.

Also – M—! Ich grüsse dich, in der Ewigkeit. Aber hier, im Herzblut, hast du Gift und Leid nachgelassen – to use your own romantic language.

INDIANS AND AN ENGLISHMAN (1922)

Supposing one fell onto the moon, and found them talking English, it would be something the same as falling out of the open world plump down here in the middle of America. 'Here' means New Mexico, the Southwest, wild and woolly and artistic and sage-brush desert.

It is all rather like comic opera played with solemn intensity. All the wildness and woolliness and westernity and motor-cars and art and sage and savage are so mixed up, so incongruous, that it is a farce, and everybody knows it. But they refuse to play it as farce. The wild and woolly section insists on being heavily dramatic, bold and bad on purpose; the art insists on being real American and artistic; motor-cars insist on being thrilled, moved to the marrow; highbrows insist on being ecstatic; Mexicans insist on being Mexicans, squeezing the last black drop of macabre joy out of life; and Indians wind themselves in white cotton sheets like Hamlet's father's ghost, with a lurking smile.

And here am I, a lone lorn Englishman, tumbled out of the known world of the British Empire onto this stage: for it persists in seeming like a stage to me, and not like the proper world.

Whatever makes a proper world, I don't know. But surely two elements are necessary: a common purpose and a common sympathy. I can't see any common purpose. The Indians and Mexicans don't even seem very keen on dollars. That full moon of a silver dollar doesn't strike me as overwhelmingly hypnotic out here. As for a common sympathy or understanding, that's beyond imagining. West is wild and woolly and bad-on-purpose; commerce is a little self-conscious about its own pioneering importance – Pioneers! O Pioneers! – highbrow is bent on getting to the bottom of everything and saving the lost soul down there in the depths; Mexican is bent on being Mexican and not gringo; and the Indian is all the things that all the others aren't. And so everybody smirks at everybody else, and says tacitly: 'Go on; you do your little stunt, and I'll do mine,' and they're like the various troupes in a circus, all performing at once, with nobody for Master of Ceremonies.

It seems to me, in this country, everything is taken so damn seriously that nothing remains serious. Nothing is so farcical as insistent drama. Everybody is lurkingly conscious of this. Each section or troupe is quite willing to admit that all the other sections are buffoon stunts. But it itself is the real thing, solemnly bad in its badness, good in its goodness, wild in its wildness, woolly in its woolliness, arty in its artiness, deep in its depths – in a word, earnest.

In such a masquerade of earnestness, a bewildered straggler out of the far-flung British Empire, myself! Don't let me for a moment pretend to *know* anything. I know less than nothing. I simply gasp like a bumpkin in a circus ring, with the horse-lady leaping over my head, the Apache war-whooping in my ear, the Mexican staggering under crosses and bumping me as he goes by, the artist whirling colours across my dazzled vision, the highbrows solemnly declaiming at me from all the cross-roads. If, dear reader, you, being the audience who has paid to come in, feel that you must take up an attitude to me, let it be one of amused pity.

One has to take sides. First, one must be either pro-Mexican or pro-Indian; then, either art or intellect; then, Republican or Democrat; and so on. But as for me, poor lamb, if I bleat at all in the circus ring, it will be my own shorn lonely bleat of a lamb who's lost his mother.

The first Indians I really saw were the Apaches in the Apache Reservation of this state. We drove in a motor-car, across desert and mesa, down cañons and up divides and along arroyos and so forth, two days, till at afternoon our two Indian men ran the car aside from the trail and sat under the pine tree to comb their long black hair and roll it into the two roll-plaits that hang in front of their shoulders, and put on all their silver-and-turquoise jewellery and their best blankets: because we were nearly there. On the trail were horsemen passing, and wagons with Ute Indians and Navajos.

'*De donde viene Usted?*' . . .

We came at dusk from the high shallows and saw on a low crest the points of Indian tents, the tepees, and smoke, and silhouettes of tethered horses and blanketed figures moving. In the shadow a rider was following a flock of white goats that flowed like water. The car ran to the top of the crest, and there was a hollow basin with a lake in the distance, pale in the dying light. And this shallow upland basin, dotted with Indian tents, and the fires flickering in front, and crouching blanketed figures, and horsemen crossing the dusk from tent to tent, horsemen in big steeple hats sitting glued on their ponies, and bells tinkling, and dogs yapping, and tilted wagons trailing in on the trail below, and a smell of wood-smoke and of cooking, and wagons coming in from far off, and tents pricking on the ridge of the round *vallum*, and horsemen dipping down and emerging again, and more red sparks of fires glittering, and crouching bundles of women's figures squatting at a fire before a little tent made of boughs, and little girls in full petticoats hovering, and wild barefoot boys throwing bones at thin-tailed dogs, and tents away in the distance, in the growing dark, on the slopes, and the trail crossing the floor of the hollows in the low dusk.

There you had it all, as in the hollow of your hand. And to my heart, born in England and kindled with Fenimore Cooper, it wasn't the wild and woolly West, it was the nomad nations gathering still in the continent of hemlock trees and prairies. The Apaches came and talked to us, in their steeple black hats and plaits wrapped with beaver fur, and their silver and beads and turquoise. Some talked strong American, and some talked only Spanish. And they had strange lines in their faces.

The two kivas, the rings of cut aspen trees stuck in the ground like the walls of a big hut of living trees, were on the plain, at either end of the race-track. And as the sun went down, the drums began to beat, the drums with their strong-weak, strong-weak pulse that beat on the plasm of one's tissue. The car slid down to the south kiva. Two elderly men held the drum, and danced the pàt-pat, pàt-pat quick beat on flat feet, like birds that move from the feet only, and sang with wide mouths: Hie! Hie! Hie! Hy-a! Hy-a! Hy-a! Hie! Hie! Hie! Ay-away-away-a! Strange dark faces with wide, shouting mouths and rows of small, close-set teeth, and strange lines on the faces, part ecstasy, part mockery, part humorous, part devilish, and the strange, calling, summoning sound in a wild song-shout, to the thud-thud of the drum. Answer of the same from the other kiva, as of a challenge accepted. And from the gathering darkness around, men drifting slowly in, each carrying an aspen twig, each joining to cluster close in two rows upon the drum, holding each his aspen twig inwards, their faces all together, mouths all open in the song-shout, and all of them all the time going on the two feet, pàt-pat, pàt-pat, to the thud-thud of the drum and the strange, plangent yell of the chant, edging inch by inch, pàt-pat, pàt-pat, pàt-pat, sideways in a cluster along the track, towards the distant cluster of the challengers from the other kiva, who were sing-shouting and edging onwards, sideways, in the dusk, their faces all together, their leaves all inwards, towards the drum, and their feet going pàt-pat, pàt-pat on the dust, with their buttocks stuck out a little, faces all inwards, shouting open-mouthed to the drum, and half laughing, half mocking, half devilment, half fun. *Hie! Hie! Hie! Hie-away-awaya!* The strange yell, song, shout rising so lonely in the dusk, as if pine trees could suddenly, shaggily sing. Almost a pre-animal sound, full of triumph in life, and devilment against other life, and mockery, and humorousness, and the pàt-pat, pàt-pat of the rhythm. Sometimes more youths coming up, and as they draw near laughing, they give the war-whoop, like a turkey giving a startled shriek and then gobble-gobbling with laughter – Ugh! – the shriek half laughter, then the gobble-gobble-gobble like a great demoniac chuckle. The chuckle in the war-whoop. – They produce the gobble from the deeps of the stomach, and say it makes them feel good.

Listening, an acute sadness, and a nostalgia, unbearably yearning for something, and a sickness of the soul came over me. The gobble-gobble chuckle in the whoop surprised me in my very tissues. Then I got used to it, and could hear in it the humanness, the playfulness, and then, beyond that, the mockery and the diabolical, pre-human, pine-tree fun of cutting dusky throats and letting the blood spurt out unconfined. Gobble-agobble-agobble, the unconfined loose blood, gobble-agobble, the dead, mutilated lump, gobble-agobble-agobble, the fun, the greatest man-fun. The war-whoop!

So I felt. I may have been all wrong, and other folk may feel much more natural and reasonable things. But so I felt. And the sadness and the nostalgia of the song-calling, and the resinous continent of pine trees and turkeys, the feet of birds treading a dance, far off, when man was dusky and not individualized.

I am no ethnologist. The point is, what is the feeling that passes from an Indian to me, when we meet? We are both men, but how do we feel together? I shall never forget that first evening when I first came into contact with Red Men, away in the Apache country. It was not what I had thought it would be. It was something of a shock. Again something in my soul broke down, letting in a bitterer dark, a pungent awakening to the lost past, old darkness, new terror, new root-griefs, old root-richnesses.

The Apaches have a cult of water-hatred; they never wash flesh or rag. So never in my life have I smelt such an unbearable sulphur-human smell as comes from them when they cluster: a smell that takes the breath from the nostrils.

We drove the car away half a mile or more, back from the Apache hollow, to a lonely ridge, where we pitched camp under pine trees. Our two Indians made the fire, dragged in wood, then wrapped themselves in their best blankets and went off to the tepees of their friends. The night was cold and starry.

After supper I wrapped myself in a red serape up to the nose, and went down alone to the Apache encampment. It is good, on a chilly night in a strange country, to be wrapped almost to the eyes in a good Navajo blanket. Then you feel warm inside yourself, and as good as invisible, and the dark air thick with enemies. So I stumbled on, startling the hobbled horses that jerked aside from me. Reaching the rim-crest one saw many fires burning in red spots round the slopes of the hollow, and against the fires many crouching figures. Dogs barked, a baby cried from a bough shelter, there was a queer low crackle of voices. So I stumbled alone over the ditches and past the tents, down to the kiva. Just near was a shelter with a big fire in front, and a man, an Indian, selling drinks, no doubt Budweiser beer and grape-juice, non-intoxicants. Cowboys in chaps and big hats were drinking too, and one screechy, ungentle cowgirl in khaki. So I went on in the dark up the opposite slope. The dark Indians passing in the night peered at me. The air was full of a sort of sportiveness, playfulness, that had a jeering, malevolent vibration in it, to my fancy. As if this play were another kind of harmless-harmful warfare, overbearing. Just the antithesis of what I understand by jolliness: ridicule. Comic sort of bullying. No jolly, free laughter. Yet a great deal of laughter. But with a sort of gibe in it.

This, of course, may just be the limitation of my European fancy. But that was my feeling. One felt a stress of will, of human wills, in the dark air, gibing even in the comic laughter. And a sort of unconscious animosity.

Again a sound of a drum down below, so again I stumbled down to the kiva. A bunch of young men were clustered – seven or eight round a drum, and standing with their faces together, loudly and mockingly singing the song-yells, some of them treading the pàt-pat, some not bothering. Just behind was the blazing fire and the open shelter of the drink-tent, with Indians in tall black hats and long plaits in front of their shoulders, and bead-braided waistcoats, and hands in their pockets; some swathed in sheets, some in brilliant blankets, and all grinning, laughing. The cowboys with big spurs still there, horses' bridles trailing, and cowgirl screeching her laugh. One felt an inevitable silent gibing, animosity in each group, one for the other. At the same time, an absolute avoidance of any evidence of this.

The young men round the drum died out and started again. As they died out, the strange uplifted voice in the kiva was heard. It seemed to me the outside drumming and singing served to cover the voice within the kiva.

The kiva of young green trees was just near, two paces only. On the ground outside, boughs and twigs were strewn round to prevent anyone's coming close to the enclosure. Within was the firelight. And one could see through the green of the leaf-screen, men round a fire inside there, and one old man, the same old man always facing the open entrance, the fire between him and it. Other Indians sat in a circle, of which he was the key. The old man had his dark face lifted, his head bare, his two plaits falling on his shoulders. His close-shutting Indian lips were drawn open, his eyes were as if half-veiled, as he went on and on, on and on, in a distinct, plangent, recitative voice, male and yet strangely far-off and plaintive, reciting, reciting, reciting like a somnambulist, telling, no doubt, the history of the tribe interwoven with the gods. Other Apaches sat round the fire. Those nearest the old teller were stationary, though one chewed gum all the time and one ate bread-cake and others lit cigarettes. Those nearer the entrance rose after a time, restless. At first some strolled in, stood a minute, then strolled out, desultory. But as the night went on, the ring round the fire inside the wall of green young trees was complete, all squatting on the ground, the old man with the lifted face and parted lips and half-unseeing eyes going on and on, across the fire. Some men stood lounging with the half self-conscious ease of the Indian behind the seated men. They lit cigarettes. Some drifted out. Another filtered in. I stood wrapped in my blanket in the cold night, at some little distance from the entrance, looking on.

A big young Indian came and pushed his face under my hat to see who or what I was.

'*Buenos!*'

'*Buenos!*'

'*Qué quiere?*'

'*No hablo español.*'

'Oh, only English, eh? You can't come in here.'

'I don't want to.'

'This Indian church.'

'Is it?'

'I don't let people come, only Apache, only Indian.'

'You keep watch?'

'I keep watch, yes; Indian church, eh?'

'And the old man preaches?'

'Yes, he preaches.'

After which I stood quite still and uncommunicative. He waited for a further development. There was none. So, after giving me another look, he went to talk to other Indians, *sotto voce*, by the door. The circle was complete; groups stood behind the squatting ring, some men were huddled in blankets, some sitting just in trousers and shirt, in the warmth near the fire, some wrapped close in white cotton sheets. The firelight shone on the dark, unconcerned faces of the listeners, as they chewed gum, or ate bread, or smoked a cigarette. Some had big silver earrings swinging, and necklaces of turquoise. Some had waistcoats all bead braids. Some wore store shirts and store trousers, like Americans. From time to time one man pushed another piece of wood on the fire.

They seemed to be paying no attention; it all had a very perfunctory appearance. But they kept silent, and the voice of the old reciter went on blindly, from his lifted, bronze mask of a face with its wide-opened lips. They furl back their teeth as they speak, and they use a sort of resonant tenor voice that has a plangent, half-sad, twanging sound, vibrating deep from the chest. The old man went on and on, for hours, in that urgent, far-off voice. His hair was grey, and parted, and his two round plaits hung in front of his shoulders on his shirt. From his ears dangled pieces of blue turquoise, tied with string. An old green blanket was wrapped round above his waist, and his feet in old moccasins were crossed before the fire. There was a deep pathos, for me, in the old, mask-like, virile figure, with its metallic courage of persistence, old memory, and its twanging male voice. So far, so great a memory. So dauntless a persistence in the piece of living red earth seated on the naked earth, before the fire; this old, bronze-resonant man with his eyes as if glazed in old memory, and his voice issuing in endless plangent monotony from the wide, unfurled mouth.

And the young men, who chewed chewing-gum and listened without listening. The voice no doubt registered on their under-consciousness, as they looked around, and lit a cigarette, and spat sometimes aside. With their day-consciousness they hardly attended.

As for me, standing outside, beyond the open entrance, I was no enemy of theirs; far from it. The voice out of the far-off time was not for my ears. Its language was unknown to me. And I did not wish to know. It was enough to hear the sound issuing plangent from the bristling darkness of the far past, to see the bronze mask of the face lifted, the white, small, close-packed teeth showing all the time. It was not for me, and I knew it. Nor had I any curiosity to understand. The soul is as old as the oldest day, and has its own hushed echoes, its own far-off tribal under-standings sunk and incorporated. We do not need to live the past over again. Our darkest tissues are twisted in this old tribal experience, our warmest blood came out of the old tribal fire. And they vibrate still in answer, our blood, our tissue. But me, the conscious me, I have gone a long road since then. And as I look back, like memory terrible as bloodshed, the dark faces round the fire in the night, and one blood beating in me and them. But I don't want to go back to them, ah, never. I never want to deny them or break with them. But there is no going back. Always onward, still further. The great devious onward flowing stream of conscious human blood. From them to me, and from me on.

I don't want to live again the tribal mysteries my blood has lived long since. I don't want to know as I have known, in the tri-bal exclusiveness. But every drop of me trembles still alive to the old sound, every thread in my body quivers to the frenzy of the old mystery. I know my derivation. I was born of no virgin, of no Holy Ghost. Ah, no, these old men telling the tribal tale were my fathers. I have a dark-faced, bronze-voiced father far back in the resinous ages. My mother was no virgin. She lay in her hour with this dusky-lipped tribe-father. And I have not forgotten him. But he, like many an old father with a changeling son, he would like to deny me. But I stand on the far edge of their firelight, and am neither denied nor accepted. My way is my own, old red father; I can't cluster at the drum any more.

TAOS (1922)

The Indians say Taos is the heart of the world. Their world, maybe. Some places seem temporary on the face of the earth: San Francisco, for example. Some places seem final. They have a true nodality. I never felt that so powerfully as, years ago, in London. The intense powerful nodality of that great heart of the world. And during the war that heart, for me, broke. So it is. Places can lose their living nodality. Rome, to me, has lost hers. In Venice one feels the magic of the glamorous old node that once united East and West, but it is the beauty of an after-life.

Taos pueblo still retains its old nodality. Not like a great city. But, in its way, like one of the monasteries of Europe. You cannot come upon the ruins of the old great monasteries of England, beside their waters, in some lovely valley, now remote, without feeling that here is one of the choice spots of the earth, where the spirit dwelt. To me it is so important to remember that when Rome collapsed, when the great Roman Empire fell into smoking ruins, and bears roamed in the streets of Lyon and wolves howled in the deserted streets of Rome, and Europe really was a dark ruin, then, it was not in castles or manors or cottages that life remained vivid. Then those whose souls were still alive withdrew together and gradually built monasteries, and these monasteries and convents, little communities of quiet labour and courage, isolated, helpless, and yet never overcome in a world flooded with devastation, these alone kept the human spirit from disintegration, from going quite dark, in the Dark Ages. These men made the Church, which again made Europe, inspiring the martial faith of the Middle Ages.

Taos pueblo affects me rather like one of the old monasteries. When you get there you feel something final. There is an arrival. The nodality still holds good.

But this is the pueblo. And from the north side to the south side, from the south side to the north side, the perpetual silent wandering intentness of a full-skirted, black-shawled, long-fringed woman in her wide white deerskin boots, the running of children, the silent sauntering of dark-faced men, bare-headed, the two plaits in front of their thin shoulders, and a white sheet like a sash swathed round their loins. They must have something to swathe themselves in.

And if it were sunset, the men swathing themselves in their sheets like shrouds, leaving only the black place of the eyes visible. And women, darker than ever, with shawls over their heads, busy at the ovens. And cattle being driven to sheds. And men and boys trotting in from the fields, on ponies. And as the night is dark, on one of the roofs, or more often on the bridge, the inevitable drum-drum-drum of the tomtom, and young men in the dark lifting their voices to the song, like wolves or coyotes crying in music.

There it is, then, the pueblo, as it has been since heaven knows when. And the slow dark weaving of the Indian life going on still, though perhaps more waveringly. And oneself, sitting there on a pony, a far-off stranger with gulfs of time between me and this. And yet, the old nodality of the pueblo still holding, like a dark ganglion spinning invisible threads of consciousness. A sense of dryness, almost of weariness, about the pueblo. And a sense of the inalterable. It brings a sick sort of feeling over me, always, to get into the Indian vibration. Like breathing chlorine.

The next day, in the morning, we went to help erect the great stripped maypole. It was the straight, smoothed yellow trunk of a big tree. Of course one of the white boys took the bossing of the show. But the Indians were none too ready to obey, and their own fat dark-faced boss gave counter-orders. It was the old, amusing contradiction between the white and the dark races. As for me, I just gave a hand steadying the pole as it went up, outsider at both ends of the game.

An American girl came with a camera, and got a snap of us all struggling in the morning light with the great yellow trunk. One of the Indians went to her abruptly, in his quiet, insidious way.

'You give me that Kodak. You ain't allowed take no snaps here. You pay fine – one dollar.'

She was frightened, but she clung to her camera.

'You're not going to take my Kodak from me,' she said.

'I'm going to take that film out. And you pay one dollar fine, see?'

The girl relinquished the camera; the Indian took out the film.

'Now you pay me one dollar, or I don't give you back the Kodak.'

Rather sullenly, she took out her purse and gave the two silver half-dollars. The Indian returned the camera, pocketed the money, and turned aside with a sort of triumph. Done it over one specimen of the white race.

There were not very many Indians helping to put up the pole.

'I never see so few boys helping put up the pole,' said Tony Romero to me.

'Where are they all?' I asked. He shrugged his shoulders.

Dr West, a woman doctor from New York who has settled in one of the villages, was with us. Mass was being said inside the church, and she would have liked to go in. She is well enough known, too. But two Indians were at the church door, and one put his elbow in front of her.

'You Catholic?'

'No, I'm not.'

'Then you can't come in.'

The same almost jeering triumph in giving the white man – or the white woman – a kick. It is the same the whole world over, between dark-skin and white. Dr West, of course, thinks everything Indian wonderful. But she wasn't used to being rebuffed, and she didn't like it. But she found excuses.

'Of course,' she said, 'they're quite right to exclude the white people, if the white people can't behave themselves. It seems there were some Americans, boys and girls, in the church yesterday, insulting the images of the saints, shrieking, laughing, and saying they looked like monkeys. So now *no* white people are allowed inside the church.'

I listened, and said nothing. I had heard the same story at Buddhist temples in Ceylon. For my own part, I have long since passed the stage when I want to crowd up and stare at anybody's spectacle, white man's or dark man's.

I stood on one of the first roofs of the north pueblo. The iron bell of the church began to bang-bang-bang. The sun was down beyond the far-off, thin clear line of the western mesa, the light had ceased glowing on the piñon-dotted foot-hills beyond the south pueblo. The square beneath was thick with people. And the Indians began to come out of church.

Two Indian women brought a little dressed-up Madonna to her platform in the green starting-bower. Then the men slowly gathered round the drum. The bell clanged. The tomtom beat. The men slowly uplifted their voices. The wild music resounded strangely against the banging of that iron bell, the silence of the many faces, as the group of Indians in their sheets and their best blankets, and in their ear-rings and brilliant scarlet trousers, or emerald trousers, or purple trousers, trimmed with beads, trod the slow bird-dance sideways, in feet of beaded moccasins, or yellow doeskin moccasins, singing all the time like drumming coyotes, slowly down and across the bridge to the south side, and up the incline to the south kiva. One or two Apaches in their beaded waistcoats and big black hats were among the singers, distinguishable by their thick build also. An old Navajo chief was among the encouragers.

As dusk fell, the singers came back under a certain house by the south kiva, and as they passed under the platform they broke and dispersed; it was over. They seemed as if they were grinning subtly as they went: grinning at being there in all that white crowd of inquisitives. It must have been a sort of ordeal to sing and tread the slow dance between that solid wall of silent, impassive white faces. But the Indians seemed to take no notice. And the crowd only silently, impassively watched. Watched with that strange, static American quality of *laissez-faire* and of indomitable curiosity.

THE FUTURE OF THE NOVEL (1922–23)

You talk about the future of the baby, little cherub, when he's in the cradle cooing; and it's a romantic, glamorous subject. You also talk, with the parson, about the future of the wicked old grandfather who is at last lying on his death-bed. And there again you have a subject for much vague emotion, chiefly of fear this time.

How do we feel about the novel? Do we bounce with joy thinking of the wonderful novelistic days ahead? Or do we grimly shake our heads and hope the wicked creature will be spared a little longer? Is the novel on his death-bed, old sinner? Or is he just toddling round his cradle, sweet little thing? Let us have another look at him before we decide this rather serious case.

There he is, the monster with many faces, many branches to him, like a tree: the modern novel. And he is almost dual, like Siamese twins. On the one hand, the pale-faced, high-browed, earnest novel, which you have to take seriously; on the other, that smirking, rather plausible hussy, the popular novel.

Let us just for the moment feel the pulses of *Ulysses* and of Miss Dorothy Richardson and M. Marcel Proust, on the earnest side of Briareus; on the other, the throb of *The Sheik* and Mr Zane Grey, and, if you will, Mr Robert Chambers and the rest. Is *Ulysses* in his cradle? Oh, dear! What a grey face! And *Pointed Roofs*, are they a gay little toy for nice little girls? And M. Proust?

Alas! You can hear the death-rattle in their throats. They can hear it themselves. They are listening to it with acute interest, trying to discover whether the intervals are minor thirds or major fourths. Which is rather infantile, really.

So there you have the 'serious' novel, dying in a very long-drawn-out fourteen-volume death-agony, and absorbedly, childishly interested in the phenomenon. 'Did I feel a twinge in my little toe, or didn't I?' asks every character of Mr Joyce or of Miss Richardson or M. Proust. Is my aura a blend of frankincense and orange pekoe and boot-blacking, or is it myrrh and bacon-fat and Shetland tweed? The audience round the death-bed gapes for the answer. And when, in a sepulchral tone, the answer comes at length, after hundreds of pages: 'It is none of these, it is abysmal chloro-coryambasis,' the audience quivers all over, and murmurs: "That's just how I feel myself.'

Which is the dismal, long-drawn-out comedy of the death-bed of the serious novel. It is self-consciousness picked into such fine bits that the bits are most of them invisible, and you have to go by smell. Through thousands and thousands of pages Mr Joyce and Miss Richardson tear themselves to pieces, strip their smallest emotions to the finest threads, till you feel you are sewed inside a wool mattress that is being slowly shaken up, and you are turning to wool along with the rest of the woolliness.

It's awful. And it's childish. It really is childish, after a certain age, to be absorbedly self-conscious. One has to be self-conscious at seventeen: still a little self-conscious at twenty-seven; but if we are going it strong at thirty-seven, then it is a sign of arrested development, nothing else. And if it is still continuing at forty-seven, it is obvious senile precocity.

And there's the serious novel: senile-precocious. Absorbedly, childishly concerned with *what I am*. 'I am this, I am that, I am the other. My reactions are such, and such, and such. And, oh, Lord, if I liked to watch myself closely enough, if I liked to analyse my feelings minutely, as I unbutton my gloves, instead of saying crudely I unbuttoned them, then I could go on to a million pages instead of a thousand. In fact, the more I come to think of it, it is gross, it is uncivilized bluntly to say: I unbuttoned my gloves. After all, the absorbing adventure of it! Which button did I begin with?' etc.

The people in the serious novels are so absorbedly concerned with themselves and what they feel and don't feel, and how they react to every mortal button; and their audience as frenziedly absorbed in the application of the author's discoveries to their own reactions: 'That's me! That's exactly it! I'm just finding myself in this book!' Why, this is more than death-bed, it is almost post-mortem behaviour.

Some convulsion or cataclysm will have to get this serious novel out of its self-consciousness. The last great war made it worse. What's to be done? Because, poor thing, it's really young yet. The novel has never become fully adult. It has never quite grown to years of discretion. It has always youthfully hoped for the best, and felt rather sorry for itself on the last page. Which is just childish. The childishness has become very long-drawn-out. So very many adolescents who drag their adolescence on into their forties and their fifties and their sixties! There needs some sort of surgical operation, somewhere.

Then the popular novels – the *Sheiks* and *Babbitts* and Zane Grey novels. They are just as self-conscious, only they do have more illusions about themselves. The heroines do think they are lovelier, and more fascinating, and purer. The heroes do see themselves more heroic, braver, more chivalrous, more fetching. The mass of the populace 'find themselves' in the popular novels. But nowadays it's a funny sort of self they find. A Sheik with a whip up his sleeve, and a heroine with weals on her back, but adored in the end, adored, the whip out of sight, but the weals still faintly visible.

It's a funny sort of self they discover in the popular novels. And the essential moral of *If Winter Comes*, for example, is so shaky. 'The gooder you are, the worse it is for you, poor you, oh, poor you. Don't you be so blimey good, it's not good enough.' Or *Babbitt:* 'Go on, you make your pile, and then pretend you're too good for it. Put it over the rest of the grabbers that way. They're only pleased with themselves when they've made their pile. You go one better.'

Always the same sort of baking-powder gas to make you rise: the soda counteracting the cream of tartar, and the tartar counteracted by the soda. Sheik heroines, duly whipped, wildly adored. Babbitts with solid fortunes, weeping from self-pity. Winter-Comes heroes as good as pie, hauled off to jail. *Moral:* Don't be too good, because you'll go to jail for it. *Moral:* Don't feel sorry for yourself till you've made your pile and don't need to feel sorry for yourself. *Moral:* Don't let him adore you till he's whipped you into it. Then you'll be partners in mild crime as well as in holy matrimony.

Which again is childish. Adolescence which can't grow up. Got into the self-conscious rut and going crazy, quite crazy in it. Carrying on their adolescence into middle age and old age, like the looney Cleopatra in *Dombey and Son*, murmuring 'Rose-coloured curtains' with her dying breath.

The future of the novel? Poor old novel, it's in a rather dirty, messy tight corner. And it's either got to get over the wall or knock a hole through it. In other words, it's got to grow up. Put away childish things like: 'Do I love the girl, or don't I?' – 'Am I pure and sweet, or am I not?' – 'Do I unbutton my right glove first, or my left?' – 'Did my mother ruin my life by refusing to drink the cocoa which my bride had boiled for her?' These questions and their answers don't really interest me any more, though the world still goes sawing them over. I simply don't care for any of these things now, though I used to. The purely emotional and self-analytical stunts are played out in me. I'm finished. I'm deaf to the whole band. But I'm neither *blasé* nor cynical, for all that. I'm just interested in something else.

Supposing a bomb were put under the whole scheme of things, what would we be after? What feelings do we want to carry through into the next epoch? What feelings will carry us through? What is the underlying impulse in us that will provide the motive power for a new state of things, when this democratic-industrial-lovey-dovey-darling-take-me-to-mamma state of things is bust?

What next? That's what interests me. 'What now?' is no fun any more.

If you wish to look into the past for what-next books, you can go back to the Greek philosophers. Plato's Dialogues are queer little novels. It seems to me it was the greatest pity in the world, when philosophy and fiction got split. They used to be one, right from the days of myth. Then they went and parted, like a nagging married couple, with Aristotle and Thomas Aquinas and that beastly Kant. So the novel went sloppy, and philosophy went abstract-dry. The two should come together again – in the novel.

You've got to find a new impulse for new things in mankind, and it's really fatal to find it through abstraction. No, no; philosophy and religion, they've both gone too far on the algebraical tack: Let X stand for sheep and Y for goats: then X minus Y equals Heaven, and X plus Y equals Earth, and Y minus X equals Hell. Thank you! But what coloured shirt does X have on?

The novel has a future. It's got to have the courage to tackle new propositions without using abstractions; it's got to present us with new, really new feelings, a whole line of new emotion, which will get us out of the emotional rut. Instead of snivelling about what is and has been, or inventing new sensations in the old line, it's got to break a way through, like a hole in the wall. And the public will scream and say it is sacrilege: because, of course, when you've been jammed for a long time in a tight corner, and you get really used to its stuffiness and its tightness, till you find it suffocatingly cozy; then, of course, you're horrified when you see a new glaring hole in what was your cosy wall. You're horrified. You back away from the cold stream of fresh air as if it were killing you. But gradually, first one and then another of the sheep filters through the gap, and finds a new world outside.

PARIS LETTER (1924)

I promised to write a letter to you from Paris. Probably I should have forgotten, but I saw a little picture – or sculpture – in the Tuileries, of Hercules slaying the Centaur, and that reminded me. I had so much rather the Centaur had slain Hercules, and men had never developed souls. Seems to me they're the greatest ailment humanity ever had. However, they've got it.

Paris is still monumental and handsome. Along the river where its splendours are, there's no denying its man-made beauty. The poor, pale little Seine runs rapidly north to the sea, the sky is pale, pale jade overhead, greenish and Parisian, the trees of black wire stand in rows, and flourish their black wire brushes against a low sky of jade-pale cobwebs, and the huge dark-grey palaces rear up their masses of stone and slope off towards the sky still with a massive, satisfying suggestion of pyramids. There is something noble and man-made about it all.

My wife says she wishes that grandeur still squared its shoulders on the earth. She wishes she could sit sumptuously in the river windows of the Tuileries, and see a royal spouse – who wouldn't be me – cross the bridge at the head of a tossing, silk and silver cavalcade. She wishes she had a bevy of ladies-in-waiting around her, as a peacock has its tail, as she crossed the weary expanses of pavement in the Champs Elysées.

Well, she can have it. At least, she can't. The world has lost its faculty for splendour, and Paris is like an old, weary peacock that sports a bunch of dirty twigs at its rump, where it used to have a tail. Democracy has collapsed into more and more democracy, and men, particularly Frenchmen, have collapsed into little, rather insignificant, rather wistful, rather nice and helplessly commonplace little fellows who rouse one's mother-instinct and make one feel they should be tucked away in bed and left to sleep, like Rip Van Winkle, till the rest of the storms rolled by.

It's a queer thing to sit in the Tuileries on a Sunday afternoon and watch the crowd drag through the galleries. Instead of a gay and wicked court, the weary, weary crowd, that looks as if it had nothing at heart to keep it going. As if the human creature had been dwindling and dwindling through the processes of democracy, amid the ponderous ridicule of the aristocratic setting; till soon he will dwindle right away.

Oh, those galleries. Oh, those pictures and those statues of nude, nude women: nude, nude, insistently and hopelessly nude. At last the eyes fall in absolute weariness, the moment they catch sight of a bit of pink-and-white painting, or a pair of white marble *fesses*. It becomes an inquisition; like being forced to go on eating pink marzipan icing. And yet there is a fat and very undistinguished bourgeois with a little beard and a fat and hopelessly petit-bourgeoise wife and awful little girl, standing in front of a huge heap of twisting marble, while he, with a goose-grease unctuous simper, strokes the marble hip of the huge marble female, and points out its niceness *to his wife*. She is not in the least jealous. She knows, no doubt, that her own hip and the marble hip are the only ones he will stroke without paying prices, one of which, and the last he could pay, would be the price of spunk.

It seems to me the French are just worn out. And not nearly so much with the late great war as with the pink nudities of women. The men are just worn out, making offerings on the shrine of Aphrodite in elastic garters. And the women are worn out, keeping the men up to it. The rest is all nervous exasperation.

And the table. One shouldn't forget that other, four-legged mistress of man, more unwitherable than Cleopatra. The table. The good kindly tables of Paris, with Coquilles Saint Martin, and escargots and oysters and Chateaubriands and the good red wine. If they can afford it, the men sit and eat themselves pink. And no wonder. But the Aphrodite in a hard black hat opposite, when she has eaten herself also pink, is going to insist on further delights, to which somebody has got to play up. Weariness isn't the word for it.

May the Lord deliver us from our own enjoyments, we gasp at last. And he won't. We actually have to deliver ourselves.

One goes out again from the restaurant comfortably fed and soothed with a food and drink, to find the pale-jade sky of Paris crumbling in a wet dust of rain; motor-cars skidding till they turn clean around, and are facing south when they were going north: a boy on a bicycle coming smack, and picking himself up with his bicycle pump between his legs: and the men still fishing, as if it were a Sisyphus penalty, with long sticks fishing for invisible fishes in the Seine: and the huge buildings of the Louvre and the Tuileries standing ponderously, with their Parisian suggestion of pyramids.

And no, in the old style of grandeur I never want to be grand. That sort of regality, that builds itself up in piles of stone and masonry, and prides itself on living inside the monstrous heaps, once they're built, is not for me. My wife asks why she can't live in the Petit Palais, while she's in Paris. Well, even if she might, she'd live alone.

I don't believe any more in democracy. But I can't believe in the old sort of aristocracy, either, nor can I wish it back, splendid as it was. What I believe in is the old Homeric aristocracy, when the grandeur was inside the man, and he lived in a simple wooden house. Then, the men that were grand inside themselves, like Ulysses, were the chieftains and the aristocrats by instinct and by choice. At least we'll hope so. And the Red Indians only knew the aristocrat by instinct. The leader was leader in his own being, not because he was somebody's son or had so much money.

It's got to be so again. They say it won't work. I say, why not? If men could once recognize the natural aristocrat when they set eyes on him, they can still. They can still choose him if they would.

But this business of dynasties is weariness. House of Valois, House of Tudor! Who would want to be a House, or a bit of a House! Let a man be a man, and damn the House business. I'm absolutely a democrat as far as that goes.

But that men are all brothers and all equal is a greater lie than the other. Some men are always aristocrats. But it doesn't go by birth. A always contains B, but B is not contained in C.

Democracy, however, says that there is no such thing as an aristocrat. All men have two legs and one nose, ergo, they are all alike. Nosily and leggily, maybe. But otherwise, very different.

Democracy says that B is not contained in C, and neither is it contained in A. B, that is, the aristocrat, does not exist.

Now this is palpably a greater lie than the old dynastic life. Aristocracy truly does not go by birth. But it still goes. And the tradition of aristocracy will help it a lot.

The aristocrats tried to fortify themselves inside these palaces and these splendours. Regal Paris built up the external evidences of her regality. But the two-limbed man inside these vast shells died, poor worm, of over-encumbrance.

The natural aristocrat has got to fortify himself inside his own will, according to his own strength. The moment he builds himself external evidences, like palaces, he builds himself in, and commits his own doom. The moment he depends on his jewels, he has lost his virtue.

It always seems to me that the next civilization won't want to raise these ponderous, massive, deadly buildings that refuse to crumble away with their epoch and weigh men helplessly down. Neither palaces nor cathedrals nor any other hugenesses. Material simplicity is after all the highest sign of civilization. Here in Paris one knows it finally. The ponderous and depressing museum that is regal Paris. And living humanity like poor worms struggling inside the shell of history, all of them inside the museum. The dead life and the living life, all one museum.

Monuments, museums, permanencies, and ponderosities are all anathema. But brave men are for ever born, and nothing else is worth having.

A LETTER FROM GERMANY (1924)

We are going back to Paris tomorrow, so this is the last moment to write a letter from Germany. Only from the fringe of Germany, too.

It is a miserable journey from Paris to Nancy, through that Marne country, where the country still seems to have had the soul blasted out of it, though the dreary fields are ploughed and level, and the pale wire trees stand up. But it is all void and null. And in the villages, the smashed houses in the street rows, like rotten teeth between good teeth.

You come to Strasburg, and the people still talk Alsatian German, as ever, in spite of French shop-signs. The place feels dead. And full of cotton goods, white goods, from Mülhausen, from the factories that once were German. Such cheap white cotton goods, in a glut.

The cathedral front rearing up high and flat and fanciful, a sort of darkness in the dark, with round rose windows and long, long prisons of stone. Queer, that men should have ever wanted to put stone upon fanciful stone to such a height, without having it fall down. The Gothic! I was always glad when my card-castle fell. But these Goths and Alemans seemed to have a craze for peaky heights.

The Rhine is still the Rhine, the great divider. You feel it as you cross. The flat, frozen, watery places. Then the cold and curving river. Then the other side, seeming so cold, so empty, so frozen, so forsaken. The train stands and steams fiercely. Then it draws through the flat Rhine plain, past frozen pools of flood-water, and frozen fields, in the emptiness of this bit of occupied territory.

Immediately you are over the Rhine, the spirit of place has changed. There is no more attempt at the bluff of geniality. The marshy places are frozen. The fields are vacant. There seems nobody in the world.

It is as if the life had retreated eastwards. As if the Germanic life were slowly ebbing away from contact with western Europe, ebbing to the deserts of the east. And there stand the heavy, ponderous, round hills of the Black Forest, black with an inky blackness of Germanic trees, and patched with a whiteness of snow. They are like a series of huge, involved black mounds, obstructing the vision eastwards. You look at them from the Rhine plain, and know that you stand on an actual border, up against something.

The moment you are in Germany, you know. It feels empty, and, somehow, menacing. So must the Roman soldiers have watched those black, massive round hills: with a certain fear, and with the knowledge that they were at their own limit. A fear of the invisible natives. A fear of the invisible life lurking among the woods. A fear of their own opposite.

So it is with the French: this almost mystic fear. But one should not insult even one's fears.

Germany, this bit of Germany, is very different from what it was two-and-a-half years ago, when I was here. Then it was still open to Europe. Then it still looked to western Europe for a reunion, for a sort of reconciliation. Now that is over. The inevitable, mysterious barrier has fallen again, and the great leaning of the Germanic spirit is once more eastwards, towards Russia, towards Tartary. The strange vortex of Tartary has become the positive centre again, the positivity of western Europe is broken. The positivity of our civilization has broken. The influences that come, come invisibly out of Tartary. So that all Germany reads *Beasts, Men and Gods* with a kind of fascination. Returning again to the fascination of the destructive East, that produced Attila.

So it is at night. Baden-Baden is a little quiet place, all its guests gone. No more Turgenievs or Dostoievskys or Grand Dukes or King Edwards coming to drink the waters. All the outward effect of a world-famous watering-place. But empty now, a mere Black Forest village with the wagon-loads of timber going through, to the French.

The Rentenmark, the new gold mark of Germany, is abominably dear. Prices are high in England, but English money buys less in Baden than it buys in London, by a long chalk. And there is no work – consequently no money. Nobody buys anything, except absolute necessities. The shop-keepers are in despair. And there is less and less work.

Everybody gives up the telephone – can't afford it. The tram-cars don't run, except about three times a day to the station. Up to the Annaberg, the suburb, the lines are rusty, no trams ever go. The people can't afford the ten pfennigs for the fare. Ten pfennigs is an important sum now: one penny. It is really a hundred milliards of marks.

Money becomes insane, and people with it.

At night the place is almost dark, economizing light. Economy, economy, economy – that too becomes an insanity. Luckily the government keeps bread fairly cheap.

But at night you feel strange things stirring in the darkness, strange feelings stirring out of this still-unconquered Black Forest. You stiffen your backbone and you listen to the night. There is a sense of danger. It is not the people. They don't seem dangerous. Out of the very air comes a sense of danger, a queer, *bristling* feeling of uncanny danger.

Something has happened. Something has happened which has not yet eventuated. The old spell of the old world has broken, and the old, bristling, savage spirit has set in. The war did not break the old peace-and-production hope of the world, though it gave it a severe wrench. Yet the old peace-and-production hope still governs, at least the consciousness. Even in Germany it has not quite gone.

But it feels as if, virtually, it were gone. The last two years have done it. The hope in peace-and-production is broken. The old flow, the old adherence is ruptured. And a still older flow has set in. Back, back to the savage polarity of Tartary, and away from the polarity of civilized Christian Europe. This, it seems to me, has already happened. And it is a happening of far more profound import than any actual *event*. It is the father of the next phase of events.

And the feeling never relaxes. As you travel up the Rhine valley, still the same latent sense of danger, of silence, of suspension. Not that the people are actually planning or plotting or preparing. I don't believe it for a minute. But something has happened to the human soul, beyond all help. The human soul recoiling now from unison, and making itself strong elsewhere. The ancient spirit of pre-historic Germany coming back, at the end of history.

The same in Heidelberg. Heidelberg full, full, full of people. Students the same, youths with rucksacks the same, boys and maidens in gangs come down from the hills. The same, and not the same. These queer gangs of *Young Socialists*, youths and girls, with their non-materialistic professions, their half-mystic assertions, they strike one as strange. Something primitive, like loose, roving gangs of broken, scattered tribes, so they affect one. And the swarms of people somehow produce an impression of silence, of secrecy, of stealth. It is as if everything and everybody recoiled away from the old unison, as barbarians lurking in a wood recoil out of sight. The old habits remain. But the bulk of the people have no money. And the whole stream of feeling is reversed.

So you stand in the woods above the town and see the Neckar flowing green and swift and slippery out of the gulf of Germany, to the Rhine. And the sun sets slow and scarlet into the haze of the Rhine valley. And the old, pinkish stone of the ruined castle across looks sultry, the marshalry is in shadow below, the peaked roofs of old, tight Heidelberg compressed in its river gateway glimmer and glimmer out. There is a blue haze.

And it all looks as if the years were wheeling swiftly backwards, no more onwards. Like a spring that is broken, and whirls swiftly back, so time seems to be whirling with mysterious swiftness to a sort of death. Whirling to the ghost of the old Middle Ages of Germany, then to the Roman days, then to the days of the silent forest and the dangerous, lurking barbarians.

Something about the Germanic races is unalterable. White-skinned, elemental, and dangerous. Our civilization has come from the fusion of the dark-eyes with the blue. The meeting and mixing and mingling of the two races has been the joy of our ages. And the Celt has been there, alien, but necessary as some chemical reagent to the fusion. So the civilization of Europe rose up. So these cathedrals and these thoughts.

But now the Celt is the disintegrating agent. And the Latin and southern races are falling out of association with the northern races, the northern Germanic impulse is recoiling towards Tartary, the destructive vortex of Tartary.

It is a fate; nobody now can alter it. It is a fate. The very blood changes. Within the last three years, the very constituency of the blood has changed, in European veins. But particularly in Germanic veins.

At the same time, we have brought it about ourselves – by a Ruhr occupation, by an English nullity, and by a German false will. We have done it ourselves. But apparently it was not to be helped.

Quos vult perdere Deus, dementat prius.

PAN IN AMERICA (1924)

At the beginning of the Christian era, voices were heard off the coasts of Greece, out to sea, on the Mediterranean, wailing: 'Pan is dead! Great Pan is dead!'

The father of fauns and nymphs, satyrs and dryads and naiads was dead, with only the voices in the air to lament him. Humanity hardly noticed.

But who was he, really? Down the long lanes and overgrown ridings of history we catch odd glimpses of a lurking rustic god with a goat's white lightning in his eyes. A sort of fugitive, hidden among leaves, and laughing with the uncanny derision of one who feels himself defeated by something lesser than himself.

An outlaw, even in the early days of the gods. A sort of Ishmael among the bushes.

Yet always his lingering title: The Great God Pan. As if he was, or had been, the greatest.

Lurking among the leafy recesses, he was almost more demon than god. To be feared, not loved or approached. A man who should see Pan by daylight fell dead, as if blasted by lightning.

Yet you might dimly see him in the night, a dark body within the darkness. And then, it was a vision filling the limbs and the trunk of a man with power, as with new, strong-mounting sap. The Pan-power! You went on your way in the darkness secretly and subtly elated with blind energy, and you could cast a spell, by your mere presence, on women and on men. But particularly on women.

In the woods and the remote places ran the children of Pan, all the nymphs and fauns of the forest and the spring and the river and the rocks. These, too, it was dangerous to see by day. The man who looked up to see the white arms of a nymph flash as she darted behind the thick wild laurels away from him followed helplessly. He was a nympholept. Fascinated by the swift limbs and the wild, fresh sides of the nymph, he followed for ever, for ever, in the endless monotony of his desire. Unless came some wise being who could absolve him from the spell.

But the nymphs, running among the trees and curling to sleep under the bushes, made the myrtles blossom more gaily, and the spring bubble up with greater urge, and the birds splash with a strength of life. And the lithe flanks of the faun gave life to the oak-groves, the vast trees hummed with energy. And the wheat sprouted like green rain returning out of the ground, in the little fields, and the vine hung its black drops in abundance, urging a secret.

Gradually men moved into cities. And they loved the display of people better than the display of a tree. They liked the glory they got of overpowering one another in war. And, above all, they loved the vainglory of their own words, the pomp of argument and the vanity of ideas.

So Pan became old and grey-bearded and goat-legged, and his passion was degraded with the lust of senility. His power to blast and to brighten dwindled. His nymphs became coarse and vulgar.

Till at last the old Pan died, and was turned into the devil of the Christians. The old god Pan became the Christian devil, with the cloven hoofs and the horns, the tail, and the laugh of derision. Old Nick, the Old Gentleman who is responsible for all our wickednesses, but especially our sensual excesses – this is all that is left of the Great God Pan.

It is strange. It is a most strange ending for a god with such a name. Pan! All! That which is everything has goat's feet and a tail! With a black face!

This really is curious.

Yet this was all that remained of Pan, except that he acquired brimstone and hell-fire, for many, many centuries. The nymphs turned into the nasty-smelling witches of a Walpurgis night, and the fauns that danced became sorcerers riding the air, or fairies no bigger than your thumb.

But Pan keeps on being reborn, in all kinds of strange shapes. There he was, at the Renaissance. And in the eighteenth century he had quite a vogue. He gave rise to an 'ism,' and there were many pantheists, Wordsworth one of the first. They worshipped Nature in her sweet-and-pure aspect, her Lucy Gray aspect.

'Oft have I heard of Lucy Gray,' the school-child began to recite, on examination-day.

'So have I,' interrupted the bored inspector.

Lucy Gray, alas, was the form that William Wordsworth thought fit to give to the Great God Pan.

And then he crossed over to the young United States: I mean Pan did. Suddenly he gets a new name. He becomes the Oversoul, the Allness of everything. To this new Lucifer Gray of a Pan Whitman sings the famous *Song of Myself*: 'I am All, and All is Me.' That is: 'I am Pan, and Pan is me.'

The old goat-legged gentleman from Greece thoughtfully strokes his beard, and answers: 'All A is B, but all B is not A.' Aristotle did not live for nothing. All Walt is Pan, but all Pan is not Walt.

This, even to Whitman, is incontrovertible. So the new American pantheism collapses.

Then the poets dress up a few fauns and nymphs, to let them run riskily – oh, would there were any risk! – in their private 'grounds.' But, alas, these tame guinea-pigs soon became boring. Change the game.

We still *pretend* to believe that there is One mysterious Something-or-other back of Everything, ordaining all things for the ultimate good of humanity. It wasn't back of the Germans in 1914, of course, and whether it's back of the bolshevist is still a grave question. But still, it's back of *us*, so that's all right.

Alas, poor Pan! Is this what you've come to? Legless, hornless, faceless, even smileless, you are less than everything or anything, except a lie.

And yet here, in America, the oldest of all, old Pan is still alive. When Pan was greatest, he was not even Pan. He was nameless and unconceived, mentally. Just as a small baby new from the womb may say Mama! Dada! whereas in the womb it said nothing; so humanity, in the womb of Pan, said nought. But when humanity was born into a separate idea of itself, it said *Pan*.

In the days before man got too much separated off from the universe, he *was* Pan, along with all the rest.

As a tree still is. A strong-willed, powerful thing-in-itself, reaching up and reaching down. With a powerful will of its own it thrusts green hands and huge limbs at the light above, and sends huge legs and gripping toes down, down between the earth and rocks, to the earth's middle.

Here, on this little ranch under the Rocky Mountains, a big pine tree rises like a guardian spirit in front of the cabin where we live. Long, long ago the Indians blazed it. And the lightning, or the storm, has cut off its crest. Yet its column is always there, alive and changeless, alive and changing. The tree has its own aura of life. And in winter the snow slips off it, and in June it sprinkles down its little catkin-like pollen-tips, and it hisses in the wind, and it makes a silence within a silence. It is a great tree, under which the house is built. And the tree is still within the allness of Pan. At night, when the lamplight shines out of the window, the great trunk dimly shows, in the near darkness, like an Egyptian column, supporting some powerful mystery in the over-branching darkness. By day, it is just a tree.

It is just a tree. The chipmunks skelter a little way up it, the little black-and-white birds, tree-creepers, walk quick as mice on its rough perpendicular, tapping; the bluejays throng on its branches, high up, at dawn, and in the afternoon you hear the faintest rustle of many little wild doves alighting in its upper remoteness. It is a tree, which is still Pan.

And we live beneath it, without noticing. Yet sometimes, when one suddenly looks far up and sees those wild doves there, or when one glances quickly at the inhuman-human hammering of a woodpecker, one realizes that the tree is asserting itself as much as I am. It gives out life, as I give out life. Our two lives meet and cross one another, unknowingly: the tree's life penetrates my life, and my life the tree's. We cannot live near one another, as we do, without affecting one another.

The tree gathers up earth-power from the dark bowels of the earth, and a roaming sky-glitter from above. And all unto itself, which is a tree, woody, enormous, slow but unyielding with life, bristling with acquisitive energy, obscurely radiating some of its great strength.

It vibrates its presence into my soul, and I am with Pan. I think no man could live near a pine tree and remain quite suave and supple and compliant. Something fierce and bristling is communicated. The piny sweetness is rousing and defiant, like turpentine, the noise of the needles is keen with æons of sharpness. In the volleys of wind from the western desert, the tree hisses and resists. It does not lean eastward at all. It resists with a vast force of resistance, from within itself, and its column is a ribbed, magnificent assertion.

I have become conscious of the tree, and of its interpenetration into my life. Long ago, the Indians must have been even more acutely conscious of it, when they blazed it to leave their mark on it.

I am conscious that it helps to change me, vitally. I am even conscious that shivers of energy cross my living plasm, from the tree, and I become a degree more like unto the tree, more bristling and turpentiney, in Pan. And the tree gets a certain shade and alertness of my life, within itself.

Of course, if I like to cut myself off, and say it is all bunk, a tree is merely so much lumber not yet sawn, then in a great measure I shall *be* cut off. So much depends on one's attitude. One can shut many, many doors of receptivity in oneself; or one can open many doors that are shut.

I prefer to open my doors to the coming of the tree. Its raw earth-power and its raw sky-power, its resinous erectness and resistance, its sharpness of hissing needles and relentlessness of roots, all that goes to the primitive savageness of a pine tree, goes also to the strength of man.

Give me of your power, then, oh tree! And I will give you of mine.

And this is what men must have said, more naïvely, less sophisticatedly, in the days when all was Pan. It is what, in a way, the aboriginal Indians still say, and still *mean*, intensely: especially when they dance the sacred dance, with the tree; or with the spruce twigs tied above their elbows.

Give me your power, oh tree, to help me in my life. And I will give you my power: even symbolized in a rag torn from my clothing.

This is the oldest Pan.

Or again, I say: 'Oh you, you big tree, standing so strong and swallowing juice from the earth's inner body, warmth from the sky, beware of me. Beware of me, because I am strongest. I am going to cut you down and take your life and make you into beams for my house, and into a fire. Prepare to deliver up your life to me.'

Is this any less true than when the lumberman glances at a pine tree, sees if it will cut good lumber, dabs a mark or a number upon it, and goes his way absolutely without further thought or feeling? Is he truer to life? Is it truer to life to insulate oneself entirely from the influence of the tree's life, and to walk about in an inanimate forest of standing lumber, marketable in St Louis, Mo.? Or is it truer to life to know, with a pantheistic sensuality, that the tree has its own life, its own assertive existence, its own living relatedness to me: that my life is added to, or militated against, by the tree's life?

Which is really truer?

Which is truer, to live among the living, or to run on wheels?

And who can sit with the Indians around a big camp-fire of logs, in the mountains at night, when a man rises and turns his breast and his curiously-smiling bronze face away from the blaze, and stands voluptuously warming his thighs and buttocks and loins, his back to the fire, faintly smiling the inscrutable Pan-smile into the dark trees surrounding, without hearing him say, in the Pan voice: 'Aha! Tree! Aha! Tree! Who has triumphed now? I drank the heat of your blood into my face and breast, and now I am drinking it into my loins and buttocks and legs, oh tree! I am drinking your heat right through me, oh tree! Fire is life, and I take your life for mine. I am drinking it up, oh tree, even into my buttocks. Aha! Tree! I am warm! I am strong! I am happy, tree, in this cold night in the mountains!'

And the old man, glancing up and seeing the flames flapping in flamy rags at the dark smoke, in the upper fire-hurry towards the stars and the dark spaces between the stars, sits stonily and inscrutably: yet one knows that he is saying: 'Go back, oh fire! Go back like honey! Go back, honey of life, to where you came from, before you were hidden in the tree. The trees climb into the sky and steal the honey of the sun, like bears stealing from a hollow tree-trunk. But when the tree falls and is put on to the fire, the honey flames and goes straight back to where it came from. And the smell of burning pine is as the smell of honey.'

So the old man says, with his lightless Indian eyes. But he is careful never to utter one word of the mystery. Speech is the death of Pan, who can but laugh and sound the reed-flute.

Is it better, I ask you, to cross the room and turn on the heat at the radiator, glancing at the thermometer and saying: 'We're just a bit below the level, in here'? Then to go back to the newspaper!

What can a man do with his life but live it? And what does life consist in, save a vivid relatedness between the man and the living universe that surrounds him? Yet man insulates himself more and more into mechanism, and repudiates everything but the machine and the contrivance of which he himself is master, god in the machine.

Morning comes, and white ash lies in the fire-hollow, and the old man looks at it broodingly.

'The fire is gone,' he says in the Pan silence, that is so full of unutterable things. 'Look! there is no more tree. We drank his warmth, and he is gone. He is way, way off in the sky, his smoke is in the blueness, with the sweet smell of a pine-wood fire, and his yellow flame is in the sun. It is morning, with the ashes of night. There is no more tree. Tree is gone. But perhaps there is fire among the ashes. I shall blow it, and it will be alive. There is always fire, between the tree that goes and the tree that stays. One day I shall go –'

So they cook their meat, and rise, and go in silence.

There is a big rock towering up above the trees, a cliff. And silently a man glances at it. You hear him say, without speech:

'Oh, you big rock! If a man fall down from you, he dies. Don't let me fall down from you. Oh, you big pale rock, you are so still, you know lots of things. You know a lot. Help me, then, with your stillness. I go to find deer. Help me find deer.'

And the man slips aside, and secretly lays a twig, or a pebble, some little object in a niche of the rock, as a pact between him and the rock. The rock will give him some of its radiant-cold stillness and enduring presence, and he makes a symbolic return, of gratitude.

Is it foolish? Would it have been better to invent a gun, to shoot his game from a great distance, so that he need not approach it with any of that living stealth and preparedness with which one live thing approaches another? Is it better to have a machine in one's hands, and so avoid the life-contact: the trouble! the pains! Is it better to see the rock as a mere nothing, not worth noticing because it has no value, and you can't eat it as you can a deer?

But the old hunter steals on, in the stillness of the eternal Pan, which is so full of soundless sounds. And in his soul he is saying: 'Deer! Oh, you thin-legged deer! I am coming! Where are you, with your feet like little stones bounding down a hill? I know you. Yes, I know you. But you don't know me. You don't know where I am, and you don't know me, anyhow. But I know you. I am thinking of you. I shall get you. I've got to get you. I got to; so it will be. – I shall get you, and shoot an arrow right in you.'

In this state of abstraction, and subtle, hunter's communion with the quarry – a weird psychic connexion between hunter and hunted – the man creeps into the mountains.

And even a white man who is a born hunter must fall into this state. Gun or no gun! He projects his deepest, most primitive hunter's consciousness abroad, and finds his game, not by accident, nor even chiefly by looking for signs, but primarily by a psychic attraction, a sort of telepathy: the hunter's telepathy. Then when he finds his quarry, he aims with a pure, spellbound volition. If there is no flaw in his abstracted huntsman's *will*, he cannot miss. Arrow or bullet, it flies like a movement of pure will, straight to the spot. And the deer, once she has let her quivering alertness be overmastered or stilled by the hunter's subtle, hypnotic, *following* spell, she cannot escape.

This is Pan, the Pan-mystery, the Pan-power. What can men who sit at home in their studies, and drink hot milk and have lamb's-wool slippers on their feet, and write anthropology, what *can* they possibly know about men, the men of Pan?

Among the creatures of Pan there is an eternal struggle for life, between lives. Man, defenceless, rapacious man, has needed the qualities of every living thing, at one time or other. The hard, silent abidingness of rock, the surging resistance of a tree, the still evasion of a puma, the dogged earth-knowledge of the bear, the light alertness of the deer, the sky-prowling vision of the eagle: turn by turn man has needed the power of every living thing. Tree, stone, or hill, river, or little stream, or waterfall, or salmon in the fall – man can be master and complete in himself, only by assuming the living powers of each of them, as the occasion requires.

He used to make himself master by a great effort of will, and sensitive, intuitive cunning, and immense labour of body.

Then he discovered the 'idea.' He found that all things were related by certain *laws*. The moment man learned to abstract, he began to make engines that would do the work of his body. So, instead of concentrating upon his quarry, or upon the living things which made his universe, he concentrated upon the engines or instruments which should intervene between him and the living universe, and give him mastery.

This was the death of the great Pan. The idea and the engine came between man and all things, like a death. The old connexion, the old Allness, was severed, and can never be ideally restored. Great Pan is dead.

Yet what do we live for, except to live? Man has lived to conquer the phenomenal universe. To a great extent he has succeeded. With all the mechanism of the human world, man is to a great extent master of all life, and of most phenomena.

And what then? Once you have conquered a thing, you have lost it. Its real relation to you collapses.

A conquered world is no good to man. He sits stupefied with boredom upon his conquest.

We need the universe to live again, so that we can live with it. A conquered universe, a dead Pan, leaves us nothing to live with.

You have to abandon the conquest, before Pan will live again. You have to live to live, not to conquer. What's the good of conquering even the North Pole, if after the conquest you've nothing left but an inert fact? Better leave it a mystery.

It was better to be a hunter in the woods of Pan, than it is to be a clerk in a city store. The hunter hungered, laboured, suffered tortures of fatigue. But at least he lived in a ceaseless living relation to his surrounding universe.

At evening, when the deer was killed, he went home to the tents, and threw down the deer-meat on the swept place before the tent of his women. And the women came out to greet him softly, with a sort of reverence, as he stood before the meat, the life-stuff. He came back spent, yet full of power, bringing the life-stuff. And the children looked with black eyes at the meat, and at that wonder-being, the man, the bringer of meat.

Perhaps the children of the store-clerk look at their father with a *tiny* bit of the same mystery. And perhaps the clerk feels a fragment of the old glorification, when he hands his wife the paper dollars.

But about the tents the women move silently. Then when the

cooking-fire dies low, the man crouches in silence and toasts meat on a stick, while the dogs lurk round like shadows and the children watch avidly. The man eats as the sun goes down. And as the glitter departs, he says: 'Lo, the sun is going, and I stay. All goes, but still I stay. Power of deer-meat is in my belly, power of sun is in my body. I am tired, but it is with power. There the small moon gives her first sharp sign. So! So! I watch her. I will give her something; she is very sharp and bright, and I do not know her power. Lo! I will give the woman something for this moon, which troubles me above the sunset, and has power. Lo! how very curved and sharp she is! Lo! how she troubles me!'

Thus, always aware, always watchful, subtly poising himself in the world of Pan, among the powers of the living universe, he sustains his life and is sustained. There is no boredom, because *everything* is alive and active, and danger is inherent in all movement. The contact between all things is keen and wary: for wariness is also a sort of reverence, or respect. And nothing, in the world of Pan, may be taken for granted.

So when the fire is extinguished, and the moon sinks, the man says to the woman: 'Oh, woman, be very soft, be very soft and deep towards me, with the deep silence. Oh, woman, do not speak and stir and wound me with the sharp horns of yourself. Let me come into the deep, soft places, the dark, soft places deep as between the stars. Oh, let me lose there the weariness of the day: let me come in the power of the night. Oh, do not speak to me, nor break the deep night of my silence and my power. Be softer than dust, and darker than any flower. Oh, woman, wonderful is the craft of your softness, the distance of your dark depths. Oh, open silently the deep that has no end, and do not turn the horns of the moon against me.'

This is the might of Pan, and the power of Pan.

And still, in America, among the Indians, the oldest Pan is alive. But here, also, dying fast.

It is useless to glorify the savage. For he will kill Pan with his own hands, for the sake of a motor-car. And a bored savage, for whom Pan is dead, is the stupefied image of all boredom.

And we cannot return to the primitive life, to live in tepees and hunt with bows and arrows.

Yet live we must. And once life has been conquered, it is pretty difficult to live. What are we going to do, with a conquered universe? The Pan relationship, which the world of man once had with all the world, was better than anything man has now. The savage, today, if you give him the chance, will become more mechanical and unliving than any civilized man. But civilized man, having conquered the universe, may as well leave off bossing it. Because, when all is said and done, life itself consists in a live relatedness between man and his universe: sun, moon, stars, earth, trees, flowers, birds, animals, men, everything – and not in a 'conquest' of anything by anything. Even the conquest of the air makes the world smaller, tighter, and more airless.

And whether we are a store-clerk or a bus-conductor, we can still choose between the living universe of Pan, and the mechanical conquered universe of modern humanity. The machine has no windows. But even the most mechanized human being has only got his windows nailed up, or bricked in.

THE BAD SIDE OF BOOKS
INTRODUCTION TO *A BIBLIOGRAPHY OF THE WRITINGS OF D. H. LAWRENCE* (1924)

There doesn't seem much excuse for me, sitting under a little cedar tree at the foot of the Rockies, looking at the pale desert disappearing westward, with hummocks of shadow rising in the stillness of incipient autumn, this morning, the near pine trees perfectly still, the sunflowers and the purple Michaelmas daisies moving for the first time, this morning, in an invisible breath of breeze, to be writing an introduction to a bibliography.

Books to me are incorporate things, voices in the air, that do not disturb the haze of autumn, and visions that don't blot the sunflowers. What do I care for first or last editions? I have never read one of my own published works. To me, no book has a date, no book has a binding.

What do I care if 'e' is somewhere upside down, or 'g' comes from the wrong font? I really don't.

And when I force myself to remember, what pleasure is there in that? The very first copy of *The White Peacock* that was ever sent out, I put into my mother's hands when she was dying. She looked at the outside, and then at the title-page, and then at me, with darkening eyes. And though she loved me so much, I think she doubted whether it could be much of a book, since no one more important than I had written it. Somewhere, in the helpless privacies of her being, she had wistful respect for me. But for me in the face of the world, not much. This David would never get a stone across at Goliath. And why try? Let Goliath alone! Anyway, she was beyond reading my first immortal work. It was put aside, and I never wanted to see it again. She never saw it again.

After the funeral, my father struggled through half a page, and it might as well have been Hottentot.

'And what dun they gi'e thee for that, lad?'

'Fifty pounds, father.'

'Fifty pounds!' He was dumbfounded, and looked at me with shrewd eyes, as if I were a swindler. 'Fifty pounds! An' tha's niver done a day's hard work in thy life.'

I think to this day, he looks upon me as a sort of cleverish swindler, who gets money for nothing: a sort of Ernest Hooley. And my sister says, to my utter amazement: 'You always were lucky!'

Somehow, it is the actual corpus and substance, the actual paper and rag volume of any of my works, that calls up these personal feelings and memories. It is the miserable tome itself which somehow delivers me to the vulgar mercies of the world. The voice inside is mine for ever. But the beastly marketable chunk of published volume is a bone which every dog presumes to pick with me.

William Heinemann published *The White Peacock*. I saw him once; and then I realized what an immense favour he was doing me. As a matter of fact, he treated me quite well.

I remember at the last minute, when the book was all printed and ready to bind: some even bound: they sent me in great haste a certain page with a marked paragraph. Would I remove this paragraph, as it might be considered 'objectionable,' and substitute an exactly identical number of obviously harmless words.

Hastily I did so. And later, I noticed that the two pages, on one of which was the altered paragraph, were rather loose, not properly bound into the book. Only my mother's copy had the paragraph unchanged.

I have wondered often if Heinemann's just altered the 'objectionable' bit in the first little batch of books they sent out, then left the others as first printed. Or whether they changed all but the one copy they sent me ahead.

It was my first experience of the objectionable. Later, William Heinemann said he thought *Sons and Lovers* one of the dirtiest books he had ever read. He refused to publish it. I should not have thought the deceased gentleman's reading had been so circumspectly narrow.

I forget the first appearance of *The Trespasser* and *Sons and Lovers*. I always hide the fact of publication from myself as far as possible. One writes, even at this moment, to some mysterious presence in the air. If that presence were not there, and one thought of even a single solitary actual reader, the paper would remain for ever white.

But I always remember how, in a cottage by the sea, in Italy, I rewrote almost entirely that play, *The Widowing of Mrs Holroyd*, right on the proofs which Mitchell Kennerley had sent me. And he nobly forbore with me.

But then he gave me a nasty slap. He published *Sons and Lovers* in America, and one day, joyful, arrived a cheque for twenty pounds. Twenty pounds in those days was a little fortune: and as it was a windfall, it was handed over to Madame; the first pin-money she had seen. Alas and alack, there was an alteration in the date of the cheque, and the bank would not cash it. It was returned to Mitchell Kennerley, but that was the end of it. He never made good, and never to this day made any further payment for *Sons and Lovers*. Till this year of grace 1924, America has had that, my most popular book, for nothing – as far as I am concerned.*

Then came the first edition of *The Rainbow*. I'm afraid I set my rainbow in the sky too soon, before, instead of after, the deluge. Methuen published that book, and he almost wept before the magistrate, when he was summoned for bringing out a piece of indecent literature. He said he did not know the dirty thing he had been handling, he had not read the work, his reader had mis-advised him – and Peccavi! Peccavi! wept the now be-knighted gentleman. Then around me arose such a fussy sort of interest, as when a really scandalous bit of scandal is being whispered about one. In print my fellow-authors kept scrupulously silent, lest a bit of the tar might stick to them. Later Arnold Bennett and May Sinclair raised a kindly protest. But John Galsworthy told me, very calmly and *ex cathedra*, he thought the book a failure as a work of art. They think as they please. But why not wait till I ask them, before they deliver an opinion to me? Especially as impromptu opinions by elderly authors are apt to damage him who gives as much as him who takes.

There is no more indecency or impropriety in *The Rainbow* than there is in this autumn morning – I, who say so, ought to know. And when I open my mouth, let no dog bark.

So much for the first edition of *The Rainbow*. The only copy of any of my books I ever keep is my copy of Methuen's *Rainbow*. Because the American editions have all been mutilated. And this is almost my favourite among my novels: this, and *Women in Love*. And I should really be best pleased if it were never reprinted at all, and only those blue, condemned volumes remained extant.

Since *The Rainbow*, one submits to the process of publication

---

* In a letter to Mr Edward Garnett, dated April 22, 1914, Lawrence acknow-ledges the receipt of £35 from Mr Mitchell Kennerley. *Letters of D. H. Lawrence*, p. 192 (American edition).

as to a necessary evil: as souls are said to submit to the necessary evil of being born into the flesh. The wind bloweth where it listeth. And one must submit to the processes of one's day. Personally, I have no belief in the vast public. I believe that only the winnowed few can care. But publishers, like thistle, must set innumerable seeds on the wind, knowing most will miscarry.

To the vast public, the autumn morning is only a sort of stage background against which they can display their own mechanical importance. But to some men still the trees stand up and look around at the daylight, having woven the two ends of darkness together into visible being and presence. And soon, they will let go the two ends of darkness again, and disappear. A flower laughs once, and having had his laugh, chuckles off into seed, and is gone. Whence? Whither? Who knows, who cares? That little laugh of achieved being is all.

So it is with books. To every man who struggles with his own soul in mystery, a book that is a book flowers once, and seeds, and is gone. First editions or forty-first are only the husks of it.

Yet if it amuses a man to save the husks of the flower that opened once for the first time, one can understand that too. It is like the costumes that men and women used to wear, in their youth, years ago, and which now stand up rather faded in museums. With a jolt they reassemble for us the day-to-day actuality of the bygone people, and we see the trophies once more of man's eternal fight with inertia.

ON COMING HOME (1924–25)

> Breathes there a man with soul so dead
> Who never to himself hath said
> This is my own, my native land –

With a vengeance!

It is four years since I saw, under a little winter snow, the death-grey coast of Kent go out. After four years, down, down on the horizon, with the last sunset still in the west, right down under the eyelid of the shut cold sky, the faintest spark, like a message. It is the Land's End light. And I, who am a bit short-sighted, saw it, almost first. One sees by divination. The infinitesimal sparking of the Land's End light, so absolutely remote, as one approaches from over the sea, from the Gulf of Mexico, after sunset.

I won't pretend my heart was dead. It exploded again in my chest. 'This is my own, my native land!' My God, what lies behind that spark of light!

One goes out on deck again, two hours later, to find a vast light towering out of the dark, as if someone were swinging an immense white beam of communication in the black boughs of the tree of night. And the ship creeps invisible under the pure white branches of the light of men, down on the little lustre of the sea. We are entering Plymouth Sound.

'Breathes there a man with soul so dead – ?'

There are the small lights on the soft blackness that must be land. Far off, ahead, a tiny row of lights that must be the Hoe. And the ship slowly pulses forward, at half speed, venturing in.

England! So still! So remote-seeming! Across what mysterious belt of isolation does England lie! 'It doesn't seem like a big civilized country,' says the Cuban behind me. 'It seems as if there were no people in it.'

'Yes!' cries the German woman. 'So still! So still! As if one could never come to it.'

And that is how it seems, as you slowly steam up the Sound in the night, and watch the little lights that must be land, on the unspeaking darkness. The darkness doesn't speak, as the darkness of the coast of America, or of Spain for example, speaks in the night when you are passing.

Slowly the ship lapses to silence in mid-water. A tender lit up with red and white and yellow lights – the German woman calls it the Christmas-tree boat – hovers round the stern and comes up on the leeward side. It looks curiously empty, in spite of its lights. And with strange quick quietness, the English sailors make fast. Queer to hear English voices below on the tender, so curiously quiet and withheld, against the noise of Spanish and German we are used to on board.

It is the same with English voices of sailors making fast the ropes, as with the sight of land. They do not stir the darkness. They do not come through. Quickly, quietly, the ladder is put up. Quickly, quietly, the police and passport people come on board. All is strangely still, and the ship, which at tea-time was still lively with mixed nationalities, seems deserted. England is on board – everything has fallen silent.

Quietly, quickly, softly, everything is done, and we are landed. There is a strange absence of something, an absentness is felt in everything and in everybody. I think, in the ordinary come-and-go of life, only the Englishman is really civilized. So, the soft, quiet, vague landing, the vague looking at the luggage, the vague finding oneself in the hotel in Plymouth. Everything soft, vague, with the quiet of accomplished civilization. Accomplished, that is, in these matters of landing from a ship and finding oneself in an hotel.

And it is the first night ashore, in the curious stillness. I cannot say wherein lies the almost deathly sense of stillness one gets, returning to England from the west. Landing in San Francisco gave me the feeling of intolerable crackling noise. But London gives me a dead muffled sense of stillness, as if nothing had any resonance. Everything muffled, or muted, and no sharp contact, no sharp reaction anywhere. As if all the traffic went on deep sand, heavily, straining the heart, and hushed.

I must confess, this curious mutedness of my native land frightens me more than the noise of New York or of Mexico City. Since the sparking of the Land's End light, and the great strong beaming of the lighthouse overhead, tall overhead like a great tree, at the entrance to the Sound, I have not had one single sharp impression in England. Everything seems sand-bagged, like when a ship hangs bags of sand over her side to deaden the bump with the wharf. So it is here. Every impact, every contact is sand-bagged, deadened. Everything that everybody says is modified beforehand, to prevent any kind of bump. Everything that everybody feels is keyed down, and muted, so as not to impinge on anybody else's feelings.

And this, in the end, becomes a madness. One sits in the breakfast car in the train, coming to London. There is a strange tension. What is the curious unease that holds the car spellbound? In America the Pullmans, being much heavier, don't shake like our cars. And there seems more room, inside and out, morally and physically. It is possible the American manners are not so good, though I doubt if I agree, even there. The silent bad manners of the Englishman when he happens to decide that he is not among his own 'sort,' take a lot of beating. But of course, he never says or does anything, so he is perfectly safe and proper in his circumstance.

But there one sits in a breakfast car on the Great Western. The train shakes terribly. The waiters are quick and soft and attentive, but the food isn't very good, and one feels as if one were some sort of ghost being waited on by men who have long ago gone to sleep, and are serving one in their sleep. The place feels tight: one would like to smash something. Outside, a tight little landscape goes by, just unbelievable, with sunshine like thin water, a horizon half a mile away, and everything crowded forward into one's face till one gasps for space and breath, and tries to jerk one's head back, as one does when someone pushes his face right under one's hat-brim. Too horribly close!

Inside, we eat kippers and bacon. The place is full. The other people, mostly men, all keep themselves modified and muted, as if they didn't want their aura to stray beyond the four legs of their chair. Inside this charmed circle of their self-constraint they seem to sit and smile with pleasant English faces. And, of course, they are all trying to be a bit 'grander' than they really are: to give the impression that they have more servants in the kitchen than they really have, and so on. That is part of the English naïveté! If they have two servants, they want to give the impression of four: not less than four.

Essentially, however, and apart from being 'grand,' each one of them sits complacent inside a crystal bubble, smiling and eating and sprinkling sugar on porridge, and then half-furtively glancing through the transparency of their bubble, to see if there is anything outside. They will never allow anything outside: except, of course, other bubbles of varying 'grandness.'

In the small things of life, the Englishman is the only perfectly civilized being. But God save me from such civilization. God in heaven deliver me. The trick lies in tensely withholding oneself, tensely withholding one's aura, till it forms a perfect and transparent little globe around one. At the centre of this little globe sits the Englishman, his own little god unto himself, terribly complacent, and at the same time, terribly self-deprecating. He seems to say: My dear man, I know I am no more than what I am. I wouldn't trespass on what you are, not for worlds. Oh, not for worlds! Because when all's said and done, what you are means nothing to me. I am god inside my own crystal world, the strictly limited domain of myself, which after all no one can deny is my own. I am only god within the bubble of my own self-contained being, dear sir; but there, god I am, so how could I possibly desire to trespass? I only urge that all other people shall be as self-contained and as little inclined to trespass. And they may be gods inside their own bubbles if they like.

Hence the feeling of intolerable shut-in-edness. One enters from the open sea, to the Channel: first box. Into Plymouth Sound: second box. Into the customs place: third box. Into the hotel: fourth. Into the dining car of the train: fifth. And so on and so on, like those Chinese boxes that fit one inside the other, and at the very middle is a tiny porcelain figure half an inch long. That is how one feels. Like a tiny porcelain figure shut in inside box after box of repeated and intensified shut-in-edness. It is enough to send one mad.

That is coming home, home to one's fellow countrymen! In one sense – the small ways of life – they are the nicest and most civilized people in the world. But there they are: each one of them a perfect little accomplished figure, enclosed first and foremost within the box, or bubble, of his own self-contained ego, and afterwards in all the other boxes he has made for himself, for his own safety.

At the centre of himself he is complacent, and even 'superior.' It strikes one very hard, coming home, that every Englishman sits there feeling subtly 'superior.' He wouldn't impose anything on anybody, dear me no. That is part of his own superiority. He is too superior to make any imposition of himself in any way. But like a pleased image, there he sits at the centre of his own bubble, and feels superior. Superior to what? Oh, nothing in particular, don't you know. Just superior. And well – if you press him – superior to everything. Just damn superior to everything. There inside the bubble of his own self-constraint, his own illusion, the strange germ of his unnatural conceit.

This is my own, my native land.

He seems to have accomplished the trick of being at his ease, the gentleman in the breakfast car, sprinkling sugar on his porridge. He knows he has a pretty way of sprinkling sugar on porridge: he knows he can put the spoon back prettily into the sugar-bowl: he knows his voice is cultured and his smile charming, compared to the rest of the world. It is quite obvious he means no one ill. Surely it is obvious he would like to give every man the best that man could have. If it were his, to give, which it isn't. And finally he knows he is able to contain himself. He is an Englishman and he is himself, he is able to contain and to constrain himself, and to live within the unbroken bubble of his own self-constraint, without letting his aura stray and get at cross-purposes with other people's auras. The dear, dangerless patrician!

Yet something does stray out of him. Look into his nice, bright, apparently-smiling English eyes. They are not smiling. And look again at his nice fresh English face, that seems so pleased with life. It also is not smiling, any more than Mr Lloyd George is really smiling. The eyes are not really at ease, and the nice, fresh face is not at ease either. At the centre of the eyes, where the smile twinkles, there is fear. Even at the middle of this amiable and all-tolerant English complacency, there is fear. And the smile-wrinkles on the fresh, pleased face, they give odd quivers, and look like spite wrinkles. There strays out of him, in spite of all his self-constraining, the faint effluence of fear, and the sense of impotence, and a quiver of spite, of subdued malice. Underneath the soft civilizedness of him, fear, impotence, and malice.

> Whose heart within him ne'er hath burned
> As home his wandering steps he turned
> From travelling in a foreign land.

That's how one finds the Englishman at home. And then one understands the bitterness of Englishmen abroad in the world, especially Englishmen in responsible positions.

There is no denying this: that since the war, England's prestige has declined terribly, all over the world. Ah, says the Englishman, that's because America has the dollars. And there you hear the voice of England's own downfall.

England's prestige wasn't based on money. It was based on the imagination of men. England was supposed to be proud, and at the same time, free. Proud in her freedom, and free, to a certain extent generous, truly generous, in her pride.

This was the England that led the world. Myself, I think this was a true conception of England at her best. This was how the other nations accepted her: at her best. And the individual Englishman got his certain honour, in the world, on the strength of it.

Now? Now he still receives the remnants of honour, but mockingly, as poor Russian counts receive a little mocking distinction, now that they have to sell newspapers. The real English pride has gone, and 'superiority' takes its place: a really imbecile superiority, which the world laughs at.

As far as the wide world is concerned, England is anything but superior. She is just humiliated. From day to day she makes a more humiliated spectacle of herself in the eyes of the world.

Weak, vacillating, without purpose or policy, without even the last vestige of pride, she continues to apologize and deprecate on the platform of the world.

And of course individual Englishmen abroad feel it. You rarely meet an Englishman far from home, but he is burning with impatience, disgust, and even contempt, of home. Home seems a shoddy place. And when you get here, it's even shoddier than it seems from afar.

If, abroad, you meet an Englishman in office, he is speechless, almost cynical with rage. 'What can I do!' he says. 'What can I do, against the orders from home. I get orders that I must give no loop-hole for offence against America. All I have to do is to guard against giving offence, above all to America. I must be on my knees all the time, in front of America, begging her not to take offence, when she hasn't the faintest intention even of taking offence.'

This is from a man who has lived out in the world, and who knows that the moment you go down on your knees to a man, he spits on you: and quite right too. Men have no business on their knees.

'I have an Englishman wants to go into the United States: Washington has given him a visa, and said: Yes, you can enter whenever you like. Comes a cable from London: Prevent this man from crossing into the United States, Washington might not like it. What can one do?'

The same story everywhere. A man is building a railway with nigger labour. Some insolent Jamaica nigger – British subject, larger than life – brings a charge against his boss. Solemn trial by the British, influence from the government, the Englishman is reprimanded, and nigger smiles and spits in his face.

Long live the bottom dog! May he devour us all.

Same story from India, from Egypt, from China. At home, a lot of queer, insane, half-female-seeming men, not quite men at all, and certainly not women! The women would be far braver. Then abroad, a few Englishmen still struggling.

England seems to me the one really soft spot, the rotten spot in the empire. If ever men had to think in world terms, they have to think in world terms today. And here you get an island no bigger than a back garden, chock-full of people who never realize there is anything outside their back garden, pretending to direct the destinies of the world. It is pathetic and ridiculous. And the 'superiority' is bathetic to lunacy.

These poor 'superior' gentry, all that is left to them is to blame the Americans. It amazes me, the rancour with which English people speak of Americans. Just because the republican eagle of the west doesn't choose to be a pelican for other people's convenience. Why should it?

After all, rancour is a bad sign in a superior person. It is a sign of impotence. The superior Englishman feels impotent against the American dollar, so he is wildly rancorous, in private, when America can't hear him.

Now I am an Englishman. And I know that if my countrymen still have a soul to sell, they'll sell it for American dollars, and drive a hard bargain.

Which is what I call being truly superior to the dollar.

This is my own, my native land.*

It was such a brave country, for so many years: the old brave, reckless, manly England. Even a man with dyed whiskers, like

---

* Lawrence has misquoted Scott's *The Lay of the Last Minstrel*. The accepted reading of these first six lines of Canto VI is: 'Breathes there the man, with soul so dead,/Who never to himself hath said,/This is my own, my native land!/Whose heart hath ne'er within him burn'd,/As home his footsteps he hath turn'd,/From wandering on a foreign strand!' Eds.

Palmerston. Too brave and reckless to be treacherous. My England.

Look at us now. Not a man left inside all the millions of pairs of trousers. Not a man left. A host of would-be-amiable cowards shut up each in his own bubble of conceit, and the whole lot within box after box of safeguards.

One could shout with laughter at the figures inside these endless safety boxes. Except that one is still English, and therefore flabbergasted. My own, my native land just leaves me flabbergasted.

ART AND MORALITY (1925)

It is a part of the common claptrap that 'art is immoral.' Behold, everywhere, artists running to put on jazz underwear, to demoralize themselves; or, at least, to *débourgeoiser* themselves.

For the bourgeois is supposed to be the fount of morality. Myself, I have found artists far more morally finicky.

Anyhow, what has a water-pitcher and six insecure apples on a crumpled tablecloth got to do with bourgeois morality? Yet I notice that most people, who have not learnt the trick of being arty, feel a real moral repugnance for a Cézanne still-life. They think it is not *right*.

For them, it isn't.

Yet how can they feel, as they do, that it is subtly *immoral*?

The very same design, if it was humanized, and the tablecloth was a draped nude and the water-pitcher a nude semi-draped, weeping over the draped one, would instantly become highly moral. Why?

Perhaps from painting better than from any other art we can realize the subtlety of the distinction between what is dumbly *felt* to be moral, and what is felt to be immoral. The moral instinct in the man in the street.

But instinct is largely habit. The moral instinct of the man in the street is largely an emotional defence of an old habit.

Yet what can there be in a Cézanne still-life to rouse the aggressive moral instinct of the man in the street? What ancient habit in man do these six apples and a water-pitcher succeed in hindering?

A water-pitcher that isn't so very much like a water-pitcher, apples that aren't very appley, and a tablecloth that's not particularly much of a tablecloth. I could do better myself!

Probably! But then, why not dismiss the picture as a poor attempt? Whence this anger, this hostility? The derisive resentment?

Six apples, a pitcher, and a tablecloth can't suggest improper *behaviour*. They don't – not even to a Freudian. If they did, the man in the street would feel much more at home with them.

Where, then, does the immorality come in? Because come in it does.

Because of a very curious habit that civilized man has been forming down the whole course of civilization, and in which he is now hard-boiled. The slowly formed habit of seeing just as the photographic camera sees.

You may say, the object reflected on the retina is *always* photographic. It may be, I doubt it. But whatever the image on the retina may be, it is rarely, even now, the photographic image of the object which is actually *taken in* by the man who sees the object. He does not, even now, see for himself. He sees what the Kodak has taught him to see. And man, try as he may, is not a Kodak.

When a child sees a man, what does the child *take in*, as an impression? Two eyes, a nose, a mouth of teeth, two straight legs, two straight arms: a sort of hieroglyph which the human child has used through all the ages to represent man. At least, the old hieroglyph was still in use when I was a child.

Is this what the child actually *sees*?

If you mean by seeing, consciously registering, then this is what the child actually sees. The photographic image may be there all right, upon the retina. But there the child leaves it: outside the door, as it were.

Through many ages, mankind has been striving to register the image on the retina *as it is*: no more glyphs and hieroglyphs. We'll have the real objective reality.

And we have succeeded. As soon as we succeed, the Kodak is invented, to prove our success. Could lies come out of a black box, into which nothing but light had entered? Impossible! It takes life to tell a lie.

Colour also, which primitive man cannot really *see*, is now seen by us, and fitted to the spectrum.

Eureka! We have seen it, with our own eyes.

When we see a red cow, we see a red cow. We are quite sure of it, because the unimpeachable Kodak sees exactly the same.

But supposing we had all of us been born blind, and had to get our image of a red cow by touching her, and smelling her, hearing her moo, and 'feeling' her? Whatever should we think of her? Whatever sort of image should we have of her, in our dark minds? Something very different, surely!

As vision developed towards the Kodak, man's idea of himself developed towards the snapshot. Primitive man simply didn't know *what* he was: he was always half in the dark. But we have learned to see, and each of us has a complete Kodak idea of himself.

You take a snap of your sweetheart, in the field among the buttercups, smiling tenderly at the red cow with a calf, and dauntlessly offering a cabbage-leaf.

Awfully nice, and absolutely 'real.' There is your sweetheart, complete in herself, enjoying a sort of absolute objective reality: complete, perfect, all her surroundings contributing to her, incontestable. She is really a 'picture.'

This is the habit we have formed: of visualizing *everything*. Each man to himself is a picture. That is, he is a complete little objective reality, complete in himself, existing by himself, absolutely, in the middle of the picture. All the rest is just setting, background. To every man, to every woman, the universe is just a setting to the absolute little picture of himself, herself.

This has been the development of the conscious ego in man, through several thousand years: since Greece first broke the spell of 'darkness.' Man has learnt to *see* himself. So now, he *is* what he sees. He makes himself in his own image.

Previously, even in Egypt, men had not learnt to *see straight*. They fumbled in the dark, and didn't quite know where they were, or what they were. Like men in a dark room, they only *felt* their own existence surging in the darkness of other creatures.

We, however, have learned to see ourselves for what we are, as the sun sees us. The Kodak bears witness. We see as the All-Seeing Eye sees, with the universal vision. And we *are* what is seen: each man to himself an identity, an isolated absolute, corresponding with a universe of isolated absolutes. A picture! A Kodak snap, in a universal film of snaps.

We have achieved universal vision. Even god could not see *differently* from what we see: only more extensively, like a telescope, or more intensively, like a microscope. But the same vision. A vision of images which are real, and each one limited to itself.

We behave as if we had got to the bottom of the sack, and seen the Platonic Idea with our own eyes, in all its photographically developed perfection, lying in the bottom of the sack of the universe. Our own ego!

The identifying of ourselves with the visual image of ourselves has become an instinct; the habit is already old. The picture of me, the me that is *seen*, is me.

As soon as we are supremely satisfied about it, somebody starts to upset us. Comes Cézanne with his pitcher and his apples, which not only are not life-like, but are a living lie. The Kodak will prove it.

The Kodak will take all sorts of snaps, misty, atmospheric, sun-dazed, dancing – all quite different. Yet the image is *the* image. There is only more or less sun, more or less vapour, more or less light and shade.

The All-Seeing Eye sees with every degree of intensity and in every possible kind of mood: Giotto, Titian, El Greco, Turner, all so different, yet all the true image in the All-Seeing Eye.

This Cézanne still-life, however, is *contrary* to the All-Seeing Eye. Apples, to the eye of God, could not look like that, nor could a tablecloth, nor could a pitcher. So, it is *wrong*.

Because man, since he grew out of a personal God, has taken over to himself all the attributes of the Personal Godhead. It is the all-seeing human eye which is now the Eternal Eye.

And if apples don't *look* like that, in any light or circumstance, or under any mood, then they shouldn't be painted like that.

Oh, *là-là-là!* The apples *are* just like that, to me! cries Cézanne. They *are* like that, no matter what they look like.

Apples are always apples! says Vox Populi, Vox Dei.

Sometimes they're a sin, sometimes they're a knock on the head, sometimes they're a bellyache, sometimes they're part of a pie, sometimes they're sauce for the goose.

And you can't see a bellyache, neither can you see a sin, neither can you see a knock on the head. So paint the apple in these aspects, and you get – probably, or approximately – a Cézanne still-life.

What an apple looks like to an urchin, to a thrush, to a browsing cow, to Sir Isaac Newton, to a caterpillar, to a hornet, to a mackerel who finds one bobbing on the sea, I leave you to conjecture. But the All-Seeing must have mackerel's eyes, as well as man's.

And this is the immorality in Cézanne: he begins to see more than the All-Seeing Eye of humanity can possibly see, Kodak-wise. If you can see in the apple a bellyache and a knock on the head, and paint these in the image, among the prettiness, then it is the death of the Kodak and the movies, and must be immoral.

It's all very well talking about decoration and illustration, significant form, or tactile values, or plastique, or movement, or space-composition, or colour-mass relations, afterwards. You might as well force your guest to eat the menu card, at the end of the dinner.

What art has got to do, and will go on doing, is to reveal things in their different relationships. That is to say, you've got to see in the apple the bellyache, Sir Isaac's knock on the cranium, the vast, moist wall through which the insect bores to lay her eggs in the middle, and the untasted, unknown quality which Eve saw hanging on a tree. Add to this the glaucous glimpse that the mackerel gets as he comes to the surface, and Fantin-Latour's apples are no more to you than enamelled rissoles.

The true artist doesn't substitute immorality for morality. On the contrary, he *always* substitutes a finer morality for a grosser. And as soon as you see a finer morality, the grosser becomes relatively immoral.

The universe is like Father Ocean, a stream of all things slowly moving. We move, and the rock of ages moves. And since we move and move for ever, in no discernible direction, there is no centre to the movement, to us. To us, the centre shifts at every moment. Even the pole-star ceases to sit on the pole. *Allons!* there is no road before us!

There is nothing to do but to maintain a true relationship to the things we move with and amongst and against. The apple, like the moon, has still an unseen side. The movement of Ocean will turn it round to us, or us to it.

There is nothing man can do but maintain himself in true relationship to his contiguous universe. An ancient Rameses can sit in stone absolute, absolved from visual contact, deep in the silent ocean of sensual contact. Michelangelo's Adam can open his eyes for the first time, and see the old man in the skies, objectively. Turner can tumble into the open mouth of the objective universe of light, till we see nothing but his disappearing heels. As the stream carries him, each in his own relatedness, each one differently, so a man must go through life.

Each thing, living or unliving, streams in its own odd, intertwining flux, and nothing, not even man nor the God of man, nor anything that man has thought or felt or known, is fixed or abiding. All moves. And nothing is true, or good, or right, except in its own living relatedness to its own circumambient universe; to the things that are in the stream with it.

Design in art, is a recognition of the relation between various things, various elements in the creative flux. You can't *invent* a design. You recognize it, in the fourth dimension. That is, with your blood and your bones, as well as with your eyes.

Egypt had a wonderful relation to a vast living universe, only dimly visual in its reality. The dim eye-vision and the powerful blood-feeling of the Negro African, even today, gives us strange images, which our eyes can hardly see, but which we know are surpassing. The big silent statue of Rameses is like a drop of water, hanging through the centuries in dark suspense, and never static. The African fetish-statues have no movement, visually represented. Yet one little motionless wooden figure stirs more than all the Parthenon frieze. It sits in the place where no Kodak can snap it.

As for us, we have our Kodak-vision, all in bits that group or jig. Like the movies, that jerk but never move. An endless shifting and rattling together of isolated images, 'snaps,' miles of them, all of them jigging, but each one utterly incapable of movement or change, in itself. A kaleidoscope of inert images, mechanically shaken.

And this is our vaunted 'consciousness,' made up, really, of inert visual images and little else: like the cinematograph.

Let Cézanne's apples go rolling off the table for ever. They live by their own laws, in their own *ambiente*, and not by the laws of the Kodak – or of man. They are casually related to man. But to those apples, man is by no means the absolute.

A new relationship between ourselves and the universe means a new morality. Taste the unsteady apples of Cézanne, and the nailed-down apples of Fantin-Latour are apples of Sodom. If the *status quo* were paradise, it would indeed be a sin to taste the new apples; but since the *status quo* is much more prison than paradise, we can go ahead.

MORALITY AND THE NOVEL
(1925)

The business of art is to reveal the relation between man and his circumambient universe, at the living moment. As mankind is always struggling in the toils of old relationships, art is always ahead of the 'times,' which themselves are always far in the rear of the living moment.

When van Gogh paints sunflowers, he reveals, or achieves, the vivid relation between himself, as man, and the sunflower, as sunflower, at that quick moment of time. His painting does not represent the sunflower itself. We shall never know what the sunflower itself is. And the camera will *visualize* the sunflower far more perfectly than van Gogh can.

The vision on the canvas is a third thing, utterly intangible and inexplicable, the offspring of the sunflower itself and van Gogh himself. The vision on the canvas is for ever incommensurable with the canvas, or the paint, or van Gogh as a human organism, or the sunflower as a botanical organism. You cannot weigh nor measure nor even describe the vision on the canvas. It exists, to tell the truth, only in the much-debated fourth dimension. In dimensional space it has no existence.

It is a revelation of the perfected relation, at a certain moment, between a man and a sunflower. It is neither man-in-the-mirror nor flower-in-the-mirror, neither is it above or below or across anything. It is in between everything, in the fourth dimension.

And this perfected relation between man and his circumambient universe is life itself, for mankind. It has the fourth-dimensional quality of eternity and perfection. Yet it is momentaneous.

Man and the sunflower both pass away from the moment, in the process of forming a new relationship. The relation between all things changes from day to day, in a subtle stealth of change. Hence art, which reveals or attains to another perfect relationship, will be for ever new.

At the same time, that which exists in the non-dimensional space of pure relationship is deathless, lifeless, and eternal. That is, it gives us the *feeling* of being beyond life or death. We say an Assyrian lion or an Egyptian hawk's head 'lives.' What we really mean is that it is beyond life, and therefore beyond death. It gives us that feeling. And there is something inside us which must also be beyond life and beyond death, since that 'feeling' which we get from an Assyrian lion or an Egyptian hawk's head is so infinitely precious to us. As the evening star, that spark of pure relation between night and day, has been precious to man since time began.

If we think about it, we find that our life *consists in* this achieving of a pure relationship between ourselves and the living universe about us. This is how I 'save my soul' by accomplishing a pure relationship between me and another person, me and other people, me and a nation, me and a race of men, me and the animals, me and the trees or flowers, me and the earth, me and the skies and sun and stars, me and the moon: an infinity of pure relations, big and little, like the stars of the sky: that makes our eternity, for each one of us, me and the timber I am sawing, the lines of force I follow; me and the dough I knead for bread, me and the very motion with which I write, me and the bit of gold I have got. This, if we knew it, is our life and our eternity: the subtle, perfected relation between me and my whole circumambient universe.*

And morality is that delicate, for ever trembling and changing *balance* between me and my circumambient universe, which precedes and accompanies a true relatedness.

Now here we see the beauty and the great value of the novel. Philosophy, religion, science, they are all of them busy nailing things down, to get a stable equilibrium. Religion, with its nailed-down One God, who says *Thou shalt, Thou shan't*, and hammers home every time; philosophy, with its fixed ideas; science with its 'laws': they, all of them, all the time, want to nail us on to some tree or other.

But the novel, no. The novel is the highest example of subtle inter-relatedness that man has discovered. Everything is true in its own time, place, circumstance, and untrue outside of its own place, time, circumstance. If you try to nail anything down, in the novel, either it kills the novel, or the novel gets up and walks away with the nail.

Morality in the novel is the trembling instability of the balance. When the novelist puts his thumb in the scale, to pull down the balance to his own predilection, that is immorality.

The modern novel tends to become more and more immoral, as the novelist tends to press his thumb heavier and heavier in the pan: either on the side of love, pure love: or on the side of licentious 'freedom.'

The novel is not, as a rule, immoral because the novelist has any dominant *idea*, or *purpose*. The immorality lies in the novelist's helpless, unconscious predilection. Love is a great emotion. But if you set out to write a novel, and you yourself are in the throes of

---

* As an inscription discovered in a copy of James Mason's *Fra Angelico*, this paragraph was published separately under the title 'The Universe and Me' by the Powgen Press, New York, 1935.

the great predilection for love, love as the supreme, the only emotion worth living for, then you will write an immoral novel.

Because *no* emotion is supreme, or exclusively worth living for. *All* emotions go to the achieving of a living relationship between a human being and the other human being or creature or thing he becomes purely related to. All emotions, including love and hate, and rage and tenderness, go to the adjusting of the oscillating, unestablished balance between two people who amount to anything. If the novelist puts his thumb in the pan, for love, tenderness, sweetness, peace, then he commits an immoral act: he *prevents* the possibility of a pure relationship, a pure relatedness, the only thing that matters: and he makes inevitable the horrible reaction, when he lets his thumb go, towards hate and brutality, cruelty and destruction.

Life is so made that opposites sway about a trembling centre of balance. The sins of the fathers are visited on the children. If the fathers drag down the balance on the side of love, peace, and production, then in the third or fourth generation the balance will swing back violently to hate, rage, and destruction. We must balance as we go.

And of all the art forms, the novel most of all demands the trembling and oscillating of the balance. The 'sweet' novel is more falsified, and therefore more immoral, than the blood-and-thunder novel.

The same with the smart and smudgily cynical novel, which says it doesn't matter what you do, because one thing is as good as another, anyhow, and prostitution is just as much 'life' as anything else.

This misses the point entirely. A thing isn't life just because somebody does it. This the artist ought to know perfectly well. The ordinary bank clerk buying himself a new straw that isn't 'life' at all: it is just existence, quite all right, like everyday dinners: but not 'life.'

By life, we mean something that gleams, that has the fourth-dimensional quality. If the bank clerk feels really piquant about his hat, if he establishes a lively relation with it, and goes out of the shop with the new straw on his head, a changed man, be-aureoled, then that is life.

The same with the prostitute. If a man establishes a living relation to her, if only for one moment, then it is life. But if it *doesn't*: if it is just money and function, then it is not life, but sordidness, and a betrayal of living.

If a novel reveals true and vivid relationships, it is a moral work, no matter what the relationships may consist in. If the novelist *honours* the relationship in itself, it will be a great novel.

But there are so many relationships which are not real. When the man in *Crime and Punishment* murders the old woman for sixpence, although it is *actual* enough, it is never quite real. The balance between the murderer and the old woman is gone entirely; it is only a mess. It is actuality, but it is not 'life,' in the living sense.

The popular novel, on the other hand, dishes up a réchauffé of old relationships: *If Winter Comes*. And old relationships dished up are likewise immoral. Even a magnificent painter like Raphael does nothing more than dress up in gorgeous new dresses relationships which have already been experienced. And this gives a gluttonous kind of pleasure to the mass: a voluptuousness, a wallowing. For centuries, men say of their voluptuously ideal woman: 'She is a Raphael Madonna.' And women are only just learning to take it as an insult.

A new relation, a new relatedness hurts somewhat in the attaining; and will always hurt. So life will always hurt. Because real voluptuousness lies in re-acting old relationships, and at the best, getting an alcoholic sort of pleasure out of it, slightly depraving.

Each time we strive to a new relation, with anyone or anything, it is bound to hurt somewhat. Because it means the struggle

with and the displacing of old connexions, and this is never pleasant. And moreover, between living things at least, an adjustment
means also a fight, for each party, inevitably, must 'seek its own'
in the other, and be denied. When, in the two parties, each of
them seeks his own, her own, absolutely, then it is a fight to the
death. And this is true of the thing called 'passion.' On the other
hand, when, of the two parties, one yields utterly to the other,
this is called sacrifice, and it also means death. So the Constant
Nymph died of her eighteen months of constancy.

It isn't the nature of nymphs to be constant. She should have
been constant in her nymph-hood. And it is unmanly to accept
sacrifices. He should have abided by his own manhood.

There is, however, the third thing, which is neither sacrifice
nor fight to the death: when each seeks only the true relatedness
to the other. Each must be true to himself, herself, his own
manhood, her own womanhood, and let the relationship work
out of itself. This means courage above all things: and then discipline. Courage to accept the life-thrust from within oneself,
and from the other person. Discipline, not to exceed oneself any
more than one can help. Courage, when one has exceeded oneself, to accept the fact and not whine about it.

Obviously, to read a really new novel will *always* hurt, to
some extent. There will always be resistance. The same with
new pictures, new music. You may judge of their reality by the
fact that they do arouse a certain resistance, and compel, at
length, a certain acquiescence.

The great relationship, for humanity, will always be the relation between man and woman. The relation between man and
man, woman and woman, parent and child, will always be
subsidiary.

And the relation between man and woman will change for
ever, and will for ever be the new central clue to human life. It
is the *relation itself* which is the quick and the central clue to life,

not the man, nor the woman, nor the children that result from the relationship, as a contingency.

It is no use thinking you can put a stamp on the relation between man and woman, to keep it in the *status quo*. You can't. You might as well try to put a stamp on the rainbow or the rain.

As for the bond of love, better put it off when it galls. It is an absurdity, to say that men and women *must love*. Men and women will be for ever subtly and changingly related to one another; no need to yoke them with any 'bond' at all. The only morality is to have man true to his manhood, woman to her womanhood, and let the relationship form of itself, in all honour. For it is, to each, *life itself.*

If we are going to be moral, let us refrain from driving pegs through anything, either through each other or through the third thing, the relationship, which is for ever the ghost of both of us. Every sacrificial crucifixion needs five pegs, four short ones and a long one, each one an abomination. But when you try to nail down the relationship itself, and write over it *Love* instead of *This is the King of the Jews*, then you can go on putting in nails for ever. Even Jesus called it the Holy Ghost, to show you that you can't lay salt on its tail.

The novel is a perfect medium for revealing to us the changing rainbow of our living relationships. The novel can help us to live, as nothing else can: no didactic Scripture, anyhow. If the novelist keeps his thumb out of the pan.

But when the novelist *has* his thumb in the pan, the novel becomes an unparalleled perverter of men and women. To be compared only, perhaps, to that great mischief of sentimental hymns, like 'Lead, Kindly Light,' which have helped to rot the marrow in the bones of the present generation.

THE NOVEL (1925)

Somebody says the novel is doomed. Somebody else says it is the green bay tree getting greener. Everybody says something, so why shouldn't I!

Mr Santayana sees the modern novel expiring because it is getting so thin; which means, Mr Santayana is bored.

I am rather bored myself. It becomes harder and harder to read the *whole* of any modern novel. One reads a bit, and knows the rest; or else one doesn't want to know any more.

This is sad. But again, I don't think it's the novel's fault. Rather the novelists'.

You can put anything you like in a novel. So why do people *always* go on putting the same thing? Why is the *vol au vent* always chicken! Chicken *vol au vents* may be the rage. But who sickens first shouts first for something else.

The novel is a great discovery: far greater than Galileo's telescope or somebody else's wireless. The novel is the highest form of human expression so far attained. Why? Because it is so incapable of the absolute.

In a novel, everything is relative to everything else, if that novel is art at all. There may be didactic bits, but they aren't the novel. And the author may have didactic 'purpose' up his sleeve. Indeed most great novelists have, as Tolstoi had his Christian-socialism, and Hardy his pessimism, and Flaubert his intellectual desperation. But even a didactic purpose so wicked as Tolstoi's or Flaubert's cannot put to death the novel.

You can tell me, Flaubert had a 'philosophy', not 'purpose'. But what is a novelist's philosophy but a purpose on a rather higher level? And since every novelist who amounts to anything has a philosophy – even Balzac – any novel of importance has a purpose. If only the 'purpose' be large enough, and not at outs with the passional inspiration.

Vronsky sinned, did he? But also the sinning was a consummation devoutly to be wished. The novel makes that obvious: in spite of old Leo Tolstoi. And the would-be-pious Prince in *Resurrection* is a muff, with his piety that nobody wants or believes in.

There you have the greatness of the novel itself. It won't *let* you tell didactic lies, and put them over. Nobody in the world is anything but delighted when Vronsky gets Anna Karénina. Then what about the sin? – Why, when you look at it, all the tragedy comes from Vronsky's and Anna's fear of *society*. The monster was social, not phallic at all. They couldn't live in the pride of their sincere passion, and spit in Mother Grundy's eye. And that, that cowardice, was the real 'sin'. The novel makes it obvious, and knocks all old Leo's teeth out. 'As an officer I am still useful. But as a man, I am a ruin,' says Vronsky – or words to that effect. Well what a skunk, collapsing as a man and a male, and remaining merely as a social instrument; an 'officer', God love us! – merely because people at the opera turn backs on him! As if people's backs weren't preferable to their faces, anyhow!

And old Leo tries to make out it was all because of the phallic sin. Old liar! Because where would any of Leo's books be, without the phallic splendour? And then to blame the column of blood, which really gave him all his life riches! The Judas! Cringe to a mangy, bloodless Society, and try to dress up that dirty old Mother Grundy in a new bonnet and face-powder of Christian-Socialism. Brothers indeed! Sons of a castrated Father!

The novel itself gives Vronsky a kick in the behind, and knocks old Leo's teeth out, and leaves us to learn.

It is such a bore that nearly all great novelists have a didactic purpose, otherwise a philosophy, directly opposite to their passional inspiration. In their passional inspiration, they are all phallic worshippers. From Balzac to Hardy, it is so. Nay, from Apuleius to E. M. Forster. Yet all of them, when it comes to their philosophy, or what they think-they-are, they are all crucified Jesuses. What a bore! And what a burden for the novel to carry!

But the novel has carried it. Several thousands of thousands of lamentable crucifixions of self-heroes and self-heroines. Even the silly duplicity of *Resurrection*, and the wickeder duplicity of Salammbô, with that flayed phallic Matho, tortured upon the Cross of a gilt Princess.

You can't fool the novel. Even with man crucified upon a woman: his 'dear cross'. The novel will show you how dear she was: dear at any price. And it will leave you with a bad taste of disgust against these heroes who *turn* their women into a 'dear cross', and *ask* for their own crucifixion.

You can fool pretty nearly every other medium. You can make a poem pietistic, and still it will be a poem. You can write *Hamlet* in drama: if you wrote him in a novel, he'd be half comic, or a trifle suspicious: a suspicious character, like Dostoevsky's Idiot. Somehow, you sweep the ground a bit too clear in the poem or the drama, and you let the human Word fly a bit too freely. Now in a novel there's always a tom-cat, a black tom-cat that pounces on the white dove of the Word, if the dove doesn't watch it; and there is a banana-skin to trip on; and you know there is a water-closet on the premises. All these things help to keep the balance.

If, in Plato's *Dialogues*, somebody had suddenly stood on his head and given smooth Plato a kick in the wind, and set the whole school in an uproar, then Plato would have been put into a much truer relation to the universe. Or if, in the midst of the *Timaeus*, Plato had only paused to say: 'And now, my dear Cleon – (or whoever it was) – I have a bellyache, and must retreat to the privy: this too is part of the Eternal Idea of man,' then we never need have fallen so low as Freud.

And if, when Jesus told the rich man to take all he had and give it to the poor, the rich man had replied: *'All right, old sport! You are poor, aren't you? Come on, I'll give you a fortune. Come on!'* Then a great deal of snivelling and mistakenness would have been spared us all, and we might never have produced a Marx and a Lenin. If only Jesus had *accepted* the fortune!

Yes, it's a pity of pities that Matthew, Mark, Luke, and John didn't write straight novels. They did write novels; but a bit crooked. The *Evangels* are wonderful novels, by authors 'with a purpose'. Pity there's so much Sermon-on-the-Mounting.

> Matthew, Mark, Luke, and John
> Went to bed with their breeches on! –

as every child knows. Ah, if only they'd taken them off!

Greater novels, to my mind, are the books of the Old Testament, Genesis, Exodus, Samuel, Kings, by authors whose purpose was so big, it didn't quarrel with their passionate inspiration. The purpose and the inspiration were almost one. Why, in the name of everything bad, the two ever should have got separated, is a mystery! But in the modern novel they are hopelessly divorced. When there *is* any inspiration there, to be divorced from.

This, then, is what is the matter with the modern novel. The modern novelist is possessed, hag-ridden, by such a stale old 'purpose', or idea-of-himself, that his inspiration succumbs. Of course he denies having any didactic purpose at all: because a purpose is supposed to be like catarrh, something to be ashamed of. But he's got it. They've all got it: the same snivelling purpose.

They're all little Jesuses in their own eyes, and their 'purpose' is to prove it. Oh Lord! – *Lord Jim*! *Sylvestre Bonnard*! *If Winter Comes*! *Main Street*! *Ulysses*! *Pan*! They are all pathetic or sympathetic or antipathetic little Jesuses *accomplis* or *manqués*. And there is a heroine who is always 'pure', usually, nowadays, on the muck-heap! Like the Green Hatted Woman. She is all the time at the feet of Jesus, though her behaviour there may be misleading. Heaven knows what the Saviour really makes of it: whether she's a Green Hat or a Constant Nymph (eighteen months of constancy, and her heart failed), or any of the rest of 'em. They are all, heroes and heroines, novelists and she-novelists, little Jesuses or Jesusesses. They may be wallowing in the mire: but then didn't Jesus harrow Hell! *A la bonne heure!*

Oh, they are all novelists with an idea of themselves! Which is a 'purpose', with a vengeance! For what a weary, false, sickening idea it is nowadays! The novel gives them away. They can't fool the novel.

Now really, it's time we left *off* insulting the novel any further. If your purpose is to prove your own Jesus qualifications, and the thin stream of your inspiration is 'sin', then dry up, for the interest is dead. *Life as it is!* What's the good of pretending that the lives of a set of tuppenny Green Hats and Constant Nymphs is Life-as-it-is, when the novel itself proves that all it amounts to is life as it is isn't life, but a sort of everlasting and intricate and boring habit: of Jesus peccant and *Jesusa peccante*.

These wearisome sickening little personal novels! After all, they aren't novels at all. In every great novel, who is the hero all the time? Not any of the characters, but some unnamed and nameless flame behind them all. Just as God is the pivotal interest in the books of the Old Testament. But just a trifle too intimate, too *frère et cochon*, there. In the great novel, the felt but unknown flame stands behind all the characters, and in their words and gestures there is a flicker of the presence. If you are *too personal, too human*, the flicker fades out, leaving you with something awfully lifelike, and as lifeless as most people are.

We have to choose between the quick and the dead. The quick is God-flame, in everything. And the dead is dead. In this room where I write, there is a little table that is dead: it doesn't even weakly exist. And there is a ridiculous little iron stove, which for some unknown reason is quick. And there is an iron wardrobe trunk, which for some still more mysterious reason is quick. And there are several books, whose mere corpus is dead, utterly dead and non-existent. And there is a sleeping cat, very quick. And a glass lamp, alas, is dead.

What makes the difference? *Quién sabe!* But difference there is. And I *know* it.

And the sum and source of all quickness we will call God. And the sum and total of all deadness we may call human.

And if one tries to find out wherein the quickness of the quick lies, it is in a certain weird relationship between that which is quick and – I don't know; perhaps all the rest of things. It seems to consist in an odd sort of fluid, changing, grotesque or beauti-ful relatedness. That silly iron stove somehow *belongs*. Whereas this thin-shanked table doesn't belong. It is a mere disconnected lump, like a cut-off finger.

And now we see the great, great merits of the novel. It can't exist without being 'quick'. The ordinary unquick novel, even if it be a best seller, disappears into absolute nothingness, the dead burying their dead with surprising speed. For even the dead like to be tickled. But the next minute, they've forgotten both the tickling and the tickler.

Secondly, the novel contains no didactic absolute. All that is quick, and all that is said and done by the quick, is in some way godly. So that Vronsky's taking Anna Karenina we must count godly, since it is quick. And that Prince in *Resurrection*, following the convict girl, we must count dead. The convict train is quick and alive. But that would-be-expiatory Prince is as dead as lumber.

The novel itself lays down these laws for us, and we spend our time evading them. The man in the novel must be 'quick'. And this means one thing, among a host of unknown meaning: it means he must have a quick relatedness to all the other things in the novel: snow, bed-bugs, sunshine, the phallus, trains, silk-hats, cats, sorrow, people, food, diphtheria, fuchsias, stars, ideas, God, tooth-paste, lightning, and toilet-paper. He must be in quick relation to all these things. What he says and does must be relative to them all.

And this is why Pierre, for example, in *War and Peace*, is more dull and less quick than Prince André. Pierre is quite nicely related to ideas, tooth-paste, God, people, foods, trains, silk-hats, sorrow, diphtheria, stars. But his relation to snow and sunshine, cats, lightning and the phallus, fuchsias and toilet-paper, is sluggish and mussy. He's not quick enough.

The really quick, Tolstoi loved to kill them off or muss them over. Like a true Bolshevist. One can't help feeling Natasha is rather mussy and unfresh, married to that Pierre.

Pierre was what we call 'so human.' Which means 'so limited.' Men clotting together into social masses in order to limit their individual liabilities: this is humanity. And this is Pierre. And this is Tolstoi, the philosopher with a very nauseating Christian-brotherhood idea of himself. Why limit man to a Christian-brotherhood? I myself, I could belong to the sweetest Christian-brotherhood one day, and ride after Attila with a raw beefsteak for my saddle-cloth, to see the red cock crow in flame over all Christendom, next day.

And that is man! That, really, was Tolstoi. That, even, was Lenin, God in the machine of Christian-brotherhood, that hashes men up into social sausage-meat.

Damn all absolutes. Oh damn, damn, damn all absolutes! I tell you, no absolute is going to make the lion lie down with the lamb: unless, like the limerick, the lamb is inside.

> They returned from the ride
> With lamb Leo inside
> And a smile on the face of the tiger!
> Sing fol-di-lol-lol!
> Fol-di-lol-lol!
> Fol-di-lol-ol-di-lol-olly!

For man, there is neither absolute nor absolution. Such things should be left to monsters like the right-angled triangle, which does only exist in the ideal consciousness. A man can't have a square on his hypotenuse, let him try as he may.

Ay! Ay! Ay! – Man handing out absolutes to man, as if we were all books of geometry with axioms, postulates and definitions in front. God with a pair of compasses! Moses with a set square! Man a geometric bifurcation, not even a radish!

Holy Moses!

'Honour they father and thy mother!' That's awfully cute! But supposing they are not honourable? How then, Moses?

Voice of thunder from Sinai: *'Pretend to honour them!'*

'Love thy neighbour as thyself.'

Alas, my neighbour happens to be mean and detestable.

Voice of the lambent Dove, cooing: *'Put it over him, that you love him.'*

Talk about the cunning of serpents! I never saw even a serpent kissing his instinctive enemy.

Pfui! I wouldn't blacken my mouth, kissing my neighbour, who, I repeat, to me is mean and detestable.

Dove, go home!

The Goat and Compasses, indeed!

Everything is relative. Every Commandment that ever issued out of the mouth of God or man, is strictly relative: adhering to the particular time, place and circumstance.

And this is the beauty of the novel; everything is true in its own relationship, and no further.

For the relatedness and interrelatedness of all things flows and changes and trembles like a stream, and like a fish in the stream the characters in the novel swim and drift and float and turn belly-up when they're dead.

So, if a character in a novel wants two wives – or three – or thirty: well, that is true of that man, at that time, in that circumstance. It may be true of other men, elsewhere and elsewhen. But to infer that all men at all times want two, three, or thirty wives; or that the novelist himself is advocating furious polygamy; is just imbecility.

It has been just as imbecile to infer that, because Dante worshipped a remote Beatrice, every man, all men, should go worshipping remote Beatrices.

And that wouldn't have been so bad, if Dante had put the thing in its true light. Why do we slur over the actual fact that Dante had a cosy bifurcated wife in his bed, and a family of lusty little Dantinos? Petrarch, with his Laura in the distance, had *twelve* little legitimate Petrarchs of his own, between his knees. Yet all we hear is *Laura! Laura! Beatrice! Beatrice! Distance! Distance!*

What bunk ! Why didn't Dante and Petrarch chant in chorus:

> Oh be my spiritual concubine
>> Beatrice! ⎤
>> Laura! ⎦
> My old girl's got several babies that are mine,
> But *thou* be my spiritual concubine,
>> Beatrice! ⎤
>> Laura! ⎦

Then there would have been an honest relation between all the bunch. Nobody grudges the gents their spiritual concubines. But keeping a wife and family – twelve children – up one's sleeve, has always been recognized as a dirty trick.

Which reveals how *immoral* the absolute is! Invariably keeping some vital fact dark ! Dishonourable!

Here we come upon the third essential quality of the novel. Unlike the essay, the poem, the drama, the book of philosophy, or the scientific treatise: all of which may beg the question, when they don't downright filch it; the novel inherently is and must be:

1. Quick.
2. Interrelated in all its parts, vitally, organically.
3. Honourable.

I call Dante's *Commedia* slightly dishonourable, with never a mention of the cosy bifurcated wife, and the kids. And *War and Peace* I call downright dishonourable, with that fat, diluted Pierre for a hero, stuck up as preferable and desirable, when everybody knows that he *wasn't* attractive, even to Tolstoi.

Of course Tolstoi, being a great creative artist, was true to his characters. But being a man with a philosophy, he wasn't true to his *own character*.

Character is a curious thing. It is the flame of a man, which burns brighter or dimmer, bluer or yellower or redder, rising or sinking or flaring according to the draughts of circumstance and the changing air of life, changing itself continually, yet remaining one single, separate flame, flickering in a strange world: unless it be blown out at last by too much adversity.

If Tolstoi had looked into the flame of his own belly, he would have seen that he didn't really like the fat, fuzzy Pierre, who was a poor tool, after all. But Tolstoi was a personality even more than a character. And a personality is a self-conscious *I am*: being all that is left in us of a once-almighty Personal God. So being a personality and almighty *I am*, Leo proceeded deliberately to lionize that Pierre, who was a domestic sort of house-dog.

Doesn't anybody call that dishonourable on Leo's part? He might just as well have been true to *himself*! But no! His self-conscious personality was superior to his own belly and knees, so he thought he'd improve on himself by creeping inside the skin of a lamb; the doddering old lion that he was! Leo! Léon!

Secretly, Leo worshipped the human male, man as a column of rapacious and living blood. He could hardly meet three lusty, roisterous young guardsmen in the street, without crying with envy: and ten minutes later, fulminating on them black oblivion and annihilation, utmost moral thunder-bolts.

How boring, in a great man! And how boring, in a great nation like Russia, to let its old-Adam manhood be so improved upon by these reformers, who all feel themselves short of something, and therefore live by spite, that at last there's nothing left but a lot of shells of men, improving themselves steadily emptier and emptier, till they rattle with words and formulae, as if they'd swallowed the whole encyclopædia of socialism.

But wait ! There is life in the Russians. Something new and strange will emerge out of their weird transmogrification into Bolshevists.

When the lion swallows the lamb, fluff and all, he usually gets a pain, and there's a rumpus. But when the lion tries to force himself down the throat of the huge and popular lamb – a nasty old sheep, really – then it's a phenomenon. Old Leo did it: wedged himself bit by bit down the throat of woolly Russia. And now out of the mouth of the bolshevist lambkin still waves an angry, mistaken, tufted leonine tail, like an agitated exclamation mark.

Meanwhile it's a deadlock.

But what a dishonourable thing for that claw-biting little Leo to do! And in his novels you see him at it. So that the papery lips of *Resurrection* whisper: '*Alas! I would have been a novel. But Leo spoiled me.*'

Count Tolstoi had that last weakness of a great man: he wanted the absolute: the absolute of love, if you like to call it that. Talk about the 'last infirmity of noble minds'! It's a perfect epidemic of senility. He wanted to *be* absolute: a universal brother. Leo was too tight for Tolstoi. He wanted to puff, and puff, and puff, till he became Universal Brotherhood itself, the great gooseberry of our globe.

Then pop went Leo! And from the bits sprang up bolshevists.

It's all bunk. No man can be absolute. No man can be absolutely good or absolutely right, nor absolutely lovable, nor absolutely beloved, nor absolutely loving. Even Jesus, the paragon, was only relatively good and relatively right. Judas could take him by the nose.

No god, that men can conceive of, could possibly be absolute or absolutely right. All the gods that men ever discovered are still God: and they contradict one another and fly down one another's throats, marvellously. Yet they are *all* God: the incalculable Pan.

It is rather nice, to know what a lot of gods there are, and have been, and will be, and that they are all of them God all the while. Each of them utters an absolute: which, in the ears of all the rest of them, falls flat. This makes even eternity lively.

But man, poor man, bobbing like a cork in the stream of time, must hitch himself to some absolute star of righteousness overhead. So he throws out his line, and hooks on. Only to find, after a while, that his star is slowly falling: till it drops into the stream of time with a fizzle, and there's *another* absolute star gone out.

Then we scan the heavens afresh.

As for the babe of love, we're simply tired of changing its napkins. Put the brat down, and let it learn to run about, and manage its own little breeches.

But it's nice to think that all the gods are God all the while. And if a god only genuinely feels to you like God, then it *is* God. But if it doesn't feel quite, quite altogether like God to you, then wait awhile, and you'll hear him fizzle.

The novel knows all this, irrevocably. 'My dear,' it kindly says, 'one God is relative to another god, until he gets into a machine; and then it's a case for the traffic cop!'

'But what am I to do!' cries the despairing novelist. 'From Amon and Ra to Mrs Eddy, from Ashtaroth and Jupiter to Annie Besant, I don't know where I am.'

'Oh yes you do, my dear!' replies the novel. 'You are where you are, so you needn't hitch yourself on to the skirts either of Ashtaroth or Eddy. If you meet them, say *how-do-you-do!* to them quite courteously. But don't hook on, or I shall turn you down.'

'Refrain from hooking on!' says the novel.

'But be honourable among the host!' he adds.

Honour! Why, the gods are like the rainbow, all colours and shades. Since light itself is invisible, a manifestation has got to be pink or black or blue or white or yellow or vermilion, or 'tinted'.

You may be a theosophist, and then you will cry: *Avaunt! Thou dark-red aura! Away!!! – Oh come! Thou pale-blue or thou primrose aura, come!*

This you may cry if you are a theosophist. And if you put a theosophist in a novel, he or she may cry *avaunt!* to the heart's content.

But a theosophist cannot be a novelist, as a trumpet cannot be a regimental band. A theosophist, or a Christian, or a Holy Roller, may be *contained* in a novelist. But a novelist may not put up a fence. The wind bloweth where it listeth, and auras will be red when they want to.

As a matter of fact, only the Holy Ghost knows truly what righteousness is. And heaven only knows what the Holy Ghost is! But it sounds all right. So the Holy Ghost hovers among the flames, from the red to the blue and the black to the yellow, putting brand to brand and flame to flame, as the wind changes, and life travels in flame from the unseen to the unseen, men will never know how or why. Only travel it must, and not die down in nasty fumes.

And the honour, which the novel demands of you, is only that you shall be true to the flame that leaps in you. When that Prince in *Resurrection* so cruelly betrayed and abandoned the girl, at the beginning of her life, he betrayed and wetted on the flame of his own manhood. When, later, he bullied her with his repentant benevolence, he again betrayed and slobbered upon the flame of his waning manhood, till in the end his manhood is extinct, and he's just a lump of half-alive elderly meat.

It's the oldest Pan-mystery. God is the flame-life in all the universe; multifarious, multifarious flames, all colours and beauties and pains and sombrenesses. Whichever flame flames in your manhood, that is you, for the time being. It is your manhood, don't make water on it, says the novel. A man's manhood is to honour the flames in him, and to know that none of them is absolute: even a flame is only relative.

But see old Leo Tolstoi wetting on the flame. As if even his wet were absolute!

Sex is flame, too, the novel announces. Flame burning against every absolute, even against the phallic. For sex is so much more than phallic, and so much deeper than functional desire. The flame of sex singes your absolute, and cruelly scorches your ego. What, will you assert your ego in the universe? Wait till the flames of sex leap at you like striped tigers.

They returned from the ride
With the lady inside,
And a smile on the face of the tiger.

You will play with sex, will you! You will tickle yourself with sex as with an ice-cold drink from a soda-fountain! You will pet your best girl, will you, and spoon with her, and titillate yourself and her, and do as you like with your sex?

Wait! Only wait till the flame you have dribbled on flies back at you; later! Only wait!

Sex is a life-flame, a dark one, reserved and mostly invisible. It is a deep reserve in a man, one of the core-flames of his manhood.

What, would you play with it? Would you make it cheap and nasty!

Buy a king-cobra, and try playing with that.

Sex is even a majestic reserve in the sun.

Oh, give me the novel! Let me hear what the novel says.

As for the novelist, he is usually a dribbling liar.

WHY THE NOVEL MATTERS (1925)

We have curious ideas of ourselves. We think of ourselves as a body with a spirit in it, or a body with a soul in it, or a body with a mind in it. *Mens sana in corpore sano.* The years drink up the wine, and at last throw the bottle away, the body, of course, being the bottle.

It is a funny sort of superstition. Why should I look at my hand, as it so cleverly writes these words, and decide that it is a mere nothing compared to the mind that directs it? Is there really any huge difference between my hand and my brain? Or my mind? My hand is alive, it flickers with a life of its own. It meets all the strange universe in touch, and learns a vast number of things, and knows a vast number of things. My hand, as it writes these words, slips gaily along, jumps like a grasshopper to dot an *i*, feels the table rather cold, gets a little bored if I write too long, has its own rudiments of thought, and is just as much *me* as is my brain, my mind, or my soul. Why should I imagine that there is a *me* which is more *me* than my hand is? Since my hand is absolutely alive, me alive.

Whereas, of course, as far as I am concerned, my pen isn't alive at all. My pen *isn't me* alive. Me alive ends at my finger-tips.

Whatever is me alive is me. Every tiny bit of my hands is alive, every little freckle and hair and fold of skin. And whatever is me alive is me. Only my finger-nails, those ten little weapons between me and an inanimate universe, they cross the mysterious Rubicon between me alive and things like my pen, which are not alive, in my own sense.

So, seeing my hand is all alive, and me alive, wherein is it just a bottle, or a jug, or a tin can, or a vessel of clay, or any of the rest of that nonsense? True, if I cut it it will bleed, like a can of cherries. But then the skin that is cut, and the veins that bleed, and the bones that should never be seen, they are all just as alive as the blood that flows. So the tin can business, or vessel of clay, is just bunk.

And that's what you learn, when you're a novelist. And that's what you are very liable *not* to know, if you're a parson, or a philosopher, or a scientist, or a stupid person. If you're a parson, you talk about souls in heaven. If you're a novelist, you know that paradise is in the palm of your hand, and on the end of your nose, because both are alive; and alive, and man alive, which is more than you can say, for certain, of paradise. Paradise is after life, and I for one am not keen on anything that is *after* life. If you are a philosopher, you talk about infinity, and the pure spirit which knows all things. But if you pick up a novel, you realize immediately that infinity is just a handle to this self-same jug of a body of mine; while as for knowing, if I find my finger in the fire, I know that fire burns, with a knowledge so emphatic and vital, it leaves Nirvana merely a conjecture. Oh, yes, my body, me alive, *knows*, and knows intensely. And as for the sum of all knowledge, it can't be anything more than an accumulation of all the things I know in the body, and you, dear reader, know in the body.

These damned philosophers, they talk as if they suddenly went off in steam, and were then much more important than they are when they're in their shirts. It is nonsense. Every man, philosopher included, ends in his own finger-tips. That's the end of his man alive. As for the words and thoughts and sighs and aspirations that fly from him, they are so many tremulations in the ether, and not alive at all. But if the tremulations reach another man alive, he may receive them into his life, and his life may take on a new colour, like a chameleon creeping from a brown rock on to a green leaf. All very well and good. It still doesn't alter the fact that the so-called spirit, the message or teaching of the philosopher or the saint, isn't alive at all, but just a tremulation upon the ether, like a radio message. All this spirit stuff is just tremulations upon the ether. If you, as man alive, quiver from the tremulation of the ether into new life, that is because you are man alive, and you take sustenance and stimulation into your alive man in a myriad ways. But to say that the message, or the spirit which is communicated to you, is more important than your living body, is nonsense. You might as well say that the potato at dinner was more important.

Nothing is important but life. And for myself, I can absolutely see life nowhere but in the living. Life with a capital L is only man alive. Even a cabbage in the rain is cabbage alive. All things that are alive are amazing. And all things that are dead are subsidiary to the living. Better a live dog than a dead lion. But better a live lion than a live dog. *C'est la vie!*

It seems impossible to get a saint, or a philosopher, or a scientist, to stick to this simple truth. They are all, in a sense, renegades. The saint wishes to offer himself up as spiritual food for the multitude. Even Francis of Assisi turns himself into a sort of angel-cake, of which anyone may take a slice. But an angel-cake is rather less than man alive. And poor St Francis might well apologize to his body, when he is dying: 'Oh, pardon me, my body, the wrong I did you through the years!' It was no wafer, for others to eat.

The philosopher, on the other hand, because he can think, decides that nothing but thoughts matter. It is as if a rabbit, because he can make little pills, should decide that nothing but little pills matter. As for the scientist, he has absolutely no use for me so long as I am man alive. To the scientist, I am dead. He puts under the microscope a bit of dead me, and calls it me. He takes me to pieces, and says first one piece, and then another piece, is me. My heart, my liver, my stomach have all been scientifically me, according to the scientist; and nowadays I am either a brain, or nerves, or glands, or something more up-to-date in the tissue line.

Now I absolutely flatly deny that I am a soul, or a body, or a mind, or an intelligence, or a brain, or a nervous system, or a bunch of glands, or any of the rest of these bits of me. The whole is greater than the part. And therefore, I, who am man alive, am greater than my soul, or spirit, or body, or mind, or consciousness, or anything else that is merely a part of me. I am a man, and alive. I am man alive, and as long as I can, I intend to go on being man alive.

For this reason I am a novelist. And being a novelist, I consider myself superior to the saint, the scientist, the philosopher, and the poet, who are all great masters of different bits of man alive, but never get the whole hog.

The novel is the one bright book of life. Books are not life. They are only tremulations on the ether. But the novel as a tremulation can make the whole man alive tremble. Which is more than poetry, philosophy, science, or any other book-tremulation can do.

The novel is the book of life. In this sense, the Bible is a great confused novel. You may say, it is about God. But it is really about man alive. Adam, Eve, Sarai, Abraham, Isaac, Jacob, Samuel, David, Bath-Sheba, Ruth, Esther, Solomon, Job, Isaiah, Jesus, Mark, Judas, Paul, Peter: what is it but man alive, from start to finish? Man alive, not mere bits. Even the Lord is another man alive, in a burning bush, throwing the tablets of stone at Moses's head.

I do hope you begin to get my idea, why the novel is supremely important, as a tremulation on the ether. Plato makes the perfect ideal being tremble in me. But that's only a bit of me. Perfection is only a bit, in the strange make-up of man alive. The Sermon on the Mount makes the selfless spirit of me quiver. But that, too, is only a bit of me. The Ten Commandments set the old Adam shivering in me, warning me that I am a thief and a murderer, unless I watch it. But even the old Adam is only a bit of me.

I very much like all these bits of me to be set trembling with life and the wisdom of life. But I do ask that the whole of me shall tremble in its wholeness, some time or other.

And this, of course, must happen in me, living.

But as far as it can happen from a communication, it can only happen when a whole novel communicates itself to me. The Bible – but *all* the Bible – and Homer, and Shakespeare: these are the supreme old novels. These are all things to all men. Which means that in their wholeness they affect the whole man alive, which is the man himself, beyond any part of him. They set the whole tree trembling with a new access of life, they do not just stimulate growth in one direction.

I don't want to grow in any one direction any more. And, if I can help it, I don't want to stimulate anybody else into some particular direction. A particular direction ends in a *cul-de-sac*. We're in a *cul-de-sac* at present.

I don't believe in any dazzling revelation, or in any supreme Word. 'The grass withereth, the flower fadeth, but the Word of the Lord shall stand for ever.' That's the kind of stuff we've drugged ourselves with. As a matter of fact, the grass withereth, but comes up all the greener for that reason, after the rains. The flower fadeth, and therefore the bud opens. But the Word of the Lord, being man-uttered and a mere vibration on the ether, becomes staler and staler, more and more boring, till at last we turn a deaf ear and it ceases to exist, far more finally than any withered grass. It is grass that renews its youth like the eagle, not any Word.

We should ask for no absolutes, or absolute. Once and for all and for ever, let us have done with the ugly imperialism of any absolute. There is no absolute good, there is nothing absolutely right. All things flow and change, and even change is not absolute. The whole is a strange assembly of apparently incongruous parts, slipping past one another.

Me, man alive, I am a very curious assembly of incongruous parts. My yea! of today is oddly different from my yea! of yesterday. My tears of tomorrow will have nothing to do with my tears of a year ago. If the one I love remains unchanged and unchanging, I shall cease to love her. It is only because she changes and startles me into change and defies my inertia, and is herself staggered in her inertia by my changing, that I can continue to love her. If she stayed put, I might as well love the pepper-pot.

In all this change, I maintain a certain integrity. But woe betide me if I try to put my finger on it. If I say of myself, I am this, I am that! – then, if I stick to it, I turn into a stupid fixed thing like a lamp-post. I shall never know wherein lies my integrity, my individuality, my me. I *can* never know it. It is useless to talk about my ego. That only means that I have made up an *idea* of myself, and that I am trying to cut myself out to pattern. Which is no good. You can cut your cloth to fit your coat, but you can't clip bits off your living body, to trim it down to your idea. True, you can put yourself into ideal corsets. But even in ideal corsets, fashions change.

Let us learn from the novel. In the novel, the characters can do nothing but *live*. If they keep on being good, according to pattern, or bad, according to pattern, or even volatile, according to pattern, they cease to live, and the novel falls dead. A character in a novel has got to live, or it is nothing.

We, likewise, in life have got to live, or we are nothing.

What we mean by living is, of course, just as indescribable as what we mean by *being*. Men get ideas into their heads, of what they mean by Life, and they proceed to cut life out to pattern. Sometimes they go into the desert to seek God, sometimes they go into the desert to seek cash, sometimes it is wine, woman, and song, and again it is water, political reform, and votes. You never know what it will be next: from killing your neighbour with hideous bombs and gas that tears the lungs, to supporting a Foundlings Home and preaching infinite Love, and being co-respondent in a divorce.

In all this wild welter, we need some sort of guide. It's no good inventing Thou Shalt Nots!

What then? Turn truly, honourably to the novel, and see wherein you are man alive, and wherein you are dead man in life. You may love a woman as man alive, and you may be making love to a woman as sheer dead man in life. You may eat your dinner as man alive, or as a mere masticating corpse. As man alive you may have a shot at your enemy. But as a ghastly simulacrum of life you may be firing bombs into men who are neither your enemies nor your friends, but just things you are dead to. Which is criminal, when the things happen to be alive.

To be alive, to be man alive, to be whole man alive: that is the point. And at its best, the novel, and the novel supremely, can help you. It can help you not to be dead man in life. So much of a man walks about dead and a carcass in the street and house, today: so much of women is merely dead. Like a pianoforte with half the notes mute.

But in the novel you can see, plainly, when the man goes dead, the woman goes inert. You can develop an instinct for life, if you will, instead of a theory of right and wrong, good and bad.

In life, there is right and wrong, good and bad, all the time. But what is right in one case is wrong in another. And in the novel you see one man becoming a corpse, because of his so-called goodness, another going dead because of his so-called wickedness. Right and wrong is an instinct: but an instinct of the whole consciousness in a man, bodily, mental, spiritual at once. And only in the novel are *all* things given full play, or at least, they may be given full play, when we realize that life itself, and not inert safety, is the reason for living. For out of the full play of all things emerges the only thing that is anything, the wholeness of a man, the wholeness of a woman, man alive, and live woman.

THE NOVEL AND THE FEELINGS
(1925)

We think we are so civilized, so highly educated and civilized. It is farcical. Because, of course, all our civilization consists in harping on one string. Or at most on two or three strings. Harp, harp, harp, twingle, twingle-twang! That's our civilization, always on one note.

The note itself is all right. It's the exclusiveness of it that is awful. Always the same note, always the same note! 'Ah, how can you run after other women when your wife is so delightful, a lovely plump partridge?' Then the husband laid his hand on his waistcoat, and a frightened look came over his face. 'Nothing but partridge?' he exclaimed.

Toujours perdrix! It was up to that wife to be a goose and a cow, an oyster and an inedible vixen, at intervals.

Wherein are we educated? Come now, in what are we educated? In politics, in geography, in history, in machinery, in soft drinks and in hard, in social economy and social extravagance: ugh! a frightful universality of knowings.

But it's all France without Paris, *Hamlet* without the Prince, and bricks without straw. For we know nothing, or next to nothing, about ourselves. After hundreds of thousands of years we have learned how to wash our faces and bob our hair, and that is about all we *have* learned, *individually*. Collectively, of course, as a species, we have combed the round earth with a tooth-comb, and pulled down the stars almost within grasp. And then what?

Here sit I, a two-legged individual with a risky temper, knowing all about – take a pinch of salt – Tierra del Fuego and Relativity and the composition of celluloid, the appearance of the anthrax bacillus and solar eclipses, and the latest fashion in shoes; and it don't do me *no* good: as the charlady said of near beer. It doesn't leave me feeling no less lonesome inside! as the old English-woman said, long ago, of tea without rum.

Our knowledge, like the prohibition beer, is always near. But it never gets there. It leaves us feeling just as lonesome inside.

We are hopelessly uneducated in ourselves. We pretend that when we know a smattering of the Patagonian idiom we have in so far educated ourselves. What nonsense! The leather of my boots is just as effectual in turning me into a bull, or a young steer. Alas! we wear our education just as externally as we wear our boots, and to far less profit. It is all external education, anyhow.

What am I, when I am at home? I'm supposed to be a sensible human being. Yet I carry a whole waste-paper basket of ideas at the top of my head, and in some other part of my anatomy, the dark continent of myself. I have a whole stormy chaos of 'feelings.' And with these self-same feelings I simply don't get a chance. Some of them roar like lions, some twist like snakes, some bleat like snow-white lambs, some warble like linnets, some are absolutely dumb, but swift as slippery fishes, some are oysters that open on occasion: and lo! here am I, adding another scrap of paper to the ideal accumulation in the waste-paper bas-ket, hoping to settle the matter that way.

The lion springs on me! I wave an idea at him. The serpent casts a terrifying glance at me, and I hand him a Moody and Sankey hymn-book. Matters go from bad to worse.

The wild creatures are coming forth from the darkest Africa inside us. In the night you can hear them bellowing. If you are a big game-hunter, like Billy Sunday, you may shoulder your elephant gun. But since the forest is inside all of us, and in every forest there's a whole assortment of big game and dangerous creatures, it's one against a thousand. We've managed to keep clear of the darkest Africa inside us, for a long time. We've been so busy finding the North Pole and converting the Patagonians, loving our neighbour and devising new means of exterminating him, listening-in and shutting-out.

But now, my dear, dear reader, Nemesis is blowing his nose. And muffled roarings are heard out of darkest Africa, with stifled shrieks.

I say feelings, not emotions. Emotions are things we more or less recognize. We see love, like a woolly lamb, or like a decorative decadent panther in Paris clothes: according as it is sacred or profane. We see hate, like a dog chained to a kennel. We see fear, like a shivering monkey. We see anger, like a bull with a ring through his nose, and greed, like a pig. Our emotions are our domesticated animals, noble like the horse, timid like the rabbit, but all completely at our service. The rabbit goes into the pot, and the horse into the shafts. For we are creatures of circumstance, and must fill our bellies and our pockets.

Convenience! Convenience! There are convenient emotions and inconvenient ones. The inconvenient ones we chain up, or put a ring through their nose. The convenient ones are our pets. Love is our pet favourite.

And that's as far as our education goes, in the direction of feelings. We have no language for the feelings, because our feelings do not even exist for us.

Yet what is a man? Is he really just a little engine that you stoke with potatoes and beef-steak? Does all the strange flow of life in him come out of meat and potatoes, and turn into the so-called physical energy?

Educated! We are not even *born*, as far as our feelings are concerned.

You can eat till you're bloated, and 'get ahead' till you're a by-word, and still, inside you, will be the darkest Africa whence come roars and shrieks.

Man is not a little engine of cause and effect. We must put that out of our minds for ever. The *cause* in man is something we shall never fathom. But there it is, a strange dark continent that we do not explore, because we do not even allow that it exists. Yet all the time, it is within us: the *cause* of us, and of our days.

And our feelings are the first manifestations within the aboriginal jungle of us. Till now, in sheer terror of ourselves, we have turned our backs on the jungle, fenced it in with an enormous entanglement of barbed wire, and declared it did not exist.

But alas! we ourselves only exist because of the life that bounds and leaps into our limbs and our consciousness, from out of the original dark forest within us. We may wish to exclude this inbounding, inleaping life. We may wish to be as our domesticated animals are, tame. But let us remember that even our cats and dogs have, in each generation, to be tamed. They are not now a tame species. Take away the control, and they will cease to be tame. They will not tame *themselves*.

Man is the only creature who has deliberately tried to tame himself. He has succeeded. But alas! it is a process you cannot set a limit to. Tameness, like alcohol, destroys its own creator. Tameness is an effect of control. But the tamed thing loses the power of control, in itself. It must be controlled from without. Man has pretty well tamed himself, and he calls his tameness civilization. True civilization would be something very different. But man is now tame. Tameness means the loss of the peculiar power of command. The tame are always commanded by the untame. Man has tamed himself, and so has lost his power for command, the power to give himself direction. He has no choice in himself. He is tamed, like a tame horse waiting for the rein.

Supposing all horses were suddenly rendered masterless,

what would they do? They would run wild. But supposing they were left still shut up in their fields, paddocks, corrals, stables, what would they do? They would go insane.

And that is precisely man's predicament. He is tamed. There are no untamed to give the commands and the direction. Yet he is shut up within all his barbed wire fences. He can only go insane, degenerate.

What is the alternative? It is nonsense to pretend we can untame ourselves in five minutes. That, too, is a slow and strange process, that has to be undertaken seriously. It is nonsense to pretend we can break the fences and dash out into the wilds. There are no wilds left, comparatively, and man is a dog that returns to his vomit.

Yet unless we proceed to connect ourselves up with our own primeval sources, we shall degenerate. And degenerating, we shall break up into a strange orgy of feelings. They will be decomposition feelings, like the colours of autumn. And they will precede whole storms of death, like leaves in a wind.

There is no help for it. Man cannot tame himself and then stay tame. The moment he tries to stay tame he begins to degenerate, and gets the second sort of wildness, the wildness of destruction, which may be autumnal-beautiful for a while, like yellow leaves. Yet yellow leaves can only fall and rot.

Man tames himself in order to learn to un-tame himself again. To be civilized, we must not deny and blank out our feelings. Tameness is not civilization. It is only burning down the brush and ploughing the land. Our civilization has hardly realized yet the necessity for ploughing the soul. Later, we sow wild seed. But so far, we've only been burning off and rooting out the old wild brush. Our civilization, as far as our own souls go, has been a destructive process, up to now. The landscape of our souls is a charred wilderness of burnt-off stumps, with a green bit of water here, and a tin shanty with a little iron stove.

Now we have to sow wild seed again. We have to cultivate our feelings. It is no good trying to be popular, to let a whole rank tangle of liberated, degenerate feelings spring up. It will give us no satisfaction.

And it is no use doing as the psychoanalysts have done. The psychoanalysts show the greatest fear of all, of the innermost primeval place in man, where God is, if He is anywhere. The old Jewish horror of the true Adam, the mysterious 'natural man,' rises to a shriek in psychoanalysis. Like the idiot who foams and bites his wrists till they bleed. So great is the Freudian hatred of the oldest, old Adam, from whom God is not yet separated off, that the psychoanalyst sees this Adam as nothing but a monster of perversity, a bunch of engendering adders, horribly clotted.

This vision is the perverted vision of the degenerate tame: tamed through thousands of shameful years. The old Adam is the for ever untamed: he who is of the tame hated, with a horror of fearful hate: but who is held in innermost respect by the fearless.

In the oldest of the old Adam, was God: behind the dark wall of his breast, under the seal of the navel. Then man had a revulsion against himself, and God was separated off, lodged in the outermost space.

Now we have to return. Now again the old Adam must lift up his face and his breast, and un-tame himself. Not in viciousness nor in wantonness, but having God within the walls of himself. In the very darkest continent of the body there is God. And from Him issue the first dark rays of our feeling, wordless, and utterly previous to words: the innermost rays, the first messengers, the primeval, honourable beasts of our being, whose voice echoes wordless and for ever wordless down the darkest avenues of the soul, but full of potent speech. Our own inner meaning.

Now we have to educate ourselves, not by laying down laws and inscribing tables of stone, but by listening. Not listening-in to noises from Chicago or Timbuktu. But listening-in to the voices of the honourable beasts that call in the dark paths of the veins of our body, from the God in the heart. Listening inwards, inwards, not for words nor for inspiration, but to the lowing of the innermost beasts, the feelings, that roam in the forest of the blood, from the feet of God within the red, dark heart.

And how? How? How shall we even begin to educate ourselves in the feelings?

Not by laying down laws, or commandments, or axioms and postulates. Not even by making assertions that such and such is blessed. Not by words at all.

If we can't hear the cries far down in our own forests of dark veins, we can look in the real novels, and there listen-in. Not listen to the didactic statements of the author, but to the low, calling cries of the characters, as they wander in the dark woods of their destiny.

REFLECTIONS ON THE DEATH OF A PORCUPINE (1925)

There are many bare places on the little pine trees, towards the top, where the porcupines have gnawed the bark away and left the white flesh showing. And some trees are dying from the top.

Everyone says porcupines should be killed; the Indians, Mexicans, Americans all say the same.

At full moon a month ago, when I went down the long clearing in the brilliant moonlight, through the poor dry herbage a big porcupine began to waddle away from me, towards the trees and the darkness. The animal had raised all its hairs and bristles, so that by the light of the moon it seemed to have a tall, swaying, moonlit aureole arching its back as it went. That seemed curiously fearsome, as if the animal were emitting itself demon-like on the air.

It waddled very slowly, with its white spiky spoon-tail steering flat, behind the round bear-like mound of its back. It had a lumbering, beetle's, squalid motion, unpleasant. I followed it into the darkness of the timber, and there, squat like a great tick, it began scrapily to creep up a pine-trunk. It was very like a great aureoled tick, a bug, struggling up.

I stood near and watched, disliking the presence of the creature. It is a duty to kill the things. But the dislike of killing him was greater than the dislike of him. So I watched him climb.

And he watched me. When he had got nearly the height of a man, all his long hairs swaying with a bristling gleam like an aureole, he hesitated, and slithered down. Evidently he had decided, either that I was harmless, or else that it was risky to go up any further, when I could knock him off so easily with a pole. So he slithered podgily down again, and waddled away with the same bestial, stupid motion of that white-spiky repulsive spoon-tail. He was as big as a middle-sized pig: or more like a bear.

I let him go. He was repugnant. He made a certain squalor in the moonlight of the Rocky Mountains. As all savagery has a touch of squalor, that makes one a little sick at the stomach. And anyhow, it seemed almost more squalid to pick up a pine-bough and push him over, hit him and kill him.

A few days later, on a hot, motionless morning when the pine-trees put out their bristles in stealthy, hard assertion; and I was not in a good temper, because Black-eyed Susan, the cow, had disappeared into the timber, and I had had to ride hunting her, so it was nearly nine o'clock before she was milked: Madame came in suddenly out of the sunlight, saying: 'I got such a shock! There are two strange dogs, and one of them has got the most awful beard, all round his nose.'

She was frightened, like a child, at something unnatural.

'Beard! Porcupine quills, probably! He's been after a porcupine.'

'Ah!' she cried in relief. 'Very likely! Very likely!' – then with a change of tone; 'Poor thing, will they hurt him?'

'They will. I wonder when he came.'

'I heard dogs bark in the night.'

'Did you? Why didn't you say so? I should have known Susan was hiding –'

The ranch is lonely, there is no sound in the night, save the innumerable noises of the night, that you can't put your finger on; cosmic noises in the far deeps of the sky, and of the earth.

I went out. And in the full blaze of sunlight in the field, stood two dogs, a black-and-white, and a big, bushy, rather handsome sandy-red dog, of the collie type. And sure enough, this latter did look queer and a bit horrifying, his whole muzzle set round with white spines, like some ghastly growth; like an unnatural beard.

The black-and-white dog made off as I went through the fence. But the red dog whimpered and hesitated, and moved on hot bricks. He was fat and in good condition. I thought he might belong to some shepherds herding sheep in the forest ranges, among the mountains.

He waited while I went up to him, wagging his tail and whimpering, and ducking his head, and dancing. He daren't rub his nose with his paws any more: it hurt too much. I patted his head and looked at his nose, and he whimpered loudly.

He must have had thirty quills, or more, sticking out of his nose, all the way round: the white, ugly ends of the quills protruding an inch, sometimes more, sometimes less, from his already swollen, blood-puffed muzzle.

The porcupines here have quills only two or three inches long. But they are devilish; and a dog will die if he does not get them pulled out. Because they work further and further in, and will sometimes emerge through the skin away in some unexpected place.

Then the fun began. I got him in the yard: and he drank up the whole half-gallon of the chickens' sour milk. Then I started pulling out the quills. He was a big, bushy, handsome dog, but his nerve was gone, and every time I got a quill out, he gave a yelp. Some long quills were fairly easy. But the shorter ones, near his lips, were deep in, and hard to get hold of, and hard to pull out when you did get hold of them. And with every one that came out, came a little spurt of blood and another yelp and writhe.

The dog wanted the quills out: but his nerve was gone. Every time he saw my hand coming to his nose, he jerked his head away. I quieted him, and stealthily managed to jerk out another quill, with the blood all over my fingers. But with every one that came out, he grew more tiresome. I tried and tried and tried to get hold of another quill, and he jerked and jerked, and writhed and whimpered, and ran under the porch floor.

It was a curiously unpleasant, nerve-trying job. The day was blazing hot. The dog came out and I struggled with him again for an hour or more. Then we blindfolded him. But either he smelled my hand approaching his nose, or some weird instinct told him. He jerked his head, this way, that way, up, down, side-ways, roundwise, as one's fingers came slowly, slowly, to seize a quill.

The quills on his lips and chin were deep in, only about a quarter of an inch of white stub protruding from the swollen, blood-oozed, festering black skin. It was very difficult to jerk them out.

We let him lie for an interval, hidden in the quiet cool place under the porch floor. After half an hour, he crept out again. We got a rope round his nose, behind the bristles, and one held while the other got the stubs with the pliers. But it was too try-ing. If a quill came out, the dog's yelp startled every nerve. And he was frightened of the pain, it was impossible to hold his head still any longer.

After struggling for two hours, and extracting some twenty quills, I gave up. It was impossible to quiet the creature, and I had had enough. His nose on the top was clear: a punctured, puffy, blood-darkened mess; and his lips were clear. But just on his round little chin, where the few white hairs are, was still a bunch of white quills, eight or nine, deep in.

We let him go, and he dived under the porch, and there he lay invisible: save for the end of his bushy, foxy tail, which moved when we came near. Towards noon he emerged, ate up the chicken-food, and stood with that doggish look of dejection, and fear, and friendliness, and greediness, wagging his tail.

But I had had enough.

'Go home!' I said. 'Go home! Go home to your master, and let him finish for you.'

He would not go. So I led him across the blazing hot clearing, in the way I thought he should go. He followed a hundred yards, then stood motionless in the blazing sun. He was not going to leave the place.

And I! I simply did not want him.

So I picked up a stone. He dropped his tail, and swerved towards the house. I knew what he was going to do. He was going to dive under the porch, and there stick, haunting the place.

I dropped my stone, and found a good stick under the cedar tree. Already in the heat was that sting-like biting of electricity, the thunder gathering in the sheer sunshine, without a cloud, and making one's whole body feel dislocated.

I could not bear to have that dog around any more. Going quietly to him, I suddenly gave him one hard hit with the stick, crying: 'Go home!' He turned quickly, and the end of the stick caught him on his sore nose. With a fierce yelp, he went off like a wolf, downhill, like a flash, gone. And I stood in the field full of pangs of regret, at having hit him, unintentionally, on his sore nose.

But he was gone.

And then the present moon came, and again the night was clear. But in the interval there had been heavy thunder-rains, the ditch was running with bright water across the field, and the night, so fair, had not the terrific, mirror-like brilliancy, touched with terror, so startling bright, of the moon in the last days of June.

We were alone on the ranch. Madame went out into the clear night, just before retiring. The stream ran in a cord of silver across the field, in the straight line where I had taken the irrigation ditch. The pine tree in front of the house threw a black shadow. The mountain slope came down to the fence, wild and alert.

'Come!' said she excitedly. 'There is a big porcupine drinking at the ditch. I thought at first it was a bear.'

When I got out he had gone. But among the grasses and the coming wild sunflowers, under the moon, I saw his greyish halo, like a pallid living bush, moving over the field, in the distance, in the moonlit *clair-obscur*.

We got through the fence, and following, soon caught him up. There he lumbered, with his white spoon-tail spiked with bristles, steering behind almost as if he were moving backwards, and this was his head. His long, long hairs above the quills quivering with a dim grey gleam, like a bush.

And again I disliked him.

'Should one kill him?'

She hesitated. Then with a sort of disgust:

'Yes!'

I went back to the house, and got the little twenty-two rifle. Now never in my life had I shot at any live thing: I never wanted to. I always felt guns very repugnant: sinister, mean. With difficulty I had fired once or twice at a target: but resented doing even so much. Other people could shoot if they wanted to. Myself, individually, it was repugnant to me even to try.

But something slowly hardens in a man's soul. And I knew now it had hardened in mine. I found the gun, and with rather trembling hands got it loaded. Then I pulled back the trigger and followed the porcupine. It was still lumbering through the grass. Coming near, I aimed.

The trigger stuck. I pressed the little catch with a safety-pin I found in my pocket, and released the trigger. Then we followed the porcupine. He was still lumbering towards the trees. I went sideways on, stood quite near to him, and fired, in the clear-dark of the moonlight.

And as usual I aimed too high. He turned, went scuttling back whence he had come.

I got another shell in place, and followed. This time I fired full into the mound of his round back, below the glistening grey halo. He seemed to stumble on to his hidden nose, and struggled a few strides, ducking his head under like a hedgehog.

'He's not dead yet! Oh, fire again!' cried Madame.

I fired, but the gun was empty.

So I ran quickly, for a cedar pole. The porcupine was lying still, with subsiding halo. He stirred faintly. So I turned him and hit him hard over the nose; or where, in the dark, his nose should have been. And it was done. He was dead.

And in the moonlight, I looked down on the first creature I had ever shot.

'Does it seem mean?' I asked aloud, doubtful.

Again Madame hesitated. Then: 'No!' she said resentfully.

And I felt she was right. Things like the porcupine, one must be able to shoot them, if they get in one's way.

One must be able to shoot. I, myself, must be able to shoot, and to kill.

For me, this is a *volta face*. I have always preferred to walk round my porcupine, rather than kill it.

Now, I know it's no good walking round. One must kill.

I buried him in the adobe hole. But some animal dug down and ate him; for two days later there lay the spines and bones spread out, with the long skeletons of the porcupine-hands.

The only nice thing about him – or her, for I believe it was a female, by the dugs on her belly – were the feet. They were like longish, alert black hands, paw-hands. That is why a porcupine's tracks in the snow look almost as if a child had gone by, leaving naked little human foot-prints, like a little boy.

So, he is gone: or she is gone. But there is another one, bigger and blacker-looking, among the west timber. That too is to be shot. It is part of the business of ranching: even when it's only a little half-abandoned ranch like this one.

Wherever man establishes himself, upon the earth, he has to fight for his place against the lower orders of life. Food, the basis of existence, has to be fought for even by the most idyllic of farmers. You plant, and you protect your growing crop with a gun. Food, food, how strangely it relates man with the animal and vegetable world! How important it is! And how fierce is the fight that goes on around it.

The same when one skins a rabbit, and takes out the inside, one realizes what an enormous part of the animal, comparatively, is intestinal, what a big part of him is just for food-apparatus; for *living on* other organisms.

And when one watches the horses in the big field, their noses to the ground, bite-bite-biting at the grass, and stepping absorbedly on, and bite-bite-biting without ever lifting their noses, cropping off the grass, the young shoots of alfalfa, the dandelions, with a blind, relentless, unwearied persistence, one's whole life pauses. One suddenly realizes again how all creatures devour, and *must* devour the lower forms of life.

So Susan, swinging across the field, snatches off the tops of the little wild sunflowers as if she were mowing. And down they go, down her black throat. And when she stands in her cowy oblivion chewing her cud, with her lower jaw swinging peacefully, and I am milking her, suddenly the camomiley smell of her breath, as she glances round with glaring, smoke-blue eyes, makes me realize it is the sunflowers that are her ball of cud. Sunflowers! And they will go to making her glistening black hide, and the thick cream on her milk.

And the chickens, when they see a great black beetle, that the Mexicans call a *toro*, floating past, they are after it in a rush. And if it settles, instantly the brown hen stabs it with her beak. It is a great beetle two or three inches long: but in a second it is in the crop of the chicken. Gone!

And Timsy, the cat, as she spies on the chipmunks, crouches

in another sort of oblivion, soft, and still. The chipmunks come to drink the milk from the chickens' bowl. Two of them met at the bowl. They were little squirrely things with stripes down their backs. They sat up in front of one another, lifting their inquisitive little noses and humping their backs. Then each put its two little hands on the other's shoulders, they reared up, gazing into each other's faces; and finally they put their two little noses together, in a sort of kiss.

But Miss Timsy can't stand this. In a soft, white-and-yellow leap she is after them. They skip, with the darting jerks of chipmunks, to the wood-heap, and with one soft, high-leaping sideways bound Timsy goes through the air. Her snow-flake of a paw comes down on one of the chipmunks. She looks at it for a second. It squirms. Swiftly and triumphantly she puts her two flowery little white paws on it, legs straight out in front of her, back arched, gazing concentratedly yet whimsically. Chipmunk does not stir. She takes it softly in her mouth, where it dangles softly, like a lady's tippet. And with a proud, prancing motion the Timsy sets off towards the house, her white little feet hardly touching the ground.

But she gets shooed away. We refuse to loan her the sitting-room any more, for her gladiatorial displays. If the chippy must be 'butchered to make a Timsy holiday', it shall be outside. Disappointed, but still high-stepping, the Timsy sets off towards the clay oven by the shed.

There she lays the chippy gently down, and soft as a little white cloud lays one small paw on its striped back. Chippy does not move. Soft as thistle-down she raises her paw a tiny, tiny bit, to release him.

And all of a sudden, with an elastic jerk, he darts from under the white release of her paw. And instantly, she is up in the air and down she comes on him, with the forward thrusting bolts of her white paws. Both creatures are motionless.

Then she takes him softly in her mouth again, and looks round, to see if she can slip into the house. She cannot. So she trots towards the wood-pile.

It is a game, and it is pretty. Chippy escapes into the wood-pile, and she softly, softly reconnoitres among the faggots.

Of all the animals, there is no denying it, the Timsy is the most pretty, the most fine. It is not her mere *corpus* that is beautiful; it is her bloom of aliveness. Her 'infinite variety'; the soft, snow-flakey lightness of her, and at the same time her lean, heavy ferocity. I had never realized the latter, till I was lying in bed one day moving my toe, unconsciously, under the bedclothes. Suddenly a terrific blow struck my foot. The Timsy had sprung out of nowhere, with a hurling, steely force, thud upon the bedclothes where the toe was moving. It was as if someone had aimed a sudden blow, vindictive and unerring.

'Timsy!'

She looked at me with the vacant, feline glare of her hunting eyes. It is not even ferocity. It is the dilation of the strange, vacant arrogance of power. The power is in her.

And so it is. Life moves in circles of power and of vividness, and each circle of life only maintains its orbit upon the subjection of some lower circle. If the lower cycles of life are not *mastered*, there can be no higher cycle.

In nature, one creature devours another, and this is an essential part of all existence and of all being. It is not something to lament over, nor something to try to reform. The Buddhist who refuses to take life is really ridiculous, since if he eats only two grains of rice per day, it is two grains of life. We did not make creation, *we* are not the authors of the universe. And if we see that the whole of creation is established upon the fact that one life devours another life, one cycle of existence can only come into existence through the subjugating of another cycle of existence, then what is the good of trying to pretend that it is not so? The only thing to do is to realize what is higher, and what is lower, in the cycles of existence.

It is nonsense to declare that there *is* no higher and lower. We know full well that the dandelion belongs to a higher cycle of existence than the hartstongue fern, that the ant's is a higher form of existence than the dandelion's, that the thrush is higher than the ant, that Timsy the cat is higher than the thrush, and that I, a man, am higher than Timsy.

What do we mean by higher? Strictly, we mean more alive. More vividly alive. The ant is more vividly alive than the pine tree. We know it, there is no trying to refute it. It is all very well saying that they are both alive in two different ways, and therefore they are incomparable, incommensurable. This is also true.

But one truth does not displace another. Even apparently contradictory truths do not displace one another. Logic is far too coarse to make the subtle distinctions life demands.

Truly, it is futile to compare an ant with a great pine-tree, in the absolute. Yet as far as *existence* is concerned, they are not only placed in comparison to one another, they are occasionally pitted against one another. And if it comes to a contest, the little ant will devour the life of the huge tree. If it comes to a contest.

And, in the cycles of *existence*, this is the test. From the lowest form of existence to the highest, the test question is: *Can thy neighbour finally overcome thee?*

If he can, then he belongs to a higher cycle of existence.

This is the truth behind the survival of the fittest. Every cycle of existence is established upon the overcoming of the lower cycles of existence. The real question is, wherein does *fitness* lie? Fitness for what? Fit merely to survive? That which is only fit to survive will survive only to supply food or contribute in some way to the existence of a higher form of life, which is able to do more than survive, which can really *vive*, live.

Life is more vivid in the dandelion than in the green fern, or than in a palm tree.

Life is more vivid in a snake than in a butterfly.

Life is more vivid in a wren than in an alligator.

Life is more vivid in a cat than in an ostrich.

Life is more vivid in the Mexican who drives the wagon than in the two horses in the wagon.

Life is more vivid in me than in the Mexican who drives the wagon for me.

We are speaking in terms of *existence*: that is, in terms of species, race, or type.

The dandelion can take hold of the land, the palm tree is driven into a corner, with the fern.

The snake can devour the fiercest insect.

The fierce bird can destroy the greatest reptile.

The great cat can destroy the greatest bird.

The man can destroy the horse, or any animal.

One race of man can subjugate and rule another race.

All this in terms of *existence*. As far as existence goes, that life-species is the highest which can devour, or destroy, or subjugate every other life-species against which it is pitted in contest.

This is a law. There is no escaping this law. Anyone, or any race, trying to escape it will fall a victim: will fall into subjugation.

But let us insist and insist again, we are talking now of existence, of species, of types, of races, of nations, not of single individuals, nor of *beings*. The dandelion in full flower, a little sun bristling with sun-rays on the green earth, is a nonpareil, a nonsuch. Foolish, foolish, foolish to compare it to anything else on earth. It is itself incomparable and unique.

But that is the fourth dimension, of *being*. It is in the fourth dimension, nowhere else.

Because, in the time-space dimension, any man may tread on

the yellow sun-mirror, and it is gone. Any cow may swallow it. Any bunch of ants may annihilate it.

This brings us to the inexorable law of life.

1. Any creature that attains to its own fullness of being, its own *living* self, becomes unique, a nonpareil. It has its place in the fourth dimension, the heaven of existence, and there it is perfect, it is beyond comparison.

2. At the same time, every creature exists in time and space. And in time and space it exists relatively to all other existence, and can never be absolved. Its existence impinges on other existences, and is itself impinged upon. And in the struggle for existence, if an effort on the part of any one type or species or order of life can finally destroy the other species, then the destroyer is of a more vital cycle of existence than the one destroyed. (When speaking of existence we always speak in types, species, not individuals. Species exist. But even an individual dandelion has *being*.)

3. The force which we call *vitality*, and which is the determining factor in the struggle for existence, is, however, derived also from the fourth dimension. That is to say, the ultimate source of all vitality is in that other dimension, or region, where the dandelion blooms, and which men have called heaven, and which now they call the fourth dimension: which is only a way of saying that it is not to be reckoned in terms of space and time.

4. The primary way, in our existence, to get vitality, is to absorb it from living creatures lower than ourselves. It is thus transformed into a new and higher creation. (There are many ways of absorbing: devouring food is one way, love is often another. The best way is a pure relationship, which includes the *being* on each side, and which allows the transfer to take place in a living flow, enhancing the life in both beings.)

5. No creature is fully itself till it is, like the dandelion, opened in the bloom of pure relationship to the sun, the entire living cosmos.

So we still find ourselves in the tangle of existence and being, a tangle which man has never been able to get out of, except by sacrificing the one to the other.

Sacrifice is useless.

The clue to all existence is being. But you can't have being without existence, any more than you can have the dandelion flower without the leaves and the long tap root.

Being is *not* ideal, as Plato would have it: nor spiritual. It is a transcendent form of existence, and as much material as existence is. Only the matter suddenly enters the fourth dimension.

All existence is dual, and surging towards a consummation into being. In the seed of the dandelion, as it floats with its little umbrella of hairs, sits the Holy Ghost in tiny compass. The Holy Ghost is that which holds the light and the dark, the day and the night, the wet and the sunny, united in one little clue. There it sits, in the seed of the dandelion.

The seed falls to earth. The Holy Ghost rouses, saying: 'Come!' And out of the sky come the rays of the sun, and out of earth come dampness and dark and the death-stuff. They are called in, like those bidden to a feast. The sun sits down at the hearth, inside the seed; and the dark, damp death-returner sits on the opposite side, with the host between. And the host says to them: '*Come! Be merry together!*' So the sun looks with desirous curiosity on the dark face of the earth, and the dark damp one looks with wonder on the bright face of the other, who comes from the sun. And the host says: '*Here you are at home! Lift me up, between you, that I may cease to be a Ghost. For it longs me to look out, it longs me to dance with the dancers.*'

So the sun in the seed, and the earthy one in the seed take hands, and laugh, and begin to dance. And their dancing is like a fire kindled, a bonfire with leaping flame. And the treading of their feet is like the running of little streams, down into the earth. So from the dance of the sun-in-the-seed with the earthy death-returner, green little flames of leaves shoot up, and hard little trickles of roots strike down. And the host laughs, and says: '*I am being lifted up! Dance harder! Oh wrestle, you two, like wonderful wrestlers, neither of which can win.*' So sun-in-the-seed and the death-returner, who is earthy, dance faster and faster and the leaves rising greener begin to dance in a ring above-ground, fiercely overwhelming any outsider, in a whirl of swords and lions' teeth. And the earthy one wrestles, wrestles with the sun-in-the-seed, so the long roots reach down like arms of a fighter gripping the power of earth, and strangles all intruders, strangling any intruder mercilessly. Till the two fall in one strange embrace, and from the centre the long flower-stem lifts like a phallus, budded with a bud. And out of the bud the voice of the Holy Ghost is heard crying: '*I am lifted up! Lo! I am lifted up! I am here!*' So the bud opens, and there is the flower poised in the very middle of the universe, with a ring of green swords below, to guard it, and the octopus, arms deep in earth, drinking and threatening. So the Holy Ghost, being a dandelion flower, looks round, and says: '*Lo! I am yellow! I believe the sun has lent me his body! Lo! I am sappy with golden, bitter blood! I believe death out of the damp black earth has lent me his blood! I am incarnate! I like my incarnation! But this is not all. I will keep this incarnation. It is good! But oh! if I can win to another incarnation, who knows how wonderful it will be! This one will have to give place. This one can help to create the next.*'

So the Holy Ghost leaves the clue of himself behind, in the seed, and wanders forth in the comparative chaos of our universe, seeking another incarnation.

And this will go on for ever. Man, as yet, is less than half grown. Even his flower-stem has not appeared yet. He is all leaves and roots, without any clue put forth. No sign of bud anywhere.

Either he will have to start budding, or he will be forsaken of the Holy Ghost: abandoned as a failure in creation, as the ich-thyosaurus was abandoned. Being abandoned means losing his vitality. The sun and the earth-dark will cease rushing together in him. Already it is ceasing. To men, the sun is becoming stale, and the earth sterile. But the sun itself will never become stale, nor the earth barren. It is only that the *clue* is missing inside men. They are like flowerless, seedless fat cabbages, nothing inside.

Vitality depends upon the clue of the Holy Ghost inside a creature, a man, a nation, a race. When the clue goes, the vitality goes. And the Holy Ghost seeks for ever a new incarnation, and subordinates the old to the new. You will know that any creature or race is still alive with the Holy Ghost, when it can subordinate the lower creatures or races, and assimilate them into a new incarnation.

No man, or creature, or race can have vivid vitality unless it be moving towards a blossoming: and the most powerful is that which moves towards the as-yet-unknown blossom.

Blossoming means the establishing of a pure, *new* relationship with all the cosmos. This is the state of heaven. And it is the state of a flower, a cobra, a jenny-wren in spring, a man when he knows himself royal and crowned with the sun, with his feet gripping the core of the earth.

This too is the fourth dimension: this state, this mysterious other reality of things in a perfected relationship. It is into this perfected relationship that every straight line curves, as if to some core, passing out of the time-space dimension.

But any man, creature, or race moving towards blossoming will have to draw immense supplies of vitality from men, or creatures below, passionate strength. And he will have to accomplish a perfected relation with all things.

There will be conquest, always. But the aim of conquest is a perfect relation of conquerors with conquered, for a new blossoming. Freedom is illusory. Sacrifice is illusory. Almightiness is illusory. Freedom, sacrifice, almightiness, these are all human side-tracks, cul-de-sacs, bunk. All that is real is the overwhelm-ingness of a new inspirational command, a new relationship with all things.

Heaven is always there. No achieved consummation is lost. Procreation goes on for ever, to support the achieved reve-lation. But the torch of revelation itself is handed on. And this is all important.

Everything living wants to procreate more living things.

But more important than this is the fact that every revelation is a torch held out, to kindle new revelations. As the dandelion holds out the sun to me, saying: *'Can you take it!'*

Every gleam of heaven that is shown – like a dandelion flower, or a green beetle – quivers with strange passion to kindle a new gleam, never yet beheld. This is not self-sacrifice: it is self-contribution: in which the highest happiness lies.

The torch of existence is handed on, in the womb of procreation.

And the torch of revelation is handed on, by every living thing, from the protococcus to a brave man or a beautiful woman, handed to whomsoever can take it. He who can take it has power beyond all the rest.

The cycle of procreation exists purely for the keeping alight of the torch of perfection, in any species: the torch being the dandelion in blossom, the tree in full leaf, the peacock in all his plumage, the cobra in all his colour, the frog at full leap, woman in all the mystery of her fathomless desirableness, man in the fulness of his power: every creature become its pure self.

One cycle of perfection urges to kindle another cycle, as yet unknown.

And with the kindling from the torch of revelation comes the inrush of vitality, and the need to consume and *consummate* the lower cycles of existence, into a new thing. This consuming and this consummating means conquest, and fearless mastery.

Freedom lies in the honourable yielding towards the new flame, and the honourable mastery of that which shall be new, over that which must yield. As I must master my horses, which are in a lower cycle of existence. And they, they are relieved and *happy* to serve. If I turn them loose into the mountain ranges, to run wild till they die, the thrill of real happiness is gone out of their lives.

Every lower order seeks in some measure to serve a higher order: and rebels against being conquered.

It is always conquest, and it always will be conquest. If the conquered be an old, declining race, they will have handed on their torch to the conqueror: who will burn his fingers badly, if he is too flippant. And if the conquered be a barbaric race, they will consume the fire of the conqueror, and leave him flameless, unless he watch it. But it is always conquest, conquered and conqueror, for ever. The Kingdom of heaven is the Kingdom of conquerors, who can serve the conquest for ever, after their own conquest is made.

In heaven, in the perfected relation, is peace: in the fourth dimension. But there is getting there. And that, for ever, is the process of conquest.

When the rose blossomed, then the great Conquest was made by the Vegetable Kingdom. But even this conqueror of conquerors, the rose, had to lend himself towards the caterpillar and the butterfly of a later conquest. A conqueror, but tributary to the later conquest.

There is no such thing as equality. In the kingdom of heaven, in the fourth dimension, each soul that achieves a perfect relationship with the cosmos, from its own centre, is perfect, and incomparable. It has no superior. It is a conqueror, and incomparable.

But every man, in the struggle of conquest towards his own consummation, must master the inferior cycles of life, and never relinquish his mastery. Also, if there be men beyond him, moving on to a newer consummation than his own, he must yield to their greater demand, and serve their greater mystery, and so be faithful to the kingdom of heaven which is within him, which is gained by conquest and by loyal service.

Any man who achieves his own being will, like the dandelion or the butterfly, pass into that other dimension which we call the fourth, and the old people called heaven. It is the state of perfected relationship. And here a man will have his peace for ever: whether he serve or command, in the process of living.

But even this entails his faithful allegiance to the kingdom of heaven, which must be for ever and for ever extended, as creation conquers chaos. So that my perfection will but serve a perfection which still lies ahead, unrevealed and unconceived, and beyond my own.

We have tried to build walls round the kingdom of heaven: but it's no good. It's only the cabbage rotting inside.

Our last wall is the golden wall of money. This is a fatal wall. It cuts us off from life, from vitality, from the alive sun and the alive earth, as *nothing* can. Nothing, not even the most fanatical dogmas of an iron-bound religion, can insulate us from the inrush of life and inspiration, as money can.

We are losing vitality: losing it rapidly. Unless we seize the torch of inspiration, and drop our moneybags, the moneyless will be kindled by the flame of flames, and they will consume us like old rags.

We are losing vitality, owing to money and money-standards. The torch in the hands of the moneyless will set our house on fire, and burn us to death, like sheep in a flaming corral.

MAN IS A HUNTER (1926)

It is a very nice law which forbids shooting in England on Sundays. Here in Italy, on the contrary, you would think there was a law ordering every Italian to let off a gun as often as possible. Before the eyelids of dawn have come apart, long before the bells of the tiny church jangle to announce daybreak, there is a sputter and crackle as of irritating fireworks, scattering from the olive gardens and from the woods. You sigh in your bed. The Holy Day has started: the huntsmen are abroad; they will keep at it till heaven sends the night, and the little birds are no more.

The very word *cacciatore*, which means hunter, stirs one's bile. Oh, Nimrod, oh, Bahram, put by your arrows:

> And Bahram, the great hunter: the wild ass
> Stamps o'er his bed, and cannot wake his sleep.

Here, an infinite number of tame asses shoot over my head, if I happen to walk in the wood to look at the arbutus berries, and they never fail to rouse my ire, no matter how fast asleep it may have been.

Man is a hunter! *L'uomo è cacciatore*: the Italians are rather fond of saying it. It sounds so virile. One sees Nimrod surging through the underbrush, with his spear, in the wake of a bleeding lion. And if it is a question of a man who has got a girl into trouble: *'L'uomo è cacciatore'* – 'man is a hunter' – what can you expect? It behoves the 'game' to look out for itself. Man is a hunter!

There used to be a vulgar song: 'If the Missis wants to go for a row, let 'er go.' Here it should be: 'If the master wants to run, with a gun, let him run.' For the pine-wood is full of them, as a dog's back with fleas in summer. They crouch, they lurk, they stand erect, motionless as virile statues, with gun on the alert. Then *bang!* they have shot something, with an astonishing amount of noise. And then they run, with fierce and predatory strides, to the spot.

There is nothing there! Nothing! The game! *La caccia!* – where is it? If they had been shooting at the ghost of Hamlet's father, there could not be a blanker and more spooky emptiness. One expects to see a wounded elephant lying on its side, writhing its trunk; at the very least, a wild boar ploughing the earth in his death-agony. But no! There is nothing, just nothing at all. Man, being a hunter, is, fortunately for the rest of creation, a very bad shot.

Nimrod, in velveteen corduroys, bandolier, cartridges, game-bag over his shoulder and gun in his hand, stands with feet apart *virilissimo*, on the spot where the wild boar should be, and gazes downwards at some imaginary point in underworld space. So! Man is a hunter. He casts a furtive glance around, under the arbutus bush, and a tail of his eye in my direction, knowing I am looking on in raillery. Then he hitches his game-bag more determinedly over his shoulder, grips his gun, and strides off uphill, large strides, virile as Hector. Perhaps even he is a Hector, Italianized into Ettore. Anyhow, he's going to be the death of something or somebody, if only he can shoot straight.

A Tuscan pine-wood is by no means a jungle. The trees are umbrella-pines, with the umbrellas open, and bare handles. They are rather parsimoniously scattered. The undergrowth, moreover, is allowed to grow only for a couple of years or so; then it is most assiduously reaped, gleaned, gathered, cleaned up clean as a lawn, for cooking Nimrod's macaroni. So that, in a *pineta*, you have a piny roof over your head, and for the rest a pretty clear run for your money. So where can the game lurk? There is hardly cover for a bumble-bee. Where can the game be that is worth all this powder? The lions and wolves and boars that must prowl perilously round all these Nimrods?

You will never know. Or not until you are going home, between the olive-trees. The hunters have been burning powder in the open, as well as in the wood: a proper fusillade. Then, on the path between the olives, you may pick up a warm, dead bullfinch, with a bit of blood on it. The little grey bird lies on its side, with its frail feet closed, and its red breast ruffled. Nimrod, having hit for once, has failed to find his quarry.

So you will know better when the servant comes excitedly and asks: 'Signore, do you want any game?' Game! Splendid idea! A couple of partridges? a hare? even a wild rabbit? Why, of course! So she arrives in triumph with a knotted red handkerchief, and the not very bulky game inside it. Untie the knots! Aha! – Alas! There, in a little heap on the table, three robins, two finches, four hedge-sparrows, and two starlings, in a fluffy, coloured, feathery little heap, all the small heads rolling limp. 'Take them away,' you say. 'We don't eat little birds.' 'But these,' she says, tipping up the starlings roughly, 'these are big ones.' 'Not these, either, do we eat.' 'No?' she exclaims, in a tone which means: '*More fools you!*' And, disgusted, disappointed at not having sold the goods, she departs with the game.

You will know best of all if you go to the market, and see whole yard-lengths of robins, like coral and onyx necklaces, and strings of bullfinches, goldfinches, larks, sparrows, nightingales, starlings, temptingly offered along with strings of sausages, these last looking like the strings of pearls in the show. If one bought the birds to wear as ornament, barbaric necklaces, it would be more conceivable. You can get quite a string of different-coloured ones for tenpence. But imagine the small mouthful of little bones each of these tiny carcasses must make!

But, after all, a partridge and a pheasant are only a bit bigger than a sparrow and a finch. And compared to a flea, a robin is big game. It is all a question of dimensions. Man is a hunter. 'If the master wants to hunt, don't you grunt; let him hunt!'

RETURN TO BESTWOOD (1926)

I came home to the Midlands for a few days, at the end of September. Not that there is any home, for my parents are dead. But there are my sisters, and the district one calls home; that mining district between Nottingham and Derby.

It always depresses me to come to my native district. Now I am turned forty, and have been more or less a wanderer for nearly twenty years, I feel more alien, perhaps, in my home place than anywhere else in the world. I can feel at ease in Canal Street, New Orleans, or in the Avenue Madero, in Mexico City, or in George Street, Sydney, in Trincomallee Street, Kandy, or in Rome or Paris or Munich or even London. But in Nottingham Road, Bestwood, I feel at once a devouring nostalgia and an infinite repulsion. Partly I want to get back to the place as it was when I was a boy, and I waited so long to be served in the Co-op I remember our Co-op number, 1553A.L., better than the date of my birth – and when I came out hugging a string net of groceries. There was a little hedge across the road from the Co-op then, and I used to pick the green buds which we called bread-and-cheese. And there were no houses in Gabes Lane. And at the corner of Queen Street, Butcher Bob was huge and fat and taciturn.

Butcher Bob is long dead, and the place is all built up. I am never quite sure where I am, in Nottingham Road. Walker Street is not very much changed, though, because the ash tree was cut down when I was sixteen, when I was ill. The houses are still only on one side the street, the fields on the other. And still one looks across at the amphitheatre of hills which I still find beautiful, though there are new patches of reddish houses, and a darkening of smoke. Crich is still on the sky line to the west, and the woods of Annesley to the north, and Coney Grey Farm still lies in front. And there is still a certain glamour about the country-side. Curiously enough, the more motor-cars and tram-cars and omnibuses there are rampaging down the roads, the more the country retreats into its own isolation, and becomes more mysteriously inaccessible.

When I was a boy, the whole population lived very much more *with* the country. Now, they rush and tear along the roads, and have joy-rides and outings, but they never seem to touch the reality of the country-side. There are many more people, for one thing: and all these new contrivances, for another.

The country seems, somehow, fogged over with people, and yet not really touched. It seems to lie back, away, unreached and asleep. The roads are hard and metalled and worn with everlasting rush. The very field-paths seem wider and more trodden and squalid. Wherever you go, there is the sordid sense of humanity.

And yet the fields and the woods in between the roads and paths sleep as in a heavy, weary dream, disconnected from the modern world.

This visit, this September, depresses me peculiarly. The weather is soft and mild, mildly sunny in that hazed, dazed, uncanny sunless sunniness which makes the Midlands peculiarly fearsome to me. I cannot, cannot accept as sunshine this thin luminous vaporousness which passes as a fine day in the place of my birth. Oh Phœbus Apollo! Surely you have turned your face aside!

But the special depression this time is the great coal strike, still going on. In house after house, the families are now living on bread and margarine and potatoes. The colliers get up before dawn, and are away into the last recesses of the country-side, scouring the country for blackberries, as if there were a famine. But they will sell the blackberries at fourpence a pound, and so they'll be fourpence in pocket.

But when I was a boy, it was utterly *infra dig.* for a miner to be picking blackberries. He would never have demeaned himself to such an unmanly occupation. And as to walking home with a little basket – he would almost rather have committed murder. The children might do it, or the women, or even the half grown youths. But a married, manly collier!

But nowadays, their pride is in their pocket, and the pocket has a hole in it.

It is another world. There are policemen everywhere, great big strange policemen with faces like a leg of mutton. Where they come from, heaven only knows: Ireland or Scotland, presumably, for they are no Englishmen. And they exist, along the country-side, in thousands. The people call them 'blue-bottles,' and 'meat-flies.' And you can hear a woman call across the street to another: 'Seen any blow-flies about?' – Then they turn to look at the alien policemen, and laugh shrilly.

And this in my native place! Truly, one no longer knows the palm of his own hand. When I was a boy, we had our own police sergeant, and two young constables. And the women would as leave have thought of calling Sergeant Mellor a 'blue-bottle' as calling Queen Victoria one. The Sergeant was a quiet, patient man, who spent his life trying to keep people out of trouble. He was another sort of shepherd, and the miners and their children were a flock to him. The women had the utmost respect for him.

But the women seem to have changed most in this, that they have no respect for anything. There was a scene in the market-place yesterday, a Mrs Hufton and a Mrs Rowley being taken off to court to be tried for insulting and obstructing the police. The police had been escorting the black-legs from the mines, after a so-called day's work, and the women had made the usual row. They were two women from decent homes. In the past they would have died of shame, at having to go to court. But now, not at all.

They had a little gang of women with them in the market-place, waving red flags and laughing loudly and using occasional bad language. There was one, the decent wife of the post-man. I had known her and played with her as a girl. But she was waving her red flag, and cheering as the motor-bus rolled up.

The two culprits got up, hilariously, into the bus.

'Good luck, old girl! Let 'em have it! Give it the blue-bottles in the neck! Tell 'em what for! Three cheers for Bestwood! Strike while the iron's hot, girls!'

'So long! So long, girls! See you soon! Merry home coming, what, eh?'

'Have a good time, now! Have a good time! Stick a pin in their fat backsides, if you can't move 'em any other road. We s'll be thinking of you!'

'So long! So long! See you soon! Who says Walker!'

'E-eh! E-eh!'

The bus rolled heavily off, with the shouting women, amid the strange hoarse cheering of the women in the little market-place. The draughty little market-place where my mother shopped on Friday evenings, in her rusty little black bonnet, and where now a group of decent women waved little red flags and hoarsely cheered two women going to court!

O mamma mia! – as the Italians say. My dear mother, your little black bonnet would fly off your head in horrified astonishment, if you saw it now. You were so keen on progress: a decent working man, and a good wage! You paid my father's union pay for him, for so many years! You believed so firmly in the Co-op! You were at your Women's Guild when they brought you word your father, the old tyrannus, was dead! At the same time, you believed so absolutely in the ultimate benevolence of all the masters, of all the upper classes. One had to be grateful to them, after all!

Grateful! You can have your cake and eat it, while the cake lasts. When the cake comes to an end, you can hand on your indigestion. Oh my dear and virtuous mother, who believed in a Utopia of goodness, so that your own people were never quite good enough for you – not even the spoiled delicate boy, myself! – oh my dear and virtuous mother, behold the indigestion we have inherited, from the cake of perfect goodness you baked too often! Nothing was good enough! We must all rise into the upper classes! Upper! Upper! Upper!

Till at last the boots are all uppers, the sole is worn out, and we yell as we walk on stones.

My dear, dear mother, you were so tragic, because you had nothing to be tragic about! We, on the other side, having a moral and social indigestion that would raise the wind for a thousand explosive tragedies, let off a mild crepitus ventris and shout: Have a good time, old girl! Enjoy yourself, old lass!

Nevertheless, we have all of us 'got on.' The reward of goodness, in my mother's far-off days, less than twenty years ago, was that you should 'get on.' *Be good, and you'll get on in life.*

Myself, a snotty-nosed little collier's lad, I call myself at home when I sit in a heavy old Cinquecento Italian villa, of which I rent only half, even then – surely I can be considered to have 'got on.' When I wrote my first book, and it was going to be published – sixteen years ago – and my mother was dying, a fairly well-known editor wrote to my mother and said, of me: 'By the time he is forty, he will be riding in his carriage.'

To which my mother is supposed to have said, sighing, 'Ay, if he lives to be forty!'

Well, I am forty-one, so there's one in the eye for that sighing remark. I was always weak in health, but my life was strong. Why had they all made up their minds that I was to die? Perhaps they thought I was too good to live. Well, in that case they were had!

And when I was forty, I was not even in my own motor-car. But I did drive my own two horses in a light buggy (my own) on a little ranch (also my own, or my wife's, through me) away on the western slope of the Rocky Mountains. And sitting in my corduroy trousers and blue shirt, calling: 'Get up Aaron! *Ambrose!*' then I thought of Justin Harrison's prophecy. Oh Oracle of Delphos! Oracle of Dodona! 'Get up, Ambrose!' Bump! went the buggy over a rock, and the pine-needles slashed my face! See him driving in his carriage, at forty! – driving it pretty badly too! Put the brake on!

So I suppose I've got on, snotty-nosed little collier's lad, of whom most of the women said: 'He's a *nice* little lad!' They don't say it now: if ever they say anything, which is doubtful. They've forgotten me entirely.

But my sister's 'getting on' is much more concrete than mine. She is almost on the spot. Within six miles of that end dwelling in The Breach, which is the house I first remember – an end house of hideous rows of miners' dwellings, though I loved it, too – stands my sister's new house, 'a lovely house!' – and her garden: 'I wish mother could see my garden in June!'

And if my mother did see it, what then? It is wonderful the flowers that bloom in these Midlands, in June. A northern Persephone seems to steal out from the Plutonic, coal-mining depths and give a real hoot of blossoms. But if my mother *did* return from the dead, and see that garden in full bloom, and the glass doors open from the hall of the new house, what then? Would she then say: It is reached! Consummatum est!

When Jesus gave up the ghost, he cried: It is finished. Consummatum est! But was it? And if so, what? What was it that was consummate?

Likewise, before the war, in Germany I used to see advertised in the newspapers a moustache-lifter, which you tied on at night and it would make your moustache stay turned up, like the immortal moustache of Kaiser Wilhelm II, whose moustache alone is immortal. This moustache-lifter was called: Es ist erreicht! In other words: It is reached! Consummatum est!

Was it? Was it reached? With the moustache-lifter?

So the ghost of my mother, in my sister's garden. I see it each time I am there, bending over the violas, or looking up at the almond tree. Actually an almond tree! And I always ask, of the grey-haired, good little ghost: 'Well what of it, my dear? What is the verdict?'

But she never answers, though I press her:

'Do look at the house, my dear! Do look at the tiled hall, and the rug from Mexico, and the brass from Venice, seen through the open doors, beyond the lilies and the carnations of the lawn beds! Do look! And do look at me, and see if I'm not a gentleman! Do say that I'm almost upper class!'

But the dear little ghost says never a word.

'Do say we've got on! Do say we've arrived. Do say it is reached, es ist erreicht, consummatum est!'

But the little ghost turns aside, she knows I am teasing her. She gives me one look, which is a look I know, and which says: 'I shan't tell you, so you can't laugh at me. You must find out for yourself.' And she steals away, to her place, wherever it may be. – 'In my father's house are many mansions. If it were not so, I would have told you.'

The black-slate roofs beyond the wind-worn young trees at the end of the garden are the same thick layers of black roofs of blackened brick houses, as ever. There is the same smell of sulphur from the burning pit bank. Smuts fly on the white violas. There is a harsh sound of machinery. Persephone couldn't quite get out of hell, so she let Spring fall from her lap along the upper workings.

But no! There are no smuts, there is even no smell of the burning pit bank. They cut the bank, and the pits are not working. The strike has been going on for months. It is September, but there are lots of roses on the lawn beds.

'Where shall we go this afternoon? Shall we go to Hardwick?'

Let us go to Hardwick. I have not been for twenty years. Let us go to Hardwick:

> Hardwick Hall
> More window than wall.

Built in the days of good Queen Bess, by that other Bess, termagant and tartar, Countess of Shrewsbury.

Butterley, Alfreton, Tibshelf – what was once the Hardwick district is now the Notts-Derby coal area. The country is the same, but scarred and splashed all over with mines and mining settlements. Great houses loom from hill-brows, old villages are smothered in rows of miners' dwellings, Bolsover Castle rises from the mass of the colliery village of Bolsover. – Böwser, we called it, when I was a boy.

Hardwick is shut. On the gates, near the old inn, where the atmosphere of the old world lingers perfect, is a notice: 'This park is closed to the public and to all traffic until further notice. No admittance.'

Of course! The strike! They are afraid of vandalism.

Where shall we go? Back into Derbyshire, or to Sherwood Forest.

Turn the car. We'll go on through Chesterfield. If I can't ride in my own carriage, I can still ride in my sister's motor-car.

It is a still September afternoon. By the ponds in the old park, we see colliers slowly loafing, fishing, poaching in spite of all notices.

And at every lane end there is a bunch of three or four policemen, 'blue-bottles,' big, big-faced, stranger policemen. Every field path, every stile seems to be guarded. There are great pits, coal mines, in the fields. And at the end of the paths coming out of the field from the colliery, along the high-road, the colliers are squatted on their heels, on the wayside grass, silent and watchful. Their faces are clean, white, and all the months of the strike have given them no colour and no tan. They are pit-bleached. They squat in silent remoteness, as if in the upper galleries of hell. And the policemen, alien, stand in a group near the stile. Each lot pretends not to be aware of the others.

It is past three. Down the path from the pit come straggling what my little nephew calls 'the dirty ones.' They are the men who have broken strike, and gone back to work. They are not many: their faces are black, they are in their pit-dirt. They linger till they have collected, a group of a dozen or so 'dirty ones,' near the stile, then they trail off down the road, the policemen, the alien 'blue-bottles,' escorting them. And the 'clean ones,' the colliers still on strike, squat by the wayside and watch without looking. They say nothing. They neither laugh nor stare. But here they are, a picket, and with their bleached faces they see without looking, and they register with the silence of doom, squatted down in rows by the road-side.

The 'dirty ones' straggle off in the lurching, almost slinking walk of colliers, swinging their heavy feet and going as if the mine-roof were still over their heads. The big blue policemen follow at a little distance. No voice is raised: nobody seems aware of anybody else. But there is the silent, hellish registering in the consciousness of all three groups, clean ones, dirty ones and blue-bottles.

So it is now all the way into Chesterfield, whose crooked spire lies below. The men who have gone back to work – they seem few, indeed – are lurching and slinking in quiet groups, home down the high-road, the police at their heels. And the pickets, with bleached faces, squat and lean and stand, in silent groups, with a certain pale fatality, like Hell, upon them.

And I, who remember the homeward-trooping of the colliers when I was a boy, the ringing of the feet, the red mouths and the quick whites of the eyes, the swinging pit bottles, and the strange voices of men from the underworld calling back and forth, strong and, it seemed to me, gay with the queer, absolved gaiety of miners – I shiver, and feel I turn into a ghost myself. The colliers were noisy, lively, with strong underworld voices such as I have never heard in any other men, when I was a boy. And after all, it is not so long ago. I am only forty-one.

But after the war, the colliers went silent: after 1920. Till 1920 there was a strange power of life in them, something wild and urgent, that one could hear in their voices. They were always excited, in the afternoon, to come up above-ground: and excited, in the morning, at going down. And they called in the darkness with strong, strangely evocative voices. And at the little local foot-ball matches, on the damp, dusky Saturday afternoons of winter, great, full-throated cries came howling from the foot-ball field, in the zest and the wildness of life.

But now, the miners go by to the foot-ball match in silence like ghosts, and from the field comes a poor, ragged shouting. These are the men of my own generation, who went to the board school with me. And they are almost voiceless. They go to the welfare clubs, and drink with a sort of hopelessness.

I feel I hardly know any more the people I come from, the colliers of the Erewash Valley district. They are changed, and I suppose I am changed. I find it so much easier to live in Italy. And they have got a new kind of shallow consciousness, all newspaper and cinema, which I am not in touch with. At the same time, they have, I think, an underneath ache and heaviness very much like my own. It must be so, because when I see them, I feel it so strongly.

They are the only people who move me strongly, and with whom I feel myself connected in deeper destiny. It is they who are, in some peculiar way, 'home' to me. I shrink away from them, and I have an acute nostalgia for them.

And now, this last time, I feel a doom over the country, and a shadow of despair over the hearts of the men, which leaves me no rest. Because the same doom is over me, wherever I go, and the same despair touches my heart.

Yet it is madness to despair, while we still have the course of destiny open to us.

One is driven back to search one's own soul, for a way out into a new destiny.

A few things I know, with inner knowledge.

I know that what I am struggling for is life, more life ahead, for myself and the men who will come after me: struggling against fixations and corruptions.

I know that the miners at home are men very much like me, and I am very much like them: ultimately, we want the same thing. I know they are, in the life sense of the word, good.

I know that there is ahead the mortal struggle for property.

I know that the ownership of property has become, now, a problem, a religious problem. But it is one we can solve.

I know I want to own a few things: my personal things. But I also know I want to own no more than those. I don't want to own a house, nor land, nor a motor-car, nor shares in anything. I don't want a fortune – not even an assured income.

At the same time, I don't want poverty and hardship. I know I need enough money to leave me free in my movements, and I want to be able to earn that money without humiliation.

I know that most decent people feel very much the same in this respect: and the indecent people must, in their indecency, be subordinated to the decent.

I know that we could, if we would, establish little by little a true democracy in England: we could nationalise the land and industries and means of transport, and make the whole thing work infinitely better than at present, *if we would*. It all depends on the spirit in which the thing is done.

I know we are on the brink of a class war.

I know we had all better hang ourselves at once, than enter on a struggle which shall be a fight for the ownership or non-ownership of property, pure and simple, and nothing beyond.

I know the ownership of property is a problem that may have to be fought out. But beyond the fight must lie a new hope, a new beginning.

I know our vision of life is all wrong. We must be prepared to have a new conception of what it means, *to live*. And everybody should try to help to build up this new conception, and everybody should be prepared to destroy, bit by bit, our old conception.

I know that man cannot live by his own will alone. With his soul, he must search for the sources of the power of life. It is life we want.

I know that where there is life, there is essential beauty. Genuine beauty, which fills the soul, is an indication of life, and genuine ugliness, which blasts the soul, is an indication of morbidity. – But prettiness is opposed to beauty.

I know that, first and foremost, we must be sensitive to life and to its movements. If there is power, it must be sensitive power.

I know that we must look after the quality of life, not the quantity. Hopeless life should be put to sleep, the idiots and the hopeless sick and the true criminal. And the birth-rate should be controlled.

I know we must take up the responsibility for the future, now. A great change is coming, and must come. What we need is some glimmer of a vision of a world that shall be, beyond the change. Otherwise we shall be in for a great débâcle.

What is alive, and open, and active, is good. All that makes for inertia, lifelessness, dreariness, is bad. This is the essence of morality.

What we should live for is life and the beauty of aliveness, imagination, awareness, and contact. To be perfectly alive is to be immortal.

I know these things, along with other things. And it is nothing very new to know these things. The only new thing would be to act on them.

And what is the good of saying these things, to men whose whole education consists in the fact that twice two are four? – which, being interpreted, means that twice tuppence is fourpence. All our education, the whole of it, is formed upon this little speck of dust.

REVIEW OF *IN OUR TIME* BY ERNEST HEMINGWAY (1927)

In Our Time is the last of the four American books, and Mr Hem ingway has accepted the goal. He keeps on making flights, but he has no illusion about landing anywhere. He knows it will be nowhere every time.

In Our Time calls itself a book of stories, but it isn't that. It is a series of successive sketches from a man's life, and makes a fragmentary novel. The first scenes, by one of the big lakes in America – probably Superior – are the best; when Nick is a boy. Then come fragments of war – on the Italian front. Then a soldier back home, very late, in the little town way west in Oklahoma. Then a young American and wife in post-war Europe; a long sketch about an American jockey in Milan and Paris; then Nick is back again in the Lake Superior region, getting off the train at a burnt-out town, and tramping across the empty country to camp by a trout-stream. Trout is the one passion life has left him – and this won't last long.

It is a short book: and it does not pretend to be about one man. But it is. It is as much as we need know of the man's life. The sketches are short, sharp, vivid, and most of them excellent. (The 'mottoes' in front seem a little affected.) And these few sketches are enough to create the man and all his history: we need know no more.

Nick is a type one meets in the more wild and woolly regions of the United States. He is the remains of the lone trapper and cow-boy. Nowadays he is educated, and through with everything. It is a state of *conscious*, accepted indifference to everything except freedom from work and the moment's interest. Mr Hemingway does it extremely well. Nothing matters. Everything happens. One wants to keep oneself loose. Avoid one thing only: getting connected up. Don't get connected up. If you get held by any-thing, break it. Don't be held. Break it, and get away. Don't get away with the idea of getting somewhere else. Just get away, for the sake of getting away. Beat it! 'Well, boy, I guess I'll beat it.' Ah, the pleasure in saying that!

Mr Hemingway's sketches, for this reason, are excellent: so short, like striking a match, lighting a brief sensational cigar-ette, and it's over. His young love-affair ends as one throws a cigarette-end away. 'It isn't fun any more.' – 'Everything's gone to hell inside me.'

It is really honest. And it explains a great deal of sentimentality. When a thing has gone to hell inside you, your sentimentalism tries to pretend it hasn't. But Mr Hemingway is through with the sentimentalism. 'It isn't fun any more. I guess I'll beat it.'

And he beats it, to somewhere else. In the end he'll be a sort of tramp, endlessly moving on for the sake of moving away from where he is. This is a negative goal, and Mr Hemingway is really good, because he's perfectly straight about it. He is like Krebs, in that devastating Oklahoma sketch: he doesn't love anybody, and it nauseates him to have to pretend he does. He doesn't even *want* to love anybody; he doesn't want to go any-where, he doesn't want to do anything. He wants just to lounge around and maintain a healthy state of nothingness inside him-self, and an attitude of negation to everything outside himself. And why shouldn't he, since that is exactly and sincerely what he feels? If he really *doesn't* care, then why should he care? Any-how, he doesn't.

FLOWERY TUSCANY (1927)

I

Each country has its own flowers, that shine out specially there. In England it is daisies and buttercups, hawthorn and cowslips. In America, it is goldenrod, stargrass, June daisies, Mayapple and asters, that we call Michaelmas daisies. In India, hibiscus and dattura and champa flowers, and in Australia mimosa, that they call wattle, and sharp-tongued strange heath-flowers. In Mexico it is cactus flowers, that they call roses of the desert, lovely and crystalline among many thorns; and also the dangling yard-long clusters of the cream bells of the yucca, like dropping froth.

But by the Mediterranean, now as in the days of the Argosy, and, we hope, for ever, it is narcissus and anemone, asphodel and myrtle. Narcissus and anemone, asphodel, crocus, myrtle, and parsley, they leave their sheer significance only by the Mediterranean. There are daisies in Italy too: at Pæstum there are white little carpets of daisies, in March, and Tuscany is spangled with celandine. But for all that, the daisy and the celandine are English flowers, their best significance is for us and for the North.

The Mediterranean has narcissus and anemone, myrtle and asphodel and grape hyacinth. These are the flowers that speak and are understood in the sun round the Middle Sea.

Tuscany is especially flowery, being wetter than Sicily and more homely than the Roman hills. Tuscany manages to remain so remote, and secretly smiling to itself in its many sleeves. There are so many hills popping up, and they take no notice of one another. There are so many little deep valleys with streams that seem to go their own little way entirely, regardless of river or sea. There are thousands, millions of utterly secluded little nooks, though the land has been under cultivation these thousands of years. But the intensive culture of vine and olive and wheat, by the ceaseless industry of naked human hands and winter-shod feet, and slow-stepping, soft-eyed oxen does not devastate a country, does not denude it, does not lay it bare, does not uncover its nakedness, does not drive away either Pan or his children. The streams run and rattle over wild rocks of secret places, and murmur through blackthorn thickets where the nightingales sing all together, unruffled and undaunted.

It is queer that a country so perfectly cultivated as Tuscany, where half the produce of five acres of land will have to support ten human mouths, still has so much room for the wild flowers and the nightingale. When little hills heave themselves suddenly up, and shake themselves free of neighbours, man has to build his garden and his vineyard, and sculp his landscape. Talk of hanging gardens of Babylon, all Italy, apart from the plains, is a hanging garden. For centuries upon centuries man has been patiently modelling the surface of the Mediterranean countries, gently rounding the hills, and graduating the big slopes and the little slopes into the almost invisible levels of terraces. Thousands of square miles of Italy have been lifted in human hands, piled and laid back in tiny little flats, held up by the drystone walls, whose stones came from the lifted earth. It is a work of many, many centuries. It is the gentle sensitive sculpture of all the landscape. And it is the achieving of the peculiar Italian beauty which is so exquisitely natural, because man, feeling his way sensitively to the fruitfulness of the earth, has moulded the earth to his necessity without violating it.

Which shows that it *can* be done. Man *can* live on the earth and by the earth without disfiguring the earth. It has been done here, on all these sculptured hills and softly, sensitively terraced slopes.

But, of course, you can't drive a steam plough on terraces four yards wide, terraces that dwindle and broaden and sink and rise a little, all according to the pitch and the breaking outline of the mother hill. Corn has got to grow on these little shelves of earth, where already the grey olive stands semi-invisible, and the grapevine twists upon its own scars. If oxen can step with that lovely pause at every little stride, they can plough the narrow field. But they will have to leave a tiny fringe, a grassy lip over the drystone wall below. And if the terraces are too narrow to plough, the peasant digging them will still leave the grassy lip, because it helps to hold the surface in the rains.

And here the flowers take refuge. Over and over and over and over has this soil been turned, twice a year, sometimes three times a year, for several thousands of years. Yet the flowers have never been driven out. There is a very rigorous digging and sifting, the little bulbs and tubers are flung away into perdition, not a weed shall remain.

Yet spring returns, and on the terrace lips, and in the stony nooks between terraces, up rise the aconites, the crocuses, the narcissus and the asphodel, the inextinguishable wild tulips. There they are, for ever hanging on the precarious brink of an existence, but for ever triumphant, never quite losing their footing. In England, in America, the flowers get rooted out, driven back. They become fugitive. But in the intensive cultivation of ancient Italian terraces, they dance round and hold their own.

Spring begins with the first narcissus, rather cold and shy and wintry. They are the little bunchy, creamy narcissus with the yellow cup like the yolk of the flower. The natives call these flowers *tazzette*, little cups. They grow on the grassy banks rather sparse, or push up among thorns.

To me they are winter flowers, and their scent is winter. Spring starts in February, with the winter aconite. Some icy day, when the wind is down from the snow of the mountains, early in February, you will notice on a bit of fallow land, under the olive trees, tight, pale-gold little balls, clenched tight as nuts, and resting on round ruffs of green near the ground. It is the winter aconite suddenly come.

The winter aconite is one of the most charming flowers. Like all the early blossoms, once her little flower emerges it is quite naked. No shutting a little green sheath over herself, like the daisy or the dandelion. Her bubble of frail, pale, pure gold rests on the round frill of her green collar, with the snowy wind trying to blow it away.

But without success. The *tramontana* ceases, comes a day of wild February sunshine. The clenched little nuggets of the aconite puff out, they become light bubbles, like small balloons, on a green base. The sun blazes on, with February splendour. And by noon, all under the olives are wide-open little suns, the aconites spreading all their rays; and there is an exquisitely sweet scent, honey-sweet, not narcissus-frosty; and there is a February humming of little brown bees.

Till afternoon, when the sun slopes, and the touch of snow comes back into the air.

But at evening, under the lamp on the table, the aconites are wide and excited, and there is a perfume of sweet spring that makes one almost start humming and trying to be a bee.

Aconites don't last very long. But they turn up in all odd places – on clods of dug earth, and in land where the broad-beans are thrusting up, and along the lips of terraces. But they like best land left fallow for one winter. There they throng, showing how quick they are to seize on an opportunity to live and shine forth.

In a fortnight, before February is over, the yellow bubbles of the aconite are crumpling to nothingness. But already in a cosy-nook the violets are dark purple, and there is a new little perfume in the air.

Like the debris of winter stand the hellebores, in all the wild places, and the butcher's broom is flaunting its last bright red berry. Hellebore is Christmas roses, but in Tuscany the flowers never come white. They emerge out of the grass towards the end of December, flowers wintry of winter, and they are delicately pale green, and of a lovely shape, with yellowish stamens. They have a peculiar wintry quality of invisibility, so lonely rising from the sere grass, and pallid green, held up like a little hand-mirror that reflects nothing. At first they are single upon a stem, short and lovely, and very wintry-beautiful, with a will not to be touched, not to be noticed. One instinctively leaves them alone. But as January draws towards February, these hellebores, these greenish Christmas roses become more assertive. Their pallid water-green becomes yellower, pale sulphur-yellow-green, and they rise up, they are in tufts, in throngs, in veritable bushes of greenish open flowers, assertive, bowing their faces with a helle-bore assertiveness. In some places they throng among the bushes and above the water of the stream, giving the peculiar pale glim-mer almost of primroses, as you walk among them, Almost of primroses, yet with a coarse hellebore leaf and an uprearing hel-lebore assertiveness, like snakes in winter.

And as one walks among them, one brushes the last scarlet off the butcher's broom. This low little shrub is the Christmas holly of Tuscany, only a foot or so high, with a vivid red berry stuck on in the middle of its sharp hard leaf. In February the last red ball rolls off the prickly plume, and winter rolls with it. The violets already are emerging from the moisture.

But before the violets make any show, there are the crocuses. If you walk up through the pine-wood, that lifts its umbrellas of pine so high, up till you come to the brow of the hill at the top, you can look south, due south, and see snow on the Apennines, and on a blue afternoon, seven layers of blue-hilled distance.

Then you sit down on that southern slope, out of the wind, and there it is warm, whether it be January or February, *tramontana* or not. There the earth has been baked by innumerable suns, baked and baked again; moistened by many rains, but never wetted for long. Because it is rocky, and full to the south, and sheering steep in the slope.

And there, in February, in the sunny baked desert of that crumbly slope, you will find the first crocuses. On the sheer aridity of crumbled stone you see a queer, alert little star, very sharp and quite small. It has opened out rather flat, and looks like a tiny freesia flower, creamy, with a smear of yellow yolk. It has no stem, seems to have been just lightly dropped on the crumbled, baked rock. It is the first hill-crocus.

II

North of the Alps, the everlasting winter is interrupted by summers that struggle and soon yield; south of the Alps, the everlasting summer is interrupted by spasmodic and spiteful winters that never get a real hold, but that are mean and dogged. North of the Alps, you may have a pure winter's day in June. South of the Alps, you may have a midsummer day in December or January or even February. The in-between, in either case, is just as it may be. But the lands of the sun are south of the Alps, for ever.

Yet things, the flowers especially, that belong to both sides of the Alps, are not much earlier south than north of the mountains. Through all the winter there are roses in the garden, lovely creamy roses, more pure and mysterious than those of summer, leaning perfect from the stem. And the narcissus in the garden are out by the end of January, and the little simple hyacinths early in February.

But out in the fields, the flowers are hardly any sooner than English flowers. It is mid-February before the first violets, the first crocus, the first primrose. And in mid-February one may find a violet, a primrose, a crocus in England, in the hedgerows and the garden corner.

And still there is a difference. There are several kinds of wild crocus in this region of Tuscany: being little spiky mauve ones, and spiky little creamy ones, that grow among the pine-trees of the bare slopes. But the beautiful ones are those of a meadow in the corner of the woods, the low hollow meadow below the steep, shadowy pine-slopes, the secretive grassy dip where the water seeps through the turf all winter, where the stream runs between thick bushes, where the nightingale sings his mightiest in May, and where the wild thyme is rosy and full of bees, in summer.

Here the lavender crocuses are most at home – here sticking out of the deep grass, in a hollow like a cup, a bowl of grass, come the lilac-coloured crocuses, like an innumerable encampment. You may see them at twilight, with all the buds shut, in the mysterious stillness of the grassy underworld, palely glimmering like myriad folded tents. So the apaches still camp, and close their tepees, in the hollows of the great hills of the West, at night.

But in the morning it is quite different. Then the sun shines strong on the horizontal green cloud-puffs of the pines, the sky is clear and full of life, the water runs hastily, still browned by the last juice of crushed olives. And there the earth's bowl of crocuses is amazing. You cannot believe that the flowers are really still. They are open with such delight, and their pistil-thrust is so red-orange, and they are so many, all reaching out wide and marvellous, that it suggests a perfect ecstasy of radiant, thronging movement, lit-up violet and orange, and surging in some invisible rhythm of concerted, delightful movement. You cannot believe they do not move, and make some sort of crystalline sound of delight. If you sit still and watch, you begin to move with them, like moving with the stars, and you feel the sound of their radiance. All the little cells of the flowers must be leaping with flowery life and utterance.

And the small brown honey-bees hop from flower to flower, dive down, try, and off again. The flowers have been already rifled, most of them. Only sometimes a bee stands on his head, kicking slowly inside the flower, for some time. He has found something. And all the bees have little loaves of pollen, bee-bread, in their elbow-joints.

The crocuses last in their beauty for a week or so, and as they begin to lower their tents and abandon camp, the violets begin to thicken. It is already March. The violets have been showing like tiny dark hounds for some weeks. But now the whole pack comes forth, among the grass and the tangle of wild thyme, till the air all sways subtly scented with violets, and the banks above where the crocuses had their tents are now swarming brilliant purple with violets. They are the sweet violets of early spring, but numbers have made them bold, for they flaunt and ruffle till the slopes are a bright blue-purple blaze of them, full in the sun, with an odd late crocus still standing wondering and erect amongst them.

And now that it is March, there is a rush of flowers. Down by the other stream, which turns sideways to the sun, and has tangles of brier and bramble, down where the hellebore has stood so wan and dignified all winter, there are now white tufts of primroses, suddenly come. Among the tangle and near the water-lip, tufts and bunches of primroses, in abundance. Yet they look more wan, more pallid, more flimsy than English primroses. They lack some of the full wonder of the northern flowers. One tends to overlook them, to turn to the great, solemn-faced purple violets that rear up from the bank, and above all, to the wonderful little towers of the grape-hyacinth.

I know no flower that is more fascinating, when it first appears, than the blue grape-hyacinth. And yet, because it lasts so long, and keeps on coming so repeatedly, for at least two months, one tends later on to ignore it, even to despise it a little. Yet that is very unjust.

The first grape-hyacinths are flowers of blue, thick and rich and meaningful, above the unrenewed grass. The upper buds are pure blue, shut tight; round balls of pure, perfect warm blue, blue, blue; while the lower bells are darkish blue-purple, with the spark of white at the mouth. As yet, none of the lower bells has withered, to leave the greenish, separate sparseness of fruiting that spoils the grape-hyacinth later on, and makes it seem naked and functional. All hyacinths are like that in the seeding.

But, at first, you have only a compact tower of night-blue clearing to dawn, and extremely beautiful. If we were tiny as fairies, and lived only a summer, how lovely these great trees of bells would be to us, towers of night and dawn-blue globes. They would rise above us thick and succulent, and the purple globes would push the blue ones up, with white sparks of ripples, and we should see a god in them.

As a matter of fact, someone once told me they were the flowers of the many-breasted Artemis; and it is true, the Cybele of Ephesus, with her clustered breasts was like a grape-hyacinth at the bosom.

This is the time, in March, when the sloe is white and misty in the hedge-tangle by the stream, and on the slope of land the peach tree stands pink and alone. The almond blossom, silvery pink, is passing, but the peach, deep-toned, bluey, not at all ethereal, this reveals itself like flesh, and the trees are like isolated individuals, the peach and the apricot.

A man said this spring: 'Oh, I *don't* care for peach blossom! It is such a vulgar pink!' One wonders what anybody means by a 'vulgar' pink. I think pink flannelette is rather vulgar. But probably it's the flannelette's fault, not the pink. And peach blossom has a beautiful sensual pink, far from vulgar, most rare and private. And pink is so beautiful in a landscape, pink houses, pink almond, pink peach and purply apricot, pink asphodels.

It is so conspicuous and so individual, that pink among the coming green of spring, because the first flowers that emerge from winter seem always white or yellow or purple. Now the celandines are out, and along the edges of the *podere*, the big, sturdy, black-purple anemones, with black hearts.

They are curious, these great, dark-violet anemones. You may pass them on a grey day, or at evening or early morning, and never see them. But as you come along in the full sunshine, they seem to be baying at you with all their throats, baying deep purple into the air. It is because they are hot and wide open now, gulping the sun. Whereas when they are shut, they have a silkiness and a curved head, like the curve of an umbrella handle, and a peculiar outward colourlessness, that makes them quite invisible. They may be under your feet, and you will not see them.

Altogether anemones are odd flowers. On these last hills above the plain, we have only the big black-purple ones, in tufts here and there, not many. But two hills away, the young green corn is blue with the lilac-blue kind, still the broad-petalled sort with the darker heart. But these flowers are smaller than our dark-purple, and frailer, more silky. Ours are substantial, thickly vegetable flowers, and not abundant. The others are lovely and silky-delicate, and the whole corn is blue with them. And they have a sweet, sweet scent, when they are warm.

Then on the priest's *podere* there are the scarlet, Adonis-blood anemones: only in one place, in one long fringe under a terrace, and there by a path below. These flowers above all you will never find unless you look for them in the sun. Their silver silk outside makes them quite invisible, when they are shut up.

Yet, if you are passing in the sun, a sudden scarlet faces on to the air, one of the loveliest scarlet apparitions in the world. The inner surface of the Adonis-blood anemone is as fine as velvet, and yet there is no suggestion of pile, not as much as on a velvet rose. And from this inner smoothness issues the red colour, perfectly pure and unknown of earth, no earthiness, and yet solid, not transparent. How a colour manages to be perfectly strong and impervious, yet of a purity that suggests condensed light, yet not luminous, at least, not transparent, is a problem. The poppy in her radiance is translucent, and the tulip in her utter redness has a touch of opaque earth. But the Adonis-blood anemone is neither translucent nor opaque. It is just pure condensed red, of a velvetiness without velvet, and a scarlet without glow.

This red seems to me the perfect premonition of summer – like the red on the outside of apple blossom – and later, the red of the apple. It is the premonition in redness of summer and of autumn.

The red flowers are coming now. The wild tulips are in bud, hanging their grey leaves like flags. They come up in myriads, wherever they get a chance. But they are holding back their redness till the last days of March, the early days of April.

Still, the year is warming up. By the high ditch the common magenta anemone is hanging its silky tassels, or opening its great magenta daisy-shape to the hot sun. It is much nearer to red than the big-petalled anemones are; except the Adonis-blood. They say these anemones sprang from the tears of Venus, which fell as she went looking for Adonis. At that rate, how the poor lady must have wept, for the anemones by the Mediterranean are common as daisies in England.

The daisies are out here too, in sheets, and they too are red-mouthed. The first ones are big and handsome. But as March goes on, they dwindle to bright little things, like tiny buttons, clouds of them together. That means summer is nearly here.

The red tulips open in the corn like poppies, only with a heavier red. And they pass quickly, without repeating themselves. There is little lingering in a tulip.

In some places there are odd yellow tulips, slender, spiky, and Chinese-looking. They are very lovely, pricking out their dulled yellow in slim spikes. But they too soon lean, expand beyond themselves, and are gone like an illusion.

And when the tulips are gone, there is a moment's pause, before summer. Summer is the next move.

III

In the pause towards the end of April, when the flowers seem to hesitate, the leaves make up their minds to come out. For some time, at the very ends of the bare boughs of fig trees, spurts of pure green have been burning like little cloven tongues of green fire vivid on the tips of the candelabrum. Now these spurts of green spread out, and begin to take the shape of hands, feeling for the air of summer. And tiny green figs are below them, like glands on the throat of a goat.

For some time, the long stiff whips of the vine have had knobby pink buds, like flower buds. Now these pink buds begin to unfold into greenish, half-shut fans of leaves with red in the veins, and tiny spikes of flower, like seed-pearls. Then, in all its down and pinky dawn, the vine-rosette has a frail, delicious scent of a new year.

Now the aspens on the hill are all remarkable with the

translucent membranes of blood-veined leaves. They are gold-brown, but not like autumn, rather like the thin wings of bats when like birds – call them birds – they wheel in clouds against the setting sun, and the sun glows through the stretched membrane of their wings, as through thin, brown-red stained glass. This is the red sap of summer, not the red dust of autumn. And in the distance the aspens have the tender panting glow of living membrane just come awake. This is the beauty of the frailty of spring.

The cherry tree is something the same, but more sturdy. Now, in the last week of April, the cherry blossom is still white, but waning and passing away: it is late this year; and the leaves are clustering thick and softly copper in their dark, blood-filled glow. It is queer about fruit trees in this district. The pear and the peach were out together. But now the pear tree is a lovely thick softness of new and glossy green, vivid with a tender fullness of apple green leaves, gleaming among all the other green of the landscape, the half-high wheat, emerald, and the grey olive, half-invisible, the browning green of the dark cypress, the black of the evergreen oak, the rolling, heavy green puffs of the stone-pines, the flimsy green of small peach and almond trees, the sturdy young green of horse-chestnut. So many greens, all in flakes and shelves and tilted tables and round shoulders and plumes and shaggles and uprisen bushes, of greens and greens, sometimes blindingly brilliant at evening, when the landscape looks as if it were on fire from inside, with greenness and with gold.

The pear is perhaps the greenest thing in the landscape. The wheat may shine lit-up yellow, or glow bluish, but the pear tree is green in itself. The cherry has white, half-absorbed flowers, so has the apple. But the plum is rough with her new foliage, and inconspicuous, inconspicuous as the almond, the peach, the apricot, which one can no longer find in the landscape, though twenty days ago they were the distinguished pink individuals of the whole countryside. Now they are gone. It is the time of green, pre-eminent green, in ruffles and flakes and slabs.

In the wood, the scrub-oak is only just coming uncrumpled, and the pines keep their hold on winter. They are wintry things, stone-pines. At Christmas, their heavy green clouds are richly beautiful. When the cypresses raise their tall and naked bodies of dark green, and the osiers are vivid red-orange, on the still blue air, and the land is lavender, then, in mid-winter, the landscape is most beautiful in colour, surging with colour.

But now, when the nightingale is still drawing out his long, wistful, yearning, teasing plaint-note, and following it up with a rich and joyful burble, the pines and the cypresses seem hard and rusty, and the wood has lost its subtlety and its mysteriousness. It still seems wintry in spite of the yellowing young oaks, and the heath in flower. But hard, dull pines above, and hard, dull, tall heath below, all stiff and resistant, this is out of the mood of spring.

In spite of the fact that the stone-white heath is in full flower, and very lovely when you look at it, it does not, casually, give the impression of blossom. More the impression of having its tips and crests all dipped in hoarfrost; or in a whitish dust. It has a peculiar ghostly colourlessness amid the darkish colourlessness of the wood altogether, which completely takes away the sense of spring.

Yet the tall white heath is very lovely, in its invisibility. It grows sometimes as tall as a man, lifting up its spires and its shadowy-white fingers with a ghostly fullness, amid the dark, rusty green of its lower bushiness; and it gives off a sweet honey-eyed scent in the sun, and a cloud of fine white stone-dust, if you touch it. Looked at closely, its little bells are most beautiful, delicate and white, with the brown-purple inner eye and the dainty pin-head of the pistil. And out in the sun at the edge of the wood, where the heath grows tall and thrusts up its spires of dim white next a brilliant, yellow-flowering vetch-bush, under a blue sky, the effect has a real magic.

And yet, in spite of all, the dim whiteness of all the flowering heath-fingers only adds to the hoariness and out-of-date quality of the pine-woods, now in the pause between spring and summer. It is the ghost of the interval.

Not that this week is flowerless. But the flowers are little lonely things, here and there: the early purple orchid, ruddy and very much alive, you come across occasionally, then the little groups of bee-orchid, with their ragged concerted indifference to their appearance. Also there are the huge bud-spikes of the stout, thick-flowering pink orchid, huge buds like fat ears of wheat, hard purple and splendid. But already odd grains of the wheat-ear are open, and out of the purple hangs the delicate pink rag of a floweret. Also there are very lovely and choice cream-coloured orchids with brown spots on the long and delicate lip. These grow in the more moist places, and have exotic tender spikes, very rare-seeming. Another orchid is a little, pretty yellow one.

But orchids, somehow, do not make a summer. They are too aloof and individual. The little slate-blue scabious is out, but not enough to raise an appearance. Later on, under the real hot sun, he will bob into notice. And by the edges of the paths there are odd rosy cushions of wild thyme. Yet these, too, are rather samples than the genuine thing. Wait another month, for wild thyme.

The same with the irises. Here and there, in fringes along the upper edge of terraces, and in odd bunches among the stones, the dark-purple iris sticks up. It is beautiful, but it hardly counts. There is not enough of it, and it is torn and buffeted by too many winds. First the wind blows with all its might from the Mediterranean, not cold, but infinitely wearying, with its rude and insistent pushing. Then, after a moment of calm, back comes a hard wind from the Adriatic, cold and disheartening. Between the two of them, the dark-purple iris flutters and tatters and curls as if it were burnt: while the little yellow rock-rose streams at the end of its thin stalk, and wishes it had not been in such a hurry to come out.

There is really no hurry. By May, the great winds will drop, and the great sun will shake off his harassments. Then the nightingale will sing an unbroken song, and the discreet, barely audible Tuscan cuckoo will be a little more audible. Then the lovely pale-lilac irises will come out in all their showering abundance of tender, proud, spiky bloom, till the air will gleam with mauve, and a new crystalline lightness will be everywhere.

The iris is half-wild, half-cultivated. The peasants sometimes dig up the roots, iris root, orris root (orris powder, the perfume that is still used). So, in May, you will find ledges and terraces, fields just lit up with the mauve light of irises, and so much scent in the air, you do not notice it, you do not even know it. It is all the flowers of iris, before the olive invisibly blooms.

There will be tufts of iris everywhere, rising up proud and tender. When the rose-coloured wild gladiolus is mingled in the corn, and the love-in-the-mist opens blue: in May and June, before the corn is cut.

But as yet it is neither May nor June, but end of April, the pause between spring and summer, the nightingale singing interruptedly, the bean-flowers dying in the bean-fields, the bean-perfume passing with spring, the little birds hatching in the nests, the olives pruned, and the vines, the last bit of late ploughing finished, and not much work to hand, now, not until the peas are ready to pick, in another two weeks or so. Then all the peasants will be crouching between the pea-rows, endlessly, endlessly gathering peas, in the long pea-harvest which lasts two months.

So the change, the endless and rapid change. In the sunny

countries, the change seems more vivid, and more complete than in the grey countries. In the grey countries, there is a grey or dark permanency, over whose surface passes change ephemeral, leaving no real mark. In England, winters and summers shadowily give place to one another. But underneath lies the grey substratum, the permanency of cold, dark reality where bulbs live, and reality is bulbous, a thing of endurance and stored-up, starchy energy.

But in the sunny countries, change is the reality and permanence is artificial and a condition of imprisonment. In the North, man tends instinctively to imagine, to conceive that the sun is lighted like a candle, in an everlasting darkness, and that one day the candle will go out, the sun will be exhausted, and the everlasting dark will resume uninterrupted sway. Hence, to the northerner, the phenomenal world is essentially tragical, because it is temporal and must cease to exist. Its very existence implies ceasing to exist, and this is the root of the feeling of tragedy.

But to the southerner, the sun is so dominant that, if every phenomenal body disappeared out of the universe, nothing would remain but bright luminousness, sunniness. The absolute is sunniness; and shadow, or dark, is only merely relative: merely the result of something getting between one and the sun.

This is the instinctive feeling of the ordinary southerner. Of course, if you start to *reason*, you may argue that the sun is a phenomenal body. Therefore it came into existence, therefore it will pass out of existence, therefore the very sun is tragic in its nature.

But this is just argument. We think, because we have to light a candle in the dark, therefore some First Cause had to kindle the sun in the infinite darkness of the beginning.

The argument is entirely shortsighted and specious. We do not know in the least whether the sun ever came into existence, and we have not the slightest possible ground for conjecturing that the sun will ever pass out of existence. All that we do know, by actual experience, is that shadow comes into being when some material object intervenes between us and the sun, and that shadow ceases to exist when the intervening object is removed. So that, of all temporal or transitory or bound-to-cease things that haunt our existence, shadow or darkness, is the one which is purely and simply temporal. We can think of death, if we like, as of something permanently intervening between us and the sun: and this is at the root of the southern, under-world idea of death. But this doesn't alter the sun at all. As far as experience goes, in the human race, the one thing that is always there is the shining sun, and dark shadow is an accident of intervention.

Hence, strictly, there is no tragedy. The universe contains no tragedy, and man is only tragical because he is afraid of death. For my part, if the sun always shines, and always will shine, in spite of millions of clouds of words, then death, somehow, does not have many terrors. In the sunshine, even death is sunny. And there is no end to the sunshine.

That is why the rapid change of the Tuscan spring is utterly free, for me, of any sense of tragedy. 'Where are the snows of yesteryear?' Why, precisely where they ought to be. Where are the little yellow aconites of eight weeks ago? I neither know nor care. They were sunny and the sun shines, and sunniness means change, and petals passing and coming. The winter aconites sunnily came, and sunnily went. What more? The sun always shines. It is our fault if we don't think so.

GERMANS AND LATINS (1927)

It is already summer in Tuscany, the sun is hot, the earth is baked hard, and the soul has changed her rhythm. The nightingales sing all day and all night – not at all sadly, but brightly, vividly, impudently, with a trilling power of assertion quite disproportionate to the size of the shy bird. Why the Greeks should have heard the nightingale weeping or sobbing is more than I can understand. Anyhow, perhaps the Greeks were looking for the tragic, rather than the rhapsodic consummation to life. They were predisposed.

Tomorrow, however, is the first of May, and already summer is here. Yesterday, in the flood of sunshine on the Arno at evening, I saw two German boys steering out of the Por Santa Maria onto the Ponte Vecchio in Florence. They were dark-haired, not blonds, but otherwise the true *Wandervögel* type, in shirts and short trousers and thick boots, hatless, coat slung in the rucksack, shirt-sleeves rolled back above the brown muscular arms, shirt-breast open from the brown, scorched breast, and the face and neck glowing sun-darkened as they strode into the flood of evening sunshine, out of the narrow street. They were talking loudly to one another in German, as if oblivious of their surroundings, in that thronged crossing of the Ponte Vecchio. And they strode with strong strides, heedless, marching past the Italians as if the Italians were but shadows. Strong, heedless, travelling intently, bent a little forward from the rucksacks in the plunge of determination to travel onwards, looking neither to right nor left, conversing in strong voices only with one another, where were they going, in the last golden light of the sun-flooded evening, over the Arno? Were they leaving town, at this hour? Were they pressing on, to get out of the Porta Romana before nightfall, going southwards?

In spite of the fact that one is used to these German youths, in Florence especially, in summer, still the mind calls a halt each time they appear and pass by. If swans or wild geese flew honking, low over the Arno in the evening light, moving with that wedge-shaped, intent, unswerving progress that is so impressive, they would create the same impression on one. They would bring that sense of remote, far-off lands which these Germans bring, and that sense of mysterious, unfathomable purpose.

Now no one knows better than myself that Munich or Frankfort-am-Main are not far-off, remote, lonely lands: on the contrary: and that these boys are not mysteriously migrating from one unknown to another. They are just wandering for wandering's sake, and moving instinctively, perhaps, towards the sun, and towards Rome, the old centre-point. There is really nothing more remarkable in it than in the English and Americans sauntering diffidently and, as it were, obscurely along the Lungarno. The English in particular seem to move under a sort of Tarnhelm, having a certain power of invisibility. They manage most of the time to efface themselves, deliberately, from the atmosphere. And the Americans, who don't try to efface themselves, give the impression of not being really there. They have left their real selves way off in the United States, in Europe they are like rather void *Doppelgänger*. I am speaking, of course, of the impression of the streets. Inside the hotels, the trains, the tearooms and the restaurants, it is another affair. There you may have a little England, very insular, or a little America, very money-rich democratic, or a little Germany, assertive, or a little

Scandinavia, domestic. But I am not speaking of indoor impressions. Merely of the streets.

And in the streets of Florence or Rome, the *Wandervögel* make a startling impression, whereas the rest of the foreigners impress one rather negatively. When I am in Germany, then Germany seems to me very much like anywhere else, especially England or America.

And when I see the *Wandervögel* pushing at evening out of the Por Santa Maria, across the blaze of sun and into the Ponte Vecchio, then Germany becomes again to me what it was to the Romans: the mysterious, half-dark land of the north, bristling with gloomy forests, resounding to the cry of wild geese and of swans, the land of the stork and the bear and the *Drachen* and the *Greifen*.

I know it is not so. Yet the impression comes back over me, as I see the youths pressing heedlessly past. And I know it is the same with the Italians. They see, as their ancestors saw in the Goths and the Vandals, *i barbari*, the barbarians. That is what the little policeman with his staff and his peaked cap thinks, as the boys from the north go by: *i barbari!* Not with dislike or contempt: not at all: but with the old, weird wonder. So he might look up at wild swans flying over the Ponte Vecchio: wild strangers from the north.

So strong is the impression the *Wandervögel* make on the imagination! It is not that I am particularly impressionable. I know the Italians feel very much as I do.

And when one sees English people with rucksacks and shirt-sleeves rolled back and hob-nailed boots, as one does sometimes, even in Tuscany, one notices them, but they make very little impression. They are rather odd than extraordinary. They are just *gli escursionisti*, quite comprehensible: part of the fresh-air movement. The Italians will laugh at them, but they know just what to think about them.

Whereas about the *Wandervögel* they do not quite know what to think, nor even what to feel: since we even only feel the things we know how to feel. And we do not know what to feel about these *Wandervögel* boys. They bring with them such a strong feeling of *somewhere else*, of an unknown country, an unknown race, a powerful, still unknown northland.

How wonderful it must have been, at the end of the old Roman Empire, for the Roman citizens to see the big, bare-limbed Goths, with their insolent-indifferent blue eyes, stand looking on at the market-places! They were there like a vision. *Non angli sed angeli*, as we were told the first great Pope said of the British slaves. Creatures from the beyond, presaging another world of men.

So it was then. So it is, to a certain extent, even now. Strange wanderers towards the sun, forerunners of another world of men. That is how one still feels, as one sees the *Wandervögel* cross the Ponte Vecchio. They carry with them another world, another air, another meaning of life. The meaning is not explicit, not as much as it is even in storks or wild geese. But there it lies, implicit.

Curious how different it is with the well-dressed Germans. They are very often quite domesticated, and in the sense that Ibsen's people are ridiculous, just a little ridiculous. They are *so* bourgeois, so much more a product of civilization than the producers of civilization. They are *so* much buttoned up inside their waistcoats, and stuck inside their trousers, and encircled in their starched collars. They are not so grotesquely self-conscious and physically withered or non-existent as the equivalent English bourgeois tourist. And they are never quite so utterly domesticated as the equivalent Scandinavian. But they have so often the unsure look of children who have been turned out in their best clothes by their mama, and told to go and enjoy themselves: Now enjoy yourselves! That is a little absurd.

The Italians, whatever they are, are what they are. So you know them, you feel that they have developed themselves into an expression of themselves, as far as they go. With the English, weird fish as they are very often, you feel the same: whatever they are, they are what they are, they can't be much different, poor dears. But with the Germans abroad, you feel: These people ought really to be something else. They are not themselves, in their Sunday clothes. They are being something they are not.

And one has the feeling even stronger, with many Russians. One feels: These people are not themselves at all. They are the roaring echoes of other people, older races, other languages. Even the things they say aren't really Russian things: they're all sorts of half-translations from Latin or French or English or God-knows-what.

Some of this feeling one has about the Germans one meets abroad: as if they were talking in translation: as if the ideas, however original, always had a faint sound of translations. As if they were never *quite* themselves.

Then, when one sees the *Wandervögel*, comes the shock of realization, and one thinks: There they go, the real Germans, seeking the sun! They have really nothing to say. They are roving, roving, roving, seeking themselves. That is it, with these 'barbarians.' They are still seeking themselves. And they have not yet found themselves. They are turning to the sun again, in the great adventure of seeking themselves.

Man does not start ready-made. He is a weird creature that slowly evolves himself through the ages. He need never stop evolving himself, for a human being who was completely himself has never even been conceived. The great Goethe was half-born, Shakespeare the same, Napoleon only a third-born. And most people are hardly born at all, into individual consciousness.

But with the Italians and the French, the mass-consciousness which governs the individual is really derived from the individual. Whereas with the German and the Russian, it seems to me not so. The mass-consciousness has been *taken over*, by great minds like Goethe or Frederick, from other people, and does not spring inherent from the Teutonic race itself. In short, the Teutonic mind, young, powerful, active, is always thinking in terms of somebody else's experience, and almost never in terms of its own experience.

Then comes a great unrest. It seems to show so plainly in the *Wandervögel*. Thinking in terms of somebody else's experience at last becomes utterly unsatisfactory. Then thought altogether falls into chaos – and then into discredit. The young don't choose to think any more. Blindly, they turn to the sun.

Because the sun is anti-thought. Thought is of the shade. In bright sunshine no man thinks. So the *Wandervögel* turn instinctively to the sun, which melts thoughts away, and sets the blood running with another, non-mental consciousness.

And this is why, at times of great change, the northern nations turn to the sun. And this is why, when revolutions come, they often come in May. It is the sun making the blood revolt against old conceptions. And this is why the nations of the sun do not live the life of thought, therefore they are more 'themselves.' In the grey shadow the northern nations mould themselves according to a few ideas until their whole life is buttoned and choked up. Then comes a revulsion. They cast off the clothes and turn to the sun, as the *Wandervögel* do, strange harbingers.

INTRODUCTION TO
MASTRO-DON GESUALDO BY
GIOVANNI VERGA (1927)

Giovanni Verga was born in the year 1840, and he died at the beginning of 1922, so that he is almost as much of a contemporary as Thomas Hardy. He seems more remote, because he left off writing many years before he died. He was a Sicilian from one of the lonely little townships in the south of the island, where his family were provincial gentlefolk. But he spent a good deal of his youth in Catania, the city on the sea, under Etna, and then he went to Naples, the metropolis; for Sicily was still part of the Bourbon kingdom of Naples.

As a young man he lived for a time in Milan and Florence, the intellectual centres, leading a more or less fashionable life and also practising journalism. A real provincial, he felt that the great world must be conquered, that it must hold some vital secret. He was apparently a great beau, and had a series of more or less distinguished love affairs, like an Alfred de Vigny or a Maupassant. In his early novels we see him in this phase. *Tigre Reale*, one of his most popular novels, is the story of a young Italian's love for a fascinating but very enigmatical (no longer so enigmatical) Russian countess of great wealth, married, but living in distinguished isolation alone in Florence. The enigmatical lady is, however, consumptive, and the end, in Sicily, is truly horrible, in the morbid and deathly tone of some of Matilde

Serao's novels. The southerners seem to go that way, macabre. Yet in Verga the savage, manly tone comes through the morbidity, and we feel how he must have loathed the humiliation of fashionable life and fashionable love affairs. He kept it up, however, till after forty, then he retired back to his own Sicily, and shut himself up away from the world. He lived in aristocratic isolation for almost another forty years, and died in Catania, almost forgotten. He was a rather short, broad-shouldered man with a big red moustache.

It was after he had left the fashionable world that he wrote his best work. And this is no longer Italian, but Sicilian. In his Italian style, he manages to get the rhythm of colloquial Sicilian, and Italy no longer exists. Now Verga turns to the peasants of his boyhood, and it is they who fill his soul. It is their lives that matter.

There are three books of Sicilian sketches and short stories, very brilliant, and drenched with the atmosphere of Sicily. They are *Cavalleria Rusticana*, *Novelle Rusticane*, and *Vagabondaggio*. They open out another world at once, the southern, sun-beaten island whose every outline is like pure memory. Then there is a small novel about a girl who is condemned to a convent: *Storia di una Capinera*. And finally, there are the two great novels, *I Malavoglia* and *Mastro-don Gesualdo*. The sketches in *Cavalleria Rusticana* had already established Verga's fame. But it was *I Malavoglia* that was hailed as a masterpiece, in Paris as well as in Italy. It was translated into French by Jose-Maria de Heredia, and after that, into English by an American lady. The English translation, which weakens the book very much, came out in America in the 'nineties, under the title *The House by the Medlar Tree*, and can still be procured.

Speaking, in conversation, the other day about Giovanni Verga, in Rome, one of the most brilliant young Italian literary men said: There is Verga, ah yes! *Some* of his things! But a thing like the *Storia di una Capinera*, now, that is ridiculous. – And it was so obvious, the young man thought all Verga a little ridiculous. Because Verga *doesn't* write about lunatics and maniacs, like Pirandello, therefore he is ridiculous. It is the attitude of the smart young. They find Tolstoi ridiculous, George Eliot ridiculous, everybody ridiculous who is not 'disillusioned.'

The *Story of a Blackcap* is indeed sentimental and overloaded with emotion. But so is Dickens' *Christmas Carol*, or *Silas Marner*. They do not therefore become ridiculous.

It is a fault in Verga, partly owing to the way he had lived his life, and partly owing to the general tendency of all European literature of the eighteen-sixties and thereabouts, to pour too much emotion, and especially too much pity, over the humble poor. Verga's novel *I Malavoglia* is really spoilt by this, and by his exaggeration of the tragic fate of his humble fisher-folk. But then it is characteristic of the southerner, that when he has an emotion he has it wholesale. And the tragic fate of the humble poor was the stunt of that day. *Les Misérables* stands as the great monument to this stunt. The poor have lately gone rather out of favour, so Hugo stands at a rather low figure, and Verga hardly exists. But when we have got over our reaction against the pity-the-poor stunt, we shall see that there is a good deal of fun in Hugo, and that *I Malavoglia* is really a very great picture of Sicilian sea-coast life, far more human and *valid* than Victor Hugo's picture of Paris.

The trouble with the Italians is, they do tend to take over other people's stunts and exaggerate them. Even when they invent a stunt of their own, for some mysterious reason it *seems* second-hand. Victor Hugo's pity-the-poor was a real Gallic gesture. Verga's pity-the-poor is just a bit too much of a good thing, and it doesn't seem to come *quite* spontaneously from him. He had been inoculated. Or he had reacted.

In his last novel, *Mastro-don Gesualdo*, Verga has slackened off in his pity-the-poor. But he is still a realist, in the grim Flaubert-ian sense of the word. A realism which, as every one now knows, has no more to do with reality than romanticism has. Realism is just one of the arbitrary views man takes of man. It sees us all as little ant-like creatures toiling against the odds of circumstance, and doomed to misery. It is a kind of aeroplane view. It became the popular outlook, and so today we actually are, millions of us, little ant-like creatures toiling against the odds of circumstance, and doomed to misery; until we take a different view of ourselves. For man always becomes what he passionately thinks he is; since he is capable of becoming almost anything.

Mastro-don Gesualdo is a great realistic novel of Sicily, as *Madame Bovary* is a great realistic novel of France. They both suffer from the defects of the realistic method. I think the inherent flaw in *Madame Bovary* – though I hate talking about flaws in great books; but the charge is really against the realistic method – is that individuals like Emma and Charles Bovary are too insignificant to carry the full weight of Gustave Flaubert's profound sense of tragedy; or, if you will, of tragic futility. Emma and Charles Bovary are two ordinary persons, chosen because they *are* ordinary. But Flaubert is by no means an ordinary person. Yet he insists on pouring his own deep and bitter tragic consciousness into the little skins of the country doctor and his dissatisfied wife. The result is a certain discrepancy, even a certain dishonesty in the attempt to be too honest. By choosing *ordinary* people as the vehicles of an extraordinarily passionate feeling of bitterness, Flaubert loads the dice, and wins by a trick which is sure to be found out against him.

Because a great soul like Flaubert's has a pure satisfaction and joy in its own consciousness, even if the consciousness be only of ultimate tragedy or misery. But the very fact of being so marvellously and vividly *aware*, awake, as Flaubert's soul was, is in itself a refutation of the all-is-misery doctrine. Since the human soul has supreme joy in true, vivid consciousness. And Flaubert's soul has this joy. But Emma Bovary's soul does not, poor thing, because she was deliberately chosen because her soul was ordinary. So Flaubert cheats us a little, in his doctrine, if not in his art. And his art is biased by his doctrine as much as any artist's is.

The same is true of *Mastro-don Gesualdo*. Gesualdo is a peasant's son, who becomes rich in his own tiny town through his own force and sagacity. He is allowed the old heroic qualities of force and sagacity. Even Emma Bovary has a certain extraordinary female energy of restlessness and unsatisfied desire. So that both Flaubert and Verga allow their heroes something of the hero, after all. The one thing they deny them is the consciousness of heroic effort.

Now Flaubert and Verga alike were aware of their own heroic effort to be truthful, to show things as they are. It was the heroic impulse which made them write their great books. Yet they deny to their protagonists any inkling of the heroic effort. It is in this sense that Emma Bovary and Gesualdo Motta are 'ordinary.' Ordinary people don't have much sense of heroic effort in life; and by the heroic effort we mean that instinctive fighting for more life to come into being, which is a basic impulse in more men than we like to admit; women too. Or it used to be. The discrediting of the heroic effort has almost extinguished that effort in the young, hence the appalling 'flatness' of their lives. It is the parents' fault. Life without the heroic effort, and without *belief* in the subtle, life-long validity of the heroic impulse, is just stale, flat and unprofitable. As the great realistic novels will show you.

Gesualdo Motta has the makings of a hero. Verga had to grant him something. I think it is in *Novelle Rusticane* that we find the long sketch or story of the little fat peasant who has become enormously rich by grinding his labourers and bleeding the Barons. It is a marvellous story, reeling with the hot atmosphere of Sicily, and the ironic fatalism of the Sicilians. And that little fat peasant must have been an actual man whom Verga knew – Verga wasn't good at inventing, he always had to have a core of actuality – and who served as the idea-germ for Gesualdo. But Gesualdo is much more attractive, much nearer the true hero. In fact, with all his energy and sagacity *and* his natural humaneness, we don't see how Gesualdo quite escaped the heroic consciousness. The original little peasant, the prototype, was a mere frog, a grabber and nothing else. He had none of Gesualdo's large humaneness. So that Verga brings Gesualdo much nearer to the hero, yet denies him still any spark of the heroic consciousness, any spark of awareness of a greater impulse within him. Men naturally have this spark, if they are the tiniest bit uncommon. The curious thing is, the moment you deny the spark, it dies, and then the heroic impulse dies with it.

It is probably true that, since the extinction of the pagan gods, the countries of the Mediterranean have never been aware of the heroic impulse in themselves, and so it has died down very low, in them. In Sicily, even now, and in the remoter Italian villages, there is what we call a low level of life, appalling. Just a squalid, unimaginative, heavy, petty-fogging, grubby sort of existence, without light or flame. It is the absence of the heroic awareness, the heroic hope.

The northerners have got over the death of the old Homeric idea of the hero, by making the hero self-conscious, and a hero by virtue of suffering and awareness of suffering. The Sicilians may have little spasms of this sort of heroic feeling, but it never lasts. It is not natural to them.

The Russians carry us to great lengths of introspective heroism. They escape the non-heroic dilemma of our age by making every man his own introspective hero. The merest scrub of a pickpocket is so phenomenally aware of his own soul, that we are made to bow down before the imaginary coruscations of suffering and sympathy that go on inside him. So is Russian literature.

Of course, your soul will coruscate with suffering and sympathy, if you think it does: since the soul is capable of anything, and is no doubt full of unimaginable coruscations which far-off future civilizations will wake up to. So far, we have only lately wakened up to the sympathy-suffering coruscation, so we are full of it. And that is why the Russians are so popular. No matter how much of a shabby little slut you may be, you can learn from Dostoevsky and Tchekov that you have got the most tender, unique soul on earth, coruscating with sufferings and impossible sympathies. And so you may be most vastly important to yourself, introspectively. Outwardly, you will say: Of course I'm an ordinary person, like everybody else. – But your very saying it will prove that you think the opposite: namely, that everybody on earth is ordinary, *except* yourself.

This is our northern way of heroism, up to date. The Sicilian hasn't yet got there. Perhaps he never will. Certainly he was nowhere near it in Gesualdo Motta's day, the mediæval Sicilian day of the middle of the last century, before Italy existed, and Sicily was still part of the Bourbon kingdom of Naples, and about as remote as the kingdom of Dahomey.

The Sicilian has no soul, except that funny little naked man who hops on hot bricks, in purgatory, and howls to be prayed out into paradise; and is in some mysterious way an *alter ego*, my me beyond the grave. This is the catholic soul, and there is nothing to do about it but to pay, and get it prayed into paradise.

For the rest, in our sense of the word, the Sicilian doesn't have any soul. He can't be introspective, because his consciousness, so to speak, doesn't have any inside to it. He can't look inside himself, because he is, as it were, solid. When Gesualdo is tormented by mean people, atrociously, all he says is: I've got bitter in my mouth. – And when he is dying, and has some awful tumour inside, he says: It is all the bitterness I have known, swelled up inside me. – That is all: a physical fact! Think what even Dmitri Karamazov would have made of it! And Dmitri Karamazov doesn't go half the lengths of the other Russian soul-twisters. Neither is he half the man Gesualdo is, although he may be much more 'interesting,' if you like soul-twisters.

In *Mastro-don Gesualdo* you have, in a sense, the same sort of tragedy as in the Russians, yet anything more un-Russian could not be imagined. Un-Russian almost as Homer. But Verga will have gods neither above nor below.

The Sicilians today are supposed to be the nearest descendants of the classic Greeks, and the nearest thing to the classic Greeks in life and nature. And perhaps it is true. Like the classic Greeks, the Sicilians have no insides, introspectively speaking. But, alas, outside they have no busy gods. It is their great loss. Because Jesus is to them only a wonder-man who was killed by foreigners and villains, and who will help you to get out of Hell, perhaps.

In the true sense of the word, the Sicily of Gesualdo is drearily godless. It needs the bright and busy gods outside. The inside gods, gods who have to be inside a man's soul, are distasteful to people who live in the sun. Once you get to Ceylon, you see that even Buddha is purely an outside god, purely objective to the natives. They have no conception of his being inside themselves.

It was the same with the Greeks, it is the same today with the Sicilians. They aren't *capable* of introspection and the inner Jesus. They leave it all to us and the Russians.

Save that he has no bright outside gods, Gesualdo is very like an old Greek: the same energy and quickness of response, the same vivid movement, the same ambition and real passion for wealth, the same easy conscience, the same queer openness, without ever really openly committing himself, and the same ancient astuteness. He is prouder, more fearless, more frank, yet more subtle than an Italian; more on his own. He is like a Greek or a traditional Englishman, in the way he just goes ahead by himself. And in that, he is Sicilian, not Italian.

And he is Greek above all, in having no inside, in the Russian sense of the word.

The tragedy is, he has no heroic gods or goddesses to fix his imagination. He has nothing, not even a country. Even his Greek ambitious desire to come out splendidly, with a final splendid look of the thing and a splendid final ring of words, turns bitter. The Sicilian aristocracy was an infinitely more paltry thing than Gesualdo himself.

It is the tragedy of a man who is forced to be ordinary, because all visions have been taken away from him. It is useless to say he should have had the northern inwardness and the Russianizing outlet. You might as well say the tall and reckless asphodel of Magna Græcia should learn to be a snowdrop. 'I'll learn you to be a toad!'

But a book exists by virtue of the vividness, the aliveness and powerful pulsing of its life-portrayal, and not by virtue of the pretty or unpretty things it portrays. *Mastro-don Gesualdo* is a great undying book, one of the great novels of Europe. If you cannot read it because it is *à terre*, and has neither nervous uplift nor nervous hysteria, you condemn yourself.

As a picture of Sicily in the middle of the last century, it is marvellous. But it is a picture done from the inside. There are no picture-postcard effects. The thing is a heavy, earth-adhering organic whole. There is nothing showy.

Sicily in the middle of the last century was an incredibly poor, lost, backward country. Spaniards, Bourbons, one after the other they had killed the life in her. The Thousand and Garibaldi had not risen over the horizon, neither had the great emigration to America begun, nor the great return, with dollars and a newish outlook. The mass of the people were poorer even than the poor Irish of the same period, and save for climate, their conditions were worse. There were some great and wealthy landlords, dukes and barons still. But they lived in Naples, or in Palermo at the nearest. In the country, there were no roads at all for wheeled vehicles, consequently no carts, nothing but donkeys and pack-mules on the trails, or a sick person in a mule litter, or armed men on horseback, or men on donkeys. The life was mediæval as in Russia. But whereas the Russia of 1850 is a vast flat country with a most picturesque life of nobles and serfs and soldiers, open and changeful, Sicily is a most beautiful country, but hilly, steep, shut-off, and abandoned, and the life is, or was, grimly unpicturesque in its dead monotony. The great nobles shunned the country, as in Ireland. And the people were sunk in bigotry, suspicion, and gloom. The life of the villages and small towns was of an incredible spiteful meanness, as life always is when there is not enough change and fresh air; and the conditions were sordid, dirty, as they always are when the human spirits sink below a certain level. It is not in such places that one looks for passion and colour. The passion and colour in Verga's stories come in the villages near the east coast, where there is change since Ulysses sailed that way. Inland, in the isolation, the lid is on, and the intense watchful malice of neighbours is infinitely worse than any police system, infinitely more killing to the soul and the passionate body.

The picture is a bitter and depressing one, while ever we stay in the dense and smelly little streets. Verga wrote what he knew and felt. But when we pass from the habitations of sordid man, into the light and marvellous open country, then we feel at once the undying beauty of Sicily and the Greek world, a morning beauty, that has something miraculous in it, of purple anemones and cyclamens, and sumach and olive trees, and the place where Persephone came above-world, bringing back spring.

And we must remember that eight-tenths of the population of Sicily is maritime or agricultural, always has been, and therefore practically the whole day-life of the people passes in the open, in the splendour of the sun and the landscape, and the delicious, elemental aloneness of the old world. This is a great *unconscious* compensation. But what a compensation, after all! – even if you don't know you've got it; as even Verga doesn't quite. But he puts it in, all the same, and you can't read *Mastro-don Gesualdo* without feeling the marvellous glow and glamour of Sicily, and the people throbbing inside the glow and the glamour like motes in a sunbeam. Out of doors, in a world like that, what is misery, after all! The great freshness keeps the men still fresh. It is the women in the dens of houses who deteriorate most.

And perhaps it is because the outside world is so lovely, that men in the Greek regions have never become introspective. They had not been driven to *that* form of compensation. With them, life pulses outwards, and the positive reality is outside. There is no turning inwards. So man becomes purely objective. And this is what makes the Greeks so difficult to understand: even Socrates. We don't understand him. We just translate him into another thing, our own thing. He is so peculiarly *objective* even in his attitude to the soul, that we could never get him if we didn't translate him into something else, and thus 'make him our own.'

And the glorious objectivity of the old Greek world still persists, old and blind now, among the southern Mediterranean peoples. It is this decayed objectivity, not even touched by mediæval mysticism, which makes a man like Gesualdo so simple, and yet so incomprehensible to us. We are apt to see him as just meaningless, just stupidly and meaninglessly getting rich, merely acquisitive. Yet, at the same time, we see him so patient with his family, with the phthisical Bianca, with his daughter, so humane, and yet so desperately enduring. In affairs, he has an unerring instinct, and he is a superb fighter. Yet in life, he seems to do the wrong thing every time. It is as if, in his life, he has no driving motive at all.

He should, of course, by every standard we know, have married Diodata. Bodily, she was the woman he turned to. She bore him sons. Yet he married her to one of his own hired men, to clear the way for his, Gesualdo's, marriage with the noble but merely pathetic Bianca Trao. And after he was married to Bianca, who was too weak for him, he still went back to Diodata, and paid her husband to accommodate him. And it never occurs to him to have any of this on his conscience. Diodata has his sons in her house, but Gesualdo, who has only one daughter by the frail Bianca, never seems to interest himself in his boys at all. There is the most amazing absence of a certain range of feeling in the man, especially feeling about himself. It is as if he had no inside. And yet we see that he most emphatically has. He has a warm and attractive presence. And he suffers bitterly, bitterly. Yet he blindly brings most of his sufferings on himself, by doing the wrong things to himself.

The idea of living for love is just entirely unknown to him, unknown as if it were a new German invention. So is the idea of living for sex. In that respect, woman is just the female of the species to him, as if he were a horse, that jumps in heat, and forgets. He never really thinks about women. Life means something else to him.

But what? What? It is so hard to see. Does he just want to *get on*, in our sense of the word? No, not even that. He has not the faintest desire to be mayor, or podesta, or that sort of thing. But he does make a duchess of his daughter. Yes, Mastro-don Gesualdo's daughter is a duchess of very aristocratic rank.

And what then? Gesualdo realizes soon enough that she is not happy. And now he is an elderly, dying man, and the impetuosity of his manhood is sinking, he begins to wonder what he should have done. What was it all about?

What *did* life mean to him, when he was in the impetuous tide of his manhood? What was he unconsciously driving at? Just blindly at nothing? Was that why he put aside Diodata, and brought on himself all that avalanche of spite, by marrying Bianca? Not that his marriage was a failure. Bianca was his wife, and he was unfailingly kind to her, fond of her, her death was bitter to him. Not being under the tyrannical sway of the idea of 'love,' he could be fond of his wife, and he could be fond of Diodata, and he needn't get into a stew about any of them.

But what was he under the sway of? What was he blindly driving at? We ask, and we realize at last that it was the old Greek impulse towards splendour and self-enhancement. Not ambition, in our sense of the word, but something more personal, more individual. That which swayed Achilles and swayed Pericles and Alcibiades: the passionate desire for individual splendour. We now call it vanity. But in the countries of the sun, where the whole outdoors consists in the splendour of the sun, it is a real thing to men, to try to make themselves splendid and like suns.

Gesualdo was blindly repeating, in his own confused way, the magnificent old gesture. But ours is not the age for splendour. We have changed all that. So Gesualdo's life amounts to nothing. Yet not, as far as I can see, to any less than the lives of the 'humble' Russians. At least he lived his life. If he thought too little about it, he helps to counterbalance all those people who think too much. Because he never has any 'profound' talk, he is not less a man than Myshkin or a Karamazov. He is possibly not more a man, either. But to me he is less distasteful. And because his life all ends in a mistake, he is not therefore any more meaningless

than Tolstoi himself. And because he simply has no idea whatsoever of 'salvation,' whether his own or anybody else's, he is not
therefore a fool. Any more than Hector and Achilles were fools;
for neither of them had any idea of salvation.

The last forlorn remnant of the Greeks, blindly but brightly
seeking for splendour and self-enhancement, instead of salvation, and choosing to surge blindly on, instead of retiring inside
himself to twist his soul into knots, Gesualdo still has a lovable
glow in his body, the very reverse of the cold marsh-gleam of
Myshkin. His life ends in a tumour of bitterness. But it was a
life, and I would rather have lived it than the life of Tolstoi's
Pierre, or the life of any Dostoevskian hero. It was not Gesualdo's fault that the bright objective gods are dead, killed by envy
and spite. It was not his fault that there was no real splendour
left in our world for him to choose, once he had the means.

WHY I DON'T LIKE LIVING IN LONDON (1928)

It begins the moment you set foot ashore, the moment you step off the boat's gangway. The heart suddenly, yet vaguely, sinks. It is no lurch of fear. Quite the contrary. It is as if the life-urge failed, and the heart dimly sank. You trail past the benevolent policeman and the inoffensive passport officials, through the fussy and somehow foolish customs – we don't *really* think it matters if somebody smuggles in two pairs of false-silk stockings – and we get into the poky but inoffensive train, with poky but utterly inoffensive people, and we have a cup of inoffensive tea from a nice inoffensive boy, and we run through small, poky but nice and inoffensive country, till we are landed in the big but unexciting station of Victoria, when an inoffensive porter puts us into an inoffensive taxi and we are driven through the crowded yet strangely dull streets of London to the cosy yet strangely poky and dull place where we are going to stay. And the first half-hour in London, after some years abroad, is really a plunge of misery. The strange, the grey and uncanny, almost deathly sense of *dullness* is overwhelming. Of course, you get over it after a while, and admit that you exaggerated. You get into the rhythm of London again, and you tell yourself that it is *not* dull. And yet you are haunted, all the time, sleeping or walking, with the uncanny feeling: It is dull! It is all dull! This life here is one vast complex of dullness! I am dull! I am being dulled! My spirit is being dulled! My life is dulling down to London dullness.

This is the nightmare that haunts you the first few weeks of London. No doubt if you stay longer you get over it, and find London as thrilling as Paris or Rome or New York. But the climate is against me. I cannot stay long enough. With pinched and wondering gaze, the morning of departure, I look out of the taxi upon the strange dullness of London's arousing; a sort of death; and hope and life only return when I get my seat in the boat-train, and I hear all the Good-byes! Good-bye! Good-bye! Thank God to say Good-bye!

Now to feel like this about one's native land is terrible. I am sure I am an exceptional, or at least an exaggerated case. Yet it seems to me most of my fellow-countrymen have the pinched, slightly pathetic look in their faces, the vague, wondering realization: It is dull! It is always essentially dull! My life is dull!

Of course, England is the easiest country in the world, easy, easy and nice. Everybody is nice, and everybody is easy. The English people on the whole are surely the *nicest* people in the world, and everybody makes everything so easy for everybody else, and there is almost nothing to resist at all. But this very easiness and this very niceness become at last a nightmare. It is as if the whole air were impregnated with chloroform or some other pervasive anæsthetic, that makes everything easy and nice, and takes the edge off everything, whether nice or nasty. As you inhale the drug of easiness and niceness, your vitality begins to sink. Perhaps not your physical vitality, but something else: the vivid flame of your individual life. England can afford to be so free and individual because no individual flame of life is sharp and vivid. It is just mildly warm and safe. You couldn't burn your fingers at it. Nice, safe, easy: the whole ideal. And yet under all the easiness is a gnawing uneasiness, as in a drug-taker.

It used not to be so. Twenty years ago London was to me thrilling, thrilling, thrilling, the vast and roaring heart of all adventure. It was not only the heart of the world, it was the heart of the world's living adventure. How wonderful the Strand, the Bank, Charing Cross at night, Hyde Park in the morning!

True, I am now twenty years older. Yet I have not lost my sense of adventure. But now all the adventure seems to me crushed out of London. The traffic is too heavy! It used to be going somewhere, on an adventure. Now it only rolls massively and overwhelmingly, going nowhere, only dully and enormously *going*. There is no adventure at the end of the 'buses' journey. The 'bus lapses into an inertia of dullness, then dully starts again. The traffic of London used to roar with the mystery of man's adventure on the seas of life, like a vast sea-shell, murmuring a thrilling, half-comprehensible story. Now it booms like monotonous, far-off guns, in a monotony of crushing something, crushing the earth, crushing out life, crushing everything dead.

And what does one do, in London? I, not having a job to attend to, lounge round and gaze in bleak wonder on the ceaseless dullness. Or I have luncheons and dinners with friends, and talk. Now my deepest private dread of London is my dread of this talk. I spend most of my days abroad, saying little, or with a bit of chatter and a silence again. But in London I feel like a spider whose thread has been caught by somebody, and is being drawn out of him, so he must spin, spin, spin, and all to no purpose. He is not even spinning his own web, for his own reasons.

So it is in London, at luncheon, dinner or tea. I don't want to talk. I don't mean to talk. Yet the talk is drawn out of me, endlessly. And the others talk, endlessly also. It is ceaseless, it is intoxicating, it is the only real occupation of us who do not jazz. And it is purely futile. It is quite as bad as ever the Russians were: talk for talk's sake, without the very faintest intention of a result in action. Utter inaction and storms of talk. That again is London to me. And the sense of abject futility in it all only deepens the sense of abject dullness, so all there is to do is to go away.

HYMNS IN A MAN'S LIFE (1928)

Nothing is more difficult than to determine what a child takes in, and does not take in, of its environment and its teaching. This fact is brought home to me by the hymns which I learned as a child, and never forgot. They mean to me almost more than the finest poetry, and they have for me a more permanent value, somehow or other.

It is almost shameful to confess that the poems which have meant most to me, like Wordsworth's 'Ode to Immortality' and Keats's Odes, and pieces of *Macbeth* or *As You Like It* or *Midsummer Night's Dream*, and Goethe's lyrics, such as 'Über allen Gipfeln ist Ruh,' and Verlaine's 'Ayant poussé la porte qui chancelle' – all these lovely poems which after all give the ultimate shape to one's life; all these lovely poems woven deep into a man's consciousness, are still not woven so deep in me as the rather banal Nonconformist hymns that penetrated through and through my childhood.

> Each gentle dove
> And sighing bough
> That makes the eve
> So fair to me
> Has something far
> Diviner now
> To draw me back

To Galilee.
O Galilee, sweet Galilee
Where Jesus loved so much to be,
O Galilee, sweet Galilee,
Come sing thy songs again to me!

To me the word Galilee has a wonderful sound. The Lake of Galilee! I don't want to know where it is. I never want to go to Palestine. Galilee is one of those lovely, glamorous worlds, not places, that exist in the golden haze of a child's half-formed imagination. And in my man's imagination it is just the same. It has been left untouched. With regard to the hymns which had such a profound influence on my childish consciousness, there has been no crystallizing out, no dwindling into actuality, no hardening into the commonplace. They are the same to my man's experience as they were to me nearly forty years ago.

The moon, perhaps, has shrunken a little. One has been forced to learn about orbits, eclipses, relative distances, dead worlds, craters of the moon, and so on. The crescent at evening still startles the soul with its delicate flashing. But the mind works automatically and says: 'Ah, she is in her first quarter. She is all there, in spite of the fact that we see only this slim blade. The earth's shadow is over her.' And, willy-nilly, the intrusion of the mental processes dims the brilliance, the magic of the first apperception.

It is the same with all things. The sheer delight of a child's apperception is based on *wonder*; and deny it as we may, knowledge and wonder counteract one another. So that as knowledge increases wonder decreases. We say again: Familiarity breeds contempt. So that as we grow older, and become more familiar with phenomena, we become more contemptuous of them. But that is only partly true. It has taken some races of men thousands of years to become contemptuous of the moon, and to the

Hindu the cow is still wondrous. It is not familiarity that breeds contempt: it is the assumption of knowledge. Anybody who looks at the moon and says, 'I know all about that poor orb,' is, of course, bored by the moon.

Now the great and fatal fruit of our civilization, which is a civilization based on knowledge, and hostile to experience, is boredom. All our wonderful education and learning is producing a grand sum-total of boredom. Modern people are inwardly thoroughly bored. Do as they may, they are bored.

They are bored because they experience nothing. And they experience nothing because the wonder has gone out of them. And when the wonder has gone out of a man he is dead. He is henceforth only an insect.

When all comes to all, the most precious element in life is wonder. Love is a great emotion, and power is power. But both love and power are based on wonder. Love without wonder is a sensational affair, and power without wonder is mere force and compulsion. The one universal element in consciousness which is fundamental to life is the element of wonder. You cannot help feeling it in a bean as it starts to grow and pulls itself out of its jacket. You cannot help feeling it in the glisten of the nucleus of the amœba. You recognize it, willy-nilly, in an ant busily tugging at a straw; in a rook, as it walks the frosty grass.

They all have their own obstinate will. But also they all live with a sense of wonder. Plant consciousness, insect consciousness, fish consciousness, all are related by one permanent element, which we may call the religious element inherent in all life, even in a flea: the sense of wonder. That is our sixth sense. And it is the *natural* religious sense.

Somebody says that mystery is nothing, because mystery is something you don't know, and what you don't know is nothing to you. But there is more than one way of knowing.

Even the real scientist works in the sense of wonder. The pity is, when he comes out of his laboratory he puts aside his wonder along with his apparatus, and tries to make it all perfectly didactic. Science in its true condition of wonder is as religious as any religion. But didactic science is as dead and boring as dogmatic religion. Both are wonderless and productive of boredom, endless boredom.

Now we come back to the hymns. They live and glisten in the depths of the man's consciousness in undimmed wonder, because they have not been subjected to any criticism or analysis. By the time I was sixteen I had criticized and got over the Christian dogma.

It was quite easy for me; my immediate forebears had already done it for me. Salvation, heaven, Virgin birth, miracles, even the Christian dogmas of right and wrong — one soon got them adjusted. I never could really worry about them. Heaven is one of the instinctive dreams. Right and wrong is something you can't dogmatize about; it's not so easy. As for my soul, I simply don't and never did understand how I could 'save' it. One can save one's pennies. But how can one save one's soul? One can only *live* one's soul. The business is to live, really alive. And this needs wonder.

So that the miracle of the loaves and fishes is just as good to me now as when I was a child. I don't care whether it is historically a fact or not. What does it matter? It is part of the genuine wonder. The same with all the religious teaching I had as a child, *apart* from the didacticism and sentimentalism. I am eternally grateful for the wonder with which it filled my childhood.

> Sun of my soul, thou Saviour dear,
> It is not night if Thou be near —

That was the last hymn at the board-school. It did not mean to me any Christian dogma or any salvation. Just the words,

'Sun of my soul, thou Saviour dear,' penetrated me with wonder and the mystery of twilight. At another time the last hymn was:

> Fair waved the golden corn
> In Canaan's pleasant land –

And again I loved 'Canaan's pleasant land.' The wonder of 'Canaan,' which could never be localized.

I think it was good to be brought up a Protestant: and among Protestants, a Nonconformist, and among Nonconformists, a Congregationalist. Which sounds pharisaic. But I should have missed bitterly a direct knowledge of the Bible, and a direct relation to Galilee and Canaan, Moab and Kedron, those places that never existed on earth. And in the Church of England one would hardly have escaped those snobbish hierarchies of class, which spoil so much for a child. And the Primitive Methodists, when I was a boy, were always having 'revivals' and being 'saved,' and I always had a horror of being saved.

So, altogether, I am grateful to my 'Congregational' upbringing. The Congregationalists are the oldest Nonconformists, descendants of the Oliver Cromwell Independents. They still had the Puritan tradition of no ritual. But they avoided the personal emotionalism which one found among the Methodists when I was a boy.

I liked our chapel, which was tall and full of light, and yet still; and colour-washed pale green and blue, with a bit of lotus pattern. And over the organ-loft, 'O worship the Lord in the beauty of holiness,' in big letters.

That was a favourite hymn, too:

> O worship the Lord, in the beauty of holiness,
> Bow down before Him, His glory proclaim;

> With gold of obedience and incense of lowliness
> Kneel and adore Him, the Lord is His name.

I don't know what the 'beauty of holiness' is exactly. It easily becomes cant, or nonsense. But if you don't think about it – and why should you? – it has a magic. The same with the whole verse. It is rather bad, really, 'gold of obedience' and 'incense of lowliness.' But in me, to the music, it still produces a sense of splendour.

I am always glad we had the Bristol hymn-book, not Moody and Sankey. And I am glad our Scotch minister on the whole avoided sentimental messes such as 'Lead, Kindly Light,' or even 'Abide with Me.' He had a healthy preference for healthy hymns.

> At even, ere the sun was set,
> The sick, O Lord, around Thee lay.
> Oh, in what divers pains they met!
> Oh, in what joy they went away!

And often we had 'Fight the good fight with all thy might.'
In Sunday School I am eternally grateful to old Mr Remington with his round white beard and his ferocity. He made us sing! And he loved the martial hymns:

> Sound the battle-cry,
> See, the foe is nigh.
> Raise the standard high
> For the Lord.

The ghastly sentimentalism that came like a leprosy over religion had not yet got hold of our colliery village. I remember when I was in Class II in the Sunday School, when I was about seven, a woman teacher trying to harrow us about the Crucifixion. And she kept saying: 'And aren't you sorry for Jesus? Aren't you sorry?' And most of the children wept. I believe I shed a crocodile tear or two, but very vivid is my memory of saying to myself: 'I don't *really* care a bit.' And I could never go back on it. I never *cared* about the Crucifixion, one way or another. Yet the *wonder* of it penetrated very deep in me.

Thirty-six years ago men, even Sunday School teachers, still believed in the fight for life and the fun of it. 'Hold the fort, for I am coming.' It was far, far from any militarism or gun-fighting. But it was the battle-cry of a stout soul, and a fine thing too.

> Stand up, stand up for Jesus,
> Ye soldiers of the Lord.

Here is the clue to the ordinary Englishman – in the Nonconformist hymns.

GIVE HER A PATTERN (1928)

The real trouble about women is that they must always go on trying to adapt themselves to men's theories of women, as they always have done. When a woman is thoroughly herself, she is being what her type of man wants her to be. When a woman is hysterical it's because she doesn't quite know what to be, which pattern to follow, which man's picture of woman to live up to.

For, of course, just as there are many men in the world, there are many masculine theories of what women should be. But men run to type, and it is the type, not the individual, that produces the theory, or 'ideal' of woman. Those very grasping gentry, the Romans, produced a theory or ideal of the matron, which fitted in very nicely with the Roman property lust. 'Cæsar's wife should be above suspicion.' – So Cæsar wife kindly proceeded to be above it, no matter how for below it the Cæsar fell. Later gentlemen like Nero produced the 'fast' theory of woman, and later ladies were fast enough for everybody. Dante arrived with a chaste and untouched Beatrice, and chaste and untouched Beatrices began to march self-importantly through the centuries. The Renaissance discovered the learned woman, and learned women buzzed mildly into verse and prose. Dickens invented the child-wife, so child-wives have swarmed ever since. He also fished out his version of the chaste Beatrice, a chaste but marriageable Agnes. George Eliot imitated this pattern, and it became confirmed. The noble woman, the pure spouse, the devoted mother took the field, and was simply worked to death. Our own poor mothers were this sort. So we younger men, having been a bit frightened of our noble mothers, tended to revert to the child-wife. We weren't very inventive. Only the child-wife must be a boyish little thing – that was the new touch we added. Because young men are definitely frightened of the real female. She's too risky a quantity. She is too untidy, like David's Dora. No, let her be a boyish little thing, it's safer. So a boyish little thing she is.

There are, of course, other types. Capable men produce the capable woman ideal. Doctors produce the capable nurse. Business men produce the capable secretary. And so you get all sorts. You can produce the masculine sense of honour (whatever that highly mysterious quantity may be) in women, if you want to.

There is, also, the eternal secret ideal of men – the prostitute. Lots of women live up to this idea: just because men want them to.

And so, poor woman, destiny makes away with her. It isn't that she hasn't got a mind – she has. She's got everything that man has. The only difference is that she asks for a pattern. Give me a pattern to follow! That will always be woman's cry. Unless of course she has already chosen her pattern quite young, then she will declare she is herself absolutely, and no man's idea of women has any influence over her.

Now the real tragedy is not that women ask and must ask for a pattern of womanhood. The tragedy is not, even, that men give them such abominable patterns, child-wives, little-boy-baby-face-girls, perfect secretaries, noble spouses, self-sacrificing mothers, pure women who bring forth children in virgin coldness, prostitutes who just make themselves low, to please the men; all the atrocious patterns of womanhood that men have supplied to woman; patterns all perverted from any real natural fulness of a human being. Man is willing to accept woman as an equal, as a man in skirts, as an angel, a devil, a baby-face, a machine, an instrument, a bosom, a womb, a pair of legs, a servant, an encyclopædia, an ideal or an obscenity; the one thing he won't accept her as is a human being, a real human being of the feminine sex.

And, of course, women love living up to strange patterns, weird patterns – the more uncanny the better. What could be more uncanny than the present pattern of the Eton-boy girl with flower-like artificial complexion? It is just weird. And for its very weirdness women like living up to it. What can be more gruesome than the little-boy-baby-face pattern? Yet the girls take it on with avidity.

But even that isn't the real root of the tragedy. The absurdity, and often, as in the Dante-Beatrice business, the inhuman nastiness of the pattern – for Beatrice had to go on being chaste and untouched all her life, according to Dante's pattern, while Dante had a cosy wife and kids at home – even that isn't the worst of it. The worst of it is, as soon as a woman has really lived up to the man's pattern, the man dislikes her for it. There is intense secret dislike for the Eton-young-man girl, among the boys, now that she is actually produced. Of course, she's very nice to show in public, absolutely the thing. But the very young men who have brought about her production detest her in private and in their private hearts are appalled by her.

When it comes to marrying, the pattern goes all to pieces. The boy marries the Eton-boy girl, and instantly he hates the *type*. Instantly his mind begins to play hysterically with all the other types, noble Agneses, chaste Beatrices, clinging Doras and lurid *filles de joie*. He is in a wild welter of confusion. Whatever pattern the poor woman tries to live up to; he'll want another. And that's the condition of modern marriage.

Modern woman isn't really a fool. But modern man is. That seems to me the only plain way of putting it. The modern man is a fool, and the modern young man a prize fool. He makes a

D. H. LAWRENCE

greater mess of his women than men have ever made. Because he absolutely doesn't know *what* he wants her to be. We shall see the changes in the woman-pattern follow one another fast and furious now, because the young men hysterically don't know what they want. Two years hence women may be in crinolines – there was a pattern for you! – or a bead flap, like naked negresses in mid-Africa – or they may be wearing brass armour, or the uniform of the Horse Guards. They may be anything. Because the young men are off their heads, and don't know what they want.

The women aren't fools, but they *must* live up to some pattern or other. They *know* the men are fools. They don't really respect the pattern. Yet a pattern they must have, or they can't exist.

Women are not fools. They have their own logic, even if it's not the masculine sort. Women have the logic of emotion, men have the logic of reason. It only works differently.

And the woman never really loses it. She may spend years living up to a masculine pattern. But in the end, the strange and terrible logic of emotion will work out the smashing of that pattern, if it has not been emotionally satisfactory. This is the partial explanation of the astonishing changes in women. For years they go on being chaste Beatrices or child-wives. Then on a sudden – bash! The chaste Beatrice becomes something quite different, the child-wife becomes a roaring lioness! The pattern didn't suffice, emotionally.

Whereas men are fools. They are based on a logic of reason, or are supposed to be. And then they go and behave, especially with regard to women, in a more-than-feminine unreasonableness. They spend years training up the little-boy-baby-face type, till they've got her perfect. Then the moment they marry her, they want something else. Oh, beware, young women, of the young men who adore you! The moment they've got you they'll want something utterly different. The moment they marry the little-boy-baby face, instantly they begin to pine for the noble

Agnes, pure and majestic, or the infinite mother with deep bosom of consolation, or the perfect business woman, or the lurid prostitute on black silk sheets: or, most idiotic of all, a combination of all the lot of them at once. And that is the logic of reason! When it comes to women, modern men are idiots. They don't know what they want, and so they never want, permanently, what they get. They want a cream cake that is at the same time ham and eggs and at the same time porridge. They are fools. If only women weren't bound by fate to play up to them!

For the fact of life is that women *must* play up to man's pattern. And she only gives her best to a man when he gives her a satisfactory pattern to play up to. But today, with a stock of ready-made, worn-out idiotic patterns to live up to, what can women give to men but the trashy side of their emotions? What could a woman possibly give to a man who wanted her to be a boy-baby face? What could she possibly give him but the dribblings of an idiot? – And, because women aren't fools, and aren't fooled even for very long at a time, she gives him some nasty cruel digs with her claws, and makes him cry for mother dear! – abruptly changing his pattern.

Bah! men are fools. If they want anything from women, let them give women a decent, satisfying idea of womanhood – not these trick patterns of washed-out idiots.

NEW MEXICO (1928)

Superficially, the world has become small and known. Poor little globe of earth, the tourists trot round you as easily as they trot round the Bois or round Central Park. There is no mystery left, we've been there, we've seen it, we know all about it. We've done the globe, and the globe is done.

This is quite true, superficially. On the superficies, horizontally, we've been everywhere and done everything, we know all about it. Yet the more we know, superficially, the less we penetrate, vertically. It's all very well skimming across the surface of the ocean, and saying you know all about the sea. There still remain the terrifying under-deeps, of which we have utterly no experience.

The same is true of land travel. We skim along, we get there, we see it all, we've done it all. And as a rule, we never once go through the curious film which railroads, ships, motor-cars, and hotels stretch over the surface of the whole earth. Peking is just the same as New York, with a few different things to look at; rather more Chinese about, etc. Poor creatures that we are, we crave for experience, yet we are like flies that crawl on the pure and transparent mucous-paper in which the world like a bon-bon is wrapped so carefully that we can never get at it, though we see it there all the time as we move about it, apparently in contact, yet actually as far removed as if it were the moon.

As a matter of fact, our great-grandfathers, who never went

anywhere, in actuality had more experience of the world than we have, who have seen everything. When they listened to a lecture with lantern-slides, they really held their breath before the unknown, as they sat in the village school-room. We, bowling along in a rickshaw in Ceylon, say to ourselves: 'It's very much what you'd expect.' We really know it all.

We are mistaken. The know-it-all state of mind is just the result of being outside the mucous-paper wrapping of civilization. Underneath is everything we don't know and are afraid of knowing.

I realized this with shattering force when I went to New Mexico.

New Mexico, one of the United States, part of the USA. New Mexico, the picturesque reservation and playground of the eastern states, very romantic, old Spanish, Red Indian, desert mesas, pueblos, cowboys, penitentes, all that film stuff. Very nice, the great South-West, put on a sombrero and knot a red kerchief round your neck, to go out in the great free spaces!

That is New Mexico wrapped in the absolutely hygienic and shiny mucous-paper of our trite civilization. That is the New Mexico known to most of the Americans who know it at all. But break through the shiny sterilized wrapping, and actually *touch* the country, and you will never be the same again.

I think New Mexico was the greatest experience from the outside world that I have ever had. It certainly changed me for ever. Curious as it may sound, it was New Mexico that liberated me from the present era of civilization, the great era of material and mechanical development. Months spent in holy Kandy, in Ceylon, the holy of holies of southern Buddhism, had not touched the great psyche of materialism and idealism which dominated me. And years, even in the exquisite beauty of Sicily, right among the old Greek paganism that still lives there, had not shattered the essential Christianity on which my character was established. Australia was a sort of dream or trance, like being under a spell, the self remaining unchanged, so long as the trance did not last too long. Tahiti, in a mere glimpse, repelled me: and so did California, after a stay of a few weeks. There seemed a strange brutality in the spirit of the western coast, and I felt: O, let me get away!

But the moment I saw the brilliant, proud morning shine high up over the deserts of Santa Fé, something stood still in my soul, and I started to attend. There was a certain magnificence in the high-up day, a certain eagle-like royalty, so different from the equally pure, equally pristine and lovely morning of Australia, which is so soft, so utterly pure in its softness, and betrayed by green parrot flying. But in the lovely morning of Australia one went into a dream. In the magnificent fierce morning of New Mexico one sprang awake, a new part of the soul woke up suddenly, and the old world gave way to a new.

There are all kinds of beauty in the world, thank God, though ugliness is homogeneous. How lovely is Sicily, with Calabria across the sea like an opal, and Etna with her snow in a world above and beyond! How lovely is Tuscany, with little red tulips wild among the corn: or bluebells at dusk in England, or mimosa in clouds of pure yellow among the grey-green dun foliage of Australia, under a soft, blue, unbreathed sky! But for a *greatness* of beauty I have never experienced anything like New Mexico. All those mornings when I went with a hoe along the ditch to the Cañon, at the ranch, and stood, in the fierce, proud silence of the Rockies, on their foothills, to look far over the desert to the blue mountains away in Arizona, blue as chalcedony, with the sage-brush desert sweeping grey-blue in between, dotted with tiny cube-crystals of houses, the vast amphitheatre of lofty, indomitable desert, sweeping round to the ponderous Sangre de Cristo, mountains on the east, and coming up flush at the pine-dotted foot-hills of the Rockies! What splendour! Only the tawny eagle could really sail out into the splendour of it all. Leo Stein once wrote to me: It is the most æsthetically-satisfying landscape I know. To me it was much more than that. It had a splendid silent terror, and a vast far-and-wide magnificence which made it way beyond mere æsthetic appreciation. Never is the light more pure and overweening than there, arching with a royalty almost cruel over the hollow, uptilted world. For it is curious that the land which has produced modern political democracy at its highest pitch should give one the greatest sense of overweening, terrible proudness and mercilessness: but so beautiful, God! so beautiful! Those that have spent morning after morning alone there pitched among the pines above the great proud world of desert will know, almost unbearably how beautiful it is, how clear and unquestioned is the might of the day. Just day itself is tremendous there. It is so easy to understand that the Aztecs gave hearts of men to the sun. For the sun is not merely hot or scorching, not at all. It is of a brilliant and unchallengeable purity and haughty serenity which would make one sacrifice the heart to it. Ah, yes, in New Mexico the heart is sacrificed to the sun and the human being is left stark, heartless, but undauntedly religious.

And that was the second revelation out there. I had looked over all the world for something that would strike *me* as religious. The simple piety of some English people, the semi-pagan mystery of some Catholics in southern Italy, the intensity of some Bavarian peasants, the semi-ecstasy of Buddhists or Brahmins: all this had seemed religious all right, as far as the parties concerned were involved, but it didn't involve me. I looked on at their religiousness from the outside. For it is still harder to feel religion at will than to love at will.

I had seen what I felt was a hint of wild religion in the so-called devil dances of a group of naked villagers from the far-remote jungle in Ceylon, dancing at midnight under the torches, glittering wet with sweat on their dark bodies as if they had been gilded, at the celebration of the Pera-hera, in Kandy, given to the Prince of Wales. And the utter dark absorption of these naked men, as they danced with their knees wide apart, suddenly affected me with a *sense* of religion, I *felt* religion for a moment. For religion is an experience, an uncontrollable sensual experience, even more so than love: I use sensual to mean an experience deep down in the senses, inexplicable and inscrutable.

But this experience was fleeting, gone in the curious turmoil of the Pera-hera, and I had no permanent feeling of religion till I came to New Mexico and penetrated into the old human race-experience there. It is curious that it should be in America, of all places, that a European should really experience religion, after touching the old Mediterranean and the East. It is curious that one should get a sense of living religion from the Red Indians, having failed to get it from Hindus or Sicilian Catholics or Cingalese.

Let me make a reservation. I don't stand up to praise the Red Indian as he reveals himself in contact with white civilization. From that angle, I am forced to admit he *may* be thoroughly objectionable. Even my small experience knows it. But also I know he *may* be thoroughly nice, even in his dealings with white men. It's a question of individuals, a good deal, on both sides.

But in this article, I don't want to deal with the everyday or superficial aspect of New Mexico, outside the mucous-paper wrapping, I *want* to go beneath the surface. But therefore the American Indian in his behaviour as an American citizen doesn't really concern me. What concerns me is what he is – or what he seems to me to be, in his ancient, ancient race-self and religious-self.

For the Red Indian seems to me much older than Greeks, or Hindus or any Europeans or even Egyptians. The Red Indian, as a civilized and truly religious man, civilized beyond taboo and totem, as he is in the south, is religious in perhaps the oldest sense, and deepest, of the word. That is to say, he is a remnant of the most deeply religious race still living. So it seems to me.

But again let me protect myself. The Indian who sells you baskets on Albuquerque station or who slinks around Taos plaza may be an utter waster and an indescribably low dog. Personally he may be even less religious than a New York sneak-thief. He may have broken with his tribe, or his tribe itself may have collapsed finally from its old religious integrity, and ceased, really to exist. Then he is only fit for rapid absorption into white civilization, which must make the best of him.

But while a tribe retains its religion and keeps up its religious practices, and while any member of the tribe shares in those practices, then there is a tribal integrity and a living tradition going back far beyond the birth of Christ, beyond the pyramids, beyond Moses. A vast old religion which once swayed the earth lingers in unbroken practice there in New Mexico, older, perhaps, than anything in the world save Australian aboriginal taboo and totem, and that is not yet religion.

You can feel it, the atmosphere of it, around the pueblos. Not, of course, when the place is crowded with sight-seers and motor-cars. But go to Taos pueblo on some brilliant snowy morning and see the white figure on the roof: or come riding through at dusk on some windy evening, when the black skirts of the silent women blow around the white wide boots, and you will feel the old, old root of human consciousness still reaching down to depths we know nothing of: and of which, only too often, we are jealous. It seems it will not be long before the pueblos are uprooted.

But never shall I forget watching the dancers, the men with the fox-skin swaying down from their buttocks, file out at San Geronimo, and the women with seed rattles following. The long, streaming, glistening black hair of the men. Even in ancient Crete long hair was sacred in a man, as it is still in the Indians.

Never shall I forget the utter absorption of the dance, so quiet, so steadily, timelessly rhythmic, and silent, with the ceaseless down-tread, always to the earth's centre, the very reverse of the upflow of Dionysiac or Christian ecstasy. Never shall I forget the deep singing of the men at the drum, swelling and sinking, the deepest sound I have heard in all my life, deeper than thunder, deeper than the sound of the Pacific Ocean, deeper than the roar of a deep waterfall: the wonderful deep sound of men calling to the unspeakable depths.

Never shall I forget coming into the little pueblo of San Filipi one sunny morning in spring, unexpectedly, when bloom was on the trees in the perfect little pueblo more old, more utterly peaceful and idyllic than anything in Theocritus, and seeing a little casual dance. Not impressive as a spectacle, only, to me, profoundly moving because of the truly terrifying religious absorption of it.

Never shall I forget the Christmas dances at Taos, twilight, snow, the darkness coming over the great wintry mountains and the lonely pueblo, then suddenly, again, like dark calling to dark, the deep Indian cluster-singing around the drum, wild and awful, suddenly rousing on the last dusk as the procession starts. And then the bonfires leaping suddenly in pure spurts of high flame, columns of sudden flame forming an alley for the procession.

Never shall I forget the khiva of birch-trees, away in the Apaché country, in Arizona this time, the tepees and flickering fires, the neighing of horses unseen under the huge dark night, and the Apaches all abroad, in their silent moccasined feet: and in the khiva, beyond a little fire, the old man reciting, reciting in the unknown Apache speech, in the strange wild Indian voice that reechoes away back to before the Flood, reciting apparently the traditions and legends of the tribe, going on and on, while the young men, the *braves* of today, wandered in, listened, and wandered away again, overcome with the power and majesty of that utterly old tribal voice, yet uneasy with their half-adherence to the modern civilization, the two things in contact. And one of these *braves* shoved his face under my hat, in the night, and stared with his glittering eyes close to mine. He'd have killed me then and there, had he dared. He didn't dare: and I knew it: and he knew it.

Never shall I forget the Indian races, when the young men, even the boys, run naked, smeared with white earth and stuck with bits of eagle fluff for the swiftness of the heavens, and the old men brush them with eagle feathers, to give them power. And they run in the strange hurling fashion of the primitive world, hurled forward, not making speed deliberately. And the race is not for victory. It is not a contest. There is no competition. It is a great cumulative effort. The tribe this day is adding up its male energy and exerting it to the utmost – for what? To get power, to get strength: to come, by sheer cumulative, hurling effort of the bodies of men, into contact with the great cosmic source of vitality which gives strength, power, energy to the men who can grasp it, energy for the zeal of attainment.

It was a vast old religion, greater than anything we know: more starkly and nakedly religious. There is no God, no conception of a god. All is god. But it is not the pantheism we are accustomed to, which expresses itself as 'God is everywhere, God is in everything.' In the oldest religion, everything was alive, not supernaturally but naturally alive. There were only deeper and deeper streams of life, vibrations of life more and more vast. So rocks were alive, but a mountain had a deeper, vaster life than a rock, and it was much harder for a man to bring his spirit, or his energy, into contact with the life of the mountain, and so draw strength from the mountain, as from a great standing well of life, than it was to come into contact with the rock. And he had to put forth a great religious effort. For the whole life-effort of man was to get his life into direct contact with the elemental life of the cosmos, mountain-life, cloud-life, thunder-life, air-life, earth-life, sun-life. To come into immediate *felt* contact, and so derive energy, power, and a dark sort of joy. This effort into sheer naked contact, *without an intermediary or mediator*, is the root meaning of religion, and at the sacred races the runners hurled themselves in a terrible cumulative effort, through the air, to come at last into naked contact with the very life of the air, which is the life of the clouds, and so of the rain.

It was a vast and pure religion, without idols or images, even mental ones. It is the oldest religion, a cosmic religion the same for all peoples, not broken up into specific gods or saviours or systems. It is the religion which precedes the god-concept, and is therefore greater and deeper than any god-religion.

And it lingers still, for a little while, in New Mexico: but long enough to have been a revelation to me. And the Indian, however objectionable he may be on occasion, has still some of the strange beauty and pathos of the religion that brought him forth and is now shedding him away into oblivion. When Trinidad, the Indian boy, and I planted corn at the ranch, my soul paused to see his brown hands softly moving the earth over the maize in pure ritual. He was back in his old religious self, and the ages stood still. Ten minutes later he was making a fool of himself with the horses. Horses were never part of the Indian's religious life, never would be. He hasn't a tithe of the feeling for them that he has for a bear, for example. So horses don't like Indians.

But there it is: the newest democracy ousting the oldest religion! And once the oldest religion is ousted, one feels the democracy and all its paraphernalia will collapse, and the oldest religion, which comes down to us from man's pre-war days, will start again. The sky-scraper will scatter on the winds like thistle-down, and the genuine America, the America of New Mexico, will start on its course again. This is an interregnum.

MYSELF REVEALED (1928)

They ask me: 'Did you find it very hard to get on and to become a success?' And I have to admit that if I can be said to have got on, and if I can be called a success, then I *did not* find it hard.

I never starved in a garret, nor waited in anguish for the post to bring me an answer from editor or publisher, nor did I struggle in sweat and blood to bring forth mighty works, nor did I ever wake up and find myself famous.

I was a poor boy. I *ought* to have wrestled in the fell clutch of circumstance, and undergone the bludgeonings of chance before I became a writer with a very modest income and a very questionable reputation. But I didn't. It all happened by itself and without any groans from me.

It seems a pity. Because I was undoubtedly a poor boy of the working classes, with no apparent future in front of me. But after all, what am I now?

I was born among the working classes and brought up among them. My father was a collier, and only a collier, nothing praiseworthy about him. He wasn't even respectable, in so far as he got drunk rather frequently, never went near a chapel, and was usually rather rude to his little immediate bosses at the pit.

He practically never had a good stall all the time he was a butty, because he was always saying tiresome and foolish things about the men just above him in control at the mine. He offended them all, almost on purpose, so how could he expect them to favour him? Yet he grumbled when they didn't.

My mother was, I suppose, superior. She came from town, and belonged really to the lower bourgeoisie. She spoke King's English, without an accent, and never in her life could even imitate a sentence of the dialect which my father spoke, and which we children spoke out of doors.

She wrote a fine Italian hand, and a clever and amusing letter when she felt like it. And as she grew older she read novels again, and got terribly impatient with *Diana of the Crossways* and terribly thrilled by *East Lynne*.

But she was a working man's wife, and nothing else, in her shabby little black bonnet and her shrewd, clear, 'different' face. And she was very much respected, just as my father was not respected. Her nature was quick and sensitive, and perhaps really superior. But she was down, right down in the working class, among the mass of poorer colliers' wives.

I was a delicate pale brat with a snuffy nose, whom most people treated quite gently as just an ordinary delicate little lad. When I was twelve I got a county council scholarship, twelve pounds a year, and went to Nottingham High School.

After leaving school I was a clerk for three months, then had a very serious pneumonia illness, in my seventeenth year, that damaged my health for life.

A year later I became a school-teacher, and after three years' savage teaching of collier lads I went to take the 'normal' course in Nottingham University.

As I was glad to leave school, I was glad to leave college. It had meant mere disillusion, instead of the living contact of men. From college I went down to Croydon, near London, to teach in a new elementary school at a hundred pounds a year.

It was while I was at Croydon, when I was twenty-three, that the girl who had been the chief friend of my youth, and who was herself a school-teacher in a mining village at home, copied out some of my poems, and without telling me, sent them to the *English Review*, which had just had a glorious re-birth under Ford Madox Hueffer.

Hueffer was most kind. He printed the poems, and asked me to come and see him. The girl had launched me, so easily, on my literary career, like a princess cutting a thread, launching a ship.

I had been tussling away for four years, getting out *The White Peacock* in inchoate bits, from the underground of my consciousness. I must have written most of it five or six times, but only in intervals, never as a task or a divine labour, or in the groans of parturition.

I would dash at it, do a bit, show it to the girl; she always admired it; then realize afterwards it wasn't what I wanted, and have another dash. But at Croydon I had worked at it fairly steadily, in the evenings after school.

Anyhow, it was done, after four or five years' spasmodic effort. Hueffer asked at once to see the manuscript. He read it immediately, with the greatest cheery sort of kindness and bluff. And in his queer voice, when we were in an omnibus in London, he shouted in my ear: 'It's got every fault that the English novel can have.'

Just then the English novel was supposed to have so many faults, in comparison with the French, that it was hardly allowed to exist at all. 'But,' shouted Hueffer in the 'bus, 'you've got GENIUS.'

This made me want to laugh, it sounded so comical. In the early days they were always telling me I had got genius, as if to console me for not having their own incomparable advantages.

But Hueffer didn't mean that. I always thought he had a bit of genius himself. Anyhow, he sent the MS. of *The White Peacock* to William Heinemann, who accepted it at once, and made me alter only four little lines whose omission would now make any-body smile. I was to have £50 when the book was published.

Meanwhile Hueffer printed more poems and some stories of mine in the *English Review*, and people read them and told me so, to my embarrassment and anger. I hated being an author, in people's eyes. Especially as I was a teacher.

When I was twenty-five my mother died, and two months later *The White Peacock* was published, but it meant nothing to me. I went on teaching for another year, and then again a bad pneumonia illness intervened. When I got better I did not go back to school. I lived henceforward on my scanty literary earnings.

It is seventeen years since I gave up teaching and started to live an independent life of the pen. I have never starved, and never even felt poor, though my income for the first ten years was no better, and often worse, than it would have been if I had remained an elementary school-teacher.

But when one has been born poor a very little money can be enough. Now my father would think I am rich, if nobody else does. And my mother would think I have risen in the world, even if I don't think so.

But something is wrong, either with me or with the world, or with both of us. I have gone far and met people, of all sorts and all conditions, and many whom I have genuinely liked and esteemed.

People, *personally*, have nearly always been friendly. Of critics we will not speak, they are different fauna from people. And I have *wanted* to feel truly friendly with some, at least, of my fellow-men.

Yet I have never quite succeeded. Whether I get on *in* the world is a question; but I certainly don't get on very well *with* the world. And whether I am a worldly success or not I really don't know. But I feel, somehow, not much of a human success.

By which I mean that I don't feel there is any very cordial or fundamental contact between me and society, or me and other people. There is a breach. And my contact is with something that is nonhuman, non-vocal.

I used to think it had something to do with the oldness and the worn-outness of Europe. Having tried other places, I know that is not so. Europe is, perhaps, the least worn-out of the continents, because it is the most lived in. A place that is lived in lives.

It is since coming back from America that I ask myself seriously: Why is there so little contact between myself and the people whom I know? Why has the contact no vital meaning?

And if I write the question down, and try to write the answer down, it is because I feel it is a question that troubles many men.

The answer, as far as I can see, has something to do with class. Class makes a gulf, across which all the best human flow is lost. It is not exactly the triumph of the middle classes that has made the deadness, but the triumph of the middle-class *thing*.

As a man from the working class, I feel that the middle class cut off some of my vital vibration when I am with them. I admit them charming and educated and good people often enough *But they just stop some part of me from working.* Some part has to be left out.

Then why don't I live with my working people? Because their vibration is limited in another direction. They are narrow, but still fairly deep and passionate, whereas the middle class is broad and shallow and passionless. Quite passionless. At the best they substitute affection, which is the great middle-class positive emotion.

But the working class is narrow in outlook, in prejudice, and narrow in intelligence. This again makes a prison. One can belong absolutely to no class.

Yet I find, here in Italy, for example, that I live in a certain silent contact with the peasants who work the land of this villa. I am not intimate with them, hardly speak to them save to say good day. And they are not working for me; I am not their *padrone*.

Yet it is they, really, who form my *ambiente*, and it is from them that the human flow comes to me. I don't want to live with them in their cottages; that would be a sort of prison. But I want them to be there, about the place, their lives going on along with mine, and in relation to mine. I don't idealize them. Enough of that folly! It is worse than setting school-children to express themselves in self-conscious twaddle. I don't expect them to make any millennium here on earth, neither now nor in the future. But I want to live near them, because their life still flows.

And now I know, more or less, why I cannot follow in the footsteps even of Barrie or of Wells, who both came from the common people also and are both such a success. Now I know why I cannot rise in the world and become even a little popular and rich.

I cannot make the transfer from my own class into the middle class. I cannot, not for anything in the world, forfeit my passional consciousness and my old blood-affinity with my fellow-men and the animals and the land, for that other thin, spurious mental conceit which is all that is left of the mental consciousness once it has made itself exclusive.

INTRODUCTION TO THESE
PAINTINGS (1928–29)

The reason the English produce so few painters is not that they are, as a nation, devoid of a genuine feeling for visual art: though to look at their productions, and to look at the mess which has been made of actual English landscape, one might really conclude that they were, and leave it at that. But it is not the fault of the God that made them. They are made with æsthetic sensibilities the same as anybody else. The fault lies in the English attitude to life.

The English, and the Americans following them, are paralysed by fear. That is what thwarts and distorts the Anglo-Saxon existence, this paralysis of fear. It thwarts life, it distorts vision, and it strangles impulse: this overmastering fear. And fear of what, in heaven's name? What is the Anglo-Saxon stock today so petrified with fear about? We have to answer that before we can understand the English failure in the visual arts: for, on the whole, it is a failure.

It is an old fear, which seemed to dig in to the English soul at the time of the Renaissance. Nothing could be more lovely and fearless than Chaucer. But already Shakespeare is morbid with fear, fear of consequences. That is the strange phenomenon of the English Renaissance: this mystic terror of the consequences, the consequences of action. Italy, too, had her reaction, at the end of the sixteenth century, and showed a similar fear. But not so profound, so overmastering. Aretino was anything but timorous: he was bold as any Renaissance novelist, and went one better.

What appeared to take full grip on the northern conscious-ness at the end of the sixteenth century was a terror, almost a horror of sexual life. The Elizabethans, grand as we think them, started it. The real 'mortal coil' in Hamlet is all sexual; the young man's horror of his mother's incest, sex carrying with it a wild and nameless terror which, it seems to me, it had never carried before. Œdipus and Hamlet are very different in this respect. In Œdipus there is no recoil in horror from sex itself: Greek drama never shows us that. The horror, when it is present in Greek tragedy, is against *destiny*, man caught in the toils of destiny. But with the Renaissance itself, particularly in England, the horror is sexual. Orestes is dogged by destiny and driven mad by the Eumenides. But Hamlet is overpowered by horrible revulsion from his physical connexion with his mother, which makes him recoil in similar revulsion from Ophelia, and almost from his father, even as a ghost. He is horrified at the merest suggestion of physical connexion, as if it were an unspeakable taint.

This, no doubt, is all in the course of the growth of the 'spiritual-mental' consciousness, at the expense of the instinctive-intuitive consciousness. Man came to have his own body in horror, especially in its sexual implications: and so he began to suppress with all his might his instinctive-intuitive conscious-ness, which is so radical, so physical, so sexual. Cavalier poetry, love poetry, is already devoid of body. Donne, after the exacer-bated revulsion-attraction excitement of his earlier poetry, becomes a divine. 'Drink to me only with thine eyes,' sings the cavalier: an expression incredible in Chaucer's poetry. 'I could not love thee, dear, so much, loved I not honour more,' sings the Cavalier lover. In Chaucer the 'dear' and the 'honour' would have been more or less identical.

But with the Elizabethans the grand rupture had started in the human consciousness, the mental consciousness recoiling in violence away from the physical, instinctive-intuitive. To the Restoration dramatist sex is, on the whole, a dirty business, but they more or less glory in the dirt. Fielding tries in vain to defend the Old Adam. Richardson with his calico purity and his underclothing excitements sweeps all before him. Swift goes mad with sex and excrement revulsion. Sterne flings a bit of the same excrement humorously around. And physical consciousness gives a last song in Burns, then is dead. Wordsworth, Keats, Shelley, the Brontës, all are post-mortem poets. The essential instinctive-intuitive body is dead, and worshipped in death – all very unhealthy. Till Swinburne and Oscar Wilde try to start a revival from the mental field. Swinburne's 'white thighs' are purely mental.

Now, in England – and following, in America – the physical self was not just fig-leafed over or suppressed in public, as was the case in Italy and on most of the Continent. In England it excited a strange horror and terror. And this extra morbidity came, I believe, from the great shock of syphilis and the realization of the consequences of the disease. Wherever syphilis, or 'pox,' came from, it was fairly new in England at the end of the fifteenth century. But by the end of the sixteenth, its ravages were obvious, and the shock of them had just penetrated the thoughtful and the imaginative consciousness. The royal families of England and Scotland were syphilitic; Edward VI and Elizabeth born with the inherited consequences of the disease. Edward VI died of it, while still a boy. Mary died childless and in utter depression. Elizabeth had no eyebrows, her teeth went rotten; she must have felt herself, somewhere, utterly unfit for marriage, poor thing. That was the grisly horror that lay behind the glory of Queen Bess. And so the Tudors died out: and another syphilitic-born unfortunate came to the throne, in the person of

James I. Mary Queen of Scots had no more luck than the Tudors, apparently. Apparently Darnley was reeking with the pox, though probably at first she did not know it. But when the Archbishop of St Andrews was christening her baby James, afterwards James I of England, the old clergyman was so dripping with pox that she was terrified lest he should give it to the infant. And she need not have troubled, for the wretched infant had brought it into the world with him, from that fool Darnley. So James I of England slobbered and shambled, and was the wisest fool in Christendom, and the Stuarts likewise died out, the stock enfeebled by the disease.

With the royal families of England and Scotland in this condition, we can judge what the noble houses, the nobility of both nations, given to free living and promiscuous pleasure, must have been like. England traded with the East and with America; England, unknowing, had opened her doors to the disease. The English aristocracy travelled and had curious taste in loves. And pox entered the blood of the nation, particularly of the upper classes, who had more chance of infection. And after it had entered the blood, it entered the consciousness, and hit the vital imagination.

It is possible that the effects of syphilis and the conscious realization of its consequences gave a great blow also to the Spanish psyche, precisely at this period. And it is possible that Italian society, which was on the whole so untravelled, had no connexion with America, and was so privately self-contained, suffered less from the disease. Someone ought to make a thorough study of the effects of 'pox' on the minds and the emotions and imaginations of the various nations of Europe, at about the time of our Elizabethans.

The apparent effect on the Elizabethans and the Restoration wits is curious. They appear to take the whole thing as a joke. The common oath, 'Pox on you!' was almost funny. But how common the oath was! How the word 'pox' was in every mind and in every mouth. It is one of the words that haunt Elizabethan speech. Taken very manly, with a great deal of Falstaffian bluff, treated as a huge joke! Pox! Why, he's got the pox! Ha-ha! What's he been after?

There is just the same attitude among the common run of men today with regard to the minor sexual diseases. Syphilis is no longer regarded as a joke, according to my experience. The very word itself frightens men. You could joke with the word 'pox.' You can't joke with the word 'syphilis.' The change of word has killed the joke. But men still joke about *clap!* which is a minor sexual disease. They pretend to think it manly, even, to have the disease, or to have had it. 'What! never had a shot of clap!' cries one gentleman to another. 'Why, where have you been all your life?' If we change the word and insisted on 'gonorrhœa,' or whatever it is, in place of 'clap,' the joke would die. And anyhow I have had young men come to me green and quaking, afraid they've caught a 'shot of clap.'

Now, in spite of all the Elizabethan jokes about pox, pox was no joke to them. A joke may be a very brave way of meeting a calamity, or it may be a very cowardly way. Myself, I consider the Elizabethan pox joke a purely cowardly attitude. They didn't think it funny, for by God it *wasn't* funny. Even poor Elizabeth's lack of eyebrows and her rotten teeth were not funny. And they all knew it. They may not have known it was the direct result of pox: though probably they did. This fact remains, that no man can contract syphilis, or any deadly sexual disease, without feeling the most shattering and profound terror go through him, through the very roots of his being. And no man can look without a sort of horror on the effects of a sexual disease in another person. We are so constituted that we are all at once horrified and terrified. The fear and dread has been so great that the pox joke was invented as an evasion, and following that, the great hush! hush! was imposed. Man was *too* frightened: that's the top and bottom of it.

But now, with remedies discovered, we need no longer be *too* frightened. We can begin, after all these years, to face the matter. After the most fearful damage has been done.

For an overmastering fear is poison to the human psyche. And this overmastering fear, like some horrible secret tumour, has been poisoning our consciousness ever since the Elizabethans, who first woke up with dread to the entry of the original syphilitic poison into the blood.

I know nothing about medicine and very little about diseases, and my facts are such as I have picked up in casual reading. Nevertheless I am convinced that the secret awareness of syphilis, and the utter secret terror and horror of it, has had an enormous and incalculable effect on the English consciousness and on the American. Even when the fear has never been formulated, there it has lain, potent and overmastering. I am convinced that *some* of Shakespeare's horror and despair, in his tragedies, arose from the shock of his consciousness of syphilis. I don't suggest for one moment Shakespeare ever contracted syphilis. I have never had syphilis myself. Yet I know and confess how profound is my fear of the disease, and more than fear, my horror. In fact, I don't think I am so very much afraid of it. I am more horrified, inwardly and deeply, at the idea of its existence.

All this sounds very far from the art of painting. But it is not so far as it sounds. The appearance of syphilis in our midst gave a fearful blow to our sexual life. The real natural innocence of Chaucer was impossible after that. The very sexual act of procreation might bring as one of its consequences a foul disease, and the unborn might be tainted from the moment of conception. Fearful thought! It is truly a fearful thought, and all the centuries of getting used to it won't help us. It remains a fearful thought, and to free ourselves from this fearful dread we should use all our wits and all our efforts, not stick our heads in the sand of some idiotic joke, or still more idiotic don't-mention-it. The fearful thought of the consequences of syphilis, or of any sexual disease, upon the unborn gives a shock to the impetus of fatherhood in any man, even the cleanest. Our consciousness is a strange thing, and the knowledge of a certain fact may wound it mortally, even if the fact does not touch us directly. And so I am certain that *some* of Shakespeare's father-murder complex, *some* of Hamlet's horror of his mother, of his uncle, of all old men came from the feeling that fathers may transmit syphilis, or syphilis-consequences, to children. I don't know even whether Shakespeare was actually aware of the consequences to a child born of a syphilitic father or mother. He may not have been, though most probably he was. But he certainly was aware of the effects of syphilis itself, especially on men. And this awareness struck at his deep sex imagination, at his instinct for fatherhood, and brought in an element of terror and abhorrence there where men should feel anything but terror and abhorrence, into the procreative act.

The terror-horror element which had entered the imagination with regard to the sexual and procreative act was at least partly responsible for the rise of Puritanism, the beheading of the king-father Charles, and the establishment of the New England colonies. If America really sent us syphilis, she got back the full recoil of the horror of it, in her puritanism.

But deeper even than this, the terror-horror element led to the crippling of the consciousness of man. Very elementary in man is his sexual and procreative being, and on his sexual and procreative being depend many of his deepest instincts and the flow of his intuition. A deep instinct of kinship joins men together, and the kinship of flesh-and-blood keeps the warm flow of intuitional awareness streaming between human beings.

Our true awareness of one another is intuitional, not mental. Attraction between people is really instinctive and intuitional, not an affair of judgment. And in mutual attraction lies perhaps the deepest pleasure in life, mutual attraction which may make us 'like' our travelling companion for the two or three hours we are together, then no more; or mutual attraction that may deepen to powerful love, and last a life-time.

The terror-horror element struck a blow at our feeling of physical communion. In fact, it almost killed it. We have become ideal beings, creatures that exist in idea, to one another, rather than flesh-and-blood kin. And with the collapse of the feeling of physical, flesh-and-blood kinship, and the substitution of our ideal, social or political oneness, came the failing of our intuitive awareness, and the great unease, the *nervousness* of mankind. We are *afraid* of the instincts. We are *afraid* of the intuition within us. We suppress the instincts, and we cut off our intuitional awareness from one another and from the world. The reason being some great shock to the procreative self. Now we know one another only as ideal or social or political entities, fleshless, bloodless, and cold, like Bernard Shaw's creatures. Intuitively we are dead to one another, we have all gone cold.

But by intuition alone can man *really* be aware of man, or of the living, substantial world. By intuition alone can man live and know either woman or world, and by intuition alone can he bring forth again images of magic awareness which we call art. In the past men brought forth images of magic awareness, and now it is the convention to admire these images. The convention says, for example, we must admire Botticelli or Giorgione, so Baedeker stars the pictures, and we admire them. But it is all a fake. Even those that get a thrill, even when they call it ecstasy, from these old pictures are only undergoing cerebral excitation. Their deeper responses, down in the intuitive and instinctive body, are not touched. They cannot be, because they are dead.

A dead intuitive body stands there and gazes at the corpse of beauty: and usually it is completely and honestly bored. Sometimes it feels a mental coruscation which it calls an ecstasy or an æsthetic response.

Modern people, but particularly English and Americans, *cannot* feel anything with the whole imagination. They can see the living body of imagery as little as a blind man can see colour. The imaginative vision, which includes physical, intuitional perception, they *have not got*. Poor things, it is dead in them. And they stand in front of a Botticelli Venus, which they know as conventionally 'beautiful,' much as a blind man might stand in front of a bunch of roses and pinks and monkey-musk, saying: 'Oh, do tell me which is red; let me feel red! Now let me feel white! Oh, let me feel it! What is this I am feeling? Monkey-musk? Is it white? Oh, do you say it is yellow blotched with orange-brown? Oh, but I can't feel it! What *can* it be? Is white velvety, or just silky?'

So the poor blind man! Yet he may have an acute perception of alive beauty. Merely by touch and scent, his intuitions being alive, the blind man may have a genuine and soul-satisfying experience of imagery. But not pictorial images. These are for ever beyond him.

So those poor English and Americans in front of the Botticelli Venus. They stare so hard; they do so *want* to see. And their eye-sight is perfect. But all they can see is a sort of nude woman on a sort of shell on a sort of pretty greenish water. As a rule they rather dislike the 'unnaturalness' or 'affectation' of it. If they are high-brows they may get a little self-conscious thrill of æsthetic excitement. But real imaginative awareness, which is so largely physical, is denied them. *Ils n'ont pas de quoi*, as the Frenchman said of the angels, when asked if they made love in heaven.

Ah, the dear high-brows who gaze in a sort of ecstasy and get a correct mental thrill! Their poor high-brow bodies stand there as dead as dust-bins, and can no more feel the sway of complete imagery upon them than they can feel any other real sway. *Ils n'ont pas de quoi.* The instincts and the intuitions are so nearly dead in them, and they fear even the feeble remains. Their fear of the instincts and intuitions is even greater than that of the English Tommy who calls: 'Eh, Jack! Come an' look at this girl standin' wi' no clothes on, an' two blokes spittin' at 'er.' That is his vision of Botticelli's Venus. It is, for him, complete, for he is void of the image-seeing imagination. But at least he doesn't have to work up a cerebral excitation, as the high-brow does, who is really just as void.

All alike, cultured and uncultured, they are still dominated by that unnamed, yet overmastering dread and hate of the instincts deep in the body, dread of the strange intuitional awareness of the body, dread of anything but ideas, which *can't* contain bacteria. And the dread all works back to a dread of the procreative body, and is partly traceable to the shock of the awareness of syphilis.

The dread of the instincts included the dread of intuitional awareness. 'Beauty is a snare' – 'Beauty is but skin-deep' – 'Handsome is as handsome does' – 'Looks don't count' – 'Don't judge by appearances' – if we only realized it, there are thousands of these vile proverbs which have been dinned into us for over two hundred years. They are all of them false. Beauty is not a snare, nor is it skin-deep, since it always involves a certain loveliness of modelling, and handsome doers are often ugly and objectionable people, and if you ignore the look of the thing you plaster England with slums and produce at last a state of spiritual depression that is suicidal, and if you don't judge by appearances, that is, if you can't trust the impression which things make on you, you are a fool. But all these base-born proverbs, born in the cash-box, hit direct against the intuitional consciousness. Naturally, man gets a great deal of his life's satisfaction from beauty, from a certain sensuous pleasure in the look of the thing. The old Englishman built his hut of a cottage with a childish joy in its appearance, purely intuitional and direct. The modern Englishman has a few borrowed ideas, simply doesn't know *what* to feel, and makes a silly mess of it: though perhaps he is improving, hopefully, in this field of architecture and house-building. The intuitional faculty, which alone relates us in direct awareness to physical things and substantial presences, is atrophied and dead, and we don't know *what* to feel. We know we ought to feel something, but what? – Oh, tell us what! And this is true of all nations, the French and Italians as much as the English. Look at new French suburbs! Go through the crockery and furniture departments in the *Dames de France* or any big shop. The blood in the body stands still, before such *crétin* ugliness. One has to decide that the modern bourgeois is a *crétin*.

This movement against the instincts and the intuition took on a moral tone in all countries. It started in hatred. Let us never forget that modern morality has its roots in hatred, a deep, evil hate of the instinctive, intuitional, procreative body. This hatred is made more virulent by fear, and an extra poison is added to the fear by unconscious horror of syphilis. And so we come to modern bourgeois consciousness, which turns upon the secret poles of fear and hate. That is the real pivot of all bourgeois consciousness in all countries: fear and hate of the instinctive, intuitional, procreative body in man or woman. But of course this fear and hate had to take on a righteous appearance, so it became moral, said that the instincts, intuitions and all the activities of the procreative body were evil, and promised a *reward* for their suppression. That is the great clue to bourgeois psychology: the reward business. It is screamingly obvious in Maria Edgeworth's tales, which must have done unspeakable damage to ordinary people. Be good, and you'll have money. Be wicked, and you'll be utterly penniless at last, and the good ones will have to offer you a little charity. This is sound working morality in the world. And it makes one realize that, even to Milton, the true hero of *Paradise Lost* must be Satan. But by this baited morality the masses were caught and enslaved to industrialism before ever they knew it; the good got hold of the goods, and our modern 'civilization' of money, machines, and wage-slaves was inaugurated. The very pivot of it, let us never forget, being fear and hate, the most intimate fear and hate, fear and hate of one's own instinctive, intuitive body, and fear and hate of every other man's and every other woman's warm, procreative body and imagination.

Now it is obvious what result this will have on the plastic arts, which depend entirely on the representation of substantial bodies, and on the intuitional perception of the *reality* of substantial bodies. The reality of substantial bodies can only be perceived by the imagination, and the imagination is a kindled state of consciousness in which intuitive awareness predominates. The plastic arts are all imagery, and imagery is the body of our imaginative life, and our imaginative life is a great joy and fulfilment to us, for the imagination is a more powerful and more comprehensive flow of consciousness than our ordinary flow. In the flow of true imagination we know in full, mentally and physically at once, in a greater, enkindled awareness. At the maximum of our imagination we are religious. And if we deny our imagination, and have no imaginative life, we are poor worms who have never lived.

In the seventeenth and eighteenth centuries we have the deliberate denial of intuitive awareness, and we see the results on the arts. Vision became more optical, less intuitive and painting began to flourish. But what painting! Watteau, Ingres, Poussin, Chardin have some real imaginative glow still. They are still somewhat free. The puritan and the intellectual has not yet struck them down with his fear and hate obsession. But look at England! Hogarth, Reynolds, Gainsborough, they all are already bourgeois. The coat is really more important than the man. It is amazing how important clothes suddenly become, how they *cover* the subject. An old Reynolds colonel in a red uniform is much more a uniform than an individual, and as for Gainsborough, all one can say is: What a lovely dress and hat! What really expensive Italian silk! This painting of garments continued in vogue, till pictures like Sargent's seem to be nothing but yards and yards of satin from the most expensive shops, having some pretty head popped on the top. The imagination is quite dead. The optical vision, a sort of flashy coloured photography of the eye, is rampant.

In Titian, in Velasquez, in Rembrandt the people are there inside their clothes all right, and the clothes are imbued with the life of the individual, the gleam of the warm procreative body comes through all the time, even if it be an old, half-blind woman or a weird, ironic little Spanish princess. But modern people are nothinging inside their garments, and a head sticks out at the top and hands stick out of the sleeves, and it is a bore. Or, as in Lawrence or Raeburn, you have something very pretty but almost a mere cliché, with very little instinctive or intuitional perception to it.

After this, and apart from landscape and water-colour, there is strictly no English painting that exists. As far as I am concerned, the pre-Raphaelites don't exist; Watts doesn't, Sargent doesn't, and none of the moderns.

There is the exception of Blake. Blake is the only painter of imaginative pictures, apart from landscape, that England has produced. And unfortunately there is so little Blake, and even in that little the symbolism is often artificially imposed. Nevertheless, Blake paints with real intuitional awareness and solid instinctive feeling. He dares handle the human body, even if he sometimes makes it a mere ideograph. And no other

Englishman has even dared handle it with alive imagination. Painters of composition-pictures in England, of whom perhaps the best is Watts, never quite get beyond the level of cliché, sentimentalism, and *funk*. Even Watts is a failure, though he made some sort of try: even Etty's nudes in York fail imaginatively, though they have some feeling for flesh. And the rest, the Leightons, even the moderns don't really do anything. They never get beyond studio models and clichés of the nude. The image never gets across to us, to seize us intuitively. It remains merely optical.

Landscape, however, is different. Here the English exist and hold their own. But, for me, personally, landscape is always waiting for something to occupy it. Landscape seems to be *meant* as a background to an intenser vision of life, so to my feeling painted landscape is background with the real subject left out.

Nevertheless, it can be very lovely, especially in water-colour, which is a more bodiless medium, and doesn't aspire to very substantial existence, and is so small that it doesn't try to make a very deep seizure on the consciousness. Water-colour will always be more of a statement than an experience.

And landscape, on the whole, is the same. It doesn't call up the more powerful responses of the human imagination, the sensual, passional responses. Hence it is the favourite modern form of expression in painting. There is no deep conflict. The instinctive and intuitional consciousness is called into play, but lightly, superficially. It is not confronted with any living, pro-creative body.

Hence the English have delighted in landscape, and have succeeded in it well. It is a form of escape for them, from the actual human body they so hate and fear, and it is an outlet for their perishing æsthetic desires. For more than a century we have produced delicious water-colours, and Wilson, Crome, Constable, Turner are all great landscape-painters. Some of Turner's landscape compositions are, to my feelings, among the finest that exist. They still satisfy me more even than van Gogh's or Cézanne's landscapes, which make a more violent assault on the emotions, and repel a little for that reason. Somehow I don't want landscape to make a violent assault on my feelings. Landscape is background with the figures left out or reduced to minimum, so let it stay back. Van Gogh's surging earth and Cézanne's explosive or rattling planes worry me. Not being profoundly interested in landscape, I prefer it to be rather quiet and unexplosive.

But, of course, the English delight in landscape is a delight in escape. It is always the same. The northern races are so innerly afraid of their own bodily existence, which they believe fantastically to be an evil thing – you could never find them feel anything but uneasy shame, or an equally shameful gloating, over the fact that a man was having intercourse with his wife, in his house next door – that all they cry for is an escape. And, especially, art must provide that escape.

It is easy in literature. Shelley is pure escape: the body is sublimated into sublime gas. Keats is more difficult – the body can still be *felt* dissolving in waves of successive death – but the death-business is very satisfactory. The novelists have even a better time. You can get some of the lasciviousness of Hetty Sorrell's 'sin,' and you can enjoy condemning her to penal servitude for life. You can thrill to Mr Rochester's *passion,* and you can enjoy having his eyes burnt out. So it is, all the way: the novel of 'passion'!

But in paint it is more difficult. You cannot paint Hetty Sorrell's sin or Mr Rochester's passion without being really shocking. And you *daren't* be shocking. It was this fact that unsaddled Watts and Millais. Both might have been painters if they hadn't been Victorians. As it is, each of them is a wash-out.

Which is the poor, feeble history of art in England, since we can lay no claim to the great Holbein. And art on the continent, in the last century? It is more interesting, and has a fuller story. An artist *can* only create what he really religiously *feels* is truth, religious truth really *felt*, in the blood and the bones. The English could never think anything connected with the body *religious* – unless it were the eyes. So they painted the social appearance of human beings, and hoped to give them wonderful eyes. But they *could* think landscape religious, since it had no sensual reality. So they felt religious about it and painted it as well as it could be painted, maybe, from their point of view.

And in France? In France it was more or less the same, but with a difference. The French, being more rational, decided that the body had its place, but that it should be rationalized. The Frenchman of today has the most reasonable and rationalized body possible. His conception of sex is basically hygienic. A certain amount of copulation is good for you. *Ça fait du bien au corps!* sums up the physical side of a Frenchman's idea of love, marriage, food, sport, and all the rest. Well, it is more sane, anyhow, than the Anglo-Saxon terrors. The Frenchman is afraid of syphilis and afraid of the procreative body, but not quite so deeply. He has known for a long time that you can take precautions. And he is not profoundly imaginative.

Therefore he has been able to paint. But his tendency, just like that of all the modern world, has been to get away from the body, while still paying attention to its hygiene, and still not violently quarrelling with it. Puvis de Chavannes is really as sloppy as all the other spiritual sentimentalizers. Renoir is jolly: *ça fait du bien au corps!* is his attitude to the flesh. If a woman didn't have buttocks and breasts, she wouldn't be paintable, he said, and he was right. *Ça fait du bien au corps!* What do you paint with, Maître? – With my penis, and be damned! Renoir didn't try to get away from the body. But he had to dodge it in some of its aspects, rob it of its natural terrors, its natural demonishness. He is delightful, but a trifle banal. *Ça fait du bien au corps!* Yet how infinitely much better he is than any English equivalent.

Courbet, Daumier, Degas, they all painted the human body. But Daumier satirized it, Courbet saw it as a toiling thing, Dégas saw it as a wonderful instrument. They all of them deny it its finest qualities, its deepest instincts, its purest intuitions. They prefer, as it were, to industrialize it. They deny it the best imaginative existence.

And the real grand glamour of modern French art, the real outburst of delight came when the body was at last dissolved of its substance, and made part and parcel of the sunlight-and-shadow scheme. Let us say what we will, but the real grand thrill of modern French art was the discovery of light, the discovery of light, and all the subsequent discoveries of the impressionists, and of the post-impressionists, even Cézanne. No matter how Cézanne may have reacted from the impressionists, it was they, with their deliriously joyful discovery of light and 'free' colour, who really opened his eyes. Probably the most joyous moment in the whole history of painting was the moment when the incipient impressionists discovered light, and with it, colour. Ah, then they made the grand, grand escape into freedom, into infinity, into light and delight. They escaped from the tyranny of solidity and the menace of mass-form. They escaped, they escaped from the dark procreative body which so haunts a man, they escaped into the open air, *plein air* and *plein soleil*: light and almost ecstasy.

Like every other human escape, it meant being hauled back later with the tail between the legs. Back comes the truant, back to the old doom of matter, of corporate existence, of the body sullen and stubborn and obstinately refusing to be transmuted into pure light, pure colour, or pure anything. It is not concerned with purity. Life isn't. Chemistry and mathematics and ideal religion are, but these are only small bits of life, which is itself bodily, and hence neither pure nor impure.

After the grand escape into impressionism and pure light, pure colour, pure bodilessness – for what is the body but a shimmer of lights and colours! – poor art came home truant and sulky, with its tail between its legs. And it is this return which now interests us. We know the escape was illusion, illusion, illusion. The cat had to come back. So now we despise the 'light' blighters too much. We haven't a good word for them. Which is nonsense, for they too are wonderful, even if their escape was into *le grand néant,* the great nowhere.

But the cat came back. And it is the home-coming tom that now has our sympathy: Renoir, to a certain extent, but mostly Cézanne, the sublime little grimalkin, who is followed by Matisse and Gauguin and Derain and Vlaminck and Braque and all the host of other defiant and howling cats that have come back, perforce, to form and substance and *thereness*, instead of delicious nowhereness.

Without wishing to labour the point, one cannot help being amused at the dodge by which the impressionists made the grand escape from the body. They metamorphosed it into a pure assembly of shifting lights and shadows, all coloured. A web of woven, luminous colour was a man, or a woman – and so they painted her, or him: a web of woven shadows and gleams. Delicious! and quite true as far as it goes. A purely optical, *visual* truth: which paint is supposed to be. And they painted delicious pictures: a little too delicious. They bore us, at the moment. They bore people like the very modern critics intensely. But very modern critics need not be so intensely bored. There is something very lovely about the good impressionist pictures. And ten years hence critics will be bored by the present run of post-impressionists, though not so passionately bored, for these post-impressionists don't move us as the impressionists moved our fathers. We have to persuade ourselves, and we have to persuade one another to be impressed by the post-impressionists, on the whole. On the whole, they rather depress us. Which is perhaps good for us.

But modern art criticism is in a curious hole. Art has suddenly gone into rebellion, against all the canons of accepted religion, accepted good form, accepted everything. When the cat came back from the delicious impressionist excursion, it came back rather tattered, but bristling and with its claws out. The glorious escape was all an illusion. There *was* substance still in the world, a thousand times be damned to it! There *was* the body, the great lumpy body. There it was. You had it shoved down your throat. What really existed was lumps, lumps. Then paint 'em. Or else paint the thin 'spirit' with gaps in it and looking merely dishevelled and 'found out.' Paint had found the spirit out.

This is the sulky and rebellious mood of the post-impressionists. They still hate the body – hate it. But, in a rage, they admit its existence, and paint it as huge lumps, tubes, cubes, planes, volumes, spheres, cones, cylinders, all the 'pure' or mathematical forms of substance. As for landscape, it comes in for some of the same rage. It has also suddenly gone lumpy. Instead of being nice and ethereal and non-sensual, it was discovered by van Gogh to be heavily, overwhelmingly substantial and sensual. Van Gogh took up landscape in heavy spadefuls. And Cézanne had to admit it. Landscape, too, after being, since Claude Lorrain, a thing of pure luminosity and floating shadow, suddenly exploded, and came tumbling back on to the canvases of artists in lumps. With Cézanne, landscape 'crystallized,' to use one of the favourite terms of the critics, and it has gone on crystallizing into cubes, cones, pyramids, and so forth ever since.

The impressionists brought the world at length, after centuries of effort, into the delicious oneness of light. At last, at last! Hail, holy Light! the great natural One, the universal, the universalizer! We are not divided, all one body we – one in Light, lovely light! No sooner had this pæan gone up than the post-impressionists, like Judas, gave the show away. They exploded the illusion, which fell back to the canvas of art in a chaos of lumps.

This new chaos, of course, needed new apologists, who therefore rose up in hordes to apologize, almost, for the new chaos. They felt a little guilty about it, so they took on new notes of effrontery, defiant as any Primitive Methodists, which, indeed, they are: the Primitive Methodists of art criticism. These evangelical gentlemen at once ran up their chapels, in a Romanesque or Byzantine shape, as was natural for a primitive and a methodist, and started to cry forth their doctrines in the decadent wilderness. They discovered once more that the æsthetic experience was an ecstasy, an ecstasy granted only to the chosen few, the elect, among whom said critics were, of course, the archelect. This was outdoing Ruskin. It was almost Calvin come to art. But let scoffers scoff, the æsthetic ecstasy was vouchsafed only to the few, the elect, and even then only when they had freed their minds of false doctrine. They had renounced the mammon of 'subject' in pictures, they went whoring no more after the Babylon of painted 'interest,' nor did they hanker after the flesh-pots of artistic 'representation.' Oh, purify yourselves, ye who would know the æsthetic ecstasy, and be lifted up to the 'white peaks of artistic inspiration.' Purify yourselves of all base hankering for a tale that is told, and of all low lust for likenesses. Purify yourselves, and know the one supreme way, the way of Significant Form. I am the revelation and the way! I am Significant Form, and my unutterable name is Reality. Lo, I am Form and I am Pure, behold, I am Pure Form. I am the revelation of

Spiritual Life, moving behind the veil. I come forth and make myself known, and I am Pure Form, behold, I am Significant Form.

So the prophets of the new era in art cry aloud to the multitude, in exactly the jargon of the revivalists, for revivalists they are. They will revive the Primitive Method-brethren, the Byzantines, the Ravennese, the early Italian and French primitives (which ones, in particular, we aren't told); these were Right, these were Pure, these were Spiritual, these were Real! And the builders of early Romanesque churches, O my brethren! these were holy men, before the world went a-whoring after Gothic. Oh, return, my brethren, to the Primitive Method. Lift up your eyes to Significant Form, and be saved.

Now myself, brought up a nonconformist as I was, I just was never able to understand the language of salvation. I never knew what they were talking about, when they raved about being saved, and safe in the arms of Jesus, and Abraham's bosom, and seeing the great light, and entering into glory: I just was puzzled, for what did it *mean*? It seemed to work out as a getting rather drunk on your own self-importance, and afterwards coming dismally sober again and being rather unpleasant. That was all I could see in actual experience of the entering-into-glory business. The term itself, like something which ought to mean something but somehow doesn't, stuck on my mind like an irritating bur, till I decided that it was just an artificial stimulant to the individual self-conceit. How could I enter into glory, when glory is just an abstraction of a human state, and not a separate reality at all? If glory means anything at all, it means the thrill a man gets when a great many people look up to him with mixed awe, reverence, delight. Today, it means Rudolph Valentino. So that the cant about entering into glory is just used fuzzily to enhance the individual sense of self-importance – one of the rather cheap cocaine-phrases.

And I'm afraid 'æsthetic ecstasy' sounds to me very much the same, especially when accompanied by exhortations. It so sounds like another great uplift into self-importance, another apotheosis of personal conceit; especially when accompanied by a lot of jargon about the pure world of reality existing behind the veil of this vulgar world of accepted appearances, and of the entry of the elect through the doorway of visual art. Too evangelical altogether, too much chapel and Primitive Methodist, too obvious a trick for advertising one's own self-glorification. The ego, as an American says, shuts itself up and paints the inside of the walls sky-blue, and thinks it is in heaven.

And then the great symbols of this salvation. When the evangelical says: Behold the lamb of God! – what on earth does he want one to behold? Are we invited to look at a lamb, with woolly, muttony appearance, frisking and making its little pills? Awfully nice, but what *has* it got to do with God or my soul? Or the cross? What *do* they expect us to see in the cross? A sort of gallows? Or the mark we use to cancel a mistake? – cross it out! That the cross by itself was supposed to *mean* something always mystified me. The same with the Blood of the Lamb. – Washed in the Blood of the Lamb! always seemed to me an extremely unpleasant suggestion. And when Jerome says: He who has once washed in the blood of Jesus need never wash again! – I feel like taking a hot bath at once, to wash off even the suggestion.

And I find myself equally mystified by the cant phrases like Significant Form and Pure Form. They are as mysterious to me as the Cross and the Blood of the Lamb. They are just the magic jargon of invocation, nothing else. If you want to invoke an æsthetic ecstasy, stand in front of a Matisse and whisper fervently under your breath: 'Significant Form! Significant Form!' – and it will come. It sounds to me like a form of masturbation, an attempt to make the body react to some cerebral formula.

No, I am afraid modern criticism has done altogether too

much for modern art. If painting survives this outburst of ecstatic evangelicism, which it will, it is because people do come to their senses, even after the silliest vogue.

And so we can return to modern French painting, without having to quake before the bogy, or the Holy Ghost of Significant Form: a bogy which doesn't exist if we don't mind leaving aside our self-importance when we look at a picture.

The actual fact is that in Cézanne modern French art made its first tiny step back to real substance, to objective substance, if we may call it so. Van Gogh's earth was still subjective earth, himself projected into the earth. But Cézanne's apples are a real attempt to let the apple exist in its own separate entity, without transfusing it with personal emotion. Cézanne's great effort was, as it were, to shove the apple away from him, and let it live of itself. It seems a small thing to do: yet it is the first real sign that man has made for several thousands of years that he is willing to admit that matter *actually* exists. Strange as it may seem, for thousands of years, in short, ever since the mythological 'Fall,' man has been preoccupied with the constant preoccupation of the denial of the existence of matter, and the proof that matter is only a form of spirit. And then, the moment it is done, and we realize finally that matter is only a form of energy, whatever that may be, in the same instant matter rises up and hits us over the head and makes us realize that it exists absolutely, since it is compact energy itself.

Cézanne felt it in paint, when he felt for the apple. Suddenly he felt the tyranny of mind, the white, worn-out arrogance of the spirit, the mental consciousness, the enclosed ego in its sky-blue heaven self-painted. He felt the sky-blue prison. And a great conflict started inside him. He was dominated by his old mental consciousness, but he wanted terribly to escape the domination. He wanted to *express* what he suddenly, convulsedly knew! the existence of matter. He terribly wanted to paint the real existence of the body, to make it artistically palpable. But he couldn't. He hadn't got there yet. And it was the torture of his life. He wanted to be himself in his own procreative body – and he couldn't. He was, like all the rest of us, so intensely and exclusively a mental creature, or a spiritual creature, or an egoist, that he could no longer identify himself with his intuitive body. He wanted to, terribly. At first he determined to do it by sheer bravado and braggadocio. But no good; it couldn't be done that way. He had, as one critic says, to become humble. But it wasn't a question of becoming humble. It was a question of abandoning his cerebral conceit and his 'willed ambition' and coming down to brass tacks. Poor Cézanne, there he is in his self-portraits, even the early showy ones, peeping out like a mouse and saying: I *am* a man of flesh, am I not? For he was not quite, as none of us are. The man of flesh has been slowly destroyed through centuries, to give place to the man of spirit, the mental man, the ego, the self-conscious I. And in his artistic soul Cézanne knew it, and wanted to rise in the flesh. He couldn't do it, and it embittered him. Yet, with his apple, he did shove the stone from the door of the tomb.

He wanted to be a man of flesh, a real man: to get out of the sky-blue prison into real air. He wanted to live, really live in the body, to know the world through his instincts and his intuitions, and to be himself in his procreative blood, not in his mere mind and spirit. He wanted it, he wanted it terribly. And whenever he tried, his mental consciousness, like a cheap fiend, interfered. If he wanted to paint a woman, his mental consciousness simply overpowered him and wouldn't let him paint the woman of flesh, the first Eve who lived before any of the fig-leaf nonsense. He couldn't do it. If he wanted to paint people intuitively and instinctively, he couldn't do it. His mental concepts shoved in front, and these he *wouldn't* paint – mere representations of what the *mind* accepts, not what the intuitions gather – and they, his mental concepts, wouldn't let him paint from intuition; they shoved in between all the time, so he painted his conflict and his failure, and the result is almost ridiculous.

Woman he was not allowed to know by intuition; his mental self, his ego, that bloodless fiend, forbade him. Man, other men, he was likewise not allowed to know – except by a few, few touches. The earth likewise he was not allowed to know: his landscapes are mostly acts of rebellion against the mental concept of landscape. After a fight tooth-and-nail for forty years, he did succeed in knowing an apple, fully; and, not quite as fully, a jug or two. That was all he achieved.

It seems little, and he died embittered. But it is the first step that counts, and Cézanne's apple is a great deal, more than Plato's Idea. Cézanne's apple rolled the stone from the mouth of the tomb, and if poor Cézanne couldn't unwind himself from his cerements and mental winding-sheet, but had to lie still in the tomb, till he died, still he gave us a chance.

The history of our era is the nauseating and repulsive history of the crucifixion of the procreative body for the glorification of the spirit, the mental consciousness. Plato was an arch-priest of this crucifixion. Art, that handmaid, humbly and honestly served the vile deed, through three thousand years at least. The Renaissance put the spear through the side of the already crucified body, and syphilis put poison into the wound made by the imaginative spear. It took still three hundred years for the body to finish: but in the eighteenth century it became a corpse, a corpse with an abnormally active mind: and today it stinketh.

We, dear reader, you and I, we were born corpses, and we are corpses. I doubt if there is even one of us who has ever known so much as an apple, a whole apple. All we know is shadows, even of apples. Shadows of everything, of the whole world, shadows even of ourselves. We are inside the tomb, and the tomb is wide and shadowy like hell, even if sky-blue by optimistic paint, so we think it is all the world. But our world is a wide tomb full of ghosts, replicas. We are all spectres, we have not been able to touch even so much as an apple. Spectres we are to one another. Spectre you are to me, spectre I am to you. Shadow you are even to yourself. And by shadow I mean idea, concept, the abstracted reality, the ego. We are not solid. We don't live in the flesh. Our instincts and intuitions are dead, we live wound round with the winding-sheet of abstraction. And the touch of anything solid hurts us. For our instincts and intuitions, which are our feelers of touch and knowing through touch, they are dead, amputated. We walk and talk and eat and copulate and laugh and evacuate wrapped in our winding-sheets, all the time wrapped in our winding-sheets.

So that Cézanne's apple hurts. It made people shout with pain. And it was not till his followers had turned him again into an abstraction that he was ever accepted. Then the critics stepped forth and abstracted his good apple into Significant Form, and henceforth Cézanne was saved. Saved for democracy. Put safely in the tomb again, and the stone rolled back. The resurrection was postponed once more.

As the resurrection will be postponed *ad infinitum* by the good bourgeois corpses in their cultured winding-sheets. They will run up a chapel to the risen body, even if it is only an apple, and kill it on the spot. They are wide awake, are the corpses, on the alert. And a poor mouse of a Cézanne is alone in the years. Who else shows a spark of awakening life, in our marvellous civilized cemetery? All is dead, and dead breath preaching with phosphorescent effulgence about æsthetic ecstasy and Significant Form. If only the dead would bury their dead. But the dead are not dead for nothing. Who buries his own sort? The dead are cunning and alert to pounce on any spark of life and bury *it*, even as they have already buried Cézanne's apple and put up to it a white tombstone of Significant Form.

For who of Cézanne's followers does anything but follow at the triumphant funeral of Cézanne's achievement? They follow him in order to bury him, and they succeed. Cézanne is deeply buried under all the Matisses and Vlamincks of his following, while the critics read the funeral homily.

It is quite easy to accept Matisse and Vlaminck and Friesz and all the rest. They are just Cézanne abstracted again. They are all just tricksters, even if clever ones. They are all mental, mental, egoists, egoists, egoists. And therefore they are all acceptable now to the enlightened corpses of connoisseurs. You needn't be afraid of Matisse and Vlaminck and the rest. They will never give your corpse-anatomy a jar. They are just shadows, minds mountebanking and playing charades on canvas. They may be quite amusing charades, and I am all for the mountebank. But of course it is all games inside the cemetery, played by corpses and *hommes d'esprit*, even *femmes d'esprit*, *like* Mademoiselle Laurencin. As for *l'esprit*, said Cézanne, I don't give a fart for it. Perhaps not! But the connoisseurs will give large sums of money. Trust the dead to pay for their amusement, when the amusement is deadly!

The most interesting figure in modern art, and the only really interesting figure, is Cézanne: and that, not so much because of his achievement as because of his struggle. Cézanne was born at Aix in Provence in 1839: small, timorous, yet sometimes bantam defiant, sensitive, full of grand ambition, yet ruled still deeper by a naïve, Mediterranean sense of truth or reality, imagination, call it what you will. He is not a big figure. Yet his struggle is truly heroic. He was a bourgeois, and one must never forget it. He had a moderate bourgeois income. But a bourgeois in Provence is much more real and human than a bourgeois in Normandy. He is much nearer the actual people, and the actual people are much less subdued by awe of his respectable bourgeois money.

Cézanne was naïve to a degree, but not a fool. He was rather insignificant, and grandeur impressed him terribly. Yet still stronger in him was the little flame of life where he *felt* things to be true. He didn't betray himself in order to get success, because he couldn't: to his nature it was impossible: he was too pure to be able to betray his own small real flame for immediate rewards. Perhaps that is the best one can say of a man, and it puts Cézanne, small and insignificant as he is, among the heroes. He would *not* abandon his own vital imagination.

He was terribly impressed by physical splendour and flamboyancy, as people usually are in the lands of the sun. He admired terribly the splendid virtuosity of Paul Veronese and Tintoretto, and even of later and less good baroque painters. He wanted to be like that – terribly he wanted it. And he tried very, very hard, with bitter effort. And he always failed. It is a cant phrase with the critics to say 'he couldn't draw.' Mr Fry says: 'With all his rare endowments, he happened to lack the comparatively common gift of illustration, the gift that any draughtsman for the illustrated papers learns in a school of commercial art.'

Now this sentence gives away at once the hollowness of modern criticism. In the first place, can one learn a 'gift' in a school of commercial art, or anywhere else? A gift surely is given, we tacitly assume, by God or Nature or whatever higher power we hold responsible for the things we have no choice in.

Was, then, Cézanne devoid of this gift? Was he simply incapable of drawing a cat so that it would look like a cat? Nonsense! Cézanne's work is full of accurate drawing. His more trivial pictures, suggesting copies from other masters, are perfectly well drawn – that is, conventionally: so are some of the landscapes, so even is that portrait of M. Geffroy and his books, which is, or was, so famous. Why these cant phrases about not being able to draw? Of course Cézanne could draw, as well as anybody else.

And he had learned everything that was necessary in the art-schools.

He *could* draw. And yet, in his terrifically earnest compositions in the late Renaissance or baroque manner, he drew so badly. Why? Not because he couldn't. And not because he was sacrificing 'significant form' to 'insignificant form,' or mere slick representation, which is apparently what artists themselves mean when they talk about drawing. Cézanne knew all about drawing: and he surely knew as much as his critics do about significant form. Yet he neither succeeded in drawing so that things looked right, nor combining his shapes so that he achieved real form. He just failed.

He failed, where one of his little slick successors would have succeeded with one eye shut. And why? Why did Cézanne fail in his early pictures? Answer that, and you'll know a little better what art is. He didn't fail because he understood nothing about drawing or significant form or æsthetic ecstasy. He knew about them all, and didn't give a spit for them.

Cézanne failed in his earlier pictures because he was trying with his mental consciousness to do something which his living Provençal body didn't want to do, or couldn't do. He terribly wanted to do something grand and voluptuous and sensuously satisfying, in the Tintoretto manner. Mr Fry calls that his 'willed ambition,' which is a good phrase, and says he had to learn humility, which is a bad phrase.

The 'willed ambition' was more than a mere willed ambition – it was a genuine desire. But it was a desire that thought it would be satisfied by ready-made baroque expressions, whereas it needed to achieve a whole new marriage of mind and matter. If we believed in reincarnation, then we should have to believe that after a certain number of new incarnations into the body of an artist, the soul of Cézanne *would* produce grand and voluptuous and sensually rich pictures – but not at all in the baroque manner. Because the pictures he actually did produce with undeniable success are the first steps in that direction, sensual and rich, with not the slightest hint of baroque, but new, the man's new grasp of substantial reality.

There was, then, a certain discrepancy between Cézanne's *notion* of what he wanted to produce, and his other, intuitive knowledge of what he *could* produce. For whereas the mind works in possibilities, the intuitions work in actualities, and what you *intuitively* desire, that is possible to you. Whereas what you mentally or 'consciously' desire is nine times out of ten impossible: hitch your wagon to a star, and you'll just stay where you are.

So the conflict, as usual, was not between the artist and his medium, but between the artist's *mind* and the artist's *intuition* and *instinct*. And what Cézanne had to learn was not humility – cant word! – but honesty, honesty with himself. It was not a question of any gift or significant form or æsthetic ecstasy: it was a question of Cézanne being himself, just Cézanne. And when Cézanne is himself he is not Tintoretto, nor Veronese, nor anything baroque at all. Yet he is something *physical*, and even sensual: qualities which he had identified with the masters of virtuosity.

In passing, if we think of Henri Matisse, a real virtuoso, and imagine him possessed with a 'willed ambition' to paint grand and flamboyant baroque pictures, then we know at once that he would not have to 'humble' himself at all, but that he would start in and paint with great success grand and flamboyant modern-baroque pictures. He would succeed because he has the gift of virtuosity. And the gift of virtuosity simply means that you don't have to humble yourself, or even be honest with yourself, because you are a clever mental creature who is capable at will of making the intuitions and instincts subserve some mental concept: in short, you can prostitute your body to your mind, your instincts and intuitions you can prostitute to your 'willed ambition,' in a sort of masturbation process, and you can produce the impotent glories of virtuosity. But Veronese and Tintoretto are real painters; they are not mere *virtuosi*, as some of the later men are.

The point is very important. Any creative act occupies the whole consciousness of a man. This is true of the great discoveries of science as well as of art. The truly great discoveries of science and real works of art are made by the whole consciousness of man working together in unison and oneness: instinct, intuition, mind, intellect all fused into one complete consciousness, and grasping what we may call a complete truth, or a complete vision, a complete revelation in sound. A discovery, artistic or otherwise, may be more or less intuitional, more or less mental; but intuition will have entered into it, and mind will have entered too. The whole consciousness is concerned in every case. – And a painting requires the activity of the whole imagination, for it is made of imagery, and the imagination is that form of complete consciousness in which predominates the intuitive awareness of forms, images, the *physical* awareness.

And the same applies to the genuine appreciation of a work of art, or the *grasp* of a scientific law, as to the production of the same. The whole consciousness is occupied, not merely the mind alone, or merely the body. The mind and spirit alone can never really grasp a work of art, though they may, in a masturbating fashion, provoke the body into an ecstasized response. The ecstasy will die out into ash and more ash. And the reason we have so many trivial scientists promulgating fantastic 'facts' is that so many modern scientists likewise work with the mind alone, and *force* the intuitions and instincts into a prostituted acquiescence. The very statement that water is H_2O is a mental *tour de force*. With our bodies we know that water is *not* H_2O, our intuitions and instincts both know it is not so. But they are bullied by the impudent mind. Whereas if we said that water, under certain circumstances, produces two volumes of hydrogen and one of oxygen, then the intuitions and instincts would agree entirely. But that water *is composed* of two volumes of hydrogen to one of oxygen we cannot physically believe. It needs something else. Something is missing. Of course, alert science does not ask us to believe the commonplace assertion of: *water* is H_2O, but school children have to believe it.

A parallel case is all this modern stuff about astronomy, stars, their distances and speeds and so on, talking of billions and trillions of miles and years and so forth: it is just occult. The mind is revelling in words, the intuitions and instincts are just left out, or prostituted into a sort of ecstasy. In fact, the sort of ecstasy that lies in absurd figures such as 2,000,000,000,000,000, 000,000,000,000 miles or years or tons, figures which abound in modern *scientific* books on astronomy, is just the sort of æsthetic ecstasy that the over-mental critics of art assert they experience today from Matisse's pictures. It is all poppycock. The body is either stunned to a corpse, or prostituted to ridiculous thrills, or stands coldly apart.

When I read how far off the suns are, and what they are made of, and so on, and so on, I believe all I am *able* to believe, with the true imagination. But when my intuition and instinct can grasp no more, then I call my mind to a halt. I am not going to accept mere mental asseverations. The mind can assert anything, and pretend it has proved it. My beliefs I test on my body, on my intuitional consciousness, and when I get a response there, then I accept. The same is true of great scientific 'laws' like the law of evolution. After years of acceptance of the 'laws' of evolution – rather desultory or 'humble' acceptance – now I realize that my vital imagination makes great reservations. I find I can't, with the best will in the world, believe that the species have 'evolved' from one common life-form. I just can't feel it, I have to violate my intuitive and instinctive awareness of something else, to make myself believe it. But since I know that my intuitions and instincts may still be held back by prejudice, I seek in the world for someone to make me intuitively and instinctively feel the truth of the 'law' – and I don't find anybody. I find scientists, just like artists, asserting things they are *mentally* sure of, in fact cocksure, but about which they are much too egoistic and ranting to be *intuitively*, *instinctively* sure. When I find a man, or a woman, intuitively and instinctively sure of anything, I am all respect. But for scientific or artistic braggarts how can one have respect? The intrusion of the egoistic element is a sure proof of intuitive uncertainty. No man who is sure by instinct and intuition *brags*, though he may fight tooth and nail for his beliefs.

Which brings us back to Cézanne, why he couldn't draw, and why he couldn't paint baroque masterpieces. It is just because he was real, and could only believe in his own expression when it expressed a moment of wholeness or completeness of consciousness in himself. He could not prostitute one part of himself to the other. He *could* not masturbate, in paint or words. And that is saying a very great deal, today; today, the great day of the masturbating consciousness, when the mind prostitutes the sensitive responsive body, and just forces the reactions. The masturbating consciousness produces all kinds of novelties, which thrill for the moment, then go very dead. It cannot produce a single genuinely new utterance.

What we have to thank Cézanne for is not his humility, but for his proud, high spirit that refused to accept the glib utterances of his facile mental self. He wasn't poor-spirited enough to be facile – nor humble enough to be satisfied with visual and emotional clichés. Thrilling as the baroque masters were to him in themselves, he realized that as soon as he reproduced them he produced nothing but cliché. The mind is full of all sorts of memory, visual, tactile, emotional memory, memories, groups of memories, systems of memories. A cliché is just a worn-out memory that has no more emotional or intuitional root, and has become a habit. Whereas a novelty is just a new grouping of clichés, a new arrangement of accustomed memories. That is why a novelty is so easily accepted: it gives the little shock or thrill of surprise, but it does not *disturb* the emotional and intuitive self. It forces you to see nothing new. It is only a novel compound of clichés. The work of most of Cézanne's successors is just novel, just a new arrangement of clichés, soon growing stale. And the clichés are Cézanne clichés, just as in Cézanne's own earlier pictures the clichés were all, or mostly, baroque clichés.

Cézanne's early history as a painter is a history of his fight with his own cliché. His consciousness wanted a new realization. And his ready-made mind offered him all the time a ready-made expression. And Cézanne, far too inwardly proud and haughty to accept the ready-made clichés that came from his mental consciousness, stocked with memories, and which appeared mocking at him on his canvas, spent most of his time smashing his own forms to bits. To a true artist, and to the living imagination, the cliché is the deadly enemy. Cézanne had a bitter fight with it. He hammered it to pieces a thousand times. And still it reappeared.

Now again we can see why Cézanne's drawing was so bad. It was bad because it represented a smashed, mauled cliché, terribly knocked about. If Cézanne had been willing to accept his own baroque cliché, his drawing would have been perfectly conventionally 'all right,' and not a critic would have had a word to say about it. But when his drawing was conventionally all right, to Cézanne himself it was mockingly all wrong, it was cliché. So he flew at it and knocked all the shape and stuffing out of it, and when it was so mauled that it was all wrong, and he was exhausted with it, he let it go; bitterly, because it still was not what he wanted. And here comes in the comic element in Cézanne's pictures. His rage with the cliché made him distort the cliché sometimes into parody, as we see in pictures like *The Pasha* and *La Femme*. 'You *will* be cliché, will you?' he gnashes. 'Then *be* it!' And he shoves it in a frenzy of exasperation over into parody. And the sheer exasperation makes the parody still funny; but the laugh is a little on the wrong side of the face.

This smashing of the cliché lasted a long way into Cézanne's life; indeed, it went with him to the end. The way he worked over and over his forms was his nervous manner of laying the ghost of his cliché, burying it. Then when it disappeared perhaps from his forms themselves, it lingered in his composition, and he had to fight with the *edges* of his forms and contours, to bury the ghost there. Only his colour he knew was not cliché. He left it to his disciples to make it so.

In his very best pictures, the best of the still-life compositions, which seem to me Cézanne's greatest achievement, the fight with the cliché is still going on. But it was in the still-life pictures he learned his final method of *avoiding* the cliché: just leaving gaps through which it fell into nothingness. So he makes his landscape succeed.

In his art, all his life long, Cézanne was tangled in a twofold activity. He wanted to express something, and before he could do it he had to fight the hydra-headed cliché, whose last head he could never lop off. The fight with the cliché is the most obvious thing in his pictures. The dust of battle rises thick, and the splinters fly wildly. And it is this dust of battle and flying of splinters which his imitators still so fervently imitate. If you give a Chinese dressmaker a dress to copy, and the dress happens to have a darned rent in it, the dressmaker carefully tears a rent in the new dress, and darns it in exact replica. And this seems to be the chief occupation of Cézanne's disciples, in every land. They absorb themselves reproducing imitation mistakes. He let off various explosions in order to blow up the stronghold of the cliché, and his followers make grand firework imitations of the explosions, without the faintest inkling of the true attack. They do, indeed, make an onslaught on representation, true-to-life representation: because the explosion in Cézanne's pictures blew them up. But I am convinced that what Cézanne himself wanted *was* representation. He *wanted* true-to-life representation. Only he wanted it *more* true to life. And once you have got photography, it is a very, very difficult thing to get representation *more* true-to-life: which it has to be.

Cézanne was a realist, and he wanted to be true to life. But he would not be content with the optical cliché. With the impressionists, purely optical vision perfected itself and fell *at once* into cliché, with a startling rapidity. Cézanne saw this. Artists like Courbet and Daumier were not purely optical, but the other element in these two painters, the intellectual element, was cliché. To the optical vision they added the concept of force-pressure, almost like an hydraulic brake, and this force-pressure concept is mechanical, a cliché, though still popular. And Daumier added mental satire, and Courbet added a touch of a sort of socialism: both cliché and unimaginative.

Cézanne wanted something that was neither optical nor mechanical nor intellectual. And to introduce into our world of vision something which is neither optical nor mechanical nor intellectual-psychological requires a real revolution. It was a revolution Cézanne began, but which nobody, apparently, has been able to carry on.

He wanted to touch the world of substance once more with the intuitive touch, to be aware of it with the intuitive awareness, and to express it in intuitive terms. That is, he wished to displace our present mode of mental-visual consciousness, the consciousness of mental concepts, and substitute a mode of consciousness that was predominantly intuitive, the awareness of touch. In the past the primitives painted intuitively, but *in the direction* of our present mental-visual, conceptual form of consciousness. They were working away from their own intuition. Mankind has never been able to trust the intuitive consciousness, and the decision to accept that trust marks a very great revolution in the course of human development.

Without knowing it, Cézanne, the timid little conventional man sheltering behind his wife and sister and the Jesuit father, was a pure revolutionary. When he said to his models: 'Be an apple! Be an apple!' he was uttering the foreword to the fall not only of Jesuits and the Christian idealists altogether, but to the collapse of our whole way of consciousness, and the substitution of another way. If the human being is going to be primarily an apple, as for Cézanne it was, then you are going to have a new world of men: a world which has very little to say, men that can sit still and just be physically there, and be truly non-moral. That was what Cézanne meant with his: 'Be an apple!' He knew perfectly well that the moment the model began to intrude her personality and her 'mind,' it would be cliché and moral, and he would have to paint cliché. The only part of her that was not banal, known *ad nauseam*, living cliché, the only part of her that was not living cliché was her appleyness. Her body, even her very sex, was known, nauseously: *connu, connu!* the endless chance of known cause-and-effect, the infinite web of the hated cliché which nets us all down in utter boredom. He knew it all, he hated it all, he refused it all, this timid and 'humble' little man. He knew, as an artist, that the only bit of a woman which nowadays escapes being ready-made and ready-known cliché is the appley part of her. Oh, be an apple, and leave out all your thoughts, all your feelings, all your mind and all your personality, which we know all about and find boring beyond endurance. Leave it all out – and be an apple! It is the appleyness of the

portrait of Cézanne's wife that makes it so permanently interesting: the appleyness, which carries with it also the feeling of
knowing the other side as well, the side you don't see, the hidden side of the moon. For the intuitive apperception of the apple
is so *tangibly* aware of the apple that it is aware of it *all round*, not
only just of the front. The eye sees only fronts, and the mind,
on the whole, is satisfied with fronts. But intuition needs all-
aroundness, and instinct needs insideness. The true imagination
is for ever curving round to the other side, to the back of presented appearance.

So to my feeling the portraits of Madame Cézanne, particularly the portrait in the red dress, are more interesting than the
portrait of M. Geffroy, or the portraits of the housekeeper or the
gardener. In the same way the *Card-Players* with two figures
please me more than those with four.

But we have to remember, in his figure-paintings, that while
he was painting the appleyness he was also deliberately painting
out the so-called humanness, the personality, the 'likeness,' the
physical cliché. He had deliberately to paint it out, deliberately
to make the hands and face rudimentary, and so on, because if
he had painted them in fully they would have been cliché. He
never got over the cliché denominator, the intrusion and inter-
ference of the ready-made concept, when it came to people, to
men and women. Especially to women he could only give a cliché response – and that maddened him. Try as he might, women
remained a known, ready-made cliché object to him, and he
could not break through the concept obsession to get at the intuitive awareness of her. Except with his wife – and in his wife he
did at least know the appleyness. But with his housekeeper he
failed somewhat. She was a bit cliché, especially the face. So
really is M. Geffroy.

With men Cézanne often dodged it by insisting on the

clothes, those stiff cloth jackets bent into thick folds, those hats, those blouses, those curtains. Some of the *Card-Players*, the big ones with four figures, seem just a trifle banal, so much occupied with painted stuff, painted clothing, and the humanness a bit cliché. Nor good colour, nor clever composition, nor 'planes' of colour, nor anything else will save an emotional cliché from being an emotional cliché, though they may, of course, garnish it and make it more interesting.

Where Cézanne did sometimes escape the cliché altogether and really give a complete intuitive interpretation of actual objects is in some of the still-life compositions. To me these good still-life scenes are purely representative and quite true to life. Here Cézanne did what he wanted to do: he made the things quite real, he didn't deliberately leave anything out, and yet he gave us a triumphant and rich intuitive vision of a few apples and kitchen pots. For once his intuitive consciousness triumphed, and broke into utterance. And here he is inimitable. His imitators imitate his accessories of tablecloths folded like tin, etc. – the unreal parts of his pictures – but they don't imitate the pots and apples, because they can't. It's the real appleyness, and you can't imitate it. Every man must create it new and different out of himself: new and different. The moment it looks 'like' Cézanne, it is nothing.

But at the same time Cézanne was triumphing with the apple and appleyness he was still fighting with the cliché. When he makes Madame Cézanne most *still*, most appley, he starts making the universe slip uneasily about her. It was part of his desire: to make the human form, the *life* form, come to rest. Not static – on the contrary. Mobile but come to rest. And at the same time he set the unmoving material world into motion. Walls twitch and slide, chairs bend or rear up a little, cloths curl like burning paper. Cézanne did this partly to satisfy his intuitive feeling that nothing is really *statically* at rest – a feeling he seems to have had strongly – as when he watched the lemons shrivel or go mildewed, in his still-life group, which he left lying there so long so that he *could* see that gradual flux of change: and partly to fight the cliché, which says that the inanimate world *is* static, and that walls *are* still. In his fight with the cliché he denied that walls are still and chairs are static. In his intuitive self he *felt* for their changes.

And these two activities of his consciousness occupy his later landscapes. In the best landscapes we are fascinated by the mysterious *shiftiness* of the scene under our eyes; it shifts about as we watch it. And we realize, with a sort of transport, how intuitively *true* this is of landscape. It is *not* still. It has its own weird anima, and to our wide-eyed perception it changes like a living animal under our gaze. This is a quality that Cézanne sometimes got marvellously.

Then again, in other pictures he seems to be saying: Landscape is not like this and not like this and not like this and not . . . etc. – and every *not* is a little blank space in the canvas, defined by the remains of an assertion. Sometimes Cézanne builds up a landscape essentially out of omissions. He puts fringes on the complicated vacuum of the cliché, so to speak, and offers us that. It is interesting in a *repudiative* fashion, but it is not the new thing. The appleyness, the intuition has gone. We have only a mental repudiation. This occupies many of the later pictures: and ecstasizes the critics.

And Cézanne was bitter. He had never, as far as his *life* went, broken through the horrible glass screen of the mental concepts, to the actual *touch* of life. In his art he had touched the apple, and that was a great deal. He had intuitively known the apple and intuitively brought it forth on the tree of his life, in paint. But when it came to anything beyond the apple, to landscape, to people, and above all to nude woman, the cliché had triumphed over him. The cliché had triumphed over him, and he was bitter, misanthropic. How not to be misanthropic when men and women are just clichés to you, and you hate the cliché? Most people, of course, love the cliché – because most people *are* the cliché. Still, for all that, there is perhaps more appleyness in man, and even in nude woman, than Cézanne was able to get at. The cliché obtruded, so he just abstracted away from it. Those last water-colour landscapes are just abstractions from the cliché. They are blanks, with a few pearly-coloured sort of edges. The blank is vacuum, which was Cézanne's last word against the cliché. It is a vacuum, and the edges are there to assert the vacuity.

And the very fact that we can reconstruct almost instantly a whole landscape from the few indications Cézanne gives, shows what a cliché the landscape is, how it exists already, ready-made, in our minds, how it exists in a pigeon-hole of the consciousness, so to speak, and you need only be given its number to be able to get it out, complete. Cézanne's last water-colour landscapes, made up of a few touches on blank paper, are a satire on landscape altogether. *They leave so much to the imagination!* – that immortal cant phrase, which means they give you the clue to a cliché and the cliché comes. That's what the cliché exists for. And that sort of imagination is just a rag-bag memory stored with thousands and thousands of old and really worthless sketches, images, etc., clichés.

We can see what a fight it means, the escape from the domination of the ready-made mental concept, the mental consciousness stuffed full of clichés that intervene like a complete screen between us and life. It means a long, long fight, that will probably last for ever. But Cézanne did get as far as the apple. I can think of nobody else who has done anything.

When we put it in personal terms, it is a fight in a man between his own ego, which is his ready-made mental self which inhabits either a sky-blue, self-tinted heaven or a black, self-tinted hell, and his other free intuitive self. Cézanne never freed himself from his ego, in his life. He haunted the fringes of experience. 'I who am so feeble in life' – but at least he knew it. At least he had the greatness to feel bitter about it. Not like the complacent bourgeois who now 'appreciate' him!

So now perhaps it is the English turn. Perhaps this is where the English will come in. They have certainly stayed out very completely. It is as if they had received the death-blow to their instinctive and intuitive bodies in the Elizabethan age, and since then they have steadily died, till now they are complete corpses. As a young English painter, an intelligent and really modest young man, said to me: 'But I do think we ought to begin to paint good pictures, now that we know pretty well all there is to know about how a picture should be made. You do agree, don't you, that technically we know almost all there is to know about painting?'

I looked at him in amazement. It was obvious that a new-born babe was as fit to paint pictures as he was. He knew technically all there was to know about pictures: all about two-dimensional and three-dimensional composition, also the colour-dimension and the dimension of values in that view of composition which exists apart from form: all about the value of planes, the value of the angle in planes, the different values of the same colour on different planes: all about edges, visible edges, tangible edges, intangible edges: all about the nodality of form-groups, the con-stellating of mass-centres: all about the relativity of mass, the gravitation and the centrifugal force of masses, the resultant of the complex impinging of masses, the isolation of a mass in the line of vision: all about pattern, line pattern, edge pattern, tone pattern, colour pattern, and the pattern of moving planes: all about texture, impasto, surface, and what happens at the edge of the canvas: also which is the æsthetic centre of the canvas, the dynamic centre, the effulgent centre, the kinetic centre, the mathematical centre, and the Chinese centre: also the points of departure in the foreground, and the points of disappearance in the background, together with the various routes between these points, namely, as the crow flies, as the cow walks, as the mind intoxicated with knowledge reels and gets there: all about spotting, what you spot, which spot, on the spot, how many spots, balance of spots, recedence of spots, spots on the explosive vision and spots on the co-ordinative vision: all about literary interest and how to hide it successfully from the policeman: all about photographic representation, and which heaven it belongs to, and which hell: all about the sex-appeal of a picture, and when you can be arrested for solicitation, when for indecency: all about the psychology of a picture, which section of the mind it appeals to, which mental state it is intended to represent, how to exclude the representation of all other states of mind from the one intended, or how, on the contrary, to give a hint of complementary states of mind fringing the state of mind portrayed: all about the chemistry of colours, when to use Winsor & Newton and when not, and the relative depth of contempt to display for Lefranc on the history of colour, past and future, whether cadmium will really stand the march of ages, whether viridian will go black, blue, or merely greasy, and the effect on our great-great-grandsons of the flake white and zinc white and white lead we have so lavishly used: on the merits and demerits of leaving patches of bare, prepared canvas, and which preparation will bleach, which blacken: on the mediums to be used, the vice of linseed oil, the treachery of turps, the meanness of gums, the innocence or the unspeakable crime of varnish: on allowing your picture to be shiny, on insisting that it should be shiny, on weeping over the merest suspicion of gloss and rubbing it with a raw potato: on brushes, and the conflicting length of the stem, the best of the hog, the length of bristle most to be desired on the many varying occasions, and whether to slash in one direction only: on the atmosphere of London, on the atmosphere of Glasgow, on the atmosphere of Rome, on the atmosphere of Paris, and the peculiar action of them all upon vermilion, cinnabar, pale cadmium yellow, mid-chrome, emerald green, Veronese green, linseed oil, turps, and Lyall's perfect medium: on quality, and its relation to light, and its ability to hold its own in so radical a change of light as that from Rome to London – all these things the young man knew – and out of it, God help him, he was going to make pictures.

Now, such innocence and such naïveté, coupled with true modesty, must make us believe that we English have indeed, at least as far as paint goes, become again as little children: very little children: tiny children: babes: nay, babes unborn. And if we have really got back to the state of the unborn babe, we are perhaps almost ready to be born. The English *may* be born again, pictorially. Or, to tell the truth, they may begin for the first time to be born: since as painters of composition pictures they don't really exist. They have reached the stage where their innocent egos are entirely and totally enclosed in pale-blue glass bottles of insulated inexperience. Perhaps now they *must* hatch out!

'Do you think we may be on the brink of a Golden Age again in England?' one of our most promising young writers asked me, with that same half-timorous innocence and naïveté of the young painter. I looked at him – he was a sad young man – and my eyes nearly fell out of my head. A golden age! He looked so ungolden, and though he was twenty years my junior, he felt also like my grandfather. A golden age! in England! a golden age! now, when even money is paper! when the enclosure in the ego is final, when they are hermetically sealed and insulated from all experience, from any *touch*, from anything *solid*.

'I suppose it's up to *you*,' said I.

And he quietly accepted it.

But such innocence, such naïveté must be a prelude to something. It's a *ne plus ultra*. So why shouldn't it be a prelude to a golden age? If the innocence and naïveté as regards artistic expression doesn't become merely idiotic, why shouldn't it become golden? The young might, out of a sheer sort of mental blankness, strike the oil of their live intuition, and get a gusher. Why not? A golden gush of artistic expression! 'Now we know pretty well everything that can be known about the technical side of pictures.' A golden age!

PORNOGRAPHY AND OBSCENITY (1929)

What they are depends, as usual, entirely on the individual. What is pornography to one man is the laughter of genius to another.

The word itself, we are told, means 'pertaining to harlots' – the graph of the harlot. But nowadays, what is a harlot? If she was a woman who took money from a man in return for going to bed with him – really, most wives sold themselves, in the past, and plenty of harlots gave themselves, when they felt like it, for nothing. If a woman hasn't got a tiny streak of a harlot in her, she's a dry stick as a rule. And probably most harlots had somewhere a streak of womanly generosity. Why be so cut and dried? The law is a dreary thing, and its judgments have nothing to do with life.

The same with the word *obscene*: nobody knows what it means. Suppose it were derived from *obscena*: that which might not be represented on the stage; how much further are you? None! What is obscene to Tom is not obscene to Lucy or Joe, and really, the meaning of a word has to wait for majorities to decide it. If a play shocks ten people in an audience, and doesn't shock the remaining five hundred, then it is obscene to ten and innocuous to five hundred; hence, the play is not obscene, by majority. But *Hamlet* shocked all the Cromwellian Puritans, and shocks nobody today, and some of Aristophanes shocks everybody today, and didn't galvanize the later Greeks at all, apparently. Man is a changeable beast, and words change their meanings with him, and things are not what they seemed, and what's what becomes what isn't, and if we think we know where we are it's only because we are so rapidly being translated to somewhere else. We have to leave everything to the majority, everything to the majority, everything to the mob, the mob, the mob. They know what is obscene and what isn't, they do. If the lower ten million doesn't know better than the upper ten men, then there's something wrong with mathematics. Take a vote on it! Show hands, and prove it by count! *Vox populi, vox Dei. Odi profanum vulgum! Profanum vulgum.*

So it comes down to this: if you are talking to the mob, the meaning of your words is the mob-meaning, decided by majority. As somebody wrote to me: the American law on obscenity is very plain, and America is going to enforce the law. Quite, my dear, quite, quite, quite! The mob knows all about obscenity. Mild little words that rhyme with spit or farce are the height of obscenity. Supposing, a printer put 'h' in the place of 'p,' by mistake, in that mere word spit? Then the great American public knows that this man has committed an obscenity, an indecency, that his act was lewd, and as a compositor he was pornographical. You can't tamper with the great public, British or American. *Vox populi, vox Dei*, don't you know. If you don't we'll let you know it. At the same time, this *vox Dei* shouts with praise over moving-pictures and books and newspaper accounts that seem, to a sinful nature like mine, completely disgusting and obscene. Like a real prude and Puritan, I have to look the other way. When obscenity becomes mawkish, which is its palatable form for the public, and when the *Vox populi, vox Dei* is hoarse with sentimental indecency, then I have to steer away, like a Pharisee, afraid of being contaminated. There is a certain kind of sticky universal pitch that I refuse to touch.

So again, it comes down to this: you accept the majority, the mob, and its decisions, or you don't. You bow down before the *Vox populi, vox Dei*, or you plug your ears not to hear its obscene howl. You perform your antics to please the vast public, *Deus ex machina*, or you refuse to perform for the public at all, unless now and then to pull its elephantine and ignominious leg.

When it comes to the meaning of anything, even the simplest word, then you must pause. Because there are two great categories of meaning, for ever separate. There is mob-meaning, and there is individual meaning. Take even the word *bread*. The mob-meaning is merely: stuff made with white flour into loaves that you eat. But take the individual meaning of the word bread: the white, the brown, the corn-pone, the home-made, the smell of bread just out of the oven, the crust, the crumb, the unleavened bread, the shew-bread, the staff of life, sour-dough bread, cottage loaves, French bread, Viennese bread, black bread, a yesterday's loaf, rye, graham, barley, rolls, *Bretzeln*, *Kringeln*, scones, damper, matsen – there is no end to it all, and the word bread will take you to the ends of time and space, and far-off down avenues of memory. But this is individual. The word bread will take the individual off on his own journey, and its meaning will be his own meaning, based on his own genuine imagination reactions. And when a word comes to us in its individual character, and starts in us the individual responses, it is great pleasure to us. The American advertisers have discovered this, and some of the cunningest American literature is to be found in advertisements of soap-suds, for example. These advertisements are *almost* prose poems. They give the word soap-suds a bubbly, shiny individual meaning, which is very skilfully poetic, would, perhaps, be quite poetic to the mind which could forget that the poetry was bait on a hook.

Business is discovering the individual, dynamic meaning of words, and poetry is losing it. Poetry more and more tends to far-fetch its word-meanings, and this results once again in mob-meanings, which arouse only a mob-reaction in the individual. For every man has a mob-self and an individual self, in varying proportions. Some men are almost all mob-self, incapable of imaginative individual responses. The worst specimens of mob-self are usually to be found in the professions, lawyers, professors, clergymen and so on. The business man, much maligned, has a tough outside mob-self, and a scared, floundering yet still alive individual self. The public, which is feeble-minded like an idiot, will never be able to preserve its individual reactions from the tricks of the exploiter. The public is always exploited and always will be exploited. The methods of exploitation merely vary. Today the public is tickled into laying the golden egg. With imaginative words and individual meanings it is tricked into giving the great goose-cackle of mob-acquiescence. *Vox populi, vox Dei*. It has always been so, and will always be so. Why? Because the public has not enough wit to distinguish between mob-meanings and individual meanings. The mass is for ever vulgar, because it can't distinguish between its own original feelings and feelings which are diddled into existence by the exploiter. The public is always profane, because it is controlled from the outside, by the trickster, and never from the inside, by its own sincerity. The mob is always obscene, because it is always second-hand.

Which brings us back to our subject of pornography and obscenity. The reaction to any word may be, in any individual, either a mob-reaction or an individual reaction. It is up to the individual to ask himself: Is my reaction individual, or am I merely reacting from my mob-self?

When it comes to the so-called obscene words, I should say that hardly one person in a million escapes mob-reaction. The first reaction is almost sure to be mob-reaction, mob-indignation, mob-condemnation. And the mob gets no further. But the real individual has second thoughts and says: Am I really shocked? Do I *really* feel outraged and indignant? And the answer of any individual is bound to be: No, I am not shocked, not outraged, nor indignant. I know the word, and take it for what it is, and I am not going to be jockeyed into making a mountain out of a mole-hill, not for all the law in the world.

Now if the use of a few so-called obscene words will startle man or woman out of a mob-habit into an individual state, well and good. And word prudery is so universal a mob-habit that it is time we were startled out of it.

But still we have only tackled obscenity, and the problem of pornography goes even deeper. When a man is startled into his individual self, he still may not be able to know, inside himself, whether Rabelais is or is not pornographic: and over Aretino or even Boccaccio he may perhaps puzzle in vain, torn between different emotions.

One essay on pornography, I remember, comes to the conclusion that pornography in art is that which is calculated to arouse sexual desire, or sexual excitement. And stress is laid on the fact, whether the author or artist *intended* to arouse sexual feelings. It is the old vexed question of intention, become so dull today, when we know how strong and influential our unconscious intentions are. And why a man should be held guilty of his conscious intentions, and innocent of his unconscious intentions, I don't know, since every man is more made up of unconscious intentions than of conscious ones. I am what I am, not merely what I think I am.

However! We take it, I assume, that *pornography* is something base, something unpleasant. In short, we don't like it. And why don't we like it? Because it arouses sexual feelings?

I think not. No matter how hard we may pretend otherwise, most of us rather like a moderate rousing of our sex. It warms us, stimulates us like sunshine on a grey day. After a century or two of Puritanism, this is still true of most people. Only the mob-habit of condemning any form of sex is too strong to let us admit it naturally. And there are, of course, many people who are genuinely repelled by the simplest and most natural stirrings of sexual feeling. But these people are perverts who have fallen into hatred of their fellow men: thwarted, disappointed, unfulfilled people, of whom, alas, our civilization contains so many. And they nearly always enjoy some unsimple and unnatural form of sex excitement, secretly.

Even quite advanced art critics would try to make us believe that any picture or book which had 'sex appeal' was *ipso facto* a bad book or picture. This is just canting hypocrisy. Half the great poems, pictures, music, stories of the whole world are great by virtue of the beauty of their sex appeal. Titian or Renoir, the Song of Solomon or *Jane Eyre*, Mozart or 'Annie Laurie,' the loveliness is all interwoven with sex appeal, sex stimulus, call it what you will. Even Michelangelo, who rather hated sex, can't help filling the Cornucopia with phallic acorns. Sex is a very powerful, beneficial and necessary stimulus in human life, and we are all grateful when we feel its warm, natural flow through us, like a form of sunshine.

So we can dismiss the idea that sex appeal in art is pornography. It may be so to the grey Puritan, but the grey Puritan is a sick man, soul and body sick, so why should we bother about his hallucinations? Sex appeal, of course, varies enormously. There are endless different kinds, and endless degrees of each kind. Perhaps it may be argued that a mild degree of sex appeal is not pornographical, whereas a high degree is. But this is a fallacy. Boccaccio at his hottest seems to me less pornographical than *Pamela* or *Clarissa Harlowe* or even *Jane Eyre*, or a host of modern books or films which pass uncensored. At the same time Wagner's *Tristan and Isolde* seems to me very near to pornography, and so, even, do some quite popular Christian hymns.

What is it, then? It isn't a question of sex appeal, merely: nor even a question of deliberate intention on the part of the author or artist to arouse sexual excitement. Rabelais sometimes had a deliberate intention, so in a different way, did Boccaccio. And I'm sure poor Charlotte Brontë, or the authoress of *The Sheik*, did not have any deliberate intention to stimulate sex feelings in the reader. Yet I find *Jane Eyre* verging towards pornography and Boccaccio seems to me always fresh and wholesome.

The late British Home Secretary, who prides himself on being a very sincere Puritan, grey, grey in every fibre, said with indignant sorrow in one of his outbursts on improper books: '– and these two young people, who had been perfectly pure up till that time, after reading this book went and had sexual intercourse together!!!' *One up to them!* is all we can answer. But the grey Guardian of British Morals seemed to think that if they had murdered one another, or worn each other to rags of nervous prostration, it would have been much better. The grey disease!

Then what is pornography, after all this? It isn't sex appeal or sex stimulus in art. It isn't even a deliberate intention on the part of the artist to arouse or excite sexual feelings. There's nothing wrong with sexual feelings in themselves, so long as they are straight-forward and not sneaking or sly. The right sort of sex stimulus is invaluable to human daily life. Without it the world grows grey. I would give everybody the gay Renaissance stories to read, they would help to shake off a lot of grey self-importance, which is our modern civilized disease.

But even I would censor genuine pornography, rigorously. It would not be very difficult. In the first place, genuine pornography is almost always underworld, it doesn't come into the open. In the second, you can recognize it by the insult it offers, invariably, to sex, and to the human spirit.

Pornography is the attempt to insult sex, to do dirt on it. This is unpardonable. Take the very lowest instance, the picture post-card sold under hand, by the underworld, in most cities. What I have seen of them have been of an ugliness to make you cry. The insult to the human body, the insult to a vital human relationship! Ugly and cheap they make the human nudity, ugly and degraded they make the sexual act, trivial and cheap and nasty.

It is the same with the books they sell in the underworld. They are either so ugly they make you ill, or so fatuous you can't imagine anybody but a cretin or a moron reading them, or writing them.

It is the same with the dirty limericks that people tell after dinner, or the dirty stories one hears commercial travellers telling each other in a smoke-room. Occasionally there is a really funny one, that redeems a great deal. But usually they are just ugly and repellent, and the so-called 'humour' is just a trick of doing dirt on sex.

Now the human nudity of a great many modern people is just ugly and degraded, and the sexual act between modern people is just the same, merely ugly and degrading. But this is nothing to be proud of. It is the catastrophe of our civilization. I am sure no other civilization, not even the Roman, has showed such a vast proportion of ignominious and degraded nudity, and ugly, squalid dirty sex. Because no other civilization has driven sex into the underworld, and nudity to the w.c.

The intelligent young, thank heaven, seem determined to alter in these two respects. They are rescuing their young nudity from the stuffy, pornographical hole-and-corner underworld of their elders, and they refuse to sneak about the sexual relation. This is a change the elderly grey ones of course deplore, but it is in fact a very great change for the better, and a real revolution.

But it is amazing how strong is the will in ordinary, vulgar people, to do dirt on sex. It was one of my fond illusions, when

425

I was young, that the ordinary healthy-seeming sort of men, in railway carriages, or the smoke-room of an hotel or a pullman, were healthy in their feelings and had a wholesome rough devil-may-care attitude towards sex. All wrong! All wrong! Experience teaches that common individuals of this sort have a disgusting attitude towards sex, a disgusting contempt of it, a disgusting desire to insult it. If such fellows have intercourse with a woman, they triumphantly feel that they have done her dirt, and now she is lower, cheaper, more contemptible than she was before.

It is individuals of this sort that tell dirty stories, carry indecent picture post-cards, and know the indecent books. This is the great pornographical class – the really common men-in-the-street and women-in-the-street. They have as great a hate and contempt of sex as the greyest Puritan, and when an appeal is made to them, they are always on the side of the angels. They insist that a film-heroine shall be a neuter, a sexless thing of washed-out purity. They insist that real sex-feeling shall only be shown by the villain or villainess, low lust. They find a Titian or a Renoir really indecent, and they don't want their wives and daughters to see it.

Why? Because they have the grey disease of sex-hatred, coupled with the yellow disease of dirt-lust. The sex functions and the excrementory functions in the human body work so close together, yet they are, so to speak, utterly different in direction. Sex is a creative flow, the excrementory flow is towards dissolution, de-creation, if we may use such a word. In the really healthy human being the distinction between the two is instant, our profoundest instincts are perhaps our instincts of opposition between the two flows.

But in the degraded human being the deep instincts have gone dead, and then the two flows become identical. *This* is the secret of really vulgar and of pornographical people: the sex flow and the excrement flow is the same to them. It happens when the psyche deteriorates, and the profound controlling instincts collapse. Then sex is dirt and dirt is sex, and sexual excitement becomes a playing with dirt, and any sign of sex in a woman becomes a show of her dirt. This is the condition of the common, vulgar human being whose name is legion, and who lifts his voice and it is the *Vox populi, vox Dei*. And this is the source of all pornography.

And for this reason we must admit that *Jane Eyre* or Wagner's *Tristan* are much nearer to pornography than is Boccaccio. Wagner and Charlotte Brontë were both in the state where the strongest instincts have collapsed, and sex has become something slightly obscene, to be wallowed in, but despised. Mr Rochester's sex passion is not 'respectable' till Mr Rochester is burned, blinded, disfigured, and reduced to helpless dependence. Then, thoroughly humbled and humiliated, it may be merely admitted. All the previous titillations are slightly indecent, as in *Pamela* or *The Mill on the Floss* or *Anna Karenina*. As soon as there is sex excitement with a desire to spite the sexual feeling, to humiliate it and degrade it, the element of pornography enters.

For this reason, there is an element of pornography in nearly all nineteenth century literature and very many so-called pure people have a nasty pornographical side to them, and never was the pornographical appetite stronger than it is today. It is a sign of a diseased condition of the body politic. But the way to treat the disease is to come out into the open with sex and sex stimulus. The real pornographer truly dislikes Boccaccio, because the fresh healthy naturalness of the Italian story-teller makes the modern pornographical shrimp feel the dirty worm he is. Today Boccaccio should be given to everybody young or old, to read if they like. Only a natural fresh openness about sex will do any good, now we are being swamped by secret or semi-secret pornography. And perhaps the Renaissance story-tellers, Boccaccio,

Lasca, and the rest, are the best antidote we can find now, just as more plasters of Puritanism are the most harmful remedy we can resort to.

The whole question of pornography seems to me a question of secrecy. Without secrecy there would be no pornography. But secrecy and modesty are two utterly different things. Secrecy has always an element of fear in it, amounting very often to hate. Modesty is gentle and reserved. Today, modesty is thrown to the winds, even in the presence of the grey guardians. But secrecy is hugged, being a vice in itself. And the attitude of the grey ones is: Dear young ladies, you may abandon all modesty, so long as you hug your dirty little secret.

This 'dirty little secret' has become infinitely precious to the mob of people today. It is a kind of hidden sore or inflammation which, when rubbed or scratched, gives off sharp thrills that seem delicious. So the dirty little secret is rubbed and scratched more and more, till it becomes more and more secretly inflamed, and the nervous and psychic health of the individual is more and more impaired. One might easily say that half the love novels and half the love films today depend entirely for their success on the secret rubbing of the dirty little secret. You can call this sex excitement if you like, but it is sex excitement of a secretive, furtive sort, quite special. The plain and simple excitement, quite open and wholesome, which you find in some Boccaccio stories is not for a minute to be confused with the furtive excitement aroused by rubbing the dirty little secret in all secrecy in modern best-sellers. This furtive, sneaking, cunning rubbing of an inflamed spot in the imagination is the very quick of modern pornography, and it is a beastly and very dangerous thing. You can't so easily expose it, because of its very furtiveness and its sneaking cunning. So the cheap and popular modern love novel and love film flourishes and is even praised by moral guardians, because you get the sneaking thrill fumbling under all the purity of dainty underclothes, without one single gross word to let you know what is happening.

Without secrecy there would be no pornography. But if pornography is the result of sneaking secrecy, what is the result of pornography? What is the effect on the individual?

The effect on the individual is manifold, and always pernicious. But one effect is perhaps inevitable. The pornography of today, whether it be the pornography of the rubber-goods shop or the pornography of the popular novel, film, and play, is an invariable stimulant to the vice of self-abuse, onanism, masturbation, call it what you will. In young or old, man or woman, boy or girl, modern pornography is a direct provocative of masturbation. It cannot be otherwise. When the grey ones wail that the young man and the young woman went and had sexual intercourse, they are bewailing the fact that the young man and the young woman didn't go separately and masturbate. Sex must go somewhere, especially in young people. So, in our glorious civilization, it goes in masturbation. And the mass of our popular literature, the bulk of our popular amusements just exists to provoke masturbation. Masturbation is the one thoroughly secret act of the human being, more secret even than excrementation. It is the one functional result of sex-secrecy, and it is stimulated and provoked by our glorious popular literature of pretty pornography, which rubs on the dirty secret without letting you know what is happening.

Now I have heard men, teachers and clergymen, commend masturbation as the solution of an otherwise insoluble sex problem. This at least is honest. The sex problem is there, and you can't just will it away. There it is, and under the ban of secrecy and taboo in mother and father, teacher, friend, and foe, it has found its own solution, the solution of masturbation.

But what about the solution? Do we accept it? Do all the grey ones of this world accept it? If so, they must now accept it openly.

We can none of us pretend any longer to be blind to the fact of masturbation, in young and old, man and woman. The moral guardians who are prepared to censor all open and plain portrayal of sex must now be made to give their only justification: We prefer that the people shall masturbate. If this preference is open and declared, then the existing forms of censorship are justified. If the moral guardians prefer that the people shall masturbate, then their present behaviour is correct, and popular amusements are as they should be. If sexual intercourse is deadly sin, and masturbation is comparatively pure and harmless, then all is well. Let things continue as they now are.

Is masturbation so harmless, though? Is it even comparatively pure and harmless? Not to my thinking. In the young, a certain amount of masturbation is inevitable, but not therefore natural. I think, there is no boy or girl who masturbates without feeling a sense of shame, anger, and futility. Following the excitement comes the shame, anger, humiliation, and the sense of futility. This sense of futility and humiliation deepens as the years go on, into a suppressed rage, because of the impossibility of escape. The one thing that it seems impossible to escape from, once the habit is formed, is masturbation. It goes on and on, on into old age, in spite of marriage or love affairs or anything else. And it always carries this secret feeling of futility and humiliation, futility and humiliation. And this is, perhaps, the deepest and most dangerous cancer of our civilization. Instead of being a comparatively pure and harmless vice, masturbation is certainly the most dangerous sexual vice that a society can be afflicted with, in the long run. Comparatively pure it may be – purity being what it is. But harmless! ! !

The great danger of masturbation lies in its merely exhaustive nature. In sexual intercourse, there is a give and take. A new stimulus enters as the native stimulus departs. Something quite new is added as the old surcharge is removed. And this is so in all sexual intercourse where two creatures are concerned, even in the homosexual intercourse. But in masturbation there is nothing but loss. There is no reciprocity. There is merely the spending away of a certain force, and no return. The body remains, in a sense, a corpse, after the act of self-abuse. There is no change, only deadening. There is what we call dead loss. And this is not the case in any act of sexual intercourse between two people. Two people may destroy one another in sex. But they cannot just produce the null effect of masturbation.

The only positive effect of masturbation is that it seems to release a certain mental energy, in some people. But it is mental energy which manifests itself always in the same way, in a vicious circle of analysis and impotent criticism, or else a vicious circle of false and easy sympathy, sentimentalities. The sentimentalism and the niggling analysis, often self-analysis, of most of our modern literature, is a sign of self-abuse. It is the manifestation of masturbation, the sort of conscious activity stimulated by masturbation, whether male or female. The outstanding feature of such consciousness is that there is no real object, there is only subject. This is just the same whether it be a novel or a work of science. The author never escapes from himself, he pads along within the vicious circle of himself. There is hardly a writer living who gets out of the vicious circle of himself – or a painter either. Hence the lack of creation, and the stupendous amount of production. It is a masturbation result, within the vicious circle of the self. It is self-absorption made public.

And of course the process is exhaustive. The real masturbation of Englishmen began only in the nineteenth century. It has continued with an increasing emptying of the real vitality and the real *being* of men, till now people are little more than shells of people. Most of the responses are dead, most of the awareness is dead, nearly all the constructive activity is dead, and all that remains is a sort of shell, a half-empty creature fatally self-preoccupied and incapable of either giving or taking. Incapable either of giving or taking, in the vital self. And this is masturbation result. Enclosed within the vicious circle of the self, with no vital contacts outside, the self becomes emptier and emptier, till it is almost a nullus, a nothingness.

But null or nothing as it may be, it still hangs on to the dirty little secret, which it must still secretly rub and inflame. For ever the vicious circle. And it has a weird, blind will of its own.

One of my most sympathetic critics wrote: 'If Mr Lawrence's attitude to sex were adopted, then two things would disappear, the love lyric and the smoking-room story.' And this, I think, is true. But it depends on which love lyric he means. If it is the: *Who is Sylvia, what is she?* – then it may just as well disappear. All that pure and noble and heaven-blessed stuff is only the counterpart to the smoking-room story. *Du bist wie eine Blume!* Jawohl! One can see the elderly gentleman laying his hands on the head of the pure maiden and praying God to keep her for ever so pure, so clean and beautiful. Very nice for him! Just pornography! Tickling the dirty little secret and rolling his eyes to heaven! He knows perfectly well that if God keeps the maiden so clean and pure and beautiful – in his vulgar sense of clean and pure – for a few more years, then she'll be an unhappy old maid, and not pure nor beautiful at all, only stale and pathetic. Sentimentality is a sure sign of pornography. Why should 'sadness strike through the heart' of the old gentleman, because the maid was pure and beautiful? Anybody but a masturbator would have been glad and would have thought: What a lovely bride for some lucky man! – But no, not the self-enclosed, pornographic masturbator. Sadness has to strike into his beastly heart! – Away with such love lyrics, we've had too much of their pornographic poison, tickling the dirty little secret and rolling the eyes to heaven.

But if it is a question of the sound love lyric, *My love is like a red, red rose – !* then we are on other ground. My love is like a red, red rose only when she's *not* like a pure, pure lily. And nowadays the pure, pure lilies are mostly festering, anyhow. Away with them and their lyrics. Away with the pure, pure lily lyric, along with the smoking-room story. They are counterparts, and the one is as pornographic as the other. *Du bist wie eine Blume* is really as pornographic as a dirty story: tickling the dirty little secret and rolling the eyes to heaven. But oh, if only Robert Burns had been accepted for what he is, then love might still have been like a red, red rose.

The vicious circle, the vicious circle! The vicious circle of masturbation! The vicious circle of self-consciousness that is never *fully* self-conscious, never fully and openly conscious, but always harping on the dirty little secret. The vicious circle of secrecy, in parents, teachers, friends – everybody. The specially vicious circle of family. The vast conspiracy of secrecy in the press, and at the same time, the endless tickling of the dirty little secret. The needless masturbation! and the endless purity! The vicious circle!

How to get out of it? There is only one way: Away with the secret! No more secrecy! The only way to stop the terrible mental itch about sex is to come out quite simply and naturally into the open with it. It is terribly difficult, for the secret is cunning as a crab. Yet the thing to do is to make a beginning. The man who said to his exasperating daughter: 'My child, the only pleasure I ever had out of you was the pleasure I had in begetting you' has already done a great deal to release both himself and her from the dirty little secret.

How to get out of the dirty little secret! It is, as a matter of fact, extremely difficult for us secretive moderns. You can't do it by being wise and scientific about it, like Dr Marie Stopes: though to be wise and scientific like Dr Marie Stopes is better than to be utterly hypocritical, like the grey ones. But by being wise and scientific in the serious and earnest manner you only tend to disinfect the dirty little secret, and either kill sex altogether with too much seriousness and intellect, or else leave it a miserable disinfected secret. The unhappy 'free and pure' love of so many people who have taken out the dirty little secret and thoroughly disinfected it with scientific words is apt to be more pathetic even than the common run of dirty-little-secret love. The danger is, that in killing the dirty little secret, you kill dynamic sex altogether, and leave only the scientific and deliberate mechanism.

This is what happens to many of those who become seriously 'free' in their sex, free and pure. They have mentalized sex till it is nothing at all, nothing at all but a mental quantity. And the final result is disaster, every time.

The same is true, in an even greater proportion, of the emancipated bohemians: and very many of the young are bohemian today, whether they ever set foot in Bohemia or not. But the bohemian is 'sex free.' The dirty little secret is no secret either to him or her. It is, indeed, a most blatantly open question. There is nothing they don't say: everything that can be revealed is revealed. And they do as they wish.

And then what? They have apparently killed the dirty little secret, but somehow, they have killed everything else too. Some of the dirt still sticks, perhaps; sex remains still dirty. But the thrill of secrecy is gone. Hence the terrible dreariness and depression of modern Bohemia, and the inward dreariness and emptiness of so many young people of today. They have killed, they imagine, the dirty little secret. The thrill of secrecy is gone. Some of the dirt remains. And for the rest, depression, inertia, lack of life. For sex is the fountain-head of our energetic life, and now the fountain ceases to flow.

Why? For two reasons. The idealists along the Marie Stopes

line, and the young bohemians of today have killed the dirty little secret as far as their personal self goes. But they are still under its dominion socially. In the social world, in the press, in literature, film, theatre, wireless, everywhere purity and the dirty little secret reign supreme. At home, at the dinner table, it is just the same. It is the same wherever you go. The young girl, and the young woman is by tacit assumption pure, virgin, sexless. *Du bist wie eine Blume.* She, poor thing, knows quite well that flowers, even lilies, have tippling yellow anthers and a sticky stigma, sex, rolling sex. But to the popular mind flowers are sexless things, and when a girl is told she is like a flower, it means she is sexless and ought to be sexless. She herself knows quite well she isn't sexless and she isn't merely like a flower. But how bear up against the great social life forced on her? She can't! She succumbs, and the dirty little secret triumphs. She loses her interest in sex, as far as men are concerned, but the vicious circle of masturbation and self-consciousness encloses her even still faster.

This is one of the disasters of young life today. Personally, and among themselves, a great many, perhaps a majority of the young people of today have come out into the open with sex and laid salt on the tail of the dirty little secret. And this is a very good thing. But in public, in the social world, the young are still entirely under the shadow of the grey elderly ones. The grey elderly ones belong to the last century, the eunuch century, the century of the mealy-mouthed lie, the century that has tried to destroy humanity, the nineteenth century. All our grey ones are left over from this century. And they rule us. They rule us with the grey, mealy-mouthed, canting lie of that great century of lies which, thank God, we are drifting away from. But they rule us still with the lie, for the lie, in the name of the lie. And they are too heavy and too numerous, the grey ones. It doesn't matter what government it is. They are all grey ones, left over from the last century, the century of mealy-mouthed liars, the century of purity and the dirty little secret.

So there is one cause for the depression of the young: the public reign of the mealy-mouthed lie, purity and the dirty little secret, which they themselves have privately overthrown. Having killed a good deal of the lie in their own private lives, the young are still enclosed and imprisoned within the great public lie of the grey ones. Hence the excess, the extravagance, the hysteria, and then the weakness, the feebleness, the pathetic silliness of the modern youth. They are all in a sort of prison, the prison of a great lie and a society of elderly liars. And this is one of the reasons, perhaps the main reason why the sex-flow is dying out of the young, the real energy is dying away. They are enclosed within a lie, and the sex won't flow. For the length of a complete lie is never more than three generations, and the young are the fourth generation of the nineteenth century lie.

The second reason why the sex-flow is dying is of course, that the young, in spite of their emancipation, are still enclosed within the vicious circle of self-conscious masturbation. They are thrown back into it, when they try to escape, by the enclosure of the vast public lie of purity and the dirty little secret. The most emancipated bohemians, who swank most about sex, are still utterly self-conscious and enclosed within the narcissus-masturbation circle. They have perhaps less sex even than the grey ones. The whole thing has been driven up into their heads. There isn't even the lurking hole of a dirty little secret. Their sex is more mental than their arithmetic; and as vital physical creatures they are more non-existent than ghosts. The modern bohemian is indeed a kind of ghost, not even narcissus, only the image of narcissus reflected on the face of the audience. The dirty little secret is most difficult to kill. You may put it to death publicly a thousand times, and still it reappears, like a crab, stealthily from under the submerged rocks of the personality.

The French, who are supposed to be so open about sex, will perhaps be the last to kill the dirty little secret. Perhaps they don't want to. Anyhow, mere publicity won't do it.

You may parade sex abroad, but you will not kill the dirty little secret. You may read all the novels of Marcel Proust, with everything there in all detail. Yet you will not kill the dirty little secret. You will perhaps only make it more cunning. You may even bring about a state of utter indifference and sex-inertia, still without killing the dirty little secret. Or you may be the most wispy and enamoured little Don Juan of modern days, and still the core of your spirit merely be the dirty little secret. That is to say, you will still be in the narcissus-masturbation circle, the vicious circle of self-enclosure. For whenever the dirty little secret exists, it exists as the centre of the vicious circle of masturbation self-enclosure. And whenever you have the vicious circle of masturbation self-enclosure, you have at the core the dirty little secret. And the most high-flown sex-emancipated young people today are perhaps the most fatally and nervously enclosed within the masturbation self-enclosure. Nor do they want to get out of it, for there would be nothing left to come out.

But some people surely do want to come out of the awful self-enclosure. Today, practically everybody is self-conscious and imprisoned in self-consciousness. It is the joyful result of the dirty little secret. Vast numbers of people don't want to come out of the prison of their self-consciousness: they have so little left to come out with. But some people, surely, want to escape this doom of self-enclosure which is the doom of our civilization. There is surely a proud minority that wants once and for all to be free of the dirty little secret.

And the way to do it is, first, to fight the sentimental lie of purity and the dirty little secret wherever you meet it, inside yourself or in the world outside. Fight the great lie of the nineteenth century, which has soaked through our sex and our bones. It means fighting with almost every breath, for the lie is ubiquitous.

Then secondly, in his adventure of self-consciousness a man must come to the limits of himself and become aware of something beyond him. A man must be self-conscious enough to know his own limits, and to be aware of that which surpasses him. What surpasses me is the very urge of life that is within me, and this life urges me to forget myself and to yield to the stirring half-born impulse to smash up the vast lie of the world, and make a new world. If my life is merely to go on in a vicious circle of self-enclosure, masturbating self-consciousness, it is worth nothing to me. If my individual life is to be enclosed within the huge corrupt lie of society today, purity and the dirty little secret, then it is worth not much to me. Freedom is a very great reality. But it means, above all things, freedom from lies. It is first, freedom from myself, from the lie of myself, from the lie of my all-importance, even to myself; it is freedom from the self-conscious masturbating thing I am, self-enclosed. And second, freedom from the vast lie of the social world, the lie of purity and the dirty little secret. All the other monstrous lies lurk under the cloak of this one primary lie. The monstrous lie of money lurks under the cloak of purity. Kill the purity-lie, and the money-lie will be defenceless.

We have to be sufficiently conscious, and self-conscious, to know our own limits and to be aware of the greater urge within us and beyond us. Then we cease to be primarily interested in ourselves. Then we learn to leave ourselves alone, in all the affective centres: not to force our feelings in any way, and never to force our sex. Then we make the great onslaught on to the outside lie, the inside lie being settled. And that is freedom and the fight for freedom.

The greatest of all lies in the modern world is the lie of purity and the dirty little secret. The grey ones left over from the nineteenth century are the embodiment of this lie. They dominate in society, in the press, in literature, everywhere. And, naturally, they lead the vast mob of the general public along with them.

Which means, of course, perpetual censorship of anything that would militate against the lie of purity and the dirty little secret, and perpetual encouragement of what may be called permissible pornography, pure, but tickling the dirty little secret under the delicate underclothing. The grey ones will pass and will commend floods of evasive pornography, and will suppress every outspoken word.

The law is a mere figment. In his article on the 'Censorship of Books,' in the *Nineteenth Century,* Viscount Brentford, the late Home Secretary, says: 'Let it be remembered that the publishing of an obscene book, the issue of an obscene post-card or pornographic photograph – are all offences against the law of the land, and the Secretary of State who is the general authority for the maintenance of law and order most clearly and definitely cannot discriminate between one offence and another in discharge of his duty.'

So he winds up, *ex cathedra* and infallible. But only ten lines above he has written: 'I agree, that if the law were pushed to its logical conclusion, the printing and publication of such books as *The Decameron*, Benvenuto Cellini's *Life*, and Burton's *Arabian Nights* might form the subject of proceedings. But the ultimate sanction of all law is public opinion, and I do not believe for one moment that prosecution in respect of books that have been in circulation for many centuries would command public support.'

Ooray then for public opinion! It only needs that a few more years shall roll. But now we see that the Secretary of State most clearly and definitely *does* discriminate between one offence and another in discharge of his duty. Simple and admitted discrimination on his part! Yet what is this public opinion? Just more lies on the part of the grey ones. They would suppress Benvenuto tomorrow, if they dared. But they would make laughing-stocks of themselves, because *tradition* backs up Benvenuto. It isn't public opinion at all. It is the grey ones afraid of making still bigger fools of themselves. But the case is simple. If the grey ones are going to be backed by a general public, then every new book that would smash the mealy-mouthed lie of the nineteenth century will be suppressed as it appears. Yet let the grey ones beware. The general public is nowadays a very unstable affair, and no longer loves its grey ones so dearly, with their old lie. And there is another public, the small public of the minority, which hates the lie and the grey ones that perpetuate the lie, and which has its own dynamic ideas about pornography and obscenity. You can't fool all the people all the time, even with purity and a dirty little secret.

And this minority public knows well that the books of many contemporary writers, both big and lesser fry, are far more pornographical than the liveliest story in *The Decameron:* because they tickle the dirty little secret and excite to private masturbation, which the wholesome Boccaccio never does. And the minority public knows full well that the most obscene painting on a Greek vase – *Thou still unravished bride of quietness* – is not as pornographical as the close-up kisses on the film, which excite men and women to secret and separate masturbation.

And perhaps one day even the general public will desire to look the thing in the face, and see for itself the difference between the sneaking masturbation pornography of the press, the film, and present-day popular literature, and then the creative portrayals of the sexual impulse that we have in Boccaccio or the Greek vase-paintings or some Pompeian art, and which are necessary for the fulfilment of our consciousness.

As it is, the public mind is today bewildered on this point, bewildered almost to idiocy. When the police raided my picture show, they did not in the least know what to take. So they took every picture where the smallest bit of the sex organ of either man or woman showed. Quite regardless of subject or meaning or anything else: they would allow anything, these dainty policemen in a picture show, except the actual sight of a fragment of the human *pudenda*. This was the police test. The dabbing on of a postage stamp – especially a green one that could be called a leaf – would in most cases have been quite sufficient to satisfy this 'public opinion.'

It is, we can only repeat, a condition of idiocy. And if the purity-with-a-dirty-little-secret lie is kept up much longer, the mass of society will really be an idiot, and a dangerous idiot at that. For the public is made up of individuals. And each individual has sex, and is pivoted on sex. And if, with purity and dirty little secrets, you drive every individual into the masturbation self-enclosure, and keep him there, then you will produce a state of general idiocy. For the masturbation self-enclosure produces idiots. Perhaps if we are all idiots, we shan't know it. But God preserve us.

THE RISEN LORD (1929)

> The risen lord, the risen lord
> has risen in the flesh,
> and treads the earth to feel the soil
> though his feet are still nesh.

The Churches loudly assert: We preach Christ crucified! – But in so doing, they preach only half of the Passion, and do only half their duty. The Creed says: 'Was crucified, dead, and buried . . . the third day He rose again from the dead.' And again, 'I believe in the resurrection of the body . . .' So that to preach Christ Crucified is to preach half the truth. It is the business of the Church to preach Christ born among men – which is Christmas; Christ crucified, which is Good Friday; and Christ Risen, which is Easter. And after Easter, till November and All Saints, and till Annunciation, the year belongs to the Risen Lord: that is, all the full-flowering spring, all summer, and the autumn of wheat and fruit, all belong to Christ Risen.

But the Churches insist on Christ Crucified, and rob us of the blossom and fruit of the year. The Catholic Church, which has given us our images, has given us the Christ-child, in the lap of woman, and again, Christ Crucified: then the Mass, the mystery of atonement through sacrifice. Yet all this is really preparatory, these are the preparatory stages of the real living religion. The Christ-child, enthroned in the lap of the Mother, is obviously only a preparatory image, to prepare us for Christ the Man. Yet a vast mass of Christians stick there.

What we have to remember is that the great religious images are only images of our own experiences, or of our own state of mind and soul. In the Catholic countries, where the Madonna-and-Child image overwhelms everything else, the man visions himself all the time as a child, a Christ-child, standing on the lap of a virgin mother. Before the war, if an Italian hurt himself, or suddenly fell into distress, his immediate cry was: *O mamma mia! mamma mia! – Oh, mother, mother! –* The same was true of many Englishmen. And what does this mean? It means that the man sees himself as a child, the innocent saviour-child enthroned on the lap of the all-pitying virgin mother. He lives according to this image of himself – the image of the guileless 'good' child sheltered in the arms of an all-sheltering mother – until the image breaks in his heart.

And during the war, this image broke in the hearts of most men, though not in the hearts of their women. During the war, the man who suffered most bitterly suffered beyond the help of wife or mother, and no wife nor mother nor sister nor any beloved could save him from the guns. This fact went home in his heart, and broke the image of mother and Christ-child, and left in its place the image of Christ crucified.

It was not so, of course, for the woman. The image did not break for her. She visioned herself still as the all-pitying, all-sheltering Madonna, on whose lap the man was enthroned, as in the old pictures, like a Christ-child. And naturally the woman did not want to abandon this vision of herself. It gave her her greatest significance; and the greatest power. Break the image, and her significance and her power were gone. But the men came back from the war and denied the image – for them it was broken. So she fought to maintain it, the great vision of man, the Christ-child, enthroned in the lap of the all-pitying virginal woman. And she fought in vain, though not without disastrous result.

For the vision of the all-pitying and all-helpful Madonna was shattered in the hearts of men, during the war. The all-pitying and all-helpful Woman actually did not, whether she could or not, prevent the guns from blowing to pieces the men who called upon her. So her image collapsed, and with it the image of the Christ-child. For the man who went through the war the resultant image inevitably was Christ Crucified, Christ tortured on the Cross. And Christ Crucified is essentially womanless.

True, many of the elderly men who never went through the war still insist on the Christ-child business, and most of the elderly women insist on their benevolent Madonna supremacy. But it is in vain. The guns broke the image in the hearts of middle-aged men, and the young were born, or are come to real consciousness, after the image was already smashed.

So there we are! We have three great image-divisions among men and women today. We have the old and the elderly, who never were exposed to the guns, still fatuously maintaining that man is the Christ-child and woman the infallible safeguard from all evil and all danger. It is fatuous, because it absolutely didn't work. Then we have the men of middle age, who were all tortured and virtually put to death by the war. They accept Christ Crucified as their image, are essentially womanless, and take the great cry: *Consummatum est! – It is finished!* – as their last word. – Thirdly, we have the young, who never went through the war. They have no illusions about it, however, and the death-cry of their elder generation: *It is finished!* rings cold through their blood. They cannot answer. They cannot even scoff. It is no joke, and never will be a joke.

And yet, neither of the great images is *their* image. They cannot accept the child-and-mother position which the old buffers still pose in. They cannot accept the Christ Crucified finality of the generations immediately ahead. For they, the young, came into the field of life after the death-cry *Consummatum est!* had rung through the world, and while the body, so to speak, was being put into the tomb. By the time the young came on to the stage, Calvary was empty, the tombs were closed, the women had lost for ever the Christ-child and the virgin savour, and it was altogether the day after, cold, bleak, empty, blank, meaningless, almost silly.

The young came into life, and found everything finished. Everywhere the empty crosses, everywhere the closed tombs, everywhere the manless, bitter or over-assertive woman, everywhere the closed grey disillusion of Christ Crucified, dead, and buried, those grey empty days between Good Friday and Easter.

And the Churches, instead of preaching the Risen Lord, go on preaching the Christ-child and Christ Crucified. Now man cannot live without some vision of himself. But still less can he live with a vision that is not true to his inner experience and inner feeling. And the vision of Christ-child and Christ Crucified are both untrue to the inner experience and feeling of the young. They don't feel that way. They show the greatest forbearance and tolerance of their elders, for whom the two images *are* livingly true. But for the post war young, neither the Christ-child nor Christ Crucified means much.

I doubt whether the Protestant Churches, which supported the war, will ever have the faith and the power of life to take the great step onwards, and preach Christ Risen. The Catholic Church might. In the countries of the Mediterranean, Easter has always been the greatest of the holy days, the gladdest and holiest, not Christmas, the birth of the Child. Easter, Christ Risen, the Risen Lord, this, to the old faith, is still the first day in the year. The Easter festivities are the most joyful, the Easter processions the finest, the Easter ceremonies the most splendid. In Sicily the women take into church the saucers of growing corn, the green blades rising tender and slim like green light, in little pools, filling round the altar. It is Adonis. It is the re-born year. It is Christ Risen. It is the Risen Lord. And in the warm south still a great joy floods the hearts of the people on Easter Sunday. They feel it, they feel it everywhere. The Lord is risen. The Lord of the rising wheat and the plum blossoms is warm and kind upon earth again, after having been done to death by the evil and the jealous ones.

The Roman Catholic Church may still unfold this part of the Passion fully, and make men happy again. For Resurrection is indeed the consummation of all the passion. Not even Atonement, the being at one with Christ through partaking in His sacrifice, consummates the Passion finally. For even after Atonement men still must live, and must go forward with the vision. After we share in the body of Christ, we rise with Him in the body. And that is the final vision that has been blurred to all the Churches.

Christ risen in the flesh! We must accept the image complete, if we accept it at all. We must take the mystery in its fulness and in fact. It is only the image of our own experience. Christ rises, when He rises from the dead, in the flesh, not merely as spirit. He rises with hands and feet, as Thomas knew for certain: and if with hands and feet, then with lips and stomach and genitals of a man. Christ risen, and risen in the whole of His flesh, not with some left out.

Christ risen in the full flesh! What for? It is here the gospels are all vague and faltering, and the Churches leave us in the lurch. Christ risen in the flesh in order to lurk obscurely for six weeks on earth, then be taken vaguely up into heaven in a cloud? Flesh, solid flesh, feet and bowels and teeth and eyes of a man, taken up into heaven in a cloud, and never put down again?

It is the only part of the great mystery which is all wrong.

The virgin birth, the baptism, the temptation, the teaching, Gethsemane, the betrayal, the crucifixion, the burial and the resurrection, these are all true according to our inward experience. They are what men and women go through, in their different ways. But floated up into heaven as flesh-and-blood, and never set down again – this nothing in all our experience will ever confirm. If aeroplanes take us up, they bring us down, or let us down. Flesh and blood belong to the earth, and only to the earth. We know it.

And Jesus was risen flesh-and-blood. He rose a man on earth to live on earth. The greatest test was still before Him: His life as a man on earth. Hitherto He had been a sacred child, a teacher, a messiah, but never a full man. Now, risen from the dead, He rises to be a man on earth, and live His life of the flesh, the great life, among other men. This is the image of our inward state today.

This is the image of the young: the Risen Lord. The teaching is over, the crucifixion is over, the sacrifice is made, the salvation is accomplished. Now comes the true life, man living his full life on earth, as flowers live their full life, without rhyme or reason except the magnificence of coming forth into fulness.

If Jesus rose from the dead in triumph, a man on earth triumphant in renewed flesh, triumphant over the mechanical anti-life convention of Jewish priests, Roman despotism, and universal money-lust; triumphant above all over His own self-absorption, self-consciousness, self-importance; triumphant and free as a man in full flesh and full, final experience, even the accomplished acceptance of His own death; a man at last full and free in flesh and soul, a man at one with death: then He rose to become at one with life, to live the great life of the flesh and the soul together, as peonies or foxes do, in their lesser way. If Jesus rose as a full man, in full flesh and soul, then He rose to take a woman to Himself, to live with her, and to know the tenderness

and blossoming of the twoness with her; He who had been hitherto so limited to His oneness, or His universality, which is the
same thing. If Jesus rose in the full flesh, He rose to know the
tenderness of a woman, and the great pleasure of her, and to
have children by her. He rose to know the responsibility and the
peculiar delight of children, and also the exasperation and nuisance of them. If Jesus rose as a full man, in the flesh, He rose to
have friends, to have a man-friend whom He would hold sometimes to His breast, in strong affection, and who would be
dearer to Him than a brother, just out of the sheer mystery of
sympathy. And how much more wonderful, this, than having
disciples! If Jesus rose a full man in the flesh, He rose to do His
share in the world's work, something He really liked doing. And
if He remembered His first life, it would neither be teaching
nor preaching, but probably carpentering again, with joy,
among the shavings. If Jesus rose a full man in the flesh, He rose
to continue His fight with the hard-boiled conventionalists like
Roman judges and Jewish priests and money-makers of every
sort. But this time, it would no longer be the fight of self-sacrifice
that would end in crucifixion. This time it would be a freed man
fighting to shelter the rose of life from being trampled on by the
pigs. This time, if Satan attempted temptation in the wilderness,
the Risen Lord would answer: Satan, your silly temptations
no longer tempt me. Luckily, I have died to that sort of self-
importance and self-conceit. But let me tell you something, old
man! Your name's Satan, isn't it? And your name is Mammon?
You are the selfish hog that's got hold of all the world, aren't
you? Well, look here, my boy, I'm going to take it all from you,
so don't worry. The world and the power and the riches thereof,
I'm going to take them all from you, Satan or Mammon or whatever your name is. Because you don't know how to use them.
The earth is the Lord's, and the fulness thereof, and it's going to
be. Men have risen from the dead and learned not to be so

greedy and self-important. We left most of that behind in the late tomb. Men have risen beyond you, Mammon, they are your risen lords. And so, you hook-nosed, glisten-eyed, ugly, money-smelling anachronism, you've got to get out. Men have not died and risen again for nothing. Whom do you think the earth belongs to, you stale old rat? The earth is the Lord's and is given to the men who have died and had the power to rise again. The earth is given to the men who have risen from the dead, risen, you old grabber, and when did you ever rise? Never! So go you down to oblivion, and give your place to the risen men, and the women of the risen men. For man has been dispossessed of the full earth and the earth's fulness long enough. And the poor women, they have been shoved about manless and meaningless long enough. The earth is the Lord's and the fulness thereof, and I, the Risen Lord, am here to take possession. For now I am fully a man, and free above all from my own self-importance. I want life, and the pure contact with life. What are riches, and glory, and honour, and might, and power, to me who have died and lost my self-importance? That's why I am going to take them all from you, Mammon, because I care nothing about them. I am going to destroy all your values, Mammon; all your money values and conceit values, I am going to destroy them all.

Because only life is lovely, and you, Mammon, prevent life. I love to see a squirrel peep round a tree; and left to you, Mammon, there will soon be no squirrels to peep. I love to hear a man singing a song to himself, and if it is an old, improper song, about the fun between lads and girls, I like it all the better. But you, beastly mealy-mouthed Mammon, you would arrest any lad that sings a gay song. I love the movement of life, and the beauty of life, O Mammon, since I am risen, I love the beauty of life intensely; columbine flowers, for example, the way they dangle, or the delicate way a young girl sits and wonders, or the rage with which a man turns and kicks a fool dog that suddenly attacks him – beautiful that, the swift fierce turn and lunge of a kick, then the quivering pause for the next attack; or even the slightly silly glow that comes over some men as they are getting tipsy – it still is a glow, beautiful; or the swift look a woman fetches me, when she would really like me to go off with her, but she is troubled; or the real compassion I saw a woman express for a man who slipped and wrenched his foot: life, the beauty, the beauty of life! But that which is anti-life, Mammon, like you, and money, and machines, and prostitution, and all that tangled mass of self-importance and greediness and self-conscious conceit which adds up to Mammon, I hate it. I hate it, Mammon, I hate you and am going to push you off the face of the earth, Mammon, you great mob-thing, fatal to men.

NOTTINGHAM AND THE MINING
COUNTRYSIDE (1929)

I was born nearly forty-four years ago, in Eastwood, a mining
village of some three thousand souls, about eight miles from
Nottingham, and one mile from the small stream, the Erewash,
which divides Nottinghamshire from Derbyshire. It is hilly
country, looking west to Crich and towards Matlock, sixteen
miles away, and east and north-east towards Mansfield and the
Sherwood Forest district. To me it seemed, and still seems, an
extremely beautiful countryside, just between the red sand-
stone and the oak-trees of Nottingham, and the cold limestone,
the ash-trees, the stone fences of Derbyshire. To me, as a child
and a young man, it was still the old England of the forest and
agricultural past; there were no motor-cars, the mines were, in
a sense, an accident in the landscape, and Robin Hood and his
merry men were not very far away.

The string of coal-mines of B.W. & Co. had been opened some
sixty years before I was born, and Eastwood had come into being
as a consequence. It must have been a tiny village at the beginning of the nineteenth century, a small place of cottages and
fragmentary rows of little four-roomed miners' dwellings, the
homes of the old colliers of the eighteenth century, who worked
in the bits of mines, foot-rill mines with an opening in the hillside into which the miners walked, or windlass mines, where the
men were wound up one at a time, in a bucket, by a donkey. The

windlass mines were still working when my father was a boy – and the shafts of some were still there, when I was a boy.

But somewhere about 1820 the company must have sunk the first big shaft – not very deep – and installed the first machinery of the real industrial colliery. Then came my grandfather, a young man trained to be a tailor, drifting from the south of England, and got the job of company tailor for the Brinsley mine. In those days the company supplied the men with the thick flannel vests, or singlets, and the moleskin trousers lined at the top with flannel, in which the colliers worked. I remember the great rolls of coarse flannel and pit-cloth which stood in the corner of my grandfather's shop when I was a small boy, and the big, strange old sewing-machine, like nothing else on earth, which sewed the massive pit-trousers. But when I was only a child the company discontinued supplying the men with pit-clothes.

My grandfather settled in an old cottage down in a quarry-bed, by the brook at Old Brinsley, near the pit. A mile away, up at Eastwood, the company built the first miners' dwellings – it must be nearly a hundred years ago. Now Eastwood occupies a lovely position on a hilltop, with the steep slope towards Derbyshire and the long slope towards Nottingham. They put up a new church, which stands fine and commanding, even if it has no real form, looking across the awful Erewash Valley at the church of Heanor, similarly commanding, away on a hill beyond. What opportunities, what opportunities! These mining villages *might* have been like the lovely hill-towns of Italy, shapely and fascinating. And what happened?

Most of the little rows of dwellings of the old-style miners were pulled down, and dull little shops began to rise along the Nottingham Road, while on the down-slope of the north side the company erected what is still known as the New Buildings, or the Square. These New Buildings consist of two great hollow squares of dwellings planked down on the rough slope of the hill, little four-room houses with the 'front' looking outward into the grim, blank street, and the 'back,' with a tiny square brick yard, a low wall, and a w.c. and ash-pit, looking into the desert of the square, hard, uneven, jolting black earth tilting rather steeply down, with these little back yards all round, and openings at the corners. The squares were quite big, and absolutely desert, save for the posts for clothes lines, and people passing, children playing on the hard earth. And they were shut in like a barracks enclosure, very strange.

Even fifty years ago the squares were unpopular. It was 'common' to live in the Square. It was a little less common to live in the Breach, which consisted of six blocks of rather more pretentious dwellings erected by the company in the valley below, two rows of three blocks, with an alley between. And it was most 'common,' most degraded of all to live in Dakins Row, two rows of the old dwellings, very old, black, four-roomed little places, that stood on the hill again, not far from the Square.

So the place started. Down the steep street between the squares, Scargill Street, the Wesleyans' chapel was put up, and I was born in the little corner shop just above. Across the other side the Square the miners themselves built the big, barn-like Primitive Methodist chapel. Along the hill-top ran the Nottingham Road, with its scrappy, ugly mid-Victorian shops. The little market-place, with a superb outlook, ended the village on the Derbyshire side, and was just left bare, with the Sun Inn on one side, the chemist across, with the gilt pestle-and-mortar, and a shop at the other corner, the corner of Alfreton Road and Nottingham Road.

In this queer jumble of the old England and the new, I came into consciousness. As I remember, little local speculators already began to straggle dwellings in rows, always in rows, across the fields: nasty red-brick, flat-faced dwellings with dark slate roofs. The bay-window period only began when I was a child. But most of the country was untouched.

There must be three or four hundred company houses in the squares and the streets that surround the squares, like a great barracks wall. There must be sixty or eighty company houses in the Breach. The old Dakins Row will have thirty to forty little holes. Then counting the old cottages and rows left with their old gardens down the lanes and along the twitchells, and even in the midst of Nottingham Road itself, there were houses enough for the population, there was no need for much building. And not much building went on when I was small.

We lived in the Breach, in a corner house. A field-path came down under a great hawthorn hedge. On the other side was the brook, with the old sheep-bridge going over into the meadows. The hawthorn hedge by the brook had grown tall as tall trees, and we used to bathe from there in the dipping-hole, where the sheep were dipped, just near the fall from the old mill-dam, where the water rushed. The mill only ceased grinding the local corn when I was a child. And my father, who always worked in Brinsley pit, and who always got up at five o'clock, if not at four, would set off in the dawn across the fields at Coney Grey, and hunt for mushrooms in the long grass, or perhaps pick up a skulking rabbit, which he would bring home at evening inside the lining of his pit-coat.

So that the life was a curious cross between industrialism and the old agricultural England of Shakespeare and Milton and Fielding and George Eliot. The dialect was broad Derbyshire, and always 'thee' and 'thou.' The people lived almost entirely by instinct, men of my father's age could not really read. And the pit did not mechanize men. On the contrary. Under the butty system, the miners worked underground as a sort of intimate community, they knew each other practically naked, and with curious close intimacy, and the darkness and the underground remoteness of the pit 'stall,' and the continual presence of danger, made the physical, instinctive, and intuitional contact between men very highly developed, a contact almost as close as touch, very real and very powerful. This physical awareness and intimate *togetherness* was at its strongest down pit. When the men came up into the light, they blinked. They had, in a measure, to change their flow. Nevertheless, they brought with them above ground the curious dark intimacy of the mine, the naked sort of contact, and if I think of my childhood, it is always as if there was a lustrous sort of inner darkness, like the gloss of coal, in which we moved and had our real being. My father loved the pit. He was hurt badly, more than once, but he would never stay away. He loved the contact, the intimacy, as men in the war loved the intense male comradeship of the dark days. They did not know what they had lost till they lost it. And I think it is the same with the young colliers of today.

Now the colliers had also an instinct of beauty. The colliers' wives had not. The colliers were deeply alive, instinctively. But they had no daytime ambition, and no daytime intellect. They avoided, really, the rational aspect of life. They preferred to take life instinctively and intuitively. They didn't even care very profoundly about wages. It was the women, naturally, who nagged on this score. There was a big discrepancy, when I was a boy, between the collier who saw, at the best, only a brief few hours of daylight – often no daylight at all during the winter weeks – and the collier's wife, who had all the day to herself when the man was down pit.

The great fallacy is, to pity the man. He didn't dream of pitying himself, till agitators and sentimentalists taught him to. He was happy: or more than happy, he was fulfilled. Or he was fulfilled on the receptive side, not on the expressive. The collier went to the pub and drank in order to continue his intimacy with his mates. They talked endlessly, but it was rather of wonders and marvels, even in politics, than of facts. It was hard facts, in the shape of wife, money, and nagging home necessities, which they fled away from, out of the house to the pub, and out of the house to the pit.

The collier fled out of the house as soon as he could, away from the nagging materialism of the woman. With the women it was always: This is broken, now you've got to mend it! or else: We want this, that and the other, and where is the money coming from? The collier didn't know and didn't care very deeply – his life was otherwise. So he escaped. He roved the countryside with his dog, prowling for a rabbit, for nests, for mushrooms, anything. He loved the countryside, just the indiscriminating feel of it. Or he loved just to sit on his heels and watch – anything or nothing. He was not intellectually interested. Life for him did not consist in facts, but in a flow. Very often, he loved his garden. And very often he had a genuine love of the beauty of flowers. I have known it often and often, in colliers.

Now the love of flowers is a very misleading thing. Most women love flowers as possessions, and as trimmings. They can't look at a flower, and wonder a moment, and pass on. If they see a flower that arrests their attention, they must at once pick it, pluck it. Possession! A possession! Something added on to *me*! And most of the so-called love of flowers today is merely this reaching out of possession and egoism: something I've *got*: something that embellishes *me*. Yet I've seen many a collier stand in his back garden looking down at a flower with that odd, remote sort of contemplation which shows a *real* awareness of the presence of beauty. It would not even be admiration, or joy, or delight, or any of those things which so often have a root in the possessive instinct. It would be a sort of contemplation: which shows the incipient artist.

The real tragedy of England, as I see it, is the tragedy of ugliness. The country is so lovely: the man-made England is so vile. I know that the ordinary collier, when I was a boy, had a peculiar sense of beauty, coming from his intuitive and instinctive consciousness, which was awakened down pit. And the fact that he met with just cold ugliness and raw materialism when he came up into daylight, and particularly when he came to the Square or the Breach, and to his own table, killed something in him, and in a sense spoiled him as a man. The woman almost invariably nagged about material things. She was taught to do it; she was encouraged to do it. It was a mother's business to see that her sons 'got on,' and it was the man's business to provide the money. In my father's generation, with the old wild England behind them, and the lack of education, the man was not beaten down. But in my generation, the boys I went to school with, colliers now, have all been beaten down, what with the din-din-dinning of Board Schools, books, cinemas, clergymen, the whole national and human consciousness hammering on the fact of material prosperity above all things.

The men are beaten down, there is prosperity for a time, in their defeat – and then disaster looms ahead. The root of all disaster is disheartenment. And men are disheartened. The men of England, the colliers in particular, are disheartened. They have been betrayed and beaten.

Now though perhaps nobody knew it, it was ugliness which really betrayed the spirit of man, in the nineteenth century. The great crime which the moneyed classes and promoters of industry committed in the palmy Victorian days was the condemning of the workers to ugliness, ugliness, ugliness: meanness and formless and ugly surroundings, ugly ideals, ugly religion, ugly hope, ugly love, ugly clothes, ugly furniture, ugly houses, ugly relationship between workers and employers. The human soul needs actual beauty even more than bread. The middle classes jeer at the colliers for buying pianos – but what is the piano, often as not, but a blind reaching out for beauty. To the woman it is a possession and a piece of furniture and something to feel superior about. But see the elderly colliers trying to learn to play, see them listening with queer alert faces to their daughter's execution of *The Maiden's Prayer*, and you will see a blind, unsatisfied craving for beauty. It is far more deep in the men than the women. The women want show. The men want beauty, and still want it.

If the company, instead of building those sordid and hideous Squares, then, when they had that lovely site to play with, there on the hill top: if they had put a tall column in the middle of the small market-place, and run three parts of a circle of arcade round the pleasant space, where people could stroll or sit, and with handsome houses behind! If they had made big, substantial houses, in apartments of five or six rooms, and with handsome entrances. If above all, they had encouraged song and dancing – for the miners still sang and danced – and provided handsome space for these. If only they had encouraged some form of beauty in dress, some form of beauty in interior life – furniture, decoration. If they had given prizes for the handsomest chair or table, the loveliest scarf, the most charming room that the men or women could make! If only they had done this, there would never have been an industrial problem. The industrial problem arises from the base forcing of all human energy into a competition of mere acquisition.

You may say the working man would not have accepted such a form of life: the Englishman's home is his castle, etc., etc. – 'my own little home.' But if you can hear every word the next-door people say, there's not much castle. And if you can see everybody in the square if they go to the w.c.! And if your one desire is to get out of your 'castle' and your 'own little home'! – well, there's not much to be said for it. Anyhow, it's only the woman who idolizes 'her own little home' – and it's always the woman at her worst, her most greedy, most possessive, most mean. There's nothing to be said for the 'little home' any more: a great scrabble of ugly pettiness over the face of the land.

As a matter of fact, till 1800 the English people were strictly a rural people – very rural. England has had towns for centuries, but they have never been real towns, only clusters of village streets. Never the real *urbs*. The English character has failed to develop the real *urban* side of a man, the civic side. Siena is a bit of a place, but it is a real city, with citizens intimately connected with the city. Nottingham is a vast place sprawling towards a million, and it is nothing more than an amorphous agglomeration. There *is* no Nottingham, in the sense that there is Siena. The Englishman is stupidly undeveloped, as a citizen. And it is partly due to his 'little home' stunt, and partly to his acceptance of hopeless paltriness in his surrounding. The new cities of America are much more genuine cities, in the Roman sense, than is London or Manchester. Even Edinburgh used to be more of a true city than any town England ever produced.

That silly little individualism of 'the Englishman's home is his castle' and 'my own little home' is out of date. It would work almost up to 1800, when every Englishman was still a villager, and a cottager. But the industrial system has brought a great change. The Englishman still likes to think of himself as a 'cottager' – 'my home, my garden.' But it is puerile. Even the farm-labourer today is psychologically a town-bird. The English are town-birds through and through, today, as the inevitable result of their complete industrialization. Yet they don't know how to build a city, how to think of one, or how to live in one. They are all suburban, pseudo-cottagy, and not one of them knows how to be truly urban – the citizen as the Romans were citizens – or the Athenians – or even the Parisians, till the war came.

And this is because we have frustrated that instinct of community which would make us unite in pride and dignity in the bigger gesture of the citizen, not the cottager. The great city means beauty, dignity, and a certain splendour. This is the side of the Englishman that has been thwarted and shockingly betrayed. England is a mean and petty scrabble of paltry dwellings called 'homes.'

I believe in their heart of hearts all Englishmen loathe their little homes – but not the women. What we want is a bigger gesture, a greater scope, a certain splendour, a certain grandeur, and beauty, big beauty. The American does far better than we, in this.

And the promoter of industry, a hundred years ago, dared to perpetrate the ugliness of my native village. And still more monstrous, promoters of industry today are scrabbling over the face of England with miles and square miles of red-brick 'homes,' like horrible scabs. And the men inside these little red rat-traps get more and more helpless, being more and more humiliated, more and more dissatisfied, liked trapped rats. Only the meaner sort of women go on loving the little home which is no more than a rat-trap to her man.

Do away with it all, then. At no matter what cost, start in to alter it. Never mind about wages and industrial squabbling. Turn the attention elsewhere. Pull down my native village to the last brick. Plan a nucleus. Fix the focus. Make a handsome gesture of radiation from the focus. And then put up big buildings, handsome, that sweep to a civic centre. And furnish them with beauty. And make an absolute clean start. Do it place by place. Make a new England. Away with little homes! Away with scrabbling pettiness and paltriness. Look at the contours of the land, and build up from these, with a sufficient nobility. The English may be mentally or spiritually developed. But as citizens of splendid cities they are more ignominious than rabbits. And they nag, nag, nag all the time about politics and wages and all that, like mean narrow housewives.

INTRODUCTION TO *THE GRAND INQUISITOR* BY F.M. DOSTOIEVSKY (1930)

It is a strange experience, to examine one's reaction to a book over a period of years. I remember when I first read *The Brothers Karamazov*, in 1913, how fascinated yet unconvinced it left me. And I remember Middleton Murry* saying to me: 'Of course the whole clue to Dostoievsky is in that Grand Inquisitor story.' And I remember saying: 'Why? It seems to me just rubbish.'

And it was true. The story seemed to me just a piece of showing off: a display of cynical-satanical pose which was simply irritating. The cynical-satanical pose always irritated me, and I could see nothing else in that black-a-vised Grand Inquisitor talking at Jesus at such length. I just felt it was all pose; he didn't really mean what he said; he was just showing off in blasphemy.

Since then I have read *The Brothers Karamazov* twice, and each time found it more depressing because, alas, more drearily true to life. At first it had been lurid romance. Now I read *The Grand Inquisitor* once more, and my heart sinks right through my shoes. I still see a trifle of cynical-satanical showing-off. But under that I hear the final and unanswerable criticism of Christ. And it is a deadly, devastating summing-up, unanswerable because borne

---

* Before this preface was published in *The Grand Inquisitor* the name of Katherine Mansfield was substituted for that of Middleton Murry.

out by the long experience of humanity. It is reality versus illusion, and the illusion was Jesus', while time itself retorts with the reality.

If there is any question: Who is the grand Inquisitor? – then surely we must say it is Ivan himself. And Ivan is the thinking mind of the human being in rebellion, thinking the whole thing out to the bitter end. As such he is, of course, identical with the Russian revolutionary of the thinking type. He is also, of course, Dostoievsky himself, in his thoughtful, as apart from his passional and inspirational self. Dostoievsky half hated Ivan. Yet, after all, Ivan is the greatest of the three brothers, pivotal. The passionate Dmitri and the inspired Alyosha are, at last, only offsets to Ivan.

And we cannot doubt that the Inquisitor speaks Dostoievsky's own final opinion about Jesus. The opinion is, baldly, this: Jesus, you are inadequate. Men must correct you. And Jesus in the end gives the kiss of acquiescence to the Inquisitor, as Alyosha does to Ivan. The two inspired ones recognize the inadequacy of their inspiration: the thoughtful one has to accept the responsibility of a complete adjustment.

We may agree with Dostoievsky or not, but we have to admit that his criticism of Jesus is the final criticism, based on the experience of two thousand years (he says fifteen hundred) and on a profound insight into the nature of mankind. Man can but be true to his own nature. No inspiration whatsoever will ever get him permanently beyond his limits.

And what are the limits? It is Dostoievsky's first profound question. What are the limits to the nature, not of Man in the abstract, but of men, mere men, everyday men?

The limits are, says the Grand Inquisitor, three. Mankind in the bulk can never be 'free,' because man on the whole makes three grand demands on life, and cannot endure unless these demands are satisfied.

1. He demands bread, and not merely as foodstuff, but as a miracle, given from the hand of God.
2. He demands mystery, the sense of the miraculous in life.
3. He demands somebody to bow down to, and somebody before whom all men shall bow down.

These three demands, for miracle, mystery and authority, prevent men from being 'free.' They are man's 'weakness.' Only a few men, the elect, are capable of abstaining from the absolute demand for bread, for miracle, mystery, and authority. These are the strong, and they must be as gods, to be able to be Christians fulfilling all the Christ-demand. The rest, the millions and millions of men throughout time, they are as babes or children or geese, they are too weak, 'impotent, vicious, worthless and rebellious' even to be able to share out the earthly bread, if it is left to them.

This, then, is the Grand Inquisitor's summing-up of the nature of mankind. The inadequacy of Jesus lies in the fact that Christianity is too difficult for men, the vast mass of men. It could only be realized by the few 'saints' or heroes. For the rest, man is like a horse harnessed to a load he cannot possibly pull. 'Hadst Thou respected him less, Thou wouldst have demanded less of him, and that would be nearer to love, for his burden would be lighter.'

Christianity, then, is the ideal, but it is impossible. It is impossible because it makes demands greater than the nature of man can bear. And therefore, to get a livable, working scheme, some of the elect, such as the Grand Inquisitor himself, have turned round to 'him,' that other great Spirit, Satan, and have established Church and State on 'him.' For the Grand Inquisitor finds that to be able to live at all, mankind must be loved more tolerantly and more contemptuously than Jesus loved it, loved, for all that, more truly, since it is loved for itself, for what it is, and not for what it ought to be. Jesus loved mankind for what it ought to be, free and limitless. The Grand Inquisitor loves it for what it is, with all its limitations. And he contends his is the kinder love. And yet he says it is Satan. And Satan, he says at the beginning, means annihilation, and not-being.

As always in Dostoievsky, the amazing perspicacity is mixed with ugly perversity. Nothing is pure. His wild love for Jesus is mixed with perverse and poisonous hate of Jesus: his moral hostility to the devil is mixed with secret worship of the devil. Dostoievsky is always perverse, always impure, always an evil thinker and a marvellous seer.

Is it true that mankind demands, and will always demand, miracle, mystery, and authority? Surely it is true. Today, man gets his sense of the miraculous from science and machinery, radio, aeroplane, vast ships, zeppelins, poison gas, artificial silk: these things nourish man's sense of the miraculous as magic did in the past. But now, man is master of the mystery, there are no occult powers. The same with mystery: medicine, biological experiment, strange feats of the psychic people, spiritualists, Christian scientists – it is all mystery. And as for authority, Russia destroyed the Tsar to have Lenin and the present mechanical despotism, Italy has the rationalized despotism of Mussolini, and England is longing for a despot.

Dostoievsky's diagnosis of human nature is simple and unanswerable. We have to submit, and agree that men are like that. Even over the question of sharing the bread, we have to agree that man is too weak, or vicious, or something, to be able to do it. He has to hand the common bread over to some absolute authority, Tsar or Lenin, to be shared out. And yet the mass of men are *incapable* of looking on bread as a mere means of sustenance, by which man sustains himself for the purpose of true living, true life being the 'heavenly bread.' It seems a strange thing that men, the mass of men, cannot understand that *life* is the great reality, that true living fills us with vivid life, 'the heavenly bread,' and earthly bread merely supports this. No, men cannot understand, never have understood that simple fact. They cannot see the distinction between bread, or property, money, and vivid life. They think that property and money are the same thing as vivid life. Only the few, the potential heroes or the 'elect,' can see the simple distinction. The mass *cannot* see it, and will never see it.

Dostoievsky was perhaps the first to realize this devastating truth, which Christ had not seen. A truth it is, none the less, and once recognized it will change the course of history. All that remains is for the elect to take charge of the bread – the property, the money – and then give it back to the masses as if it were really the gift of life. In this way, mankind might live happily, as the Inquisitor suggests. Otherwise, with the masses making the terrible mad mistake that money is life, and that therefore no one shall control the money, men shall be 'free' to get what they can, we are brought to a condition of competitive insanity and ultimate suicide.

So far, well and good, Dostoievsky's diagnosis stands. But is it then to betray Christ and turn over to Satan if the elect should at last realize that instead of refusing Satan's three offers, the heroic Christian must now accept them. Jesus refused the three offers out of pride and fear: he wanted to be greater than these, and 'above' them. But we now realize, no man, not even Jesus, is really 'above' miracle, mystery, and authority. The one thing that Jesus is truly above, is the confusion between money and life. Money is not life, says Jesus, therefore you can ignore it and leave it to the devil.

Money is not life, it is true. But ignoring money and leaving it to the devil means handing over the great mass of men to the devil, for the mass of men *cannot* distinguish between money and life. It is hard to believe: certainly Jesus didn't believe it: and yet, as Dostoievsky and the Inquisitor point out, it is so.

Well, and what then? Must we therefore go over to the devil? After all, the whole of Christianity is not contained in the rejection of the three temptations. The essence of Christianity is a love of mankind. If a love of mankind entails accepting the bitter limitation of the mass of men, their inability to distinguish between money and life, then accept the limitation, and have done with it. Then take over from the devil the money (or bread), the miracle, and the sword of Cæsar, and, for the love of mankind, give back to men the bread, with its wonder, and give them the miracle, the marvellous, and give them, in a hierarchy, someone, some men, in higher and higher degrees, to bow down to. Let them bow down, let them bow down *en masse*, for the mass, who do not understand the difference between money and life, should always bow down to the elect, who do.

And is that serving the devil? It is certainly not serving the spirit of annihilation and not-being. It is serving the great wholeness of mankind, and in that respect, it is Christianity. Anyhow, it is the service of Almighty God, who made men what they are, limited and unlimited.

Where Dostoievsky is perverse is in his making the old, old, wise governor of men a Grand Inquisitor. The recognition of the weakness of man has been a common trait in all great, wise rulers of people, from the Pharaohs and Darius through the great patient Popes of the early Church right down to the present day. They have known the weakness of men, and felt a certain tenderness. This is the spirit of all great government. But it was not the spirit of the Spanish Inquisition. The Spanish Inquisition in 1500 was a new-fangled thing, peculiar to Spain, with her curious death-lust and her bullying, and, strictly, a Spanish-political instrument, not Catholic at all, but rabidly national. The Spanish Inquisition actually was diabolic. It could not have produced a Grand Inquisitor who put Dostoievsky's sad questions to Jesus. And the man who put those sad questions to Jesus could not possibly have been a Spanish Inquisitor. He could not possibly have burnt a hundred people in an *auto-da-fé*. He would have been too wise and far-seeing.

So that, in this respect, Dostoievsky showed his epileptic and slightly criminal perversity. The man who feels a certain tenderness for mankind in its weakness or limitation is not therefore diabolic. The man who realizes that Jesus asked too much of the mass of men, in asking them to choose between earthly and heavenly bread, and to judge between good and evil, is not therefore satanic. Think how difficult it is to know the difference between good and evil! Why, sometimes it is evil to be good. And how is the ordinary man to understand that? He can't. The extraordinary men have to understand it for him. And is that going over to the devil? Or think of the difficulty in choosing between the earthly and heavenly bread. Lenin, surely a pure soul, rose to great power simply to give men – what? The earthly bread. And what was the result? Not only did they lose the heavenly bread, but even the earthly bread disappeared out of wheat-producing Russia. It is most strange. And all the socialists and the generous thinkers of today, what are they striving for? The same: to share out more evenly the earthly bread. Even *they*, who are practising Christianity *par excellence*, cannot properly choose between the heavenly and earthly bread. For the poor, they choose the earthly bread, and once more the heavenly bread is lost: and once more, as soon as it is really chosen, the earthly bread begins to disappear. It is a great mystery. But today, the most passionate believers in Christ believe that all you have to do is to struggle to give earthly bread (good houses, good sanitation, etc.) to the poor, and that is in itself the heavenly bread. But it isn't. Especially for the poor, it isn't. It is for them the loss of heavenly bread. And the poor are the vast majority. Poor things, how everybody hates them today! For benevolence is a form of hate.

What then is the heavenly bread? Every generation must answer for itself. But the heavenly bread is life, is living. Whatever makes life vivid and delightful is the heavenly bread. And the earthly bread must come as a by-product of the heavenly bread. The vast mass will never understand this. Yet it is the essential truth of Christianity, and of life itself. The few will understand. Let them take the responsibility.

Again, the Inquisitor says that it is a weakness in men, that they must have miracle, mystery and authority. But is it? Are they not bound up in our emotions, always and for ever, these three demands of miracle, mystery, and authority? If Jesus cast aside miracle in the Temptation, still there is miracle again in the Gospels. And if Jesus refused the earthly bread, still he said: 'In my Father's house are many mansions.' And for authority: 'Why call ye me Lord, Lord, and do not the things which I say?'

The thing Jesus was trying to do was to supplant physical emotion by moral emotion. So that earthly bread becomes, in a sense, immoral, as it is to many refined people today. The Inquisitor sees that this is the mistake. The earthly bread must in itself be the miracle, and be bound up with the miracle.

And here, surely, he is right. Since man began to think and to feel vividly, seed-time and harvest have been the two great sacred periods of miracle, rebirth, and rejoicing. Easter and harvest-home are festivals of the earthly bread, and they are festivals which go to the roots of the soul. For it is the earthly bread as a miracle, a yearly miracle. All the old religions saw it: the Catholic still sees it, by the Mediterranean. And this is not weakness. This is *truth*. The rapture of the Easter kiss, in old Russia, is intimately bound up with the springing of the seed and the first footstep of the new earthly bread. It is the rapture of the Easter kiss which makes the bread worth eating. It is the absence of the Easter kiss which makes the Bolshevist bread barren, dead. They eat dead bread, now.

The earthly bread is leavened with the heavenly bread. The heavenly bread is life, is contact, and is consciousness. In sowing the seed man has his contact with earth, with sun and rain: and he *must not* break the contact. In the awareness of the springing of the corn he has his ever-renewed consciousness of miracle, wonder, and mystery: the wonder of creation, procreation, and re-creation, following the mystery of death and the cold grave. It is the grief of Holy Week and the delight of Easter Sunday. And man must not, must not lose this supreme state of consciousness out of himself, or he has lost the best part of him. Again, the reaping and the harvest are another contact, with earth and sun, a rich touch of the cosmos, a living stream of activity, and then the contact with harvesters, and the joy of harvest-home. All this is life, life, it is the heavenly bread which we eat in the course of getting the earthly bread. Work is, or should be, our heavenly bread of activity, contact and consciousness. All work that is not this, is anathema. True, the work is hard; there is the sweat of the brow. But what of it? In decent proportion, this is life. The sweat of the brow is the heavenly butter.

I think the older Egyptians understood this, in the course of their long and marvellous history. I think that probably, for thousands of years, the masses of the Egyptians were happy, in the hierarchy of the State.

Miracle and mystery run together, they merge. Then there is the third thing, authority. The word is bad: a policeman has authority, and no one bows down to him. The Inquisitor means: 'that which men bow down to.' Well, they bowed down to Caesar, and they bowed down to Jesus. They will bow down, first, as the Inquisitor saw, to the one who has the power to control the bread.

The bread, the earthly bread, while it is being reaped and grown, it is life. But once it is harvested and stored, it becomes a commodity, it becomes riches. And then it becomes a danger. For men think, if they only possessed the hoard, they need not work; which means, really, they need not live. And that is the real blasphemy. For while we live we must live, we must not wither or rot inert.

So that ultimately men bow down to the man, or group of men, who can and dare take over the hoard, the store of bread, the riches, to distribute it among the people again. The lords, the givers of bread. How profound Dostoievsky is when he says that the people will forget that it is their own bread which is being given back to them. While they keep their own bread, it is not much better than stone to them – inert possessions. But given back to them from the great Giver, it is divine once more, it has the quality of miracle to make it taste well in the mouth and in the belly.

Men bow down to the lord of bread, first and foremost. For, by knowing the difference between earthly and heavenly bread, he is able calmly to distribute the earthly bread, and to give it, for the commonalty, the heavenly taste which they can never give it. That is why, in a democracy, the earthly bread loses its taste, the salt loses its savour, and there is no one to bow down to.

It is not man's weakness that he needs someone to bow down to. It is his nature, and his strength, for it puts him into touch with far, far greater life than if he stood alone. All life bows to the sun. But the sun is very far away to the common man. It needs someone to bring it to him. It needs a lord: what the Christians call one of the elect, to bring the sun to the common man, and put the sun in his heart. The sight of a true lord, a noble, a nature-hero puts the sun into the heart of the ordinary man, who is no hero, and therefore cannot know the sun direct.

This is one of the real mysteries. As the Inquisitor says, the mystery of the elect is one of the inexplicable mysteries of

Christianity, just as the lord, the natural lord among men, is one of the inexplicable mysteries of humanity throughout time. We must accept the mystery, that's all.

But to do so is not diabolic.

And Ivan need not have been so tragic and satanic. He had made a discovery about men, which was due to be made. It was the rediscovery of a fact which was known universally almost till the end of the eighteenth century, when the illusion of the perfectibility of men, of all men, took hold of the imagination of the civilized nations. It was an illusion. And Ivan has to make a restatement of the old truth, that most men *cannot* choose between good and evil, because it is so extremely difficult to know which is which, especially in crucial cases: and that most men *cannot* see the difference between life-values and money-values: they can only see money-values; even nice simple people who *live* by the life-values, kind and natural, yet can only esti-mate value in terms of money. So let the specially gifted few make the decision between good and evil, and establish the life-values against the money-values. And let the many accept the decision, with gratitude, and bow down to the few, in the hier-archy. What is there diabolical or satanic in that? Jesus kisses the Inquisitor: Thank you, you are right, wise old man! Alyosha kisses Ivan: Thank you, brother, you are right, you take a bur-den off me! So why should Dostoievsky drag in Inquisitors and *autos-da-fé*, and Ivan wind up so morbidly suicidal? Let them be glad they've found the truth again.

ELEGY (1930)

by Rebecca West

It is difficult to describe accurately the effect that D. H. Lawrence's death had on London. If one says that the effect was tremendous, one makes a suggestion of a capital in mourning, which is ludicrous. Not even among his own caste was he honoured as he should have been. I myself realized with a shock how much of what I had always put down as Lawrence's persecution mania had a solid basis, in fact, when I read obituaries in which not only was the homage due from the living to dead genius meanly denied, but the courtesy paid to any corpse was so far as possible withheld. 'Messy stuff,' was the delicate phrase bestowed by one of our greatest dailies on his poetry. He might, judging from another of them, have been a lunatic of the same sort as those who, though normal and even exceptionally gifted at most times, every now and then embarrass their friends by suddenly removing their clothes in public places. Less crass than these but just as infuriating were the articles by mediocrities whom we cannot blame for having stayed in safety, since they plainly lacked the vitality to push on the long journey to the edge of danger. They made excuses for Lawrence. It appeared to them that he saw life as a flaming mystery because he suffered from tuberculosis, though nothing seemed plainer to those who knew him best than that this malady gained its hold only because his intense perceptions had exhausted his body. It appeared to them that he wanted to crack the crust which society has allowed to form on the surface of its existence and look underneath, because he was a miner's son and had an inferiority complex about the respectable. If that were true, it were still not to be sneered at, for if a creature of such quality as Lawrence found himself in a world that by its social ordinances ignored that quality, he had a right to question those ordinances. But there was so much more than that in the spiritual drama of Lawrence's life that it is not true. Those traits in Lawrence could hardly have emerged save to those who were regarding their subject very oddly because they were looking at it through the wrong end of field glasses, wishing to see that which is much greater than themselves as much less.

The most sympathetic obituary I have yet seen was an affectionate note on him as a man which appeared in *The Times Literary Supplement*.

I desire (if I can) [says the anonymous writer] to correct the impression, which is widespread, that D. H. Lawrence was a madman of genius, savagely bent on violating sanctuaries, and bruising the finer conscience of his fellow men. To defend Lawrence's passionate convictions is no part of my hasty undertaking. These do not need to be defended, only to be understood, and understood in the light of an experience extraordinary in its depths and comprehensiveness. And again I am not invoking the beauty of his personality to excuse his work. It is right that I should make it clear that I do not consider his work needs any excuse.

It is true that the unknown goes on to say:

If it was wrong, it was passionately wrong; and to be passionately wrong is far better than to be coldly right.

a sentence which I find it impossible to record without expressing my dissent.

> If it was not right, it was not right with attendant conditions that
> have no demonstrable connection with values, and to be not
> right with these attendant conditions that have no demonstrable
> connection with values is to be more right than to be right with
> other attendant conditions that also have no demonstrable con-
> nection with values.

Such a statement seems to me wrong in itself, and unnecessary as a defence of Lawrence, since he was passionately right.
But we can follow this anonymous writer without question
when he says:

> Lawrence was the most remarkable and the most lovable man I
> have ever known. Contact with him was immediate, intimate
> and rich. When he was gay, and he was often gay – my dominant
> memory of him is of a blithe and joyful man – he seemed to
> spread a sensuous enchantment about him. By a natural magic
> he unsealed the eyes of those in his company; birds and beasts
> and flowers became new-minted as in Paradise; they stood
> revealed as what they were, and not the poor objects of our dull
> and common seeing. The most ordinary domestic act – the
> roasting of a joint of meat, the washing up of crockery, the paint-
> ing of a cottage room – in his doing became a gay sacrament.

This is the poet; and this was Lawrence.

This article is just in its estimation of his wonder: and so too
was an obituary in the *Manchester Guardian*. But, considering
the sowing, this is a meagre harvest that his genius reaps from
contemporary fame; and it might be supposed that the *Frank-
furter Zeitung* was right in the leader it published the other day,
which claimed with a sneer that Lawrence was better appreci-
ated in Germany than in England. Yet it is not so. The grief
caused by his death proves far otherwise. I do not speak of his

friends and his intimates. They had all cause to regret him for purely selfish reasons. Such a gay companion as the article in *The Times Literary Supplement* delineates is not easily replaced; nor such a friend.

> He was completely generous. At a moment when there were not ten pounds between him and destitution he thrust five of them upon a friend and because the friend refused them, flew into a transport of high-pitched rage.

It was not only with his money he was generous. He had *caritas*. That which was needed had to be given. These traits in him would explain the grief of his friends; but another explanation, which can only lie in his genius, must be found for the effect of his death on those who had never set eyes on him. I know nobody of middle age or less, above a certain standard of intellectual integrity or imaginative vigour, who is not stricken by his loss. The prevalent feeling was well described by a young man, a critic and a poet, who said to me the other day, 'I've felt rather ill ever since Lawrence died.' There is the general malaise one feels after a severe shock, after a loss that cannot be made good.

How deep the experience goes can be measured by the attempts the mind made to refuse it; for everybody I know, and myself also, refused to believe the news when it came. The first threat of trouble came to me between the acts of *This Way to Paradise*, a dramatization of Aldous Huxley's *Point Counter Point*. It is not so good as a play as it was as a novel. Curiously enough, although one usually thinks at a non-Shavian play that its intellectual content is pitiably below that of most novels, the dialectic stuff of this novel, which was far above the level of current fiction, seemed poor and unsatisfying when one heard it recited over the footlights. This was perhaps because Aldous Huxley's novels are, for all their simulation of realism, half way to poetry. The characters, and the rhythm of their appearance, give an account of the phenomena in their creator's spiritual universe. Young Quarles, the intellectual who cannot satisfy his wife Elinor's need for emotion, so that she turns to Webley, the brainless man of action, represents the fantasy that vexes man with a nightmare vision in which his environment assumes a thousand forms to take his potency away from him. If he thinks, surely the power is draining away from him in a thin flood; if he turns to action, he does but bleed from a different vein; and there are always women. Old Quarles, with his perturbed tootings, 'A babah? Surely not a babah?' was the picture of the father the son makes in rebellion, the symbol of humanity that the individual invents when he desires to make the gesture of power that is his alone. These, and all the other figures of *Point Counter Point*, were real events in Aldous Huxley's mind, and the sequence in which they appeared and reappeared revealed how his argument with himself about its values was going. It was therefore acceptable by all readers who had reached a certain level of self-consciousness, by reason of the comparison and contrasts they could find between his universe and theirs.

But when these same characters and events were presented in the terribly material medium of the stage, without any disguise of poetry, one had to judge them as if they were taking place on the plane of everyday life. Then one watched the young Quarles household only to imagine how Elinor would react to the torture, hardly to be described in the humanitarian pages of an Occidental publication, though the *Chinese Police Gazette* might like it, which one has long devised for all wives who interrupt their husbands when they are working to ask them if they remember those summer evenings in the garden at Wherever eight years ago. Old Quarles was exactly as significant in comparison with all the other senile libertines the stage has seen as his lines enable him to be, and no more. The dialectic speeches, put into the mouth of those who had diminished from real poetic creations to stage types, seemed irrelevant and papery. But certain things still emerged as important. Profound meaning rang out through lines that bore relation to matters not transplanted from the novel into the play, like bells heard across a lake from a church hidden in the hills on the other side. One was conscious of this whenever Mark Rampion, in whom Aldous Huxley has very obviously depicted Lawrence, came on the stage. One thought, 'Even Aldous Huxley, who is so far above the rest of us, feels that he has to look up to Lawrence.' When the curtain fell I said as much to my companion, who answered, 'You know Lawrence is dangerously ill.' For no reason at all I replied, 'Oh, I don't believe that, it's quite impossible,' just as lots of people, equally without reason, felt confidently, 'There's some mistake,' when they read in the newspapers about his death at Vence. What would Aldous Huxley or anybody who had seen *This Way to Paradise* have done if they had suddenly heard that the producers of the play had decided to cut out the character of Mark Rampion? All alike would have cried out that the best thing would then be gone, that the producers could not meditate such a folly. Even so did those of us who heard of Lawrence's death feel that from the spectacle of the universe, by the incredible stupidity of a destroying angel, the best thing had gone. Since we see nothing in the universe outside us which we cannot identify with what we see in the universe within us, this means that the forces which moved Lawrence seem to us the best part of our human equipment.

What were these forces? I can find an answer most easily, I find, by referring not to his work, but to my personal acquaintanceship with him, though that was slight. One spring day about ten years ago I was lunching in Florence with Reggie Turner and Norman Douglas. Reggie Turner has been described by Max

Beerbohm as Artemus in his paper on wits in *And Even Now*, and there is no need to add a line save to commemorate a supremely imaginative act of charity. When Oscar Wilde came out of prison, Reggie Turner sent him one of the most expensive and completely useless fitted dressing cases that Bond Street has ever achieved. There is need to tell over again the tale of Norman Douglas' accomplishments, because the mind finds them so incredible that it has a disposition to forget them. Besides being a master of English prose, he is one of the finest classical scholars in Europe, a great linguist (he can even speak and write Russian), a pianist, a composer, a caricaturist, a botanist, and a landscape gardener – all to the highest degree of accomplishment. By one of those ironies which forbids us to believe that nature is neutral, even when one has been forced to give up one's faith that she is kindly, Reggie Turner, in whose heart is innocence, wears the winking face of a devil off a quattrocento choir stall; and Norman Douglas, whose heart, so far as innocence is concerned, is as the Gobi Desert, looks as one who has never seen Dr Cadman would imagine him to look. There are what one has been led to believe are the stigmata of moral earnestness: the penetrating eyes under level brows, compressed lips, head set sturdily between the shoulders, as if here reason were firmly rooted in the moral law, and hair white as if the scalp itself had renounced all such vanity as colour. And indeed there is here some of the quality suggested. There is in him an austere loyalty to an interpretation of life that might, if need pushed him to it, not baulk at renunciation. Less than paganism is his religion. Things are what they are. If the landscape seems to form a pattern and the figure of a god to emerge, then that does but prove that a god is but a landscape seeming to form a pattern. That being so, all things are equal and unrelated, perpetually dissolvent back to their point of least significance. Believing this he will not forswear his belief. That day at lunch his conversation perpetually made and unmade the world till late in the afternoon; and then, though there would have seemed to an observer no reason why we should ever move, we were entertaining each other so well, we rose to our feet. Lawrence was coming in by some slow train that crawled up from Rome laden with poor folks that could not pay for speed, and would by now be installed in his hotel. To each of us, different though we were in type, it appeared of paramount importance that we should go and pay him our respects at the first possible moment.

He was staying in a poorish hotel overlooking what seems to me, since I am one of those who are so enamoured of Rome that they will not submit themselves to the magic of Florence, to be a trench of drab and turbid water wholly undeserving of the romantic prestige we have given the Arno. Make no mistake, it was the hotel that overlooked the Arno, not Lawrence. His room was one of the cheaper ones at the back. His sense of guilt which scourged him perpetually, which was the motive power of his genius, since it made him inquire what sin it was which he and all mankind have on their conscience, forbade him either enjoying comfort or having the money to pay for it, lest he should weaken. So it was a small, mean room in which he sat tapping away at a typewriter. Norman Douglas burst out in a great laugh as we went in and asked him if he were already writing an article about the present state of Florence; and Lawrence answered seriously that he was. This was faintly embarrassing, because on the doorstep Douglas had described how on arrival in a town Lawrence used to go straight from the railway station to his hotel and immediately sit down and hammer out articles about the place, vehemently and exhaustively describing the temperament of the people. This seemed obviously a silly thing to do, and here he was doing it. Douglas' laughter rang out louder than ever, and malicious as a satyr's.

But we forgot all that when Lawrence set his work aside and

laid himself out to be a good host to us. He was one of the most polite people I have ever met, in both naïve and subtle ways. The other two knew him well, but I had never seen him before. He made friends as a child might do, by shyly handing me funny little boxes he had brought from some strange place he had recently visited; and he made friends too as if he were a wise old philosopher at the end of his days, by taking notice of one's personality, showing that he recognized its quality and giving it his blessing. Also there was a promise that a shy wild thing might well give and exact from its fellows, that he would live if one would let him live. Presently he settled down to give, in a curious hollow voice, like the soft hoot of an owl, an account of the journey he had made, up from Sicily to Capri, from Capri to Rome, from Rome to Florence. There seemed no reason why he should have made these journeys, which were all as uncomfortable as cheap travelling is in Italy; nor did there seem any reason why he was presently going to Baden-Baden. Yet, if every word he said disclosed less and less reason for this journeying, it also disclosed a very definite purpose. These were the journeys that the mystics of a certain type have always found necessary. The Russian saint goes to the head of his family and says good-bye and takes his stick and walks out with no objective but the truth. The Indian fakir draws lines with his bare feet across the dust of his peninsula which describe a diagram, meaningless to the uninitiated, but significant of holiness. Lawrence travelled, it seemed, to get a certain Apocalyptic vision of mankind that he registered again and again and again, always rising to a pitch of ecstatic agony. Norman Douglas, Reggie Turner, and I, none of whom would have moved from one place to another except in the greatest comfort procurable and with a definite purpose, or have endured a disagreeable experience twice if we could possibly help it, sat in a row on the bed and nodded. We knew that what he was doing was right. We nodded and were entranced.

The next day Norman Douglas and I went for a walk with Lawrence far out into the country, past the Certosa. It was a joy for me to leave the city, for I cannot abide trams and Florence is congested with them. Impossible to pass through the streets without feeling that one is being dogged by a moaning tram one had betrayed in one's reckless youth; and it had been raining so hard that there had for long been no opportunity to walk in the country. Now there had been a day's sunshine, and the whole world was new. Irises thrust out of the wet earth like weapons suddenly brought into action. The cypresses, instead of being lank funereal plumes commemorating a foundered landscape, were exclamation marks drawn in Chinese ink, crying out at the beauty of the reborn countryside. About the grassy borders of the road there was much fine enamelwork in little flowers and weeds as one has seen it on the swards of Botticelli. Of the renascent quality of the day Lawrence became an embodiment. He was made in the angelic colours. His skin, though he had lived so much in the Southern countries, was very white, his eyes were light, his hair and beard were a pale luminous red. His body was very thin, and because of the flimsiness of his build it seemed as if a groove ran down the centre of his chest and his spine, so that his shoulder blades stood out in a pair of almost winglike projections. He moved quickly and joyously. One could imagine him as a forerunner, speeding faster than spring can go from bud to bud on the bushes, to tell the world of the season that was coming to save it from winter. Beside him Norman Douglas lumbered along stockily. Because he knew what emperor had built this road and set that city on a hill, and how the Etruscans had been like minded in their buildings before him, he made one feel that there have been so many springs that in effect there is no spring, but that that is of no great moment. Bending over a filemot-coloured flower that he had not seen since he found it on Mount Olympus, his face grew nearly as tender as a mother bending over her child. When a child tumbled at his feet from the terrace of an olive orchard, his face became neither more nor less tender than before. They moved in unison of pace along the road, these two, and chatted. They were on good terms then, Ormuzd and Ahriman.

We stopped for lunch at a place that was called the Bridge of Something: an inn that looked across a green meadow to a whitish river. We ate at a table on which a trellis of wistaria painted a shadow far more substantial than the blue mist that was its substance. The two men talked for long of a poor waif, a bastard sprig of royalty, that had recently killed himself after a life divided between conflicting passions for monastic life, unlawful pleasures, and financial fraud. He had sought refuge at the monastery of Monte Cassino, that nursery of European culture, where St Thomas Aquinas himself was educated; but soon was obliged to flee down one side of the sugar loaf mountain while the carabinieri climbed up the other with a warrant for his arrest on charges connected with the Italian law of credit. Then he had gone to Malta, and played more fantasia on the theme of debt, till his invention was exhausted. This was the man* whose recollections of service in the French Foreign Legion were published with a preface by Lawrence which provoked Norman Douglas to a savage retort that stands high among the dog fights of literary men. But then they were joined in amity while they talked of him with that grave and brotherly pitifulness that men who have found it difficult to accommodate themselves to their fellow men feel for those who have found it impossible. They broke off, I remember, to look at some lads who made their way across the meadow and began to strip by the river bank. 'The water will be icy,' said Douglas, 'it won't be warm till the snow goes off the mountains.' He began to chuckle at the thought of

* [Maurice Magnus.]

the shock that was coming to the boys who had been tempted by the first hot day. Lawrence let his breath hiss out through his teeth at the thought of their agony; but he seemed to find pleasure in it, as he would in any intense feeling.

Presently we rose and went on our way. Norman Douglas took the landlord's hand and wrung it heartily, saying a fervid good-bye. Lawrence exclaimed, 'Douglas, how can you shake hands with these people!' He meant by this that the antipathy between the Northern and the Southern peoples was so great that there could be no sincere attempt at friendship with them. Douglas answered with a grin, 'Oh, it takes something off the bill next time.' He did not mean that. It was simply the first way that came to hand of saying that he would not get excited about these fine points, that in his universe every phenomenon was of equal value. We walked away. After a minute or two I looked back through the olive trees and saw the landlord standing where we had left him, sending after us a hard black Italian stare. 'Do you know, Douglas,' said Lawrence suddenly, though he had not looked back, 'I can't help thinking that the man understood English.' 'Oh, no,' I said falsely, 'I'm sure he didn't.' But Douglas, laughing more deeply than ever said, 'I got that too.' We all walked along without speaking, ill at ease, though Douglas kept his eyes crinkled as if he were still laughing. Ormuzd and Ahriman alike did not want unnecessary explosions of the forces they well knew to be latent in their universe.

Later Lawrence began to talk of the Sicilian peasants and how full of hatred and malice he had found them. There was a great tale about some old crones who had come up at twilight to his house in Taormina with some jars of honey they had wanted him to buy, and had crouched down on his terrace while he tested their goods with malignity in their eyes, in their squatting bodies. They had meant to cheat him, for it was last year's honey and ill preserved. He detected the fraud in an instant, with his sturdy wisdom about household matters, and bade them be gone. Silently they rose and filed out through his olive trees with their jars on their shoulders; with increased malignity in their eyes and in their prowling bodies, because they had not been able to cheat him. 'Such hatred!' he cried in effect. 'Such black loathing.' Again I felt embarrassed, as I did when we discovered him pounding out articles on the momentary state of Florence with nothing more to go on than a glimpse at it. Surely he was now being almost too flatly silly, even a little mad? Of course peasants try to cheat one over honey or anything else, in Italy or anywhere else, and very natural it is, considering how meagrely the earth gives up its fruits. But as for hatred and black loathing, surely this is persecution mania? I was a little unhappy about it, which was a pity, for that made an unsatisfactory ending to what was to be my last meeting with Lawrence, though mercifully not my last contact with him. For a few months ago I received a letter from him thanking me for some little tribute I had paid him during the trouble about his pictures in London. This letter showed the utmost humility in him to take notice of such a small courtesy; and it showed more than that. With marvellous sensitiveness he had deduced from a phrase or two in my article that I was troubled by a certain problem, and he said words that in their affectionate encouragement and exquisite appositeness could not have been bettered if we had spent the ten years that had intervened since our meeting in the closest friendship.

The point about Lawrence's work that I have been unable to explain save by resorting to my personal acquaintance with him is this: that it was founded on the same basis as those of his mental movements which then seemed to me ridiculous, and which now that I have had more experience, I see as proceeding in a straight line to the distant goal of wisdom. He was tapping out an article on the state of Florence at that moment without knowing enough about it to make his views of real value. Is that the way I looked at it? Then I was naïve. I know now that he was writing about the state of his own soul at that moment, which, since our self-consciousness is incomplete, and since in consequence our vocabulary also is incomplete, he could only render in symbolic terms; and the city of Florence was as good a symbol as any other. If he was foolish in taking the material universe and making allegations about it that were true only of the universe within his own soul, then Rimbaud was a great fool also. Or to go further back, so too was Dante, who made a new Heaven and Hell and Purgatory as a symbol for the geography within his own breast, and so too was St Augustine, when in *The City of God* he writes an attack on the pagan world, which is unjust so long as it is regarded as an account of events on the material plane, but which is beyond price as an account of the conflict in his soul between that which tended to death and that which tended to life. Lawrence was in fact no different from any other great artist who has felt the urgency to describe the unseen so keenly that he has rifled the seen of its vocabulary and diverted it to that purpose; and it took courage to do that in a land swamped with naturalism as England was when Lawrence began to write.

When he cried out at Douglas for shaking hands with the inn-keeper because the North and the South were enemies, and when he saw the old crones who had come to cheat him out of an odd lira or two over the honey as maenads too venomous even to be flamboyant, I thought he was seeing lurid colours that were in his eye and not in the universe he looked on. Now I think he was doing justice to the seriousness of life, and had been rewarded with a deeper insight into its nature than most of us have. If one has the dislike of any proof that the universe has structure which is the mark of an incoherent mind, then one will find something very distasteful in his assumption that John Smith and Giovanni Grimaldi are not merely individuals, but are parts of two systems of life so fundamentally opposed that their minutest constituents must also be in opposition. If one has no purpose and therefore does not need to know the relationship between the forces of the mind and events in the external world, then it is as well to say that old women out for liras were simply old women out for liras, and leave it at that. But if one hopes that some day the mind shall govern life, then it is of value that one shall be shown a small instance of the sadism that makes the human being rejoice in killing, hurting, robbing its neighbour, and one shall be told that this is as horrible as war, since war also is the fruit of this sadism; and that therefore the mind must walk proudly and always armed, that it shall not be robbed of its power. There is nothing disconcerting about these or any other of Lawrence's attitudes, if one is a true inheritor of tradition and realizes that the greatest sons of man have always recognized that the mind which is his house is ablaze and that if the fire is not put out he will perish. Then one will rejoice that our age produced one artist who had the earnestness of the patristic writers, who like them could know no peace till he had discovered what made men lust after death. He laboured under a disadvantage compared with the fathers, in his lack of a vocabulary of symbolic terms such as was given them by theology; in the allegory of the death of the soul which ends with the death of Gerald among the mountains in *Women in Love*, he cannot tell his story save by the clumsy creation of images that do not give up their meaning till the book has been read many times. But even these struggles are of value, since they recall to one the symbolic nature of all thought. Knowledge is but a translation of reality into terms comprehensible by the human mind, a grappling with a mystery. None undertake it with the courage of Lawrence unless they very greatly care.

His claim to our reverence and gratitude was not in the least part diminished by *Lady Chatterley's Lover*. It is an appalling fact that man should speak of the functions on which depend the continued existence of his species and the tender life of the heart in words that cause shame and ugly laughter when they are spoken. When Lawrence's pity was aroused by this wound in the side of life he did what saints do: he asked for a miracle. He laid sex and those base words for it on the salver of his art and held them up before the consciousness of the world, which was his way of approaching creation, and prayed that both might be transmuted to the highest that man could use. There are many people like myself who feel that his prayer was in vain: that those words were nothing but the expressions of hatred felt by the will to die for the will to live, and they could never be converted to anything else. But people like myself are infinitely lesser than Lawrence. The presumption is that if he did not reach the truth he at least came nearer it then we did. In any case, it was the special merit of this and all his other works, as I can see by looking back at our meeting and measuring the change in my attitude towards his characteristic traits, that in no way did he underrate the gravity of the human situation.

As I write there comes to me this week's issue of *Time and Tide*, and I find in it a letter about Lawrence, from Catherine Carswell, an infrequent but gifted writer – her note on Duse in the *Adelphi* was one of the finest pieces of dramatic criticism I have ever read. Her letter is worth reprinting.

SIR:

The Picture of D. H. Lawrence suggested by the obituary notices of 'competent criticse' is of a man morose, frustrated, tortured, even a sinister failure. Perhaps this is because any other view would make his critics look rather silly. Anyhow, to those who knew him, and I knew him since 1914 as friend, hostess and guest in varying circumstances, often of the most trying kind, at home and abroad, that picture would be comic if it were not in the circumstances disgraceful.

Lawrence was as little morose as an open clematis flower, as little tortured or sinister or hysterical as a humming bird. Gay, skilful, clever at everything, furious when he felt like it but never grieved or upset, intensely amusing, without sentimentality or affectation, almost always right in his touch for the content of things or persons, he was at once the most harmonious and the most vital person I ever saw.

As to frustration, consider his achievements. In the face of formidable initial disadvantages and lifelong delicacy, poverty that lasted for three-quarters of his life and hostility that survives his death, he did nothing that he did not really want to do, and all that he most wanted to do he did. He went all over the world, he owned a ranch, he lived in the most beautiful corners of Europe, and met whom he wanted to meet and told them that they were wrong and that he was right. He painted and made things and sang and rode. He wrote something like three dozen books, of which even the worst pages dance with life that could be mistaken for no other man's, while the best are admitted, even by those who hate him, to be unsurpassed. Without vices, with most human virtues, the husband of one wife, scrupulously honest, this estimable citizen yet managed to keep free from the shackles of civilization and the cant of literary cliques. He would have laughed lightly and cursed venomously in passing at the solemn owls – each one secretly chained by the leg – who now conduct his inquest. To do his work and lead his life in spite of them took some doing, but he did it, and long after they are forgotten, sensitive and innocent people – if any are left – will turn Lawrence's pages and know from them what sort of a rare man Lawrence was.

CATHERINE CARSWELL

We must ourselves be grievously defeated if we do not regard the life of D. H. Lawrence as a spiritual victory.

NOTES ON THE TEXTS

The texts are taken from *Phoenix* (edited by Edward D. McDonald, London: Heinemann, 1936) and *Phoenix II* (edited by Warren Roberts and Harry T. Moore, London: Heinemann, 1968). For more information and for essays not included here – with texts conforming as closely as possible to Lawrence's intentions – readers are referred to the invaluable Cambridge University Press editions of: *Study of Thomas Hardy and Other Essays*, *Reflections on the Death of a Porcupine and Other Essays*, *Introductions and Reviews*, *Late Essays and Articles*, *Twilight in Italy and Other Essays*, *Mornings in Mexico and Other Essays*, *Sketches of Etruscan Places and Other Italian Essays*.

'Christs in the Tirol': written September 1912; first published in *Westminster Gazette*, 22 March 1913. (This is the second of three versions of the piece, the last one published as 'The Crucifix Across the Mountains' in *Twilight in Italy*.) *Phoenix*.

'Review of *Death in Venice* by Thomas Mann': written by June 1913; first published in *Blue Review*, July 1913. *Phoenix*.

Study of Thomas Hardy: written September–December 1914; first published in *Phoenix*.

'Whistling of Birds': written early 1917; first published in *Athenaeum*, 11 April 1919. *Phoenix*.

'Poetry of the Present': written August 1919; first published (as 'Verse Free and Unfree') in *Voices*, October 1919, and (as 'Poetry of the Present') in *The Playboy*, nos. 4 and 5, 1919; reprinted as the preface to US edition of *New Poems* (1920). *Phoenix*.

'Memoir of Maurice Magnus': written November 1921–late January 1922; first published as introduction to *Memoirs of the Foreign Legion* by 'MM'. *Phoenix II*.

'Indians and an Englishman': written September–October 1922; first published in *Dial*, February 1923. *Phoenix*.

'Taos': written September 1922; first published in *Dial*, March 1923. *Phoenix*.

'The Future of the Novel': written December 1922–January 1923; first published in *Literary Digest International Book Review*, April 1923 (as 'Surgery for the Novel – Or a Bomb'). *Phoenix*.

'Paris Letter': written January 1924; first published in *Laughing Horse*, April 1926. *Phoenix*.

'A Letter from Germany': written February 1924; first published in *New Statesman*, 13 October 1934. *Phoenix*.

'Pan in America': written May–June 1924; first published in *Phoenix*.

'The Bad Side of Books: Introduction to *A Bibliography of the Writings of D. H. Lawrence*': written 1 September 1924; first published 1925. *Phoenix*.

'On Coming Home': written end of 1924–early 1925; first published in *Phoenix II*.

'Art and Morality': written May–June 1925; first published in *Calendar of Modern Letters*, November 1925. *Phoenix*.

'Morality and the Novel': written May–June 1925; first published in *Calendar of Modern Letters*, December 1925. *Phoenix*.

'The Novel': written May–June 1925; first published in *Reflections on the Death of a Porcupine and Other Essays* (1925). *Phoenix II*.

'Why the Novel Matters': written summer–end of 1925; first published in *Phoenix*.

'The Novel and the Feelings': written summer–end of 1925; first published in *Phoenix*.

'Reflections on the Death of a Porcupine': written mid-July–mid-August 1925; first published in *Reflections on the Death of a Porcupine and Other Essays*. *Phoenix II*.

'Man Is a Hunter': written May–June 1926; first published in *Phoenix*.

'Return to Bestwood': written mid–late October 1926; first published in *Phoenix II*.

'Review of *In Our Time* by Ernest Hemingway': written by February 1927; first published as part of longer round-up of recent novels in *Calendar*, April 1927. *Phoenix*.

'Flowery Tuscany': written February–April 1927; first published in *New Criterion*, October, November, December 1927. *Phoenix*.

'Germans and Latins' (or 'Flowery Tuscany IV'): written April 1927; first published in *Phoenix*.

'Introduction to *Mastro-don Gesualdo* by Giovanni Verga': written April–May 1927; first published in Jonathan Cape's Travellers's Library edition of *Mastro-don Gesualdo* (1928). *Phoenix II*.

'Why I Don't Like Living in London': written August 1928; first published in *Evening News*, 3 September 1928. *Phoenix II* (as 'Dull London').

'Hymns in a Man's Life': written August 1928; first published in *Evening News*, 13 October 1928. *Phoenix II*.

'Give Her a Pattern': written December 1928; first published in *Vanity Fair*, May 1929. *Phoenix II*.

'New Mexico': written December 1928; first published in *Survey Graphic*, May 1931. *Phoenix*.

'Myself Revealed': written in December 1928 and partly derived from the earlier 'Which Class I Belong To' (written circa April 1927); first published in *Sunday Dispatch*, 17 February 1929. *Phoenix II* (as 'Autobiographical Sketch').

'Introduction to These Paintings': written December 1928–January 1929; first published in the exhibition catalogue *The Paintings of D. H. Lawrence* (1929). *Phoenix*.

'Pornography and Obscenity': written April 1929; first published in *This Quarter*, July–September 1929. *Phoenix*.

'The Risen Lord': written July 1929; first published in *Everyman*, 3 October 1929. *Phoenix II*.

'Nottingham and the Mining Countryside': written September 1929; first published in *New Adelphi*, June 1930. *Phoenix*.

'Introduction to *The Grand Inquisitor* by F. M. Dostoievsky': written by January 1930; first published by Elkin Mathews and Marrot, July 1930. *Phoenix*.

'Elegy' by Rebecca West: First published in *The New Adelphi*, 3 (June–August 1930) pp. 298–309; later reprinted as *D. H. Lawrence* (London: Secker, 1930).